Evidence

Evidence

Eleventh Edition

Arthur Best
Professor of Law
University of Denver
Sturm College of Law

Wolters Kluwer

Copyright © 2018 Arthur Best.

Published by Wolters Kluwer in New York.

Wolters Kluwer Legal & Regulatory U.S. serves customers worldwide with CCH, Aspen Publishers, and Kluwer Law International products. (www.WKLegaledu.com)

No part of this publication may be reproduced or transmitted in any form or by any means, electronic or mechanical, including photocopy, recording, or utilized by any information storage or retrieval system, without written permission from the publisher. For information about permissions or to request permissions online, visit us at www.WKLegaledu.com, or a written request may be faxed to our permissions department at 212-771-0803.

To contact Customer Service, e-mail customer.service@wolterskluwer.com, call 1-800-234-1660, fax 1-800-901-9075, or mail correspondence to:

Wolters Kluwer
Attn: Order Department
PO Box 990
Frederick, MD 21705

Printed in the United States of America.

1 2 3 4 5 6 7 8 9 0

ISBN 978-1-4548-9251-9

Library of Congress Cataloging-in-Publication Data

Names: Best, Arthur, author.
Title: Evidence / Arthur Best, Professor of Law, University of Denver, Sturm
    College of Law.
Description: Eleventh edition. | New York : Wolters Kluwer, [2018] | Series:
    Examples & explanations series | Includes bibliographical references and
    index.
Identifiers: LCCN 2018025512 | ISBN 9781454892519 (alk. paper)
Subjects: LCSH: Evidence (Law) — United States. | LCGFT: Study guides.
Classification: LCC KF8935.Z9 B48 2018 | DDC 347.73/6 — dc23
LC record available at https://lccn.loc.gov/2018025512

SUSTAINABLE FORESTRY INITIATIVE   Certified Sourcing
www.sfiprogram.org
SFI-00756

About Wolters Kluwer Legal & Regulatory U.S.

Wolters Kluwer Legal & Regulatory U.S. delivers expert content and solutions in the areas of law, corporate compliance, health compliance, reimbursement, and legal education. Its practical solutions help customers successfully navigate the demands of a changing environment to drive their daily activities, enhance decision quality, and inspire confident outcomes.

Serving customers worldwide, its legal and regulatory portfolio includes products under the Aspen Publishers, CCH Incorporated, Kluwer Law International, ftwilliam.com, and MediRegs names. They are regarded as exceptional and trusted resources for general legal and practice-specific knowledge, compliance and risk management, dynamic workflow solutions, and expert commentary.

To Hannah, Rachel, and Eli

Contents

Contents

Chapter 6   Expert Testimony   181

Chapter 7   Privileges   195

Chapter 8   Authentication and the Original Writing Rule   217

Chapter 9   Presumptions   231

Chapter 10   Judicial Notice   239

Preface

Evidence law is full of simple rules, complex rules, hard problems with satisfying answers, and hard problems that can never be resolved to everyone's agreement. This makes the subject difficult but rewarding. For a student beginning the course, "Participation precedes interest" might be a helpful slogan. Once you get involved with the course, you will like it, and you will master its various levels of complexity.

This text is designed to make participation easy. For every topic, it presents questions of different degrees of difficulty. It also provides clear explanations of how to analyze the questions. I hope you'll like this text, and I hope you'll like your Evidence course. Because evidence law can affect all areas of law practice, learning its rules and doctrines is a project that deserves your attention.

Arthur Best

July 2018

Acknowledgments

I am grateful to colleagues for reviewing parts of the manuscript, for sharing reactions to earlier editions, and for helping me to develop my understanding of evidence law in less formal ways as well. Thanks very much to the late Sheila Hyatt, the late Frank Jamison, and Randolph Jonakait. I also appreciate the spirit of curiosity and energetic inquiry manifested by Alfred Kil and Edith Kil.

This book is influenced strongly by the scholarship of the casebook authors whose works I have used in teaching. For their vital, though indirect, guidance, I would like to thank Ronald L. Carlson, Edward J. Imwinkelried, Eric D. Green, the late John Kaplan, Edward J. Kionka, Laird C. Kirkpatrick, Richard O. Lempert, Leon Letwin, the late David W. Louisell, Christopher B. Mueller, Charles R. Nesson, Stephen A. Saltzburg, the late Jon R. Waltz, and Olin Guy Wellborn III.

The support and skill of the editorial staff at Little, Brown and Company, Aspen Publishers, and Wolters Kluwer have been vital to the writing of this text. In particular, thanks are due to Richard Heuser, Elizabeth Kenny, Carol McGeehan, and Peter Skagestad. Finally, I am grateful to the students who have shared comments on this book's earlier editions. I appreciate their very helpful insights.

CHAPTER 1

The General Requirement of Relevance

INTRODUCTION

Learn a few simple rules and amaze your friends! There is much more than that to evidence law, but you do have to learn the basic structure to do well in an evidence course, the bar examination, or actual litigation. And it is only when you understand the explicit doctrines of evidence law that you can spot the sophisticated and complicated ambiguities that still remain even after the adoption of a code, the Federal Rules of Evidence.

The logical starting place in the study of evidence is the concept of relevance. In order to be admissible, information must be relevant to a disputed issue. This concept is the foundation of evidence law. If someone sued a police officer for alleged police brutality, could you imagine the defendant's lawyer asking the plaintiff, "What's your favorite food?" That kind of question seems strange because a person's food preferences have nothing to do with evaluating a police officer's conduct. Knowing whether the plaintiff likes particular foods cannot legitimately help the trier of fact decide whether the police officer used too much force against the plaintiff, so evidence law keeps that information out of the trial. The question is improper because it refers to something that has no reasonable connection to the substantive doctrines that govern a police brutality suit. Almost every issue in evidence law involves relevance — the idea that the party who seeks to have evidence admitted must specify what issue it relates to and show how it rationally advances the inquiry about that issue.

This chapter begins our consideration of evidence law by exploring the way it divides all the facts of the world into two categories in every case: relevant and irrelevant. Material must be relevant to be admitted into evidence at a trial. That highlights the importance of the relevance inquiry. But admissibility requires more than a showing of relevancy. There are important requirements for the form of testimony and the authentication of documents and about the degree of knowledge a witness must have concerning the topic of testimony, for example. Succeeding chapters discuss these rules as well as others that exclude relevant material for reasons based on social policies such as rules of privilege, which protect confidential communications, and the rule against hearsay, which avoids basing trial results on unreliable secondhand information. The Federal Rules of Evidence will be the main focus. They apply, of course, in federal courts. Additionally, more than 40 states have adopted evidence codes or rules modeled on the Federal Rules.

The Basic Standard and Its Application

The relevance rule restricts the trier of fact to considering only material that relates closely to facts that matter in the case. How close must the relationship be between an item of evidence and the proposition it is offered to support? The answer is necessarily vague: just close enough so the evidence could influence a rational fact finder in determining the truth or falsity of that proposition.

The Federal Rules have three main relevance provisions. Rule 402[1] requires that evidence be relevant to be admitted and that irrelevant evidence be excluded:

Relevant evidence is admissible unless any of the following provides otherwise:

- the United States Constitution;
- a federal statute;
- these rules; or
- other rules prescribed by the Supreme Court.

Irrelevant evidence is not admissible.

Rule 401 provides the following definition of relevant evidence:

Evidence is relevant if:

(a) it has any tendency to make a fact more or less probable than it would be without the evidence; and

(b) the fact is of consequence in determining the action.

---

1. Throughout this book, Rule numbers refer to provisions of the Federal Rules of Evidence.

Another provision allows the trial judge to use discretion to avoid admitting evidence under certain circumstances, even when its admission would seem to be required under Rules 401 and 402. That provision is Rule 403:

> The court may exclude relevant evidence if its probative value is substantially outweighed by a danger of one or more of the following: unfair prejudice, confusing the issues, misleading the jury, undue delay, wasting time, or needlessly presenting cumulative evidence.

The relevancy concept saves time. It narrows the topics that parties have to develop in preparation for trial. Finally, it increases the perceived legitimacy of trials by ensuring that outcomes will be based on data most people would believe have something to do with the controversy.

Suppose a plaintiff sued the owner of an office building, claiming that he had fallen and hurt himself in the lobby and that inadequate maintenance of the lobby was the proximate cause of his injury. Should our trial system allow the plaintiff to show that the office building is one floor taller than the maximum height permitted by zoning regulations? The answer to this question depends on the substantive tort law that will govern the case. The evidence will be kept out because compliance with maximum height regulations has nothing to do with an owner's liability for injuries in a building's lobby. In technical terms it is immaterial since it does not involve one of the legal issues in the case. In the language of Rule 401, it does not deal with a fact that is "of consequence in determining the action." Could the plaintiff show that the lobby walls had once been painted pink but had been repainted yellow shortly before the injury? That evidence does relate to an issue at stake in the trial, the condition of the lobby, but it could not possibly influence a decision about the building owner's efforts to maintain a safe lobby. A court would keep it out, calling it irrelevant. How would a court treat evidence that the lobby was dimly lit? That information relates to an issue in dispute in a way that could help a fact finder decide rationally whether the owner had been adequately careful to provide a safe lobby. The evidence would be admitted.

For any relevance decision, the advocates and judge must have background information in mind, a context in which to evaluate whether the offered evidence has "any tendency," in the language of Rule 401, to affect the fact finder's resolution of a disputed issue. For example, in the lobby case, evidence that the lighting was dim seems relevant to us because we know (without its being proved or evidence about it being offered) that people trip and fall more often in dark places than in places that are brightly lit. This type of information about what the world is like is necessarily a part of every relevancy decision.

The judge decides questions of admissibility under common law and under the Federal Rules. Rule 104(a) provides:

> The court must decide any preliminary question about whether a witness is qualified, a privilege exists, or evidence is admissible. In so deciding, the court is not bound by evidence rules, except those on privilege.

Subdivision (b) of the Rule is discussed later in this chapter. Because relevancy is a condition for admissibility, it is one of the issues the judge is intended to decide by himself or herself. Notice that evidence can clear the relevancy threshold with a very small showing: The judge must believe that a rational fact finder could be influenced by the material in deciding the existence of a fact. Strong influence is not required. The evidence only has to be capable of making determination of the fact more or less probable than it would be without the evidence. Thus, relevance is different from sufficiency. In McCormick's famous phrase, "A brick is not a wall."[2] Where the contribution an item of evidence could make is very slight, however, the possibility increases that a judge will exclude it under the authority of Rule 403 as wasteful of time or needlessly cumulative. In this field, judges have discretion and are rarely overruled because factual situations are so diverse and there can be a wide range of ideas about the rational relationships between various kinds of information and facts sought to be proved.

Unfair Prejudice

Evidence is subject to exclusion if the risk of unfair prejudice substantially outweighs its probative value. Rule 403 uses those terms to frame the judge's discretion. To understand this balancing, it is necessary to define both unfair prejudice and probative value. If evidence will help an opponent, parties try not to introduce it. In this sense, all evidence that a party introduces is intended to prejudice the opponent, since it is meant to help the proponent's side of the case and hurt the opponent. It is only when a fact finder might react to aspects of evidence in a way that is not supposed to be part of the evaluative process that the reaction is considered unfair prejudice.

For example, the victim in an assault case could introduce testimony that the defendant ran toward him shouting, "Get over here! I'm going to break your arm!" Naturally, a juror might dislike a person who made such a statement and might therefore be prejudiced against him. This type of prejudice is proper because it comes from the juror's belief that the

---

2. Charles T. McCormick, McCormick on Evidence 339 (John W. Strong, ed., 4th ed. 1992 (abridged ed.)).

defendant committed the alleged aggression. On the other hand, if someone testified that the defendant said to the alleged victim, "I'm going to break your arm because I belong to a cult that worships violence," jurors might develop two kinds of ideas from learning about the defendant's worship of violence. They might relate the statement about religion specifically to the alleged crime and conclude that those words were part of the crime (in the sense that they reinforced the scary effect of the threat). Jurors might also develop negative impressions about the defendant based on their feelings of aversion to people who belong to weird cults. Those impressions would be an example of unfair prejudice since they are unrelated to the probative value the religion information has with respect to the charged crime. They flow from jurors' reactions to information about the person that would cause revulsion whether or not it was linked to the events of an alleged crime, not from a belief that the defendant did commit the crime. As Chart 1 illustrates, jurors who believed that the statement was made could simultaneously draw two ideas from it. One would be that the defendant had committed the charged offense. The other would be that the defendant is a wretch and deserves to be punished no matter what. Obviously our system intends to have only the first kind of reaction, illustrated in the top row of Chart 1, play a part in the outcome of trials.

Chart 1 — Simultaneous Inferences from Evidence That Defendant Said, "I'm Going to Break Your Arm Because I Belong to a Cult That Worships Violence"

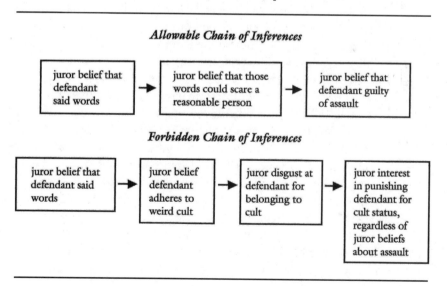

Allowable Chain of Inferences

| juror belief that defendant said words | → | juror belief that those words could scare a reasonable person | → | juror belief that defendant guilty of assault |

Forbidden Chain of Inferences

| juror belief that defendant said words | → | juror belief defendant adheres to weird cult | → | juror disgust at defendant for belonging to cult | → | juror interest in punishing defendant for cult status, regardless of juror beliefs about assault |

There is another type of unfair prejudice that the trial judge is authorized to consider under Rule 403. This is the risk that a juror will give undue probative weight to an item of evidence. For example, if there was a dispute in a products liability case about whether a plaintiff's injury had really occurred the way the plaintiff claimed, the plaintiff might seek to introduce evidence that someone else had been injured in that same way. If the defendant argued that the plaintiff's claimed injury was impossible, letting the jury know that someone else had been hurt that way would be proper since the jury could use that information to evaluate the defense of impossibility. A different treatment would be sensible if the defendant admitted that the type of accident claimed by the plaintiff was possible, but claimed that the plaintiff just had not been injured in that way. In that case, proof that one other person had been hurt that way would have only a small bearing on the likelihood that the plaintiff's claim was true, but there is a risk that jurors might believe that because something happened one time it was highly likely to have happened another time. In a case where a defendant acknowledged that the plaintiff's theory was possible, admitting evidence about a single other incident of the type claimed by the plaintiff would subject the defendant to a risk that the jury would give it too much weight.

To determine whether the risk of unfair prejudice substantially outweighs the probative value of evidence, a judge is required to do some kind of weighing. This process is not literally a measurement since there is no scale for quantifying degrees of probativeness and prejudice. In the worshipping violence example the judge would consider the other evidence the prosecution had that connected the defendant to the crime. If the prosecution had other evidence that did not entail a reference to violence worship, the probative value of that violence reference would be slight. If the judge were to instruct the witness outside the hearing of the jury that the "break your arm" statement could be repeated but that the "cult" statement must be kept from the jury, this would ensure that the prosecution had access to an important part of its case against the defendant. Additionally, it would avoid the risk of providing the jurors with information that might affect them improperly.

Appellate courts usually defer to trial court rulings based on Rule 403. Even if evidence has only slight probative value, an appellate court will rarely reject a trial court's ruling that its legitimate value exceeds the risk of unfair prejudice associated with the evidence. An unusual case, *Old Chief v. United States*,[3] illustrates how slight the probative value of evidence may have to be for an appellate court to rule that it is less than the risk of unfair prejudice. In *Old Chief*, the defendant was accused of the crime of being a felon in possession of a firearm. The defendant admitted that he was a felon, but the trial court allowed the introduction of detailed evidence about the defendant's earlier crime. This was erroneous. A full description of the prior offense had

---

3. 519 U.S. 172 (1997).

no probative value, because the defendant had conceded that he was a felon. In contrast, criminal defendants accused of violent crimes almost always seek to stipulate to the nature of wounds or other injuries suffered by the victim, but prosecutors are usually allowed to introduce gruesome photographs illustrating them. Appellate courts typically hold that a stipulation cannot fully convey the nature of the harms inflicted on the victim, so the photographs are considered to have probative value that exceeds the improper emotional effect that they create.

Examples

1. Why might rich defendants in civil cases or guilty defendants in criminal cases prefer an evidence system that did not impose a requirement that evidence be relevant?

2. Imagine a patent infringement suit. The plaintiff claims that the defendant has begun to sell a pen with an ink supply system that copies a system patented by the plaintiff more closely than patent law allows. To prove patent infringement, can the plaintiff introduce testimony that the defendant company recently moved its headquarters from one city to another?

3. Suppose the plaintiff in Example 2 offers testimony that the defendant's president bought one of the plaintiff company's pens, wrote with it, and said that he would like to invent a pen that worked as well. Would evidence of that statement be relevant?

4. In Example 2's lawsuit, suppose that the defendant company's president had paid to have a sadistic thug beat up the plaintiff and make the plaintiff tell him how to set up a production line that could make pens using the plaintiff's patented design. Could the plaintiff testify about the beating?

5. X is on trial for stealing a 1957 DeSoto automobile worth about $30,000 to collectors of classic cars. To show motive to steal and knowledge of the DeSoto's value, can the prosecution introduce evidence that X has a collection of classic cars?

Explanations

1. In a system where irrelevant evidence as well as relevant evidence was admissible, trials could last forever since only a party's endurance or financial resources would limit the amount of evidence the party could present. Theoretically, a civil defendant in a suit where the cost of losing would be very high would find it in its interest to delay the end of trial for as long as possible. The same reasoning would apply to the

guilty criminal defendant, who might well prefer daily attendance at court to serving a prison sentence.

On the other hand, the relevance principle can help defendants by preventing the jury from finding out facts about them that might make them seem unattractive: the immense wealth of a corporate defendant or a criminal defendant's long record of prior convictions.

2. No. The location of the defendant's headquarters has nothing to do with how our legal system treats the right to use particular patented inventions, so the judge should reject the testimony. Note that the judge decides questions of relevance.

3. This testimony does relate to the parties' pens. But would it help a jury decide whether the pen actually manufactured by the defendant made improper use of the plaintiff's patented invention? Its probative value is very low on the issue of patent infringement, and there might be a risk that a jury would fail to distinguish between a desire to imitate a product and a plan to misuse patented aspects of a design. Either decision made by a judge on this evidence — letting it in or keeping it out — would probably be affirmed on appeal.

4. Yes. The fact that the defendant company sought information about how to use the patented design could logically support a conclusion that the product it eventually manufactured was very close in specifications to the patented product. The fact that the defendant hired an evil person to use force against the plaintiff might cause jurors to be inclined to rule for the plaintiff just to punish the defendant for the use of force rather than because of its evaluation of the patent law issues. Nevertheless, there is a strong argument for admitting this evidence. If the plaintiff's case had lots of other evidence about the patent infringement, then it is possible that under Rule 403, a judge might decide to exclude information about the beating. But because the beating is so closely related to the defendant's manufacturing plans, it is highly likely that testimony about it would be admitted.

5. Yes. Proof that X collects cars would not support a verdict of guilty in the theft case if it were the prosecution's only evidence. But evidence does not have to be conclusive to be relevant. If X is interested in classic cars, does that make the propositions that he stole a classic car or that he knew the worth of the car more likely to be true than they would be without that information about X's interest? If the judge believes that the answer to this question is yes, then the evidence is admissible.

Limited Admissibility

Sometimes an item of evidence is relevant to one issue in a case and has no relationship at all to another issue. In that circumstance, the evidence passes the relevancy hurdle. No single piece of evidence is expected to be relevant to all the disputed issues of a case. The situation is more complicated when a single item of evidence is relevant to one issue in a case and is a type of evidence *forbidden to be considered* with respect to another issue. For example, a specialized relevancy rule prohibits admission of evidence of an alleged tortfeasor's subsequent remedial measures to prove negligence. Such remedial actions can be relevant and admissible, however, on issues other than the quality of the defendant's care. They could relate, for example, to the issues of ownership or control of the site where the injury occurred.

If a tort plaintiff seeks to introduce evidence that qualifies for the permissible relevance of showing that the defendant had control of a place where the plaintiff was hurt, our legal system is placed in a difficult position. It must deal with the possibility that a jury will make use of that information not only for the permitted purpose but also for deciding the defendant's culpability — even though a specific rule prohibits introduction of this kind of evidence to show culpability. There are two possible resolutions of the circumstance where evidence has one permissible use and another impermissible use. We could keep the evidence out. This would guarantee that the jury would not make a wrongful use of the material but would also guarantee that the proper, permitted use of the information would not occur. The other choice, which is typically the choice made by trial judges, is to let the material in and give the jury a cautionary "limiting" instruction. The limiting instruction would tell the jurors to consider the information only with respect to the topic for which it is legitimately admitted. This allows the proper use of the information, consistent with the pro-admissibility trend of modern evidence law in general and the Federal Rules in particular, while it decreases somewhat the risk that the jury will use the information improperly.

Conditional Relevance

Sometimes an item of evidence by itself will have no relevance to any issue in a trial but would be relevant if the trier of fact also had some other information. Rule 104(b) governs this situation:

> **Relevance That Depends on a Fact.** When the relevance of evidence depends on whether a fact exists, proof must be introduced sufficient to support a finding that the fact does exist. The court may admit the proposed evidence on the condition that the proof be introduced later.

To illustrate, suppose in a murder trial the prosecution sought to show that the defendant owned a red hat with a blue feather. If an eyewitness saw the murderer run from the scene wearing that kind of hat, then information about the defendant's hat would be significant circumstantial evidence of guilt. Notice, however, that the relevance of hat ownership is only apparent if there is testimony from the eyewitness. This is called "conditional relevance." The relevance of the testimony about the defendant's hat comes from the context provided by the information from the eyewitness. Judges are supposed to admit evidence of this kind if its proponent has already produced the other material that shows its relevance to the trial or if the proponent promises to produce that contextual information later. We leave it to the jury to decide whether the underlying context has been proven adequately to support consideration of the conditionally relevant information.[4] This process is mandated in Rule 104(b), which defines the situation as one in which "the relevance of evidence depends on whether a fact exists."

In the red hat illustration, the jury will make a decision about the reliability of the eyewitness testimony. If it believes that the murderer really did wear a red hat with a blue feather, it will go on to consider whether it believes the testimony which stated that the defendant owns a hat like that. If the jury does not believe that the eyewitness saw that kind of hat, it will pay no attention to the testimony it heard about the defendant's hat. Knowing that the defendant had a peculiar hat would be of no interest to a juror who did not believe that such a hat was seen at the time of the murder.

The judge does continue to have a role in the conditional relevance situation if it turns out that the proponent of the conditionally relevant information fails to produce the extra material that relates the conditionally relevant information to the case. In the red hat illustration, if the prosecutor failed to introduce eyewitness testimony about the murderer having worn a red hat, then the judge could instruct the jury to ignore whatever it had heard about the defendant's possession of a red hat. This instruction, of course, would only tell the jury to do what it would most likely have done without a specific warning, since ignoring the defendant's red hat would be natural if there was no testimony that made a red hat important to any aspect of the case.

---

4. Conditional relevance is recognized in the Rules, and judges and litigators are usually comfortable with the concept. Nevertheless, some scholars argue that the concept is analytically unsound. They point out that the relevance of *any* evidence depends on other items of evidence or other information. Whether information about the defendant's hat should be part of the jury's consideration in the hypothetical murder case is left to the jury, under the Rules. The jury will decide whether or not to think about it. In contrast, if evidence of a hatred between the defendant and the victim were introduced, the relevancy decision would not be treated as involving the Rules' concept of conditional relevance. The judge would admit it unconditionally, relying on his or her own belief that hatred is often a motive for murder.

Examples

1. In a suit between an ice cream company and the creator of a special recipe, the recipe creator claims that the ice cream company paid too little in royalties and falsified its reports of the costs of manufacturing and sales. To show that the company defrauded him, the recipe creator wants to introduce a tape recording that he claims contains a discussion by two officers of the company about the amount of profits from "this season's big project." The company objects to admission of the tape recording, claiming that "this season's big project" meant a new kind of packaging, not a recipe, and that therefore the tape is not relevant to the plaintiff's case. Discuss how the plaintiff might argue for admissibility of the tape.

2. The use of coerced confessions in criminal trials is prohibited. If a defendant objects to the admission of a confession on this basis, should the judge treat the question of whether the police used coercion as a conditional relevance issue that the jury should resolve?

3. In a rape case, the alleged victim testifies that the defendant said, "Come with me and do what I say. I'm serious. I've already been in prison for rape twice before." Is this testimony relevant to any issue in a rape case? Does it raise problems of unfair prejudice?

Explanations

1. The plaintiff would have to be able to tell the judge in good faith that he had some additional evidence showing that the conversation really involved his recipe. If the people talking on the tape were discussing packaging, then the tape would have nothing to do with the current case. If the taped executives really were discussing the plaintiff's recipe, then the information would be relevant. This is an example of conditional relevance, and the judge would properly admit the tape recording. The fact finder would consider the tape recording only if there was also persuasive evidence supporting the plaintiff's claim about what the speakers meant by "this season's big project."

2. This objection involves a factual issue about the making of the confession. But the objection does not involve the concept of relevance since the defendant is not, for the purpose of this objection, contending that the confession lacks a relationship to guilt or innocence. The defendant, for this objection, is claiming inadmissibility on the basis of a particular rule that keeps coerced confessions out of trials. The judge would decide whether the circumstances of the making of the confession were legitimate or involved forbidden coercion. If the judge decides that there was coercion, the confession would stay out and the jury would never hear about it.

If this were mistakenly treated as a conditional relevance situation, there would be an absurd result. The jury would be asked to decide whether a confession had been made voluntarily and would then be told to ignore the confession if it decided that the confession had been coerced. Notice that this puts the jury in a difficult position. A juror would be told to ignore a confession he had learned about if he decided that a preliminary factual condition our system imposes — voluntariness — was not satisfied. A juror might be able to do that, but it would require extraordinary concentration and dedication to the values on which the constitutional rule is based.In a true conditional relevance situation, jurors are never asked to do anything counterintuitive. When they are supposed to ignore information it is highly likely they will do so, because the information will not seem to them to have anything to do with the case. In the analysis of Example 1, no juror would think about the tape recording in connection with the current suit unless the juror thought the information on it involved the plaintiff's recipe. Otherwise it would not make any sense to use information about packaging to think about profits from the plaintiff's recipe. Confession cases are different. In those cases, it would make sense to think about the confession even if it had been coerced because some coerced confessions are accurate. That is why we protect defendants from being tried by jurors who have heard about their confessions in a case where the confession was coerced.

3. If there is dispute about whether the victim consented to intercourse, testimony that the defendant used coercive language would be relevant. Since the defendant's own words happen to reveal facts about his past that could cause the jury to want to punish him for that past rather than for the crime for which he is being tried, there is a possibility of unfair prejudice. The balancing test, weighing the probative value of the information against the risk of unfair prejudice, would lead to admission of the evidence, because there is not likely to be any way to prove the method of coercion other than by proving what words the alleged rapist said. Thus, the probative value of the words would be great. The risk of unfair prejudice would be treated with a limiting instruction, telling the jury to consider the words only on the issue of coercion and prohibiting the jury from considering whether or not the defendant had actually been imprisoned for rape in the past. (The problems presented by evidence of past convictions are covered by a set of specialized rules, which are discussed later in this chapter.)

Recurring Situations

Some factual propositions are involved in so many trials that precedents have developed for handling the kinds of evidence parties seek to introduce about them. Examples of these relevance inquiries are an effort to suggest that a person is guilty of a charged crime by showing that he fled the jurisdiction when arrest was imminent, or fled after arrest; use of similar occurrences to show what happened on a particular occasion; and use of statistical probabilities to prove that an event occurred.

Flight

Courts usually reason that fleeing the jurisdiction supports an inference that the defendant believed he or she was guilty, and that this supports another inference that the defendant in fact was guilty. On this analysis, flight is usually admitted as relevant to guilt. Counterarguments that are not usually successful maintain that flight should be excluded because it may show only fear of wrongful conviction, and because even a belief in guilt may not truly indicate guilt under the detailed substantive standards applicable to any given crime. A similar approach is taken to evidence about destroying evidence or trying to obtain perjured testimony.

Similar Happenings

Evidence of similar happenings is sought to be admitted in many trials. In criminal trials, prosecutors may seek to introduce evidence that a defendant has committed prior acts that are similar to the charged offense. This issue is treated in connection with "character evidence," at pages 32-40.

In tort cases, typically an accident victim will offer testimony that other people had been injured in the same way on previous occasions. This information might be relevant in a variety of ways depending on the underlying theory of the plaintiff's case. This can be illustrated with the case of a plaintiff who claims he was injured when the cap of a soft drink bottle flew off under pressure as he opened it. Proof of a significant number of similar past occurrences involving bottles sold by the defendant would support the plaintiff's contentions that (1) his injury actually was caused by a bottle cap, (2) the bottle cap was dangerous, (3) the defendant had notice of the dangerousness of the product, and (4) the defendant had an opportunity to correct the problem. Note that all of these theories of relevancy would apply in a case based on negligence, but some of them would not work in a strict liability case. Since strict liability will be imposed regardless of a defendant's notice or "wrongful conduct" in not correcting a dangerous situation, the plaintiff could not argue for the relevance of information about past injuries by claiming it showed notice to the defendant or that it supported a claim that the defendant should have acted to correct the problem. In all relevance situations, the basic substantive law or the proponent's theory of the proponent's case will have a major effect on the judge's decision on admissibility.

In determining the relevancy of similar occurrences evidence, a court will examine the surrounding circumstances of the previous incidents to compare them with the alleged facts of the incident that is the subject of the trial. If the earlier events took place under conditions with characteristics that were similar to the conditions present at the time of the event that is the basis of the suit, information about them will be considered relevant. The proponent's legal theory will affect which and how many characteristics in the past events and the litigated event must be similar to each other.

In the bottle cap example, a plaintiff who seeks recovery on negligence grounds could claim that past incidents were relevant with regard to notice. On that theory, the degree of similarity between the event that harmed the plaintiff and other earlier events could be less than would be required if the past events were claimed to be relevant to show how the plaintiff's injury occurred or to show that the product feature that harmed the plaintiff was negligently designed. If the plaintiff pleaded only a strict liability case, the plaintiff would have no basis for arguing that the past injuries were relevant to show notice. They could only be relevant to show that the plaintiff's injury really occurred in the way the plaintiff claims (by showing that the plaintiff's description of how the injury took place matched the details of past occurrences) and that the product design was hazardous. For those purposes, a high degree of similarity between the plaintiff's incident and the prior incidents would be required.

Information about similar past occurrences raises a subtle issue of the distribution of decision making between the judge and jury. This evidence is really an example of conditional relevance since information about the past events will be relevant only if a certain factual proposition is proved adequately: the similarity of settings between the past and litigated events. On this analysis, then, the judge should let the material into the trial if a juror could reasonably decide that the past event and the event being litigated are similar enough so that information from the past event could help the juror decide what really happened in the event being litigated. In theory, jurors will ignore what they learn about past mishaps if they consider them unrelated to the event examined in the trial. Even where proof of the closeness of circumstances is weak, the conditional relevance analysis leads to the idea that the judge should give the jury an opportunity to evaluate the evidence.

A further analysis is based on the fact that evidence of past injuries may be highly prejudicial. Jurors who hear about injuries to people other than the plaintiff may be inspired to make the defendant pay money to the plaintiff even if they are not persuaded there really was negligence in the plaintiff's instance. This argues against adopting a generally pro-admissibility stance on the issue of past occurrences. So even though evidence of past occurrences could be treated as an instance of conditional relevance, with most of the decision making left to juries, judges properly exclude the evidence unless they are persuaded that the showing of similarity of conditions is strong.

Statistical Proof

Another type of evidence that parties sometimes seek to introduce is testimony by experts about the probability of events. In a famous case of this type, *People v. Collins*,[5] a married couple were criminal defendants charged with robbery. The husband was a black man who sometimes wore a beard, and the wife was a white woman with blond hair. Eyewitness testimony supported the contention that the robbers were a black man with a beard and a white woman with blond hair. An expert in statistics testified for the prosecution about the probability of occurrence of many factors in the case, such as a couple being composed of two people with the combination of racial and other physical appearance attributes of the defendant couple.

The California Supreme Court found a number of problems with this. First, in calculating probabilities, it is necessary to have some empirical basis for assigning values to any event. The expert witness in *Collins* merely made guesses about the frequency of occurrence of the attributes he used for his calculations, such as how many black men have beards and how many do not. Another problem was that in calculating probabilities of combinations of different variables, the variables must be "independent." That requirement was not met in the expert's testimony. Finally, the court was concerned that jurors might improperly confuse the probability of a couple possessing the traits possessed by the defendants with the probability that the defendants were not guilty. All of these considerations led the court to be strict about the requirements of scientific accuracy in this kind of testimony because there is a strong likelihood that it will be very impressive to juries.

More modern cases involving DNA evidence raise the same problems concerning the basis and interpretation of statistical proof. For example, jurors might mistakenly believe that the rarity of a particular DNA profile is equivalent to the likelihood that a defendant committed the crime with which the examined DNA was associated. Nonetheless, it is common for

---

5. 68 Cal. 2d 319, 66 Cal. Rptr. 497 (1968).

courts to allow testimony like "the odds of a match between a random sample and the sample from the crime are only 1 out of 10,000,000."

Examples

1. A plaintiff who claimed he had been injured on the defendant's ship planned to introduce a statement from a sailor who said he had seen the injury occur. The plaintiff, the plaintiff's lawyer, and the defendant's lawyer all participated in obtaining a deposition from the sailor. On the day after taking the deposition, the defendant located crew lists showing that the "eyewitness" had not been on board the ship on the day of the injury. The plaintiff's lawyer then informed the court that he would not seek to introduce the "eyewitness" statement. The *defendant* then stated that he wanted to introduce it to show "fraud." The court replied:

   > Well, I'm not going to permit you to do that. I'm going to say that if this person perjured himself then we can do one of several things, one of which we can report it to the United States Attorney for perjury, for purposes of perjury, because it was done to influence the outcome of this case. I think that's the appropriate procedure. I don't think we are going to start introducing a document [that] you think is incorrect and intentionally incorrect in this case. . . . If it is not brought in [by the plaintiff] then I don't say it's an issue in this case for this jury to consider whether or not the plaintiff is involved. I don't know whether the plaintiff is involved in this matter. That's whose case we're trying. We're trying the plaintiff's case.[6]
   >
   > The judge was wrong. Why?

2. Warren Webster seeks damages from an amusement park, claiming that his arm was broken when one of the amusement park rides came to a sudden stop and threw him against the side of one of its cars. Webster claims that the ride was carelessly designed and carelessly operated. He also claims that the defendant amusement park should have known about the risks that the ride presented and was negligent in failing to warn about them or correct them. If Webster had evidence that other people had been hurt on the ride in the same way he claims he was hurt, it would be admissible provided that the circumstances of the earlier injuries were similar to the circumstances of Webster's injury. What if the amusement park's manager knows that in ten years of operation no one besides Webster has claimed to have been injured by the ride, and the manager knows of no other injuries? How would you argue for admissibility of this evidence of prior safety?

---

6. McQueeney v. Wilmington Trust Co., 779 F.2d 916, n.3 (3d Cir. 1985).

3. The plaintiff was hit by a carelessly driven armored truck. Unfortunately, the driver drove away from the scene of the accident. The plaintiff could not see a company's name on the truck, but remembers that it was blue. There are two companies using blue armored trucks in the area where the accident occurred; one of them has 90 trucks and the other has ten trucks. The plaintiff sues the 90-truck company claiming that there is a 90 percent chance that one of its trucks hit him. If there is no other evidence about the identity of the truck in the accident except the victim's testimony about its color and evidence showing that 90 percent of the blue armored trucks in use belong to the defendant, should the plaintiff's case get to the jury or is the defendant entitled to a directed verdict?

Explanations

1. If the jury believed that the plaintiff had known that the "eyewitness" statement was phony, the jury could infer from that belief that the plaintiff considered his case so weak that it needed help from perjured testimony. That inference could properly assist the jury in deciding whatever disputed issues of fact were involved in the case.

   The judge might have been on firmer ground if he or she had ruled that the evidence was relevant but inadmissible because without a strong link between the plaintiff personally and the attempted perjury, there are risks of wasting time and confusing the jury.

2. For the prior safe operation of the ride to be admissible evidence, the manager would have to establish that the circumstances at the time Webster claims to have been injured were highly similar to the circumstances during all the prior period about which the manager has knowledge. "Similarity" here must be interpreted to mean that the prior circumstances and the circumstances when Webster was hurt did not differ in ways that could affect safety. If that similarity is established, then safe operation in the past is directly relevant on the issue of notice since it would have suggested to the defendant that the ride was safe (not that the ride was dangerous as the plaintiff claims).

   Safe operation in the past also would support a claim by the defendant that the plaintiff is mistaken or lying about how or where his injury occurred, because a history of safe operation suggests (although it does not prove conclusively) that the ride does not cause injuries the way the plaintiff claims it did. Finally, it could support the amusement park's general contention that the ride is reasonably safe even if it did cause harm to the plaintiff on one occasion.

3. Some courts would let this plaintiff get to the jury on the probability theory. There is not really any risk that the "statistical" evidence will be overpoweringly technical and too hard for jurors to refute with their own

common sense. And information about which company with blue armored trucks owns the most blue armored trucks does relate to the question of which company's truck was involved in the accident. Yet some courts would hold that the inference one could base on the statistics is so slight that the evidence should be treated as not relevant. They might also treat the information as relevant but subject to a significant risk that the jury will give it inappropriately heavy weight; this would unfairly prejudice the defendant and could be a separate rationale for excluding the evidence.

Courts may be reluctant to create a situation in which a judgment is entered in a case that might seem entirely theoretical or suppositional to the general public. That point of view ignores the fact that most cases involve only evidence that is subject in varying degrees to error or that is based on implicit estimates of probability. Nonetheless, while a case based on eyewitness testimony may be more likely to produce the wrong result than a case based on 90 percent odds such as the problem case, many courts tolerate the risk in the eyewitness case but would be reluctant to acknowledge that probability evidence has equal reliability. (In *Kaminsky v. Hertz Corporation*, 288 N.W.2d 426 (Mich. Ct. App. 1979), the court faced a problem like the one in this question, but its task was made easier because the plaintiff remembered seeing the defendant's name on the truck. Even though some trucks with that name were not owned by the defendant, the court relied on substantive theories connected with the obligations an enterprise must bear if it allows its name to appear on trucks other than those it owns.)

Specific Exclusions
of Relevant Material

INTRODUCTION

Judges have great discretion in applying the relevance requirement and the safeguard that excludes relevant but unfairly prejudicial information. However, in certain specific circumstances they are required to keep evidence out despite its logical relevance. These are situations where the likelihood of unfair prejudice from particular types of evidence is considered so extreme that it cannot be risked or where social goals unrelated to the truth-finding process are more important than the contribution that particular types of evidence could make to that process.

Insurance

The rule regarding evidence of insurance is one of the simplest of these specialized relevance rules, so it is a good one to consider first. Rule 411 states:

> Evidence that a person was or was not insured against liability is not admissible to prove whether the person acted negligently or otherwise wrongfully. But the court may admit this evidence for another purpose, such as proving a witness's bias or prejudice or proving agency, ownership, or control.

This rule is based on a fear that jurors who know a party has insurance may find that party liable only because they believe the liability will be cost-free to the party, or that jurors will increase the amount of damages they find, secure in the belief that only an insurance company will be affected adversely. It could be argued that proof that a party has insurance does have logical relevance to the question of how carefully the party acted on a specific occasion, if one believed that people who know that they will not be financially responsible for injuries they might inflict might be more willing to take chances than people who expected that they would have to pay personally for harms they caused. That likelihood is probably slight, however. This possible logical relevance is outweighed by the fear that insurance information will distort a jury's willingness to assign liability according to a fair-minded evaluation of evidence in terms of the judge's instructions.

As a matter of fact, jurors may well have suppositions about parties' insurance, and if that is so, it might be more sensible to give them accurate information than it is to leave to their own guesswork. This argument strikes at the reasonableness of the exclusionary rule. In circumstances where insurance information comes out at trial by error, appellate judges who decide whether the error was significant enough to require retrial may be influenced by this possible weakness in the rationale for the rule. However, at common law and under the Federal Rules, the doctrine is clear, and compliance with it is not a matter of judicial discretion.

The Rule does not prohibit all possible uses of evidence about a party's insurance coverage. If it can support findings about topics other than negligent or wrongful conduct, evidence of insurance coverage is permitted to be introduced. For example, if a defense witness works for the defendant's insurance company, information about the witness's possible financial bias would be permitted to be introduced, despite the fact that it would inform the jury about the defendant's insurance coverage.

Subsequent Remedial Measures

In many trials, an injured plaintiff seeks to show that the defendant's conduct before the plaintiff's injury was careless or that the defendant's product was in some way defective. One technique a plaintiff might use to show negligence or the existence of a product defect is to introduce evidence that after the plaintiff's injury, the defendant made a repair, changed a procedure, or changed the design of a product. This use of evidence about "subsequent repairs" or "subsequent remedial measures" is forbidden by Rule 407. That Rule states:

2. Specific Exclusions of Relevant Material

When measures are taken that would have made an earlier injury or harm less likely to occur, evidence of the subsequent measures is not admissible to prove:

- negligence;
- culpable conduct;
- a defect in a product or its design; or
- a need for a warning or instruction.

But the court may admit this evidence for another purpose, such as impeachment or — if disputed — proving ownership, control, or the feasibility of precautionary measures.

If this rule did not exist, would evidence about subsequent repairs or changes meet the test of the general relevance standard under Rule 401? For example, if a plaintiff claims she slipped on the defendant's loose rug, evidence that after the accident the defendant tacked down the rug would suggest that the rug had been loose at the time of the accident and that the defendant considered it risky to leave the rug as it had been. Similarly, a manufacturer of hedge clippers might add a safety feature to the product after learning that someone had been injured using one of its clippers manufactured without that safety feature. Evidence about that change suggests that the manufacturer believed that a design incorporating the safety feature was better than a design that omitted the feature. On the other hand, tacking down the rug might have been an instance of extreme caution and therefore not a clue that the defendant was negligent in the rug's earlier maintenance. Adding the safety feature to the clippers might reflect a technological advance discovered so recently that its omission did not render the earlier design defective. Negligence law requires people to be reasonably careful, not extraordinarily careful. Strict liability law regarding design defects does not usually treat a design as defective if it lacked a feature that was not technologically or economically feasible at the time of manufacture. So, in most cases, evidence of subsequent repairs or design changes is ambiguous — it might support a relevant finding that the defendant's conduct or design was substandard, but it might also support an irrelevant finding that the defendant's subsequent conduct represented greater care than the law requires. If Rule 401's relevance standard applied to this evidence, a court would be justified in admitting it.

Despite its possible relevance, this type of evidence is excluded under Rule 407 because of two significant policy considerations. Those who support the Rule believe that if plaintiffs were able to let jurors know about changes defendants make in response to injuries, individuals and organizations would be deterred from responding to accidents by increasing their precautions. It also seems unfair, to some, for a defendant to be penalized at a trial for taking the socially desirable action of decreasing risks.

In the language of Rule 407, evidence of remedial measures "that would have made an earlier injury or harm less likely to occur" is prohibited only if it offered to prove "negligence; culpable conduct; a defect in a product or its design; or a need for a warning or instruction." The Rule's prohibition does not apply if evidence of subsequent repairs is offered to show something other than the types of findings listed in the Rule. For example, information about subsequent repairs would be admissible to show that the defendant owned or controlled the thing or the place that was involved in the accident. Evidence of subsequent remedial measures may also show that it was possible to improve whatever harmed the plaintiff; this rationale is only available, however, if the defendant controverts the feasibility of improvements.

Rule 407 is an amended version of the originally promulgated rule. It clearly applies to both negligence and strict liability causes of action, but the original version of the rule was read by a minority of courts as applying only to negligence cases. Some states, interpreting their versions of Rule 407 or interpreting the common law doctrines on which the rule is based, have declined to apply the rule to strict liability cases. A California decision[1] was the first to hold that the doctrine's policy foundation of encouraging remedial measures has no application in modern strict liability cases since manufacturers have huge incentives to make improvements whether or not those improvements will be reported to juries in tort cases — they want to continue to sell products and they want to cut down the number of future injuries caused by their products. Nevertheless, the majority of states apply Rule 407 and the general common law prohibition of evidence about subsequent repairs in strict liability cases. They reach that result primarily by emphasizing the aspects of strict liability theory that are functionally quite similar to negligence doctrines.

Compromises and Offers to Compromise

Another important exclusion of material that would otherwise be relevant and admissible concerns compromises and settlements. Statements made in negotiating most settlements, and the fact of an accomplished settlement itself, are kept from the knowledge of the trier of fact even though many settlement offers are probably a good indication that the party that offered the settlement believed that the opponent's claims were valid. In the terms of Rule 408:

> **(a) Prohibited Uses.** Evidence of the following is not admissible — on behalf of any party — either to prove or disprove the validity or amount of a

---

1. Ault v. International Harvester Co., 13 Cal. 3d 113, 117 Cal. Rptr. 812, 528 P.2d 1148 (1974).

disputed claim or to impeach by a prior inconsistent statement or a contradiction:

(1) furnishing, promising, or offering — or accepting, promising to accept, or offering to accept — a valuable consideration in compromising or attempting to compromise the claim; and

(2) conduct or a statement made during compromise negotiations about the claim — except when offered in a criminal case and when the negotiations related to a claim by a public office in the exercise of its regulatory, investigative, or enforcement authority.

(b) **Exceptions.** The court may admit this evidence for another purpose, such as proving a witness's bias or prejudice, negating a contention of undue delay, or proving an effort to obstruct a criminal investigation or prosecution.

The purpose of this rule is to encourage settlements. If it did not exist, people involved in disputes might be reluctant to talk about them for fear that their words would be used against them in later trials. The proponent of this rule's application must show that there was a disputed claim. This means that Rule 408 does *not* prevent the admission of an offer of payment like, "I know I made a mistake and there's about $500 worth of damage to your car, but I'll only pay $200." Those words admit responsibility and also concede the amount of harm caused. Unless a judge were somehow persuaded that "I'll only pay $200" was really a modification of the admission that the damage amounted to $500, Rule 408 would allow testimony about the statement.

There is a distinction between (1) offers to pay or payments and (2) statements made in connection with negotiating for a payment. The Federal Rule shields evidence about settlements or offered settlements in all cases, and *also* shields evidence about "conduct or a statement made during compromise negotiations" (except where the negotiations involved a government actor and the information is offered in a criminal case). In some jurisdictions statements made in settlement talks may be admissible unless the speaker or writer accompanies them with phrases like "this is hypothetical" or "for purposes of settlement only." The Federal Rule does not have any requirement of this type because the pro-settlement rationale of the rule is served best by a straightforward approach that does not trip up the unwary. However, where negotiations concern a claim by a government body, the Federal Rule does allow use of statements and conduct made in the negotiations in a later criminal case. Parties in this type of negotiation often know that the government may later attempt a criminal prosecution, are often represented by counsel, and may be able to negotiate to preclude disclosure.

Where Rule 408 might require exclusion of proof of *conduct or statements* related to settlements, it is important to remember that this shield applies only if the conduct or statements occurred during actual compromise negotiations.

It may sometimes be difficult to know, for example, whether a conversation was part of regular business contacts between two parties or was part of something that can properly be considered compromise negotiations. The rule is meant to facilitate settlements by shielding statements made in working them out, but it is not meant to apply to statements made in non-settlement activities. If one party has sued or threatened to sue another, then it is easy to characterize their later discussions as being part of compromise negotiations. If litigation has not been mentioned, then conversations between parties are likely to be characterized as part of ordinary business give-and-take, and the things parties say in those conversations are likely to be treated as outside the coverage of Rule 408.

It is important to remember that the purpose for which a party seeks to introduce evidence relating to a settlement can be crucial. Under Rule 408, if the proponent of testimony that would reveal the fact that some parties had agreed on a settlement can show that the information is relevant in a way other than in connection with the validity of the settled claim, the information is admissible. One such use would be in a situation where the benefits of a settlement might have made a person biased in favor of the party who agreed to the settlement. If the beneficiary of the settlement became a witness in a trial and gave testimony that benefitted the provider of the settlement, a party who opposed that testimony could have the jury learn about the settlement. The settlement would be treated as relevant to the truthfulness of the witness but not as relevant to the merits of the case.

There is another important limitation to the effect of this rule. Although Rule 408 prevents a party from telling the trier of fact that his or her opponent said a particular thing during settlement talks, a party is entitled to bring the substance of that information into the trial if it is relevant and was obtainable other than in the settlement talks. Illustratively, a party cannot testify, "My opponent told me in settlement talks that his company's trucks had suffered 50 similar brake failures before the accident that hurt me." However, that party would be allowed to introduce evidence of the prior brake failures as long as he or she did not refer to the settlement talks, even if it was the opponent's disclosures during settlement talks that gave the party the idea of obtaining that evidence. A party cannot immunize information from introduction into a trial by mentioning it in settlement talks.

Payments of Medical Expenses

People involved in an incident that causes an injury may sometimes be motivated to pay the victim's medical expenses. Insurance companies have an incentive to provide medical care for an accident victim to decrease the magnitude of the victim's injury if they think they may ultimately have financial responsibility for the harm. These payments might not be kept secret under Rule 408 since that rule applies only where there is a disputed claim. However, a different rule facilitates this type of humanitarian payment. Rule 409 provides that:

> Evidence of furnishing, promising to pay, or offering to pay medical, hospital, or similar expenses resulting from an injury is not admissible to prove liability for the injury.

Under this rule, proof about medical payments or offers of medical payments made outside of settlement negotiations is not admissible to show liability for the injury. In contrast to the broad protection provided in Rule 408 for conduct and statements related to compromise negotiations, Rule 409 offers no protection for statements made in connection with the payments. This difference in the scope of exclusion between Rules 408 and 409 is inconsequential to professionals, such as lawyers or employees of insurance companies, because they know about it and are guided by it in what they say or do not say. For individuals who have no counsel or who are inexperienced in the legal aftermath of accidents, the difference may not matter because their decision to pay for medical care is based not on legal considerations but on genuine humanitarian feelings.

Nolo Contendere and Withdrawn Guilty Pleas

The Federal Rules of Evidence, in parallel to Federal Rule of Criminal Procedure 11(e)(6), seek to facilitate plea bargaining by providing confidentiality for statements made in plea bargaining, for pleas of nolo contendere, and for guilty pleas that are later withdrawn. Rule 410 states:

> **(a) Prohibited Uses.** In a civil or criminal case, evidence of the following is not admissible against the defendant who made the plea or participated in the plea discussions:
>> **(1)** a guilty plea that was later withdrawn;
>> **(2)** a nolo contendere plea;
>> **(3)** a statement made during a proceeding on either of those pleas under Federal Rule of Criminal Procedure 11 or a comparable state procedure; or
>> **(4)** a statement made during plea discussions with an attorney for the prosecuting authority if the discussions did not result in a guilty plea or they resulted in a later-withdrawn guilty plea.
>
> **(b) Exceptions.** The court may admit a statement described in Rule 410(a)(3) or (4):

(1) in any proceeding in which another statement made during the same plea or plea discussions has been introduced, if in fairness the statements ought to be considered together; or

(2) in a criminal proceeding for perjury or false statement, if the defendant made the statement under oath, on the record, and with counsel present.

The purpose of this rule is to afford significant confidentiality to an individual's statements made in the course of negotiating a plea. However, many law enforcement officials are able to avoid the rule's effects by refusing to negotiate unless the individual waives his or her rights under the rule. The United States Supreme Court has upheld the effect of such waivers, despite arguments that Congress did not intend the rule to be waivable and that allowing it to be waived may, as a practical matter, withdraw the rule's provisions from most plea negotiations.[2]

This rule has some significant details. A guilty plea that becomes the basis for a conviction is not protected from other uses. The policy of facilitating plea bargaining is not strong enough to support a doctrine insulating convictions based on plea-bargained guilty pleas from use in other contexts. For a statement to be covered by the rule, it must have been made to a prosecutor. This is meant to prevent a defendant who makes statements to detectives or other investigators from later characterizing them as part of plea bargaining to have them excluded from admission by this rule.

Compared with the rules on compromises and payments of medical expenses, Rule 410 treats the negotiating defendant differently than the negotiating civil party or the Good Samaritan who pays an injured victim's expenses. For example, while Rule 410 applies only where a prosecutor has been involved in negotiations, for civil compromises or payments of medical expenses there are no similar limitations on the identity of those who must be involved in negotiating or handling a medical expenses payment.

If the plea bargaining leads to a nolo contendere plea or to a plea of guilty that is later withdrawn, evidence of those pleas is inadmissible to show criminal liability for the charged offense. This may facilitate plea bargaining, and the grant of secrecy is consistent with the secrecy provided to support the pro-settlement stance of Rule 408 and the pro-humanitarian payment approach of Rule 409. However, evidence of the pleas may not even be admitted to show bias or for any other purpose different from showing criminal liability for the charged offense. This is more restrictive than parallel provisions for compromises and payments of medical expenses.

Statements made in connection with plea bargaining cannot be admitted to show liability for the charged offense. This is equivalent to Rule 408's provisions for compromises, barring use of such statements to show

---

2. United States v. Mezzanatto, 513 U.S. 196 (1995).

liability. For payments of medical expenses, however, any statements that may accompany the payment or offer of payment are admissible under Rule 409. Also, according to Rule 408, statements made in compromise negotiations are not barred from admission if they are relevant for a purpose other than showing liability for the original claim or injury. In the criminal law context of Rule 410, there is a much more limited treatment of the use of bargaining statements for purposes other than proving liability for the underlying offense. Statements made during plea bargaining are admissible only to complete partial disclosures that the defendant may make and in certain perjury prosecutions. Chart 2 summarizes the important aspects of Rules 408, 409, and 410.

Chart 2 — Admissibility of Settlements, Payments, or Pleas (or Offers to Make Them) and Related Statements and Conduct

Points of Comparison	Civil Settlements	Payments and Offers to Pay Medical Expenses	Nolo Contendere and Withdrawn Guilty Pleas
Federal Rule	408	409	410
Must there be a dispute for rule to apply?	Yes	No	Impliedly
With whom must party with potential liability deal?	Anyone who can settle disputed claim	Anyone who can accept payment	Prosecutor (not police)
Can offered or actual settlement payment or plea be admitted to show liability?	No	No	No
Can offered or actual settlement payment or plea be admitted for uses other than to show liability?	Yes	Yes	No
Can related statements or conduct be admitted to show liability?	No	Yes	No
Can related statements or conduct be admitted for uses other than to show liability?	Yes	Yes	To complete partial disclosures by defendant; also certain perjury cases

2. Specific Exclusions of Relevant Material

Examples

1. Consider the following chronology:

March, 2016:	a carpenter bought a power tool
April, 2016:	the tool company redesigned that product, incorporating a finger guard
May, 2016:	the carpenter's fingers were injured while she was using the tool

   In a suit against the tool company, seeking damages under negligence and strict liability theories, can the carpenter introduce evidence of the April product improvement to show that the product as sold to her was defective or carelessly designed?

2. A customer says to a used car dealer, "I'm sorry I haven't made the last payment, and I have to admit the car runs fine, but I just can't afford it. I owe you $800 more, but will you accept $450?" In a later suit for the full $800, the customer claims he should not have to pay anything because the car was defective. To establish that there was nothing wrong with the car, can the dealer testify that the customer told him the car was fine?

3. Plaintiff sues defendant for money she claims is due under the terms of the settlement of a prior suit. How can the plaintiff establish her claim in the light of Rule 408's prohibitions about evidence of settlements?

4. In a malpractice case, the plaintiff wants to establish that the defendant doctor made a mistake in an operation by testifying that when the doctor looked at an X-ray of the plaintiff taken after the operation, he said, "This makes it look like I did the whole operation wrong." The defendant doctor objects to the testimony, claiming that it should be excluded under Rule 408 because when he said it he suspected that the patient might sue, and he wanted to establish a rapport that would help reach a compromise. Should this testimony be kept out under Rule 408? Should the judge or the jury make the decision?

5. After an accident at a railroad crossing, the state highway department cut down trees that obstructed the view of the tracks from the road. The person injured in the accident sues the railroad, claiming that the intersection was dangerous and that therefore the railroad should have instructed its engineers to slow down when they approached it. Can the plaintiff introduce evidence about the highway department's action as relevant to the dangerousness of the intersection prior to the accident?

6. In a products liability suit, the plaintiff seeks to establish that a machine's design was unreasonably dangerous. If the manufacturer added a safety

feature after the plaintiff's injury, Rule 407 prohibits introducing evidence of the change to establish negligence, culpable conduct, or product defectiveness. Suppose a witness for the manufacturer states that the product's safety features, as present in the model that injured the plaintiff, were "the best possible" or "of the highest quality." Could that provide an avenue for bringing information about the subsequent changes into the trial?

7. Andrew First and Bertha Second were walking across an intersection when they were both hit by a truck operated by defendant Cash Corporation. They were each hospitalized, and each accepted payments from Cash Corporation for the medical expenses. First later sues Cash. If Second testifies at the trial that Second and First were talking while they crossed the street and were not particularly attentive, could First introduce evidence that Cash paid Second's medical bills?

8. In a medical malpractice case, an expert testifies that in his opinion, based on an examination of the plaintiff, the defendant never injured the plaintiff. If the expert works for an insurance company that would be responsible for paying a judgment against the defendant doctor, can the plaintiff bring that fact to the attention of the jury?

Explanations

1. This example concerns the general prohibition against using evidence of subsequent remedial measures to prove negligence or strict liability for product-related injuries. The defendant made the design change in this problem subsequent to the purchase but prior to the injury. The language of Rule 407 shows that the time of injury is what counts, not the time of manufacture or sale of the product. If the change had been made after the injury, evidence of the change would have to be excluded, because the plaintiff was seeking to introduce the evidence to show negligence and strict liability. But the change was made before the injury, so evidence about it can be admitted for any purpose.

   The example also serves as a reminder that strict liability actions are thought by some state courts (a small minority) to be outside the coverage of their versions of Rule 407. In part the responses of courts to this problem have reflected their general point of view on the underlying issue of whether evidence rules can have an important effect on willingness to adopt safety measures. The courts that believe the exclusionary rule really affects people's and companies' plans for remedial measures will be inclined to apply the rule broadly to negligence and strict liability cases. In a jurisdiction that applies the rule only to negligence cases, the material could be admitted with an instruction that the jury consider it only in deciding the strict liability aspects of the case.

2. Yes. Attempting to whittle down the amount of an acknowledged debt is not the kind of conversation the rule against disclosure of settlement talks seeks to encourage. Rule 408 covers only statements and conduct in connection with claims that are disputed either as to validity or amount. In this example, there is no dispute about the quality of the car or about the total amount ($800) that is owed.

3. The plaintiff is entitled to introduce evidence of the settlement agreement. Rule 408 only precludes admission of evidence about settlements or settlement talks if the evidence is introduced as relevant to the validity or invalidity of the underlying claim that is the subject of the negotiations. In this example, the claim is not based on whatever dispute led to the settlement. It is based on a contractual undertaking (the settlement), which can be interpreted and enforced by a court without any attention to the original dispute that it was intended to resolve.

4. This is a reminder that the judge ordinarily has the responsibility to make preliminary rulings personally. Here the judge will decide whether the conversation is within Rule 408's characterization of compromise negotiations. If this task were assigned to the jury, jurors would listen to evidence about the challenged statement and the context in which it was made. Then the judge would tell them about Rule 408 and would tell them to ignore the statement if they concluded that it was made in the context of compromise negotiations. It might be hard for a juror to forget about the doctor's words, even if the juror did conclude that they had been spoken in settlement talks.

   The evidence should be admitted. The only suggestion that the doctor's words were part of settlement negotiations comes from the doctor's statement that he suspected a suit might someday be filed. This does not satisfy the requirement in Rule 408 that a dispute be involved. Furthermore, compromise negotiations must take place in order for Rule 408's protections to be invoked. If the doctor's own predictions about litigation were permitted to turn his words into protected statements for the purpose of settlement, just about any words anyone ever says to a person who later sues him would be inadmissible at trials.

   This is not a conditional relevance situation where the judge is required to let the jury do part of the work of deciding the fundamental relevance question. For conditional relevance, an item of evidence could be relevant to the trial as long as some additional condition was believed to have existed. Conditionally relevant evidence has a place in the trial if the result of some factual inquiry provides a logical link between the offered evidence and an issue at the trial. This is different from the Rule 408 problem, in which the doctor's words could be let in or kept out depending on the outcome of the factual issue about whether they were spoken in a compromise effort. There is a difference between

(a) conditional relevance where the jury gets the initial item of evidence and then decides itself whether to use it and (b) most preliminary admissibility questions. For conditional relevance, if the additional required condition is not fulfilled, there is no risk that the jury will use the originally offered evidence, because it contradicts common sense to base a decision on non-relevant information. In other situations, like those covered by Rule 408, it would definitely not contradict common sense or human nature for a juror to base a decision on significant words, even if principles based on independent social policies led the judge to instruct the jury to ignore them.

5. Yes. Ordinarily evidence of subsequent remedial measures cannot be introduced to support contentions about the quality of an actor's conduct at the time of an earlier injury. However, in this situation, the remedial measures were carried out by someone other than the defendant. Keeping them secret from the jury would not serve the public policy goal of avoiding "penalizing" those who make post-accident repairs. For that reason, most courts would admit the evidence.

6. Yes. Rule 407 prohibits the use of information about subsequent remedial measures to show culpability, negligence, or product defectiveness. It states explicitly, however, that this kind of material may be introduced for other purposes. One of the purposes listed is to show the feasibility of precautions when the defendant disputes or controverts that feasibility. The analysis of this example depends on whether the statements "highest quality" or "best possible" are equivalent to claims that there were no feasible alternatives. Many courts would characterize them that way and allow the plaintiff to introduce evidence of subsequent improvements to demonstrate that the prior design was not the "best possible" or of the "highest quality." On the other hand, if the defendant's witnesses had merely described the prior design as "good" or "excellent," it would be difficult for the plaintiff to contend that they had controverted the feasibility of alternatives.

7. Yes. The point of introducing the evidence would be to show that Second might be biased in favor of Cash Corporation. This use of the payment information is not barred by Rule 409 even though it does exclude evidence of medical payments if the evidence is introduced to show liability for the injury. Here the rationale for introducing the evidence is to show possible motivation for Second to lie or shade the testimony favorably to Cash. The evidence would be admissible, and Cash would be entitled to a limiting instruction telling the jury that it could not infer from the fact of payments to Second that Cash was responsible for the accident.

8. Yes. This would be a reference to insurance not to show culpability but to show that the witness might be biased to give testimony that favors his employer, the insurance company.

Character Evidence

If you wanted to hire someone to take care of a child, would you pay attention to information about the person's temperament? If you knew that an applicant was mean, nasty, or dishonest, would that affect your hiring decision? Most people would answer these questions "yes" since character traits do affect how we act. For instance, a dishonest person will commit more illegal acts than an honest person would. Experience suggests that it is reasonable to make inferences from a person's character traits to a person's likely conduct. However, evidence law often prohibits that use of information about a person's "character." In evidence law, *character* means the type of person someone is — honest, dishonest, generous, selfish, friendly, nasty, careless, cautious, hot-headed, or calm, for example. A basic rule (with some exceptions) is that evidence of a person's character may not be introduced to support an inference that the person acted on a specific occasion in conformity with that character.

Evidence law reflects deep ambivalence about the concept of character. Although there is an apparently broad prohibition against the use of character evidence, rules allow it to be used in many settings. The complex treatment of character is also reflected in rules about *how* character can be proved, which is an issue different from *whether* there is a role for character evidence in a particular case. This chapter and Chapter 5, "Examination and Impeachment," cover the topic of character evidence. A brief overview of the ways in which evidence law controls proof about people's character will help put the various detailed explanations in context.

Character evidence to prove a person's action in conformity with that character is often prohibited. The basic rule is that information about a person's character may not be introduced to suggest that the person did something because of a propensity to do such things. The "propensity inference," that a person did something because he or she is the type of person who would likely have done it, is often forbidden. The next paragraph describes situations where evidence law does allow propensity inferences.

Character evidence to prove a person's action in conformity with that character is often allowed. In some situations, the propensity inference is explicitly allowed. First, a criminal defendant is allowed to introduce evidence about his or her own good character to support an inference that he or she did not commit a charged crime. Once a criminal defendant does this, the prosecution may introduce rebuttal evidence about the defendant's character to suggest that he or she is guilty. Second, also in criminal trials, the defendant may show that the victim was the aggressor by introducing evidence of the victim's character for violence. The prosecution may rebut this with character evidence about the victim or about the defendant's aggressive nature. Also, it may show that a murder victim had a peaceful character to rebut a claim made in any way that the victim was an aggressor. Third, specific provisions of the Federal Rules allow proof of a defendant's sexual propensities in sex offense trials. Finally, the process of impeachment is another circumstance in which the propensity inference is permitted. Where an issue at trial is whether a witness has testified truthfully, evidence about that witness's character for truth-telling is permitted to support the inference that the witness has acted at the trial in conformity with the witness's usual respect for truth. This use of character evidence, to show truthful or deceptive conduct at a trial, is explained in the chapter on "Examination and Impeachment."

Character evidence to prove a person's character is allowed. An element of a claim or defense can explicitly involve someone's character. For example, a defendant in a defamation case, accused of falsely describing the plaintiff as evil, would be permitted to prove that the plaintiff is, in fact, evil. In that type of case, evidence intended to show the nature of a person's character is allowed.

Evidence that seems like character evidence is allowed if its relevance does not depend on an inference involving a conclusion about a person's character. The propensity bar prohibits the introduction of character evidence to support inferences that because of a person's character, the person is likely to have acted in a certain way usually linked to that character. Sometimes evidence that could support a conclusion about a person's character may have relevance independent of that type of conclusion. For example, evidence that someone charged with a crime has committed similar crimes in the past could lead a jury to think that the defendant is a criminally inclined type of person. If this were the prosecution's only justification for offering the evidence, it would be excluded by the general prohibition against propensity evidence. If the prosecution offered the evidence to show, for example, that participation in those past crimes gave the defendant skills that were specially needed in the offense for which the defendant is charged in the current trial, then admissibility would be possible. In this situation, the jury would not use the information about past conduct to determine what type of person the defendant is, but would use the information to determine that the defendant possessed a specific skill that made it more likely that he or she was the perpetrator of the charged offense.

Methods allowed for proof of character. A person's character traits can be conveyed to a finder of fact in a variety of ways. Testimony about the person's reputation or about a witness's opinion of the person is always allowed. In certain specific cases, evidence about actual instances of past conduct is allowed to support inferences about a person's character. In some situations a questioner is allowed to ask about a person's past conduct to support an inference about the person's character but is not allowed to introduce evidence (other than the response to the inquiry) about the specific past conduct.

The Propensity Inference

Suppose someone on trial for the robbery of a liquor store had robbed gas stations several times in the past. He might also have the reputation of being a thief. The propensity rule prohibits introduction of information about his reputation or the past robberies to support the inferences that he is a thief and that he therefore robbed the liquor store. Rule 404(a)(1) establishes the general exclusion by stating:

> **Prohibited Uses.** Evidence of a person's character or character trait is not admissible to prove that on a particular occasion the person acted in accordance with the character or trait.

This prohibition applies to civil cases, and to criminal cases with a small number of exceptions. For *sexual offense* civil and criminal cases, however, Rules 413, 414, and 415 reject this traditional analysis. These provisions, discussed below, permit introduction of evidence of a defendant's past sex offense to support an inference that the defendant committed another offense of that type.

There are two main reasons for the prohibition in Rule 404(a)(1). One is the belief that the propensity inference may lead to wrong conclusions. Another is a concern that the propensity inference would almost always be supported by evidence that carries a significant risk of unfair prejudice.

These reasons for excluding character evidence offered to show a person's propensity to act in a certain way can be examined using the liquor store robbery example. In that case, one might argue that the defendant's past crimes and reputation support an inference that he is a criminal type of person and disrespects private property, and that this supports an inference that he robbed a particular liquor store at a particular time. Rule 404(a)(1) rejects this line of analysis. Chart 3 shows this chain of inferences, highlighting the fact that it involves a middle conclusion about the defendant as a type of person.

The propensity inferences are questionable because "character" is a vague concept and because the effect of a person's character on a person's actions may be highly variable. Since character is likely to be multidimensional, and may mean different things to different people, it is difficult to be sure that evidence of gas station robberies really does support an inference that the robber is a thieving type of person (if there really is such a thing as a thieving type of person at all). Reputation evidence is similarly subject to a wide range of interpretations. It is also hard to know what a reputation for thievery really means in specific terms. Secondly, it is far from clear that people who are known to be thief-like rob liquor stores more often than other types of people do, since the external manifestations of any type of character by any particular person can be very varied.

condition must be satisfied in order for the past acts information to be admissible against the defendant.

In a kidnapping case, evidence that the defendant had been convicted in the past for buying narcotics could be characterized as showing that the defendant had a motive to demand ransom because he needed money to support a drug habit. In a trial for bank robbery, evidence that a person stole a car might be admissible if the car was used to commit the robbery. These uses would be described as evidence of a past bad act admissible to show a plan. Chart 6 illustrates some of the ways in which the links might be established between a defendant and past conduct, and between that conduct and conduct on the occasion under scrutiny in the trial. It shows that the proponent of evidence in this situation must always make at least two logical connections: one is between the defendant and the past conduct, and the other is between the past conduct and the charged offense.

Even if a defendant has been acquitted of past charged crimes, evidence of a possible connection with those crimes could be used against him or her in a new case. Acquittal, after all, means that the prosecution failed to prove its case beyond a reasonable doubt; it does not represent a finding that the defendant did not commit the alleged offense. So a defendant could be tried for committing a fraud through a unique set of representations and could be acquitted, yet information about the past accusations could be used in a new trial if the defendant were accused of perpetrating the same fraud against a new victim. The general relevance test—does the information make a significant fact more likely to be true than it would be in the absence of that information—is applied here, even though the ultimate decision in a criminal case is required to satisfy the beyond a reasonable doubt standard.

Chart 6 — Examples of Possible Links Between Defendant, Past Acts, and a Current Charged Offense

Person	Type of Link	One Past Event	Type of Link	Another Past Event
Defendant	Convicted of past conduct; or Described (adequately for preponderance test) as connected with past conduct; or Acquitted of past conduct	Past conduct	Marks the defendant as one with special knowledge or methods of action; or Establishes motive for committing charged offense	Charged offense

The proponent of past bad acts evidence has the burden of persuading the judge that the information has some relevance to the current trial other than to support a conclusion that the defendant is a bad person and therefore is more likely to have committed the charge offense. Additionally, because past bad acts evidence is so likely to involve a risk of unfair prejudice, the trial judge will consider the relationship between its probative value and that risk of unfair prejudice under Rule 403. In evaluating the probative value of the evidence, the court will be strongly influenced by the proponent's need for the evidence. If there are other ways to establish whatever the proponent says the past bad acts evidence will show, courts will ordinarily exclude the past bad acts and relegate the proponent to less inflammatory proof of that issue. Where other evidence is not available for the non-propensity purpose that the past bad acts evidence could serve, such as proof of a plan, a motive, or absence of mistake, then despite the risks of juror misuse of the information, the past bad acts material is properly admitted. Because evidence admitted under Rule 404(b)(2) is often strongly damaging, and because analyzing its relevance may be difficult, the rule entitles criminal defendants to notice in advance if the prosecution intends to rely on Rule 404(b)(2) for admissibility.

Note that Rules 413, 414, and 415, discussed above, allow introduction of evidence of a defendant's past sexual offenses to support an inference that the defendant committed another such offense.

"Character in Issue"

Other situations in which evidence about a person's character avoids the propensity bar are sometimes referred to as "character in issue" cases. For example, in a defamation case there may be a dispute about whether a description of the plaintiff was true. Each side can legitimately introduce evidence on that point without implicating the rule against using character evidence to support an inference that a person acts in conformity with his or her character. The point of introducing evidence about character in a case where, for example, a defendant is accused of defaming a plaintiff by describing him or her as "a thief" would be to show whether the plaintiff is a thief. This is different from using information about the plaintiff to support an inference about whether the plaintiff acted in conformity with thief-like character on any particular occasion. As Chart 7 illustrates, the chain of inferences involving character in a defamation case is different from the forbidden propensity inferences. In the defamation case, character is proved to show character. In the prohibited propensity use of character evidence, character would be used to show action in conformity with that character.

Chart 7 — Allowable Non-propensity Use of Character for "Character in Issue" Case Contrasted with Prohibited Propensity Use in Other Cases

Acceptable Chain of Inferences Where Substantive Law Makes Person's Character Relevant by Itself and Not as a Means of Inferring Something About the Person's Actions

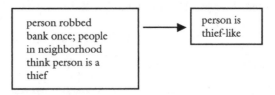

Forbidden Chain of Inferences Where Actor's Character Is Relevant Only as a Means of Inferring Something About the Person's Actions

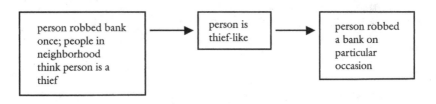

Instances are rare where data about a person's character can be relevant other than by supporting an inference about action in conformity with that character. One other example would be the litigation about the tort of negligent entrustment, where a plaintiff alleges that the defendant was culpably careless in letting a particular individual operate a car or some kind of machine. To show that the defendant was negligent, the plaintiff could introduce evidence about the character of the operator to show not that the person drove badly or operated a machine badly on a specific occasion, but to show that based on what the defendant should have known about the operator, the defendant should not have let him or her be in control of the car or machine. (Proof that the operator really did do a poor job of driving or machine work would have to be made in some non-propensity way, such as through eyewitness testimony about what actually happened.) Negligent hiring cases may sometimes fit this description since a jurisdiction's substantive law may make it negligent, for example, to hire a violent person to work as a security guard.

Habit

A concept related to character is "habit." Knowing that a driver always comes to a full stop at stop signs and looks both ways would support an inference that the driver is a cautious and law-abiding individual. If information about that habit were introduced to support that inference about character, it would usually be excluded. But evidence of habits is considered relevant to how a person acted on a specific occasion in a way that does not involve consideration of the person's general character or propensities. Rule 406 makes it clear that evidence of people's habits and organizations' routines can be proved to show conduct in conformity with them. Rule 406 states:

> Evidence of a person's habit or an organization's routine practice may be admitted to prove that on a particular occasion the person or organization acted in accordance with the habit or routine practice. The court may admit this evidence regardless of whether it is corroborated or whether there was an eyewitness.

This makes sense because of the differences between broad character traits and specific habitual conduct. For example, a decision that a person with the habit of stopping for stop signs really did stop at a stop sign on a particular occasion need not be based on an inference about the person's character traits in a broad sense. Chart 8 illustrates this.

Chart 8 — Inferences from Evidence That a Person Has a Habit of Stopping at Stop Signs

Permitted Inference

person has habit of stopping at stop signs	→	regardless of person's overall temperament, person stopped at stop sign

Forbidden, but Unnecessary, Inference

person has habit of stopping at stop signs	→	person is careful type of person in general	→	person stopped at stop sign because person is careful type of person

Where a way of acting is as specific and automatic as a "habit," the problems with ordinary character evidence disappear. There is very little ambiguity about proof that someone, for example, always locks his car door when he leaves his car. On the other hand, there is vast ambiguity about a trait such as calmness or honesty. And once a habit is proven as well as it can be, there is a strong relationship between a habit like door-locking (or obeying stop signs as illustrated in Chart 8) in general and conduct on a specific occasion. In contrast, even if a general character attribute like honesty is proven, the relationship between the trait and conduct on a specific occasion is bound to be weak. For these reasons, evidence of habits is not excluded by the propensity prohibition. Because of this, habit can be proved with any relevant evidence, including evidence about a person's specific past conduct.

In order for past conduct to be treated as habit evidence rather than as information that is relevant only as a basis for a general inference about the actor's character, a judge must be persuaded that the conduct in question is virtually automatic and has been repeated many times in the past. When that showing is made, the judge will treat the material differently from "character" evidence. "Stops at stop signs" and "quick to get angry" are examples, respectively, of habit and character evidence. In a sense, however, they are both ways of describing how a person acts in life. The main difference between them is that the stop sign conduct is easy to describe, can be demonstrated to have occurred repeatedly, and can be compared easily to whatever situation is in dispute at a trial. The conduct described as getting angry quickly may be much harder to describe accurately, and it may be difficult to show that it has been repeated in circumstances that are manifestly similar to the circumstances under study at a trial.

Form of Proof Related to Character

An important aspect of character evidence is understanding the methods of proof allowed in different contexts. Rule 405 defines the permitted techniques for proving character. This rule, it should be remembered, does not specify *whether* character evidence is legitimate in any particular circumstance. Rule 404 accomplishes that task. Rule 405 is subsidiary to Rule 404 and deals with *how* character can be proved in any situation where Rule 404 allows any attention at all to the topic of character. Rule 405 states:

> **(a) By Reputation or Opinion.** When evidence of a person's character or character trait is admissible, it may be proved by testimony about the person's reputation or by testimony in the form of an opinion. On cross-examination of the character witness, the court may allow an inquiry into relevant specific instances of the person's conduct.

(b) By Specific Instances of Conduct. When a person's character or character trait is an essential element of a charge, claim, or defense, the character or trait may also be proved by relevant specific instances of the person's conduct.

This rule applies to "character in issue" cases and to instances where Rule 404(a)(2) allows character evidence about a defendant or a victim in a criminal case. It does not apply to the propensity inferences that are forbidden by Rule 404(a)(1). Since they are prohibited, there is no style of proof through which the character on which those inferences would be based can be proved. Where Rule 404(b)(2) is a proponent's theory of relevancy, Rule 405 again has no application because it governs proof of character, while evidence is admitted under Rule 404(b)(2) only on the premise that its relevancy does not depend on conclusions about a person's character. Habit evidence is also excluded from the coverage of Rule 405 since it is defined as something different from character evidence. Finally, Rule 405 does not control the method for proof of character allowed under Rules 413, 414, and 415, since those rules treat that issue explicitly.

"Character in issue" cases are an exceptional situation in which proof of character is permitted to be in the form of information about specific conduct (as well as in the forms of reputation and opinion testimony). Assume that a worker injures a plaintiff, and the plaintiff seeks damages from the worker's employer alleging that it was negligent for the employer to entrust someone like the worker with the job that led to the plaintiff's injury. In this type of case, the worker's character will be an essential element of the plaintiff's claim (fitting Rule 405(b)'s definition) since the plaintiff alleges that it was negligent to hire a person with the worker's particular character traits. Proof of character would be used to influence the fact finder to arrive at a conclusion specifically about the worker's character (a use which is not prohibited by Rule 404(a)(1)).

On the other hand, if the issue in that plaintiff's suit was not improper hiring but allegedly improper performance by the worker, evidence about the worker's character would not be essential to the plaintiff's claim. Its only relation to an issue at the trial would be the forbidden propensity relationship: Because the worker is a certain type of person, he or she probably acted carelessly when the plaintiff was hurt. There is no basis for the plaintiff, in this second version of the case, to say that the legal theory of the case requires the jury to form a conclusion about the worker's personal traits. In the first case, a conclusion on that topic is required because it is the employer's alleged disregard of those traits that is claimed to have been negligent.

Examples

1. A 60-year-old man is on trial for sexual assault on a 14-year-old girl. The prosecution knows that he was once married to a woman significantly younger than he was and that he has also had consensual sexual relations on several occasions with women much younger than himself. If the defendant denies committing the charged crime, can the prosecution introduce evidence about his past marriage and other sexual conduct?

2. As part of its case in a bank robbery trial, the prosecution produces testimony of an eyewitness that the robbers fled the bank in a blue Chevrolet. The prosecution seeks to introduce evidence showing that the defendant had stolen a blue Chevrolet an hour before the bank robbery. In what context might this evidence be admissible, despite the general prohibition of propensity character evidence?

3. In a defamation trial, the plaintiff seeks to prove that the defendant called him a barbaric skinflint, in order to recover damages for that defamation. The defendant admits having described the plaintiff that way but asserts the defense of truth. May the defendant introduce evidence that the plaintiff has a reputation as a cheapskate? May the defendant introduce testimony about specific acts of cruelty the plaintiff has committed against animals?

4. The treasurer of a charitable organization is accused of embezzlement. Large sums of money under her control have disappeared, and she has adopted a lifestyle seemingly far more costly than her earnings would allow. In a criminal prosecution for embezzlement, may the prosecution introduce evidence that the defendant has lied to a university in applying to graduate school and has been convicted of bigamy?

5. The defendant is on trial for murder, accused of shooting the victim with a rifle. If there is evidence that a year earlier he had attempted to poison someone, can the prosecution plausibly argue that it should be allowed to introduce that evidence as relevant to the defendant's intent or identity?

6. A patient sues a doctor, claiming that the doctor carelessly forgot to warn the patient about side effects from a prescription drug. The doctor claims that she did give the patient that information. Can the doctor testify that she is very careful in all her work and therefore must have given the proper warnings? Can she testify that whenever she hands a prescription to a patient she shows the patient the name of the drug on the prescription and discusses how to take the medicine and what risks are involved in it?

7. Defendant is on trial for shoplifting, specifically for stealing a magazine from a large drug store. He claims that he had bought a large number of items, and that the owner of the store, after accepting payment for those

items, said to him, "Help yourself to a magazine on the way out." He would like to introduce testimony from witnesses showing that in the past the owner had sometimes offered free boxes of candy to three or four customers in a single day. Is this "character" evidence? Is this evidence admissible?

8. What if the defendant in Example 7 offered testimony that in the past the owner has offered free *magazines* to three or four customers in a single day? Would this evidence have a better chance of admissibility?

Explanations

1. The only logical relevance the information has to the prosecution claim is that it could lead a jury to think of the defendant as typically interested in sexual relations with women much younger than himself and that this belief could support an inference that on a particular occasion the defendant acted in conformity with that interest. This would be an instance of the forbidden propensity inference and could not be a basis for admitting the evidence in federal court. In some states there is an exception to the propensity prohibition for evidence that shows characteristic sexual depravity. While those states will not allow evidence of past robberies to be introduced in a defendant's trial for a current robbery, in a trial for a sex offense they will admit evidence of past sexual offenses on the theory that they show something about the defendant's sexual character that can reliably be a basis for decision in the current case.

2. Stealing a car could be treated as evidence showing a plan to rob a bank rather than as evidence that only has relevance to support an inference of the actor's bad character. The prosecution might be able to persuade the judge that the use of stolen cars in robberies is common enough so that a car theft can properly be linked to a later bank robbery as an element of a common plan.

   Additionally, if a witness saw the defendant steal the car and can thus identify the defendant in connection with that car, and if the witness to the robbery can identify the car but does not have the ability to identify the defendant, then the evidence linking the defendant to the car would be relevant as identification evidence. Showing the defendant's connection, then, to the earlier car theft would be for the purpose of providing circumstantial evidence of his identity as the person who robbed the bank.

3. Yes. The point of using testimony about either reputation or past acts of the plaintiff would be to support a jury inference about his character. Since the plaintiff's character is itself an issue under the substantive law of

defamation, the propensity rule has no impact on the case. Note that the theory of relevance rejected by the propensity rule would be the following: After the jury concluded something about the plaintiff's character it then went on to infer that because the plaintiff had a certain character the plaintiff probably acted in conformity with it on a specific occasion. That conclusion is not required for the defendant's defense of "truth" in the defamation case. The possibility that the jurors might reach such conclusions does not eliminate the legitimate possible use of the material that is justified by the relevance of character in defamation.

4. No. A common mistake in this situation is to notice that embezzlers are usually corrupt and deceitful people and to jump to the wrong conclusion that "deceitful character" is an element of the charged crime. To put you in jail for embezzlement, the prosecution does not have to show that you are generally a lying or stealing type of person. All the prosecution is required to do is show (beyond a reasonable doubt) that you took money that didn't belong to you. People of generally honest character may sometimes be embezzlers and so may people of criminal dispositions. But no principle of substantive criminal law establishes, as an element of the crime of embezzlement, that "bad character" is required to be shown to support a conviction. Therefore, Rule 404(a) prohibits use of this evidence.

5. The only way the past poisoning attempt would show "intent" on the occasion of the shooting incident would be if the jury reasoned that a person who tries to poison someone has an evil or murderous character and that having such a character makes it likely that on another occasion he acted in conformity with it. This is the prohibited propensity inference. Another facet of this example that makes its resolution easy is that the issue of intent can be dealt with clearly from the explicit facts of the case, namely the use of a rifle for shooting at the victim. Where conduct is ambiguous, there may be greater latitude for allowing introduction of earlier instances of similar conduct to shed light on the probable facts of the conduct on the specific occasion that is being evaluated at the trial.

Facts about the past poisoning attempt can identify the defendant as the shooter only if the jury makes the propensity inference. The past poisoning incident by the defendant makes it likely that he was involved in the shooting only if it is used by the jury as a basis for a belief that the defendant is a murdering type of person. Information about past acts known to have been committed by someone accused of a new offense can show the identity of the accused as the actual wrongdoer only if the new offense and the past acts have very strong similarities. Thus, if someone who has in the past committed crimes with a distinctive method or "signature," that fact will be admissible in a trial where he or she is accused of committing a new crime in that specific way. It shows the defendant's likely participation in the new crime without requiring a jury to reason that because he or she committed the past crimes, the defendant probably has character traits that support an inference of guilt.

6. Testimony that she is "always careful" would be kept out. It describes the doctor's character trait of being responsible and non-negligent, and for that reason is excluded from the trial if sought to be introduced to support the conclusion that on a specific occasion the doctor acted in conformity with that character. Could "being careful" be treated as a habit? To do that would be to eliminate almost all of the propensity bar since most traits of character could be described as habitual ways of being. The second kind of testimony in this problem, that the doctor gives warnings when she hands patients prescriptions, describes what the Federal Rules intend to characterize as a habit. The conduct is routine, repeated often, and does not involve reflection.

7. This testimony could support an inference that the owner is generous. If Defendant wanted the trier of fact to infer from the owner's generosity the idea that he acted generously on a specific occasion, this is precisely the type of inference the propensity rule prohibits. Could this evidence be treated as "habit" testimony? That approach would fail since the process of offering free candy involves a lot of conscious volition, was apparently infrequent, and was not shown to be a nearly automatic response to virtually every occurrence of a particular circumstance. Furthermore, Defendant is not interested in establishing that the owner offered him candy since he is charged with stealing a magazine.

8. There may be a category of evidence of conduct in between habit and character. Here Defendant's argument for admissibility would fail if he claimed that the information about past gifts of magazines indicated a habit. (The gifts involved free will, were not frequent, and were not a uniform response to all instances of a particular stimulus.) Admissibility would also be barred if the evidence was offered to establish the forbidden propensity inference. A chain of inferences from "past gifts of magazines" to "generous nature" to "probably did offer a free magazine to defendant" would be prohibited by the propensity rule because it involves reasoning from a belief about the type of person the storekeeper is. However, it is possible that Defendant can point to another chain of inferences: from "past gifts of magazines" to "frequent although not habitual magazine giver" to "probably did offer a free magazine to defendant." Defendant would have to persuade a judge that the middle conclusion, "frequent although not habitual magazine giver," is quite different from the middle conclusion, "generous type of person," which clearly implicates the rule against character evidence used to show action in conformity with character.

Some of the reasons character evidence is kept out include: Descriptions of personality attributes are sometimes very vague or likely to mean different things to different people; and it is hard to be sure what kinds of specific conduct are probably related to people's possession of various personality, or character, attributes. Here these problems loom large if the middle conclusion is "generous." The problems are much smaller if the middle conclusion is "person who sometimes gives away magazines." The effort to persuade the trier of fact that the owner really has the trait of giving away magazines sometimes is straightforward and does not involve ambiguity. The notion that past magazine giving is related to magazine giving on a specific later occasion is also fairly direct. A juror could reasonably use information about past magazine giving to evaluate the claim that the owner offered a free magazine to the defendant without reaching any conclusion about the owner's overall character trait of generosity. It is also important to notice that there is no risk of unfair prejudice here. Jurors are not likely to have feelings one way or the other about magazine giving. Also, any prejudice that might be felt would be against one of the prosecution's witnesses (the owner) and not about the defendant. Prejudice against the defendant is much more serious than prejudice against a witness in a case.

In circumstances like these, courts are frequently willing to use the non-propensity examples of Rule 404(b)(2) quite generously. Perhaps the past magazine giving would be admitted under the theory that it negated a possible mistake by the owner or that it showed a plan or method of doing business. Using these descriptions this way distorts them but serves the beneficial result of letting the evidence in.

Character of the Accused and the Victim

A defendant is allowed to introduce evidence of his or her own character to support the inference that he or she did not commit a charged crime. This permitted inference (good character shows the defendant did not commit the crime) is analytically identical to the ordinarily prohibited propensity inference (bad character shows the defendant did commit the crime). The fact that defendants control whether the propensity inferences can be used at their trials shows our system's fundamental interest in giving defendants ample opportunities to protect themselves from being found guilty. Three complications go along with this defendants' option. First, the defendant is permitted to introduce this type of character evidence only through the testimony of witnesses who state an *opinion* about the defendant's general character or report on what *reputation* the defendant has in some community. Second, the prosecutor is entitled to cross-examine these character witnesses by asking whether they have heard or know about specific past actions by the defendant. Third, when a defendant chooses to introduce testimony about his or her character, the prosecution may respond with its own witnesses about the defendant's character.

Notice that evidence law *forbids* the use of inferences from general character to conduct on specific occasions but *allows* a criminal defendant to use that precise chain of inferences to disprove guilt *and allows* a prosecutor to use it, too, if the defendant does first. The defendant's ability to inform the jury about his or her character is sometimes called the "mercy rule." A defendant must prove character by *reputation* or *opinion* evidence instead of with information about specific instances of past conduct, but a prosecutor may bring in the defendant's *past conduct* by asking the defendant's character witnesses about it. This is a confused welter of illogical rules, described by the Supreme Court in the famous *Michelson* case as "archaic, paradoxical, and full of compromises and compensations by which an irrational advantage to one side is offset by a poorly reasoned counter-privilege to the other."[3]

Understanding the Federal Rules treatment of evidence about the character of an accused and a victim requires another look at Rule 404(a). Rule 404(a)(1) states the general prohibition against using proof of character to support a conclusion about actions on a particular occasion. But Rule 404(a)(2) presents a number of exceptions. It states:

> **Exceptions for a Defendant or Victim in a Criminal Case.** The following exceptions apply in a criminal case:
>
> **(A)** a defendant may offer evidence of the defendant's pertinent trait, and if the evidence is admitted, the prosecutor may offer evidence to rebut it;
>
> **(B)** subject to the limitations in Rule 412, a defendant may offer evidence of an alleged victim's pertinent trait, and if the evidence is admitted, the prosecutor may:
>
> **(i)** offer evidence to rebut it; and
>
> **(ii)** offer evidence of the defendant's same trait; and
>
> **(C)** in a homicide case, the prosecutor may offer evidence of the alleged victim's trait of peacefulness to rebut evidence that the victim was the first aggressor.

A criminal defendant is entitled to introduce evidence of his or her "pertinent" character traits. The policy that supports this exception from the general rule excluding propensity inferences is that criminal defendants may sometimes have a very hard time refuting mistaken eyewitness testimony or developing other avenues of exculpatory proof. Recognizing these difficulties, common law tradition has allowed defendants the opportunity to have a jury know that they have acquired good reputations. At common law, a defendant's character witness can testify that the defendant has a

---

3. *Michelson v. United States*, 335 U.S. 469, 487 (1948).

generally decent, law-abiding character. The Federal Rules requirement that the trait be pertinent suggests, for example, that evidence of a defendant's trait of nonviolence would not be admitted in an embezzlement case. In a trial for theft, evidence about the defendant's honesty and typically careful treatment of other people's property would clearly be admissible. Additionally, testimony that a defendant is generally law-abiding may be treated as pertinent to any criminal charge.

Under common law, the defendant's character evidence was required to be in the form of testimony about the defendant's *reputation*. The Federal Rules have liberalized this to a slight extent, with Rule 405(a) permitting testimony based on *reputation* or *opinion*. A witness may have a basis for a personal opinion about the defendant, even if that defendant is not well-known enough in a community to have a reputation in it. The defendant is forbidden to introduce evidence of specific conduct to support inferences about his or her character. Even though a jury might develop a more accurate idea of how a person acts by learning about actual past actions (rather than by hearing summaries of reputation or opinions held by others), that type of evidence is prohibited. Besides making character evidence easier for defendants to obtain by allowing opinions as well as reports of reputations, the Federal Rules make one other pro-defendant change from the common law: A witness may describe the defendant's reputation in a particularized community such as a workplace instead of being required to report on reputation in a city or town.

Once a criminal defendant "opens the door" by introducing character evidence, the prosecutor is permitted to cross-examine the defendant's character witnesses and to introduce rival character witnesses. In cross-examining the defendant's character witnesses, the prosecutor is allowed to "inquire into" any "relevant specific instances of conduct" by the defendant (Rule 405(a)). This means that the prosecutor may ask a character witness for the defendant questions like "Have you heard that the defendant once hijacked a school bus?" or "Did you know that the defendant once hijacked a school bus?" This is a marked contrast to the rules governing the defendant's treatment of the character witness since the defendant is prohibited from asking about specific past events. However, while the prosecutor is allowed to ask about events, the prosecutor is not allowed to introduce independent proof about them and is required to accept whatever answer the character witness gives. The somewhat tortured rationale for this assortment of privileges and restrictions is that the prosecutor's questions are not intended to bring the facts of the past acts to the attention of the jury as a basis for the jury's evaluation of the *defendant*. They are meant to give the jury a basis for evaluating the *defendant's character witness* by showing how well that witness really knows the defendant's reputation or by showing what kinds of standards that witness has in mind when describing a person as having good qualities.

To respond to a defendant's character evidence, the prosecutor is also permitted to introduce testimony from other character witnesses. When this happens, the form of testimony by the prosecutor's witness is required to be the same as the form of testimony from witnesses for the defendant. That is, the witness can only report the defendant's general reputation in some community or locale and can give his own opinion of the defendant's character, but is forbidden to discuss specific instances of past acts by the defendant.

A few additional rules apply in criminal cases. Under Rule 404(a)(2)(B), the defendant is entitled to introduce evidence about the character of the victim. For example, a defendant accused of attacking someone might admit to the attack but claim that he or she had acted in self-defense. The claim of self-defense leads to two issues for which character evidence is relevant. The first is the factual question of whether the victim actually did attack the defendant. The defendant is allowed to introduce evidence showing that the victim had an aggressive or violent character to support an inference that the victim was the aggressor. In this instance, the usually forbidden propensity inference is allowed. Character evidence can also support a defendant's self-defense claim by persuading the jury that the defendant could reasonably have feared the victim because the defendant knew the victim had a reputation for violence.

When a defendant introduces character evidence on either of these rationales, the prosecution can then introduce contrary character evidence about the alleged victim to refute the defendant's showing. In homicide cases, the prosecution is sometimes entitled to introduce evidence about the victim's character even if the defendant chooses not to use that kind of material. It will be given that right if the defendant introduces non-character evidence suggesting that the victim was the aggressor. Rule 405 requires that all of this material be in the form of reputation or opinion testimony since the character of the victim is relevant only as a stepping stone to the ultimate inference about the victim's conduct.

The defendant's use of character evidence about an alleged victim also authorizes the prosecution to introduce character evidence about the defendant relevant to that same trait of character. Usually the prosecution cannot introduce character evidence about a defendant unless the defendant has already used character evidence about the defendant. However, Rule 404(a)(2)(B) provides that when the defendant uses evidence about an alleged victim's character trait, the prosecution may introduce character evidence showing that the defendant has that same trait of character. This applies regardless of whether the defendant had already introduced any evidence about his or her own character. Rule 405 controls the form of the prosecution's proof.

For sexual offense cases, Rule 413 states that "the court may admit evidence that the defendant committed any other assault." Rule 414 has similar language for child molestation, and Rule 415 has similar language for civil cases involving sexual assault or child molestation. The legislative history of these rules indicates that the proponent of this type of proof must introduce evidence of specific instances of conduct, rather than reputation or opinion evidence. A criminal defendant would be entitled to respond to evidence of his or her past acts with reputation or opinion evidence under Rule 404(a)(2)(A).

The Rule 415 provision allowing evidence of a party's past acts in civil suits involving sexual assault or child molestation is the only provision in the Federal Rules that allows introduction of character evidence in a civil case as relevant to someone's conduct out of court. It is not clear whether a civil party would be entitled to use reputation or opinion evidence in response to evidence of specific acts introduced by his or her opponent under Rule 415. Rule 404(a)(2) allows a defendant to introduce evidence of pertinent character traits, but it applies only to criminal cases.

Character of the Sexual Assault Victim

It was once common for the defendant in a sexual assault prosecution to introduce evidence about the alleged victim's character to suggest that because she was sexually experienced ("unchaste"), she had probably lied while testifying or had probably consented to sexual contact. Under the Federal Rules and in most states now, there is special treatment for this type of character evidence, typically with requirements meant to shield alleged victims from personal questions that have only slight relevance to the case. The Federal Rules allow evidence about an alleged sexual assault victim's past sexual behavior only in limited circumstances. Rule 412 provides:

> **(a) Prohibited Uses.** The following evidence is not admissible in a civil or criminal proceeding involving alleged sexual misconduct:
>
> **(1)** evidence offered to prove that a victim engaged in other sexual behavior; or
>
> **(2)** evidence offered to prove a victim's sexual predisposition.
>
> **(b) Exceptions.**
>
> **(1)** *Criminal Cases.* The court may admit the following evidence in a criminal case:
>
> **(A)** evidence of specific instances of a victim's sexual behavior, if offered to prove that someone other than the defendant was the source of semen, injury, or other physical evidence;
>
> **(B)** evidence of specific instances of a victim's sexual behavior with respect to the person accused of the sexual misconduct, if offered by the defendant to prove consent or if offered by the prosecutor; and

(C) evidence whose exclusion would violate the defendant's constitutional rights.

(2) Civil Cases. In a civil case, the court may admit evidence offered to prove a victim's sexual behavior or sexual predisposition if its probative value substantially outweighs the danger of harm to any victim and of unfair prejudice to any party. The court may admit evidence of a victim's reputation only if the victim has placed it in controversy.

(c) Procedure to Determine Admissibility.

(1) Motion. If a party intends to offer evidence under Rule 412(b), the party must:

(A) file a motion that specifically describes the evidence and states the purpose for which it is to be offered;

(B) do so at least 14 days before trial unless the court, for good cause, sets a different time;

(C) serve the motion on all parties; and

(D) notify the victim or, when appropriate, the victim's guardian or representative.

(2) Hearing. Before admitting evidence under this rule, the court must conduct an in camera hearing and give the victim and parties a right to attend and be heard. Unless the court orders otherwise, the motion, related materials, and the record of the hearing must be and remain sealed.

(d) Definition of "Victim." In this rule, "victim" includes an alleged victim.

The logical premise of this rule is that evidence of a person's past sexual conduct is rarely relevant to a question about how the person acted sexually on a specific occasion. This may conflict with the underlying premise of Rules 413, 414, and 415, which require admission of evidence of a defendant's past sexual offenses as relevant to the question of the defendant's sexual conduct on a specific occasion.

Rule 412, for criminal cases, does allow introduction of evidence of an alleged victim's past sexual conduct if it could support a claim that someone other than the defendant was the source of an injury or of semen connected with the alleged assault. If the past conduct involved the accused, evidence about it can be admitted to support a claim that the alleged victim consented to sexual behavior or to support a claim that the defendant had engaged in a pattern of misconduct with the alleged victim.

The rule also states, for criminal cases, that evidence of an alleged victim's sexual behavior in additional circumstances may be admitted if the constitution requires it to be admitted (of course, constitutional requirements would supersede the rule's restrictions, whether or not the rule stated that possibility explicitly).

The rule's provision for civil cases is less detailed than its provision for criminal cases. Rule 412(b)(2) sets up a general balancing test that compares probative value of any kind of sexual conduct proof with the dangers of unfair prejudice and harm to the alleged victim, instead of referring specifically to proof about physical injury, semen, or consent. This balancing test is different in two ways from the usual balancing test set out in Rule 403. Harm to the alleged victim is a relevant factor under Rule 412(b)(2), although it is not mentioned in Rule 403. Also, the proponent of evidence under the balancing test in Rule 412(b)(2) must show that its probative value "substantially outweighs" its dangers, while evidence is admissible under Rule 403 unless its dangers substantially outweigh its probative value. This means that when the balance is close under Rule 412(b)(2), the judge must exclude the evidence. Rule 403 is written to favor admissibility when the balance is close.

The hearing provisions in this rule are consistent with its underlying intent to protect alleged sexual assault victims from being embarrassed by questions about personal subjects that cannot be justified as part of the trial process. The hearing on admissibility of evidence of the alleged victim's past sexual conduct or predisposition is held in camera, and the record is ordinarily kept sealed. If a judge believes on the basis of such a hearing that information the defendant wants to present about the alleged victim would be properly admitted if the information is true, this presents a situation of conditional relevance. The judge would allow introduction of the evidence, since Rule 104(b) requires the jury (not the judge) to decide whether some "condition of fact" has been fulfilled.

Constitutional Restrictions on Exclusion of Defense Evidence

In a well-known case, *Chambers v. Mississippi*,[4] the Supreme Court held that "[t]he rights to confront and cross-examine witnesses and to call witnesses in one's own behalf have long been recognized as essential to due process." The defendant had been convicted of murdering a police officer despite the fact that another man (Gable McDonald) had admitted committing the crime. State rules prohibited the defendant from impeaching McDonald when he testified that he had not confessed to the murder and also prevented the defendant from introducing testimony from other witnesses about that confession. These prohibitions deprived the defendant of "a trial in accord with traditional and fundamental standards of due process." The court was influenced in reaching this conclusion by its beliefs that the rejected evidence had substantial circumstantial guarantees of trustworthiness and that the "voucher" rule, which prevented the defendant from impeaching

---

4. 410 U.S. 284 (1973).

the individual who had allegedly confessed to the crime, did not have a sound basis in policy.

Chambers does not provide clear guidance for evaluating the constitutionality of exclusion of defense evidence, in general, even though it does establish that some exclusions may be so poorly based or so strongly outcome-determinative that they are unconstitutional. In the context of rape shield statutes, the issues raised by Chambers may be significant. Where a strong argument about relevancy of a rape complainant's past sexual conduct is made, there is a possibility that the exclusionary provisions of Rule 412 may be unconstitutional. For example, if a defendant's knowledge of an alleged victim's reputation for consenting to sexual intercourse might affect a jury finding on the issue of intent to commit rape, Chambers might require that proof of that reputation be admitted if the defendant's evidence about the reputation was clear and detailed enough to support the argument for its relevance.

Another Supreme Court decision, Crane v. Kentucky,[5] held that it was unconstitutional for a state to prohibit a criminal defendant from introducing evidence intended to show that his confession had been coerced. The issue of coercion had been decided against the defendant, outside the hearing of the jury, in a judge's ruling on a motion to suppress the confession. The Supreme Court held that notwithstanding the trial court's ruling that the confession was voluntary enough to satisfy constitutional standards, the defendant's evidence supporting a contention that the confession had been coerced could have influenced the jury in evaluating the truthfulness or accuracy of the confession. In the absence of strong reasons to support the state court decision to exclude the defendant's evidence, the significant adverse impact of its exclusion on the defendant's case made the exclusion unconstitutional.

The Constitution does not require that all evidence a defendant thinks will be favorable must be admitted. In Montana v. Egelhoff,[6] the Supreme Court held that evidence of voluntary intoxication could be excluded despite the defendant's claim that it was relevant to the issue of the defendant's mental state at the time of a homicide. United States v. Scheffer[7] upheld a court-martial ruling excluding evidence of a polygraph examination that the accused sought to introduce. Exclusion was constitutional even though the tribunal applied a per se rule rejecting polygraph evidence and refused to evaluate its possible reliability.

Summary of Anti- and Pro-propensity Evidence Rules

Chart 9 lists the many anti- and pro-propensity evidence rules. It highlights the fact that although there are lots of shortcomings to the propensity

---

5. 476 U.S. 683 (1986).
6. 518 U.S. 37 (1996).
7. 523 U.S. 303 (1998).

 **Chart 9** **Can Evidence About a Person's Character Be Admitted to Show That the Person Acted in Conformity with That Character?**

No	Yes (Subject to Rule 403 Balancing)
General rule prohibits proof about a person's character to show that the person acted in conformity with that character. Rule 404(a)(1).	*About a criminal defendant* if introduced by the defendant or by prosecution to rebut that evidence. Rule 404(a)(2)(A).
Specific rule prohibits proof about the character of an alleged victim of a sex crime. Rule 412.	*About an alleged victim* if introduced by a criminal defendant or by prosecution to rebut that evidence. Rule 404(a)(2)(B)(i).
	When a criminal defendant introduces evidence about an alleged victim's character trait, evidence *about the criminal defendant's same character trait* introduced by the prosecution. Rule 404(a)(2)(B)(ii).
	About a civil or criminal defendant accused of sexual assault or child molestation. Rules 413, 414, and 415.
	About an alleged homicide victim, to rebut any evidence that victim was the first aggressor. Rule 404(a)(2)(C).
	About any witness's credibility. Rule 404(a)(3).

inference, the law has grown to tolerate it in many instances. Chart 10 shows what kinds of proof (reputation, opinion, or extrinsic evidence of acts) may be used for most of the circumstances in which evidence about character is permitted. Chart 10 does not include two special circumstances in which character evidence is admissible. One is impeachment, covered in Chapter 5. The other is character evidence introduced to prove character rather than to prove actions in conformity with character. Where a person's character is an ultimate issue in a case, all methods of proving it are permitted. It is also important to remember that when a witness provides opinion or reputation testimony about someone's character, the opposing party may question that witness about specific acts believed to have been committed by the subject of that person's testimony.

Chart 10

Character Evidence Offered to Show Conduct in Conformity with That Character on a Specific Occasion: Summary

Evidence About	May Be Introduced by	Reputation or Opinion Proof Allowed?	Extrinsic Specific Acts Proof Allowed?
Defendant's traits inconsistent with commission of charged crime	Defendant. FRE 404(a)(2)(A)	Yes	No
Defendant's traits consistent with commission of charged crime	Prosecution to rebut defendant's character evidence. FRE 404(a)(2)(A)	Yes	No
Defendant's sex-related traits in sex offense or child molestation case	Plaintiff, prosecutor, or defendant. FRE 404(a)(1), 413, 414, 415	Yes, introduced by a criminal defendant or by the prosecution to rebut such proof. FRE 404(a)(1)	Yes, introduced by any party. FRE 413, 414, 415
Victim's trait (usually trait of aggressiveness)	Defendant. FRE 404(a)(2)(B)	Yes	No
Victim's trait (usually trait of non-aggressiveness)	Prosecution to rebut defendant's character evidence about victim or (only in homicide cases) other evidence that victim was aggressor. FRE 404(a)(2)(B)(i), 404(a)(2)(C)	Yes	No
Defendant's trait identical to victim's trait shown by defendant with character evidence	Prosecution. FRE 404(a)(2)(B)(ii)	Yes	No
Victim's traits in sexual assault case	Prosecutor or defendant in specific relatively rare instances. FRE 412	No	Yes

Examples

1. Can the defendant in a burglary trial seek to show that he did not commit the crime by having witnesses testify in the following ways?

   Witness One: "He has a reputation in his neighborhood for being law-abiding."

   Witness Two: "I've known the defendant for five years, and he seems honest to me."

   Witness Three: "He has been a volunteer soccer coach for a junior high school for several years, and he's never missed a game or a practice session. The league also has him collect all the dues and handle all equipment purchases, and there's never been any problem about accounting for the money."

2. In a murder trial, before any other prosecution witnesses are presented and before any witnesses are presented by the defendant, the prosecution seeks to show the defendant's guilt by having the defendant's neighbor testify that the defendant is violent and has a reputation in the neighborhood as hot-tempered. Is this proper?

3. In a criminal case where the defendant has used character testimony to show that he is fundamentally peaceful and thus did not commit the charged crime of violence, can the prosecution present a witness who testifies that she believes the defendant has a violent nature and has no respect for law and order, and that she has developed those opinions in the course of knowing the defendant as the defendant's parole officer?

4. In a criminal trial for securities fraud, the defendant seeks to establish his innocence by presenting a witness who testifies that the defendant has a reputation for honesty. Can the prosecution ask that witness, on cross-examination, whether he has heard that the defendant was once convicted of car theft?

5. If a criminal defendant who has been convicted in the past of offenses involving dishonesty introduces character testimony in his own behalf, what use can the prosecution make of the past convictions?

6. The defendant in a criminal assault case admits using force against the victim, but claims that he was acting in reasonable self-defense. May he support that claim by testifying that the victim had a reputation for violence?

7. If the case described in Example 6 was a civil suit for damages, could the defendant introduce the same type of character evidence about the victim?

8. In a case where the defendant is accused of having sexually abused a young child, a social worker testifies that the child used terminology

about sexual matters that is not usually used by children of such a young age and that the child seemed unusually knowledgeable about sexual intercourse. The defendant seeks to introduce evidence that the alleged victim had been sexually active with several adults other than the defendant on the theory that this past experience could account for the child's familiarity with sexual matters. Does Rule 412 prevent the admission of this evidence?

9. Compare the following cases in which prosecutors seek to show that a defendant committed a crime by introducing evidence of a past act by the defendant.

> Fred First is accused of shooting a child. According to the prosecution, in 2014 he traveled to a city far from his home, entered a day care center, asked the manager for money, tried to shoot the manager when the manager did not respond quickly, and thus wounded a child who was on the floor about ten feet away from the manager. As part of its proof that First committed the crime, the prosecution seeks to introduce evidence that in 2010 First ended a long relationship with a woman and shot her child during an argument connected with the dissolution of their relationship.
>
> Sam Second is accused of attempted rape. According to the prosecution, in 2014 he traveled to a city far from his home, entered a day care center, asked the manager for money, and then attempted to rape the manager. As part of its proof that Second committed the crime, the prosecution seeks to introduce evidence that in 2010 Second ended a long relationship with a woman and attempted to rape her during an argument connected with the dissolution of their relationship.
>
> Should the prosecution in First's case and Second's case be permitted to introduce the evidence of the defendants' prior crimes? If the Rules allow different treatment of these cases, what would justify the difference?

Explanations

1. Each of the three witnesses' testimony is relevant to the defendant's character and would not have any other relevance to the case. Therefore, an initial point for analysis is whether character evidence can be used by the defendant in this situation. The answer to that inquiry is yes, since the defendant in a criminal case is exempted from the ordinary prohibition against use of the propensity inference if he wants to introduce character evidence about himself. Recall that the evidence must relate to a pertinent trait under the terms of Rule 404(a)(2)(A). "Law-abiding" and "honest" are general traits, but they are well related to a defendant's likely guilt. Respect for equipment and accurate accounting for a team's finances are traits that reduce the likelihood that the defendant was a burglar, since burglary is a crime that involves disrespect for property.

Having dealt with the issue of *whether* character evidence regarding the defendant may be introduced, the second stage of analysis is the question of *how* it can be presented. Witness One's testimony is in the form of a report of the defendant's reputation. This is the most traditional form of character evidence and is totally acceptable. Witness Two's testimony illustrates opinion testimony. Opinion testimony is an allowable method of proving character. Only Witness Three's testimony would be excluded. It relates to character, and character is a permissible topic in this trial for presentation by the defendant, but the form of presentation is wrong. Witness Three's testimony attempts to support inferences about character on the basis of information about specific conduct by the defendant in the past. This kind of testimony about specific acts is not allowed for the purpose of showing character unless character itself is an ultimate issue in a case.

2. The testimony is inadmissible. It must stay out because its only relevance depends on the forbidden propensity inference, and prosecutors are not allowed access to that inference until a defendant has "opened the door" by using it himself. If information about character were allowed in this situation, the form of the witness's testimony would have been acceptable because it is a combination of two permitted styles — reputation and opinion.

3. Because the defendant has introduced character evidence, the prosecution is entitled to respond with its own character evidence. The form of this testimony is all right because it involves the witness's own opinions. There is a risk of unfair prejudice, however, because in identifying herself as the defendant's parole officer, the witness unavoidably reveals that the defendant has been convicted of a crime and has been subject to parole supervision. Some judges might allow this testimony if there was a neutral way to describe the connection between the witness and the defendant. Others might find the risk of prejudice too great, particularly considering the low probative value of character evidence on the issue of whether the defendant actually did commit the charged offense.

4. Yes. In cross-examination of a character witness, questions that "inquire into" past conduct of the person who was the subject of the character testimony are permitted.

5. All the prosecutor can do is "inquire into" them in cross-examination of the defendant's character witnesses. Even if a character witness says he doesn't know or hasn't heard about the past convictions, the cross-examiner is required to accept that answer. Proof about the past convictions is not allowed.

6. Yes. This testimony makes two points. First, if the jury believes that the victim had a violent temperament, it may infer from that fact that the

victim actually was the initial aggressor in the incident. Second, if the jury believes that the defendant was aware of the victim's reputation at the time of the incident, it can use that fact in evaluating the force the defendant used against the victim. The reasonableness of self-defense depends on the degree of threat perceived by the self-defender.

7. No. Rule 404(a)(2) provides some exceptions to the general prohibition against using character evidence to prove conduct in conformity with that character, but the rule states explicitly that the exceptions apply only in criminal cases.

8. The detailed provisions of Rule 412 would require exclusion of this evidence since it involves sexual conduct by the victim with people other than the accused, and it does not relate to the source of semen or injury. However, *Chambers v. Mississippi* may require that the evidence be admitted on constitutional grounds. If the jury does not learn of these other possible reasons for the child's knowledge of sex and terminology related to sex, it is very likely to assume that the knowledge came from the defendant's conduct with the victim. The strong relevance of the offered evidence suggests that it should be admitted despite the social policies inherent in Rule 412 intended to protect the privacy of sexual assault victims.

9. The facts in First's case and Second's case are very similar, except that the charged and past crimes are shootings in First's case and attempted rapes in Second's case. First's case is controlled by Rule 404. The prosecution is barred from introducing evidence of the 2010 shooting to show that First is the type of person who shoots people. It is unlikely that Rule 404(b)(2) would provide an avenue for admission, although the prosecution might persuade a court that the past crime shows that First knows how to use a gun, and that establishing this makes it more likely that he committed the charged offense. If a court thinks that knowledge of guns is rare, it might be persuaded by that argument.

   Second's case is controlled by Rule 413. The prosecution is allowed to introduce evidence of the 2010 attempted rape to show that Second is the type of person who commits that kind of crime. Evidence of past sexual assaults is admissible under Rule 413 to show "any matter to which it is relevant."

   These two cases receive different treatment because Rule 413 operates to take sexual assault cases outside the ordinary framework of Rule 404. Justifications for including Rule 413 among the Federal Rules may be a belief that recidivism is more likely in sex offenses than in other offenses or that a greater need for convictions in sex offense cases than in other criminal cases justifies taking the risk that jurors may misuse information about a defendant's past.

Defining Hearsay

INTRODUCTION

The myth of hearsay is that no one understands it, and students and practicing lawyers always make mistakes about it. It does seem sometimes that the people who understand the hearsay doctrine are a kind of secret society. They have learned something that confuses other people, and they know how to manipulate their knowledge of it. This dual nature of hearsay — its appearance of difficulty to "outsiders" and its relative simplicity to initiates — may be one reason that reform proposals have often been rejected. People who have mastered hearsay may not want to give up their advantage over people who are traumatized by it.

The truth is that the hearsay rules are based on some intuitive assumptions about what kinds of communications are likely to be the most accurate. You can organize your understanding of hearsay by remembering first that "hearsay" is a type of evidence that may not be admitted, and second that exceptions to the general rule of exclusion are available in many situations. This suggests that understanding hearsay requires a grasp of its basic definition, the reasons for our system's traditional aversion to it, and the factors that lead to tolerating its use in many common situations.

Basic Rule

Statements made by people out of court often relate to issues that are disputed at trials. However, even if words people have said or written out of court contain relevant information, they can be excluded from admission. Rule 801 provides the following definitions:

> **(a) Statement.** "Statement" means a person's oral assertion, written assertion, or nonverbal conduct, if the person intended it as an assertion.
>
> **(b) Declarant.** "Declarant" means the person who made the statement.
>
> **(c) Hearsay.** "Hearsay" means a statement that:
>
> **(1)** the declarant does not make while testifying at the current trial or hearing; and
>
> **(2)** a party offers in evidence to prove the truth of the matter asserted in the statement.

Rule 802 gives a purpose to those definitions, stating:

> Hearsay is not admissible unless any of the following provides otherwise:
>
> - a federal statute;
> - these rules; or
> - other rules prescribed by the Supreme Court.

Thus, out-of-court statements are defined as *hearsay* and are *inadmissible* if a party seeks to have them admitted to establish that their content is true. Unless there is an exception to the rule of exclusion, a party cannot have a witness quote what anyone ever said outside of court, and a party cannot introduce a document containing words written out of court. Information from such statements is kept out of trials because the original speaker's absence makes it hard for the jury to decide if the original speaker (1) had an adequate opportunity to perceive or learn about the subject of the out-of-court statement, (2) had a clear memory of the subject of the out-of-court statement, (3) meant to tell the truth, and (4) understood the typical meanings of the words he or she used. If the original speaker is present, the jury can see him or her and draw some conclusions about these issues. Also, if the original speaker is present, cross-examination is possible. Many people think that cross-examination is a particularly strong technique for uncovering flaws in a person's perception, memory, honesty, and use of words.

Testimony that quotes an out-of-court statement is hearsay only if the out-of-court words are introduced to prove the truth of what they assert. For example, an issue at a trial was whether Mr. Driver had drunk beer at a party before driving a car. Testimony by a witness at the trial that while he was at the party he heard Mr. Host say, "Driver has been drinking beer all night," would be relevant because it supports the proposition that Driver had been drinking. This would be an example of hearsay since the purpose of offering proof that the out-of-court words were said would be to support the exact proposition that they assert — that Driver had been drinking before he drove. The idea behind the hearsay rule is that having someone repeat another person's out-of-court statements is a poor way to have the jury find out the truth about the subject of the out-of-court words.

Out-of-court words treated as hearsay can be written as well as spoken. If an issue at a trial was whether a patient had received morphine in a hospital, a statement in a hospital record showing that morphine was administered would be relevant evidence. But it would also be hearsay, since it is a written out-of-court statement conveying the idea that the patient received morphine, and the purpose of introducing it would be to support the conclusion that the patient received morphine.[1]

The person who makes the out-of-court statement is usually referred to as the declarant. In the typical hearsay situation, a person testifies at a trial and seeks to repeat the declarant's words. Those words are the declarant's statement. When a declarant's statement is in writing, a litigant seeks to bring the out-of-court words into the trial by introducing the document that contains them rather than by having a person testify about having heard the declarant say the words. Suppose that a plaintiff sued a construction company, claiming that something had fallen from a building under construction and had damaged his car parked on the street below. If the car owner sought to establish what had happened by having a witness testify that a pedestrian who saw the event said later that an object had fallen from the building onto the plaintiff's car, the testimony would be hearsay and would be rejected. Note that the person testifying (the witness) is a witness not to the accident but to another event: the speaking by the pedestrian. In standard hearsay terminology, the pedestrian (who was a witness to the accident but who is not a witness in court) is called the declarant. If the pedestrian came to the trial, he or she would be allowed to testify about recollections of the event. However, bringing the pedestrian's knowledge into the trial by having another person quote some of the pedestrian's words violates the rule against hearsay.

Basic Rationale for Excluding Hearsay

Information you get from a person directly is likely to be more accurate than information you get from that person through an intermediary. If you wanted to know about an automobile accident, for example, and there was a person — Mr. Observer — who claimed to have information about it, what might you do? Your first choice would be to talk to Mr. Observer. In

---

1. The record would be admissible under an exception to the hearsay exclusionary rule. That admissibility, however, does not change the fact that evidence law doctrines would characterize the statement as hearsay.

a conversation, you would find out how Mr. Observer initially saw or learned what he thinks he knows about the accident. You could evaluate the clarity of his memory. If he used words that were ambiguous or if he seemed to be using ordinary words in an unusual way, you could ask him to make his meaning clear. It is also possible that in talking with Mr. Observer, you could get an impression of his honesty. Mr. Observer might say, "The red car was going very fast, and it slammed into the blue car." You could ask him how he knew about the accident. He might tell you how close he was to the scene of the accident, and this would give you an idea about how clearly he might have been able to see what he thinks he saw. You could ask him to describe the weather at the time, or give you details about the style of the cars, to estimate how strong his memory is. Since words like "fast" and "slammed" are ambiguous, you could ask Mr. Observer questions that would give you an idea of what he really means when he says a car moves fast or slams into another car. Finally, by seeing Mr. Observer's style of responding to your questions, you might develop an opinion about how honestly he was reporting what he believed he knew.

Notice that the probing questions to determine the reliability of Observer's words involve checking on how well he saw the event and how well he remembers what he saw. These factors control the accuracy of whatever beliefs Observer has about the past event at the time he talks about it. The probes to check on Observer's sincerity and on the ambiguity of his language focus on another part of the communication process. They highlight the possibility that a person who has an accurate belief about some past event might still use words to describe it that convey a false impression of that accurate belief. *Perception, memory, sincerity, and ambiguity* are sometimes called the *testimonial infirmities*. They are called infirmities because they represent the possible sources for incorrect descriptions of past reality in testimony or in non-testimonial communications. Checking on all of them is possible when you have a firsthand communication with a speaker. If you have only another person's report of what a speaker once said, checking on the possible infirmities is much harder. At trials, the extent to which a statement's accuracy may have been impaired by any of the testimonial infirmities will be exposed, usually, through cross-examination.

Of course, an alternate method of getting Mr. Observer's information would be the indirect process of talking to someone else — Ms. Friend — who had talked to Mr. Observer. Ms. Friend could tell you what Mr. Observer had told her about the accident. For example, she could say, "Mr. Observer said to me, 'I saw the red car drive very fast and slam into the blue car' when we had lunch together last week." Getting Mr. Observer's information this way would deprive you of a chance to ask exactly how he saw the event and to ask questions that might test his memory, the meanings he intended to convey with the words he used, and his honesty.

3. Defining Hearsay

This second method, where one person's knowledge about something is conveyed to a listener by a second person repeating or quoting what the first person has said, is prohibited in trials by the rule against hearsay. The jury must learn what people know by hearing them talk about their knowledge and by hearing them respond to cross-examination that illuminates the possible weaknesses in their original perceptions, their recollection, their current choice of words, and their honesty. If Mr. Observer's information is relevant at a trial, it must (ordinarily) be presented at the trial by Mr. Observer testifying in person. Ms. Friend is not allowed to appear at the trial and tell the trier of fact what Mr. Observer once told her. In private life, a person who wanted to know about the automobile accident would prefer to learn about it from Mr. Observer directly but might be satisfied to have Ms. Friend provide a secondhand version of Mr. Observer's knowledge by quoting him. Evidence law rejects that choice in general on the theory that the opportunities for clarification and reliability checks that are lost when testimony quotes out-of-court statements are so valuable that the goals of fairness and accuracy in trials are best served by prohibiting the testimony.

The hearsay rule contradicts the general freedom that evidence law gives parties to select their own kinds of proof. A party can usually try to prove its case with any kind of evidence it can find, subject only to the requirement that the material be relevant. A witness with weak eyesight can testify about something he saw at a great distance. To suggest that a person stole something, circumstantial evidence is permitted that the object was in a place at one time and was missing from that place after the person had access to it. Our system relies on the self-interest of litigants to encourage them to use the most efficient and persuasive styles of proof. Also, we expect that adversaries will alert juries if the evidence their opponents choose to use is weak in terms of the conclusions it is presented to support. But the reliability problems of out-of-court statements are thought to be so great that common law decisions and the Federal Rules of Evidence take the position that a rule of exclusion will produce the fairest results overall.[2]

Despite the strong policy grounds for excluding hearsay, the Federal Rules and common law do allow it to be admitted in many circumstances covered by exceptions to the general principle of exclusion. The exceptions apply where there are reasons to think that the out-of-court statement was particularly likely to be accurate or truthful so that the impossibility of probing the original speaker's statements is not so harmful. An additional rationale for some exceptions is the belief that the risks that out-of-court

---

2. There are some other examples of evidence doctrines that move away from relying on the competitiveness of litigation and the common sense of juries to protect against cases being decided on weak evidence. One is the original writing rule, discussed at pages 220-223. Others are the specialized relevance rules, controlling the use of evidence of subsequent remedial measures or of evidence of a person's past bad acts, discussed at pages 20-22 and 32-40.

words may convey a false meaning are outweighed by other factors. In a murder trial, for example, the dying victim's accusatory statement naming someone as the murderer is admissible since it has often been thought that people at the point of death have no motive to lie and may be afraid (for religious reasons) to lie. Also, the risks of using the out-of-court words are less severe than the unfairness of excluding from a trial a victim's last words identifying the murderer.

Detailed Analysis of Statements Typically *Not* Offered to Prove the Truth of What They Assert

When an out-of-court statement is relevant without regard to whether it conveys accurate information, then the hearsay prohibition does not operate and testimony about the statement is allowed. How can a litigant ever claim that an out-of-court statement is relevant without also claiming that the jury should believe the substance of what the speaker said? Suppose a party needed to prove that security guards were patrolling a warehouse on a particular evening. A janitor could testify that as he passed the warehouse door he heard the guards talking to each other. The janitor would be permitted to quote the words the guards said because proof that the words were said is relevant to an issue at the trial (were the guards in the warehouse?), and using the words as relevant to that issue does not require that the content of the guards' statements be true or be believed by the jury. No matter what the guards said, and no matter whether it was true or false, the fact that they were speaking supports the proposition for which the janitor's testimony is sought to be introduced: The guards were present in the warehouse. The guards' words would be introduced not to show that what they asserted was true, but just to show that the words were said.

The plaintiff's case in a defamation suit provides another clear example. The plaintiff must prove that the defendant said something defamatory about the plaintiff, but when the plaintiff has someone testify about the defendant's out-of-court statement, the plaintiff is *not* seeking to have the jury believe that the statement was accurate. The plaintiff needs to have the jury believe that the allegedly defamatory words were uttered, not that they were a truthful report of some aspect of reality. The plaintiff's position is that *words were said*, not that the *words were true*. For this reason, the hearsay rule allows quotation of the defendant's out-of-court statement.

Warnings are another example of out-of-court words that are relevant because they were spoken whether or not they are "true." A defendant who is sued for carelessly failing to guard a dangerous machine might introduce evidence that she told the plaintiff, "Look out for the sharp edge." If the plaintiff's degree of care is relevant under the substantive law of the case, proof that the defendant gave a warning would be admissible. There is neither truth nor falsity in the "look out" statement. It is important in the case merely because it was made. If the speaker meant to lie when she said it, that doesn't matter. If the speaker meant to say "pointed" instead of "sharp," that doesn't matter either. If the speaker had the impression that the machine had one kind of danger but was really mistaken about it, that misperception or lack of clear memory is also completely unimportant since on the question of the plaintiff's conduct and his response to words of warning, it is the fact that the words "look out for the sharp edge" were once spoken that provides information for the jury to consider. None of the testimonial infirmities are involved in this kind of testimony. The out-of-court speaker's perceptions, memory, sincerity, and possible use of words in an idiosyncratic way would have no impact on the significance of the fact, if the jury believes it to be a fact, that those warning words were once spoken by her.

The language of contracts is another instance of out-of-court words being used in a non-hearsay way. When a litigant introduces evidence that a party, out of court, wrote or spoke words that created a contract, the litigant is not, in theory, relying on those words to establish their own truth. If the contract is enforced, it will not be because the party's promise was taken as "true" by the court. The contract will be enforced if legal principles independent from the "truth" or "falsity" of the party's words require that those words once spoken or written constitute a contract.

The contracts example belongs to a category sometimes called verbal acts or verbal parts of acts. If you say, "This is a gift," and hand someone some money, it is a gift in some jurisdictions under property law doctrines. In those places, testimony that the donor said, "This is a gift," would not be hearsay because the statement would be introduced merely to show that the words were said (the jurisdiction's substantive law takes over the task of converting the saying of those words to a decision about ownership of the money). In some other jurisdictions the money might only be a gift if the donor meant it to be a gift. Then, proof of what the donor said would be hearsay since it would be intended to support a conclusion about the donor's state of mind at the time he or she handed over the money. This hearsay would be admissible under an exception for statements reflecting a speaker's mental state.

Words introduced just to show their effect on the hearer or reader are another broad class of non-hearsay in which out-of-court words can be relevant without their proponent asking the trier of fact to treat them as true. Warnings are in this class, as are any other kinds of statements that are relevant just because a party was exposed to them. In a tort suit claiming that a manufacturer should have changed its design because it had received reports of injuries earlier than the plaintiff's injury, the reports of those other injuries would be relevant in two ways, of which one would constitute hearsay and one would be non-hearsay. To show that the out-of-court reports accurately conveyed information about those past injuries, the reports would be hearsay, since that use depends on their information being true. To show that the manufacturer had received information that a reasonable manufacturer would investigate, the reports are not hearsay since that use does not require that the reports have contained accurate information; it only requires that there is a showing that the manufacturer actually did receive the reports.

Criticizing a manufacturer's response to reports of injuries does not require reliance on the accuracy of the reports, as long as it is shown that they apparently were made concerning the same kind of product that allegedly injured the plaintiff. This same analysis would apply where a person's motivation for committing a crime was at stake: If that person sought to establish that he was acting in response to a threat, testimony that someone once said to him, "Commit this crime or I'll kill you," would be admissible. It would be significant in the trial because of the effect those out-of-court words allegedly had on the person charged with the crime, not because of the truth or falsity of the details of the threat.

Where proof that words were said is relevant in a trial, without regard to whether or not the content of the words provides a true account of some past reality, a witness may quote those words. Proof such as a witness's testimony that words of warning or words of a business agreement were said, when they are being introduced not to prove that they were true but just to prove that they were said, does not involve any hearsay problems. A witness can report to the jury that the words were uttered, just as a witness can report any other event that a witness has observed. Testimony that a witness heard a person say, "Look out," is just like testimony that a witness saw a person wearing a blue sweater or running across a street. The hearsay rule's preference for having the actual speaker present in court and available to answer clarifying questions has no application where the proponent's effort is to prove that words were *said* rather than that words were *true*.

Visual Aids

Visual aids may help in one of the crucial issues of hearsay analysis: whether the declarant's words are being offered into evidence to prove the truth of what they assert or merely to prove that they were said. This distinction defines hearsay, since the hearsay exclusion only operates when the out-of-court words are offered as evidence of their truth. A detailed analysis of the components inherent in people's communications may clarify this inquiry.

3. Defining Hearsay

When a person talks about something she thinks she knows, her words reflect an effort to convey information about something she believes. Her belief, in turn, is formed (partly) by some aspect of reality she observed in the past. In analyzing statements people make (in court or out of court), three stages can be outlined.

1. The speaker's words about a past event;
2. The speaker's belief about the past event; and
3. The real past event.

Someone, for example, who once saw a ship sail might say, "I saw the ship sail." That statement would involve the speaker's choice of words to convey an idea. The speaker would have to mean by "ship" what most people mean by that word, and the speaker would have to intend to get that typical meaning across to his audience. If the speaker meant to be honest and used words carefully, the speaker's statement would be a full and clear version of his belief about having seen the ship. Does the fact that he believes he saw the ship sail mean that the ship really sailed? The speaker's belief is based on some past perception of reality and on his ability to remember that past perception. Depending on how clearly he was able to see what he thought was a ship sailing, and on how well he is able to remember things he has seen in the past, his belief about having seen the ship sail might or might not be an accurate report of past reality.

It is possible to think through what a juror does when he or she hears testimony, focusing on these same three factors: the speaker's current words, the speaker's current belief, and past events. The juror hears the speaker speak. The juror then must decide whether the speaker's *words* are an accurate reflection of what the speaker believes is true and whether the speaker's current *belief* really is an accurate reflection of a *past event*, taking into account how well the speaker was able to perceive what he was looking at and how well the speaker is able to remember what he saw. Chart 11 illustrates these stages of past perception, current belief, and current spoken words. It shows how a speaker may come to say certain words about a past event and also how a juror who hears those words must inferentially work through the same process that the speaker used if the juror's purpose is to learn about the past event from the speaker. An expanded illustration, Chart 12, also illustrates how issues such as lying, use of ambiguous words, poor memory, and poor original perception of an event can affect the accuracy of what a person says about an event. In the expanded version, the "testimonial infirmities" are inserted to show how they might affect the reliability of a speaker's words.

Chart 11 — Links Between Words and Perceptions

Relationship between observer's words and past reality	Relationship between hearing observer's words and forming a belief about past reality (juror)
SPEAKER	JUROR
Describes a recollection of ship	Hears speaker's words
Description is based on a belief	Decides if words truthfully and clearly portray what speaker remembers
Belief is based on past perception	Decides if speaker's past perception was likely to have been accurate and whether (if it was accurate) the speaker's current memory is a good reflection of that former accurate perception

Chart 12 — Location of "Testimonial Infirmities" in the Steps Between Observer's Words and Past Reality

Speaker describes a recollection of ship

↓

Are the words clear?
Is the speaker intending to be honest in describing the recollection?

↓

Speaker's description is based on a belief

↓

Is the belief based on an accurate memory of past perception?
Was the past perception achieved well or was it subject to flaws?

↓

Speaker's belief is based on past perception

These charts can help solve the "truth of the matter asserted" issue in identifying hearsay. The hearsay rule only excludes out-of-court statements sought to be introduced as a basis for a finding that the information they contain is true. A way to remember this is to see that on the charts, depending on the way in which an out-of-court statement is claimed to be relevant, a jury will have to decide one or more of the following issues: (1) did a speaker make the statement someone says in court he made, (2) what was the out-of-court speaker's belief when he spoke, or (3) what did the out-of-court speaker perceive about something. If the only issue for which the out-of-court words are sought to be introduced is the first of these issues — whether the words were spoken or written — then the hearsay rule allows admission of the words. In that situation the words are not introduced to establish that their meaning is true, and as the charts illustrate, none of the testimonial infirmities are involved.

The testimonial infirmities come into play only when the proponent of admission of the out-of-court words wants the jury to rely on them to form an opinion about what the out-of-court speaker believed or what the out-of-court speaker had perceived. In contrast, whenever a statement made out of court could illuminate an issue without the jurors deciding that it is an accurate representation of the speaker's belief or that it is an accurate report of some past reality perceived by the speaker, the hearsay rule does not apply. This makes sense because using words that fit this description avoids all four of the testimonial infirmities illustrated in the chart.

The stages of past perception, current belief, and communication about that belief are illustrated in these charts in a vertical column. You could also think of them in any of the ways shown in Chart 13.

All these visualizations incorporate the same fundamental idea. If the out-of-court words can be characterized as relevant at the trial without any requirement that they are an accurate representation of the speaker's belief or that the speaker's belief was an accurate representation of some past reality, then the hearsay issue disappears. If no consideration is required past the first point of the triangle, past the statement point on the horizontal row, or into the brain of the speaker in the human illustration, then the testimonial infirmities are not implicated and the policies inherent in the hearsay rules do not require exclusion of the statement.

Detailed Analysis of What Constitutes a Statement

The hearsay prohibition applies to spoken and written words. It also applies to actions that are intended to convey a meaning. The Federal Rules call such actions "assertive conduct." In our society, nodding your head up and down is usually understood to convey the assertion of agreement or the meaning *yes*. Head nodding is conduct primarily meant to express an idea. In contrast,

Chart 13 Round Up the Usual Diagrams

1. Statement ⟶ Belief ⟶ Past Reality

2. Past Reality ⟶ Belief ⟶ Statement

3.

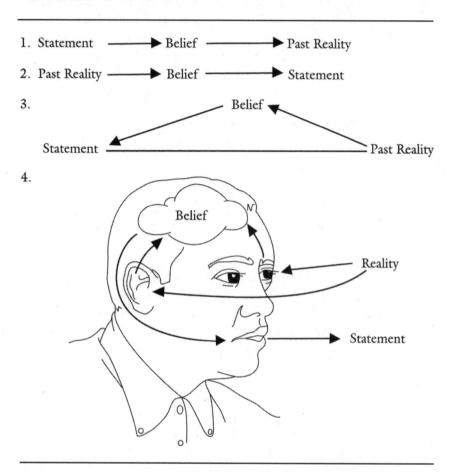

4.

most conduct is "nonassertive," intended to accomplish something but not to convey information. However, nonassertive conduct may still indicate what a person thinks about a subject. In some jurisdictions, but not those following the Federal Rules, testimony about conduct that was not intended to express an idea is defined as hearsay if it is relevant because the action indicates that the actor believed something to be true. The way non-communicative action can be relevant at a trial is illustrated by an effort to prove that a ship was seaworthy by introducing testimony that an experienced ship captain examined it and then sailed on it. Would the report of that captain's actions be hearsay? Under the Federal Rules, the answer is no. Because the captain was intending to take a trip on a ship rather than make an assertion, the conduct can be described without any hearsay concerns. In jurisdictions that apply a broader definition of hearsay, testimony describing what the captain did would be called hearsay because in order to be relevant it must be treated as an expression of what the captain believed to be true about the ship.

The Federal Rules call it hearsay for a witness to testify that the captain once said, "This is a fine ship," but they allow a witness to say that he or she saw the captain examine the ship and then sail on it. This is because sailing on a ship is nonassertive conduct, conduct meant to accomplish something but not to effect a communication or make an assertion. The drafters of the Federal Rules believed that the risk of insincerity in *statements* by an out-of-court *speaker* is greater than the risk of insincerity in the *actions* of an out-of-court *actor*. A speaker is always conscious that his or her words relate to the topic they talk about. An actor, by contrast, may not be as clearly aware that others may interpret his or her actions as revealing what he or she believes to be true. Certainly, if one were interested in lying about a topic, one would lie about it while speaking on that subject. It is less clear that a person who wanted to lie about something would shape nonverbal conduct in ways that would produce deceptive impressions. Furthermore, where an actor's conduct is sought to be relied on in a trial as evidence of some fact the actor may have believed, the actor will usually have done something in real life that was consistent with the supposed underlying belief. The fact that actions expose people to consequences is an additional guarantee that actions will be based on an actor's honest beliefs about reality. These distinctions between words and actions are the main justification for the Federal Rules position in Rule 801(a) that excludes nonassertive conduct from the definition of hearsay. They mainly affect the testimonial issue of truth telling, which suggests that of all the four aspects of conveying information (perception, memory, choice of words, and sincerity), the drafters considered sincerity (or truth-telling) to be the most important.

Since speech itself can be thought of as a kind of conduct, the Federal Rules treatment of nonassertive conduct requires analysis of another issue, the unintended implications of people's assertions. Recall that the Federal Rules exclude from the definition of hearsay testimony about conduct that is relevant because of what it reveals about the actor's beliefs as long as the actor did not intend to be communicating about those beliefs. By implication, another exclusion from the Federal Rules definition of hearsay is testimony about an out-of-court statement that is offered to prove something the speaker did not intend to assert. Obviously, out-of-court words may sometimes be relevant for what they imply rather than what they assert directly. However, it may be difficult to distinguish between a statement claimed to be relevant because of a fact it asserts and a statement claimed to be relevant because it is circumstantial evidence of some fact.

For example, in a suit alleging that a landlord failed to obey a regulation requiring that apartments have adequate heat during winter months, the plaintiff might seek to introduce testimony about the following out-of-court statements made by people in an apartment as part of the plaintiff's proof that the apartment was very cold:

1. "It's very cold in here."
2. "This is a great place for polar bears."
3. "I need to put on a sweater."

Everyone would call the first of these statements hearsay, because the declarant stated that the apartment was very cold, and the statement is sought to be introduced to show that the apartment was very cold. The second statement ("polar bears") is also hearsay. Even though there are differences between the exact out-of-court words and the proposition they are offered to support ("polar bears" is not the same as "very cold"), everyone would agree that the sense of the declarant's words, the meaning the declarant meant to convey, was that the apartment was very cold. For that reason, the statement is hearsay when offered as proof that the apartment was too cold. A speaker's use of humor or metaphor does not prevent evidence law from analyzing the statement as being equivalent, for hearsay purposes, to a statement like the first example, "It's very cold in here."

The third statement, "I need to put on a sweater," would be relevant on the issue of the temperature of the apartment, because someone who plans to dress warmly probably is basing that plan on a belief that the apartment is cold. However, in line with the Federal Rules treatment of nonassertive conduct, it could be argued that the statement is not an assertion about the temperature of the apartment. Since its main subject was how the speaker would be dressed, the likelihood that the statement might be a false characterization of something else (the temperature of the apartment) is reduced. Under the Federal Rules, the statement about the sweater would be an example of what the Advisory Committee Note called "verbal conduct that is assertive but offered as a basis for inferring something other than the matter asserted."

A famous common law case, *Wright v. Doe d. Tatham*,[3] represents a point of view opposed to the Federal Rules position on this issue. To prove that a person had been of sound mind at the time he wrote a will, the proponent of the will sought to introduce letters that various individuals had written to the testator at that time. The explicit subject matter of the letters was not claimed to be relevant. The proponent of the will sought to introduce them to support the inference that the writers believed that the person to whom they were writing was sane, since the letters were straightforward and friendly and involved routine matters of business. After a number of appeals, it was decided that admission of the letters was wrong. They were the equivalent of out-of-court statements by the writers that they thought the

---

3. 7 Ad. & E. 313, 112 Eng. Rep. 488 (Exchequer Chamber 1837).

fact that the call was made to the location is highly suggestive that the place is used for taking bets. In this analysis, the accuracy of the speaker's perceptions and the honesty of the speaker do not matter. On the other hand, if the speaker did not believe that he or she was making the call to a bookie joint, the fact that the call was received does not logically support the idea that the location of the phone actually was a bookie joint.

The statement could be treated as an example of an unintended assertion like the letters to the testator in *Wright*. Taken this way, it is assumed that the statement is relevant because it incorporates the idea, "I think this is a bookie joint," and the truthfulness and accurate perception of the speaker becomes important. Some common law jurisdictions would keep the statement out since it is only relevant to the extent that it incorporates the speaker's unstated belief, "This phone is used by a bookie." Under the Federal Rules, if the judge decided that the statement really meant something about placing a bet, and that this is different from a subsidiary inferable, meaning that the speaker believed the location to be a bookie joint, then the statement would be outside the definition of hearsay. In this analysis, the speaker's statement is admissible as incorporating the speaker's actual belief that the phone is used for a bookie joint, but because the speaker did not explicitly articulate that belief there is an adequate guarantee of trustworthiness to justify treating it as non-hearsay.

In a famous case, *Bridges v. State*,[4] a defendant was accused of having committed a crime against a child. The trial court admitted testimony quoting the child's out-of-court description of the room in which the crime occurred. Proof was also introduced that the defendant lived in a room that met the child's description. Admission of the child's statement was approved in an opinion that characterized it as circumstantial evidence. It can be argued that the words show she had been in that room not because that is the meaning of her out-of-court assertion, but because — regardless of the meaning attributed to her statement — her ability to say anything that contained a description of the room provided circumstantial evidence that she had been there. Testimony was introduced showing that the child would not have had any way to know about the room unless she had, in fact, been taken there by the defendant.

Monograms, inscriptions, and commercial signage: for example, to prove that a hit-and-run vehicle belonged to ABC Pizza, testimony that writing on the side of the vehicle said "ABC Pizza."

If a hit-and-run victim wants to prove that he or she was hit by a truck owned by ABC Pizza, evidence that the truck said "ABC Pizza" on it would be relevant. Would it be hearsay? Since the words are equivalent to a

---

4. 19 N.W.2d 529 (Wis. 1945).

statement, "This truck is operated by ABC Pizza," it is clear that they are sought to be introduced to prove the truth of what they assert. Therefore, the words meet the standard definition of hearsay. (If ABC Pizza is a party to the case, and the words are offered against ABC Pizza, then the hearsay rule will not be an obstacle. Under a hearsay exemption, discussed in Chapter 4, a party's own words are never barred by the hearsay rule when offered by the opposing party.) If the words are hearsay, how could the plaintiff ever have the jury find out that the truck had that writing on it? The trick is to find some way to argue that the words are not being introduced to rely on the truth of their assertion that the truck is operated by ABC Pizza. One approach would be to find evidence from some other source that trucks with the words "ABC Pizza" on them are operated by ABC Pizza. Then, testimony that the hit-and-run truck had "ABC Pizza" on it could be offered just to prove that the words were on the truck without any requirement that their underlying meaning be taken as true merely because of what the words say. Once it is established that the hit-and-run truck said "ABC Pizza" and that ABC Pizza did own trucks with that type of writing on them, the problem of trying to draw meaning from the out-of-court words disappears. The analysis becomes the same as if the victim saw a truck with blue and yellow spots and there was testimony that the defendant operated trucks with blue and yellow spots. Where the identifying characteristics of a thing are a monogram or inscription, or someone's name, the hearsay rule is implicated if a party tries to use the writing to show that its meaning is true. If a party just uses a writing to show that the writing existed, and uses other proof to suggest that things with that writing have certain attributes (such as ownership by the person named in the monogram or inscription), there is no hearsay problem.

> **Surveys:** for example, to prove that the defendant manufacturer's product was deceptively similar to the plaintiff's, testimony that survey respondents identified the defendant's product as the plaintiff's.

It may violate trademark or unfair competition law for one company to make its product look too much like the product of another company. One element of the cause of action may be proof that the appearance of the defendant's product deceived customers into thinking that it was the plaintiff's. A plaintiff in a case like this will often commission a survey to discover if people in the marketplace think that the defendant's product is made by the plaintiff. The hearsay problem in this context involves testimony by the director of the consumer survey, stating that some percentage of survey respondents identified the defendant's product as the plaintiff's. Does this involve quotation of out-of-court statements? While there is no direct quotation, the testimony is entirely based on what other people (the survey respondents) have said out of court. For this reason, the hearsay problem

Basic Instances of Hearsay and Non-hearsay

3. Homeowner's house is burned down in a fire that was caused by a defective lighting fixture. Homeowner thinks that the fixture was made by Waybright Corporation and sues that company for damages. A painter once said to Homeowner, while standing on a ladder near the light, "This is a Waybright fixture." On the issue of whether Waybright made the fixture, would it be hearsay for Homeowner to state what the painter said?

4. Homeowner (from Example 3) puts the painter on the witness stand. The painter testifies: "Two years ago, when I was painting Homeowner's house, I saw her lighting fixture and I told her it was a Waybright fixture." Does this testimony contain hearsay?

5. Could the painter (from Examples 3 and 4) testify that when he painted the room the fixture was in, it looked to him like the fixture was installed securely?

6. An insurance company wants to prove that an insured believed he was suffering from arthritis at the time he applied for insurance that was only available to people who did not suffer from arthritis. Could a witness testify for the insurance company that she saw the insured sitting in a waiting room at a hospital's arthritis clinic on a date earlier than the date of the insurance application?

7. Plaintiff sues Defendant for trespass. The plaintiff said to the defendant the day before the alleged trespass, "I'm glad to meet you; you're nice. You're never a trespasser on my land, and you can visit it whenever you want to." Would it be hearsay evidence for the defendant to testify that the plaintiff said, "You're never a trespasser"?

8. Mr. Victim was injured in an industrial accident and seeks damages from Mr. Maintainer, a self-employed contractor who allegedly did a negligent job of maintaining the machine that hurt him. Shortly after the injury, a government inspector checked the machine and said, "I'd never let that Mr. Maintainer do any work for me." Would testimony by Mr. Victim that the inspector said that be hearsay, if it was introduced to prove that Mr. Maintainer did bad work?

9. Harry Hasty and Clarence Clever started an office-cleaning company that became successful. Hasty sold his share of the business to Clever and agreed not to contact any of the company's customers for a period of two years. Three weeks later, Clever suspected that Hasty was approaching customers of the business and offering to do their office cleaning. In a suit seeking damages for violation of the noncompetition agreement, Clever sought to show that Hasty solicited business from Clever's customers. Clever had a note written to him by one of his

cleaning employees. It said, "Yesterday when I was cleaning the offices of Maximum Corporation, their office manager told me that Harry Hasty was calling them up and visiting them, trying to get them to stop using our company and start hiring Hasty to do their cleaning." Would the note be hearsay, if introduced by Clever?

10. Accused of negligently hiring an incompetent nurse, a doctor would like to testify that one of the nurse's former employers had stated in an employment reference that the nurse "does excellent work." Would the reference comment be hearsay on the issue of the doctor's reasonableness in hiring the nurse? Would it be hearsay on the issue of whether the nurse is skillful?

11. To show that an extortion defendant knew the alleged victim, the prosecution seeks to introduce a piece of paper found in the defendant's apartment with the victim's address and telephone number on it. Is the note hearsay?

12. Ms. Spectator sues the owner of a large field where a motorcycle race was held. She claims that she was hit by a motorcycle while watching the race from a hill that was marked out as safe for viewing. The defendant claims that she thought that spot was appropriate for spectators because the organizers of the race told her the race would be on flat parts of the land and never told her anything about using the hill. An investigator, hired by the owner, interviewed all the people who organized the race. Would it involve hearsay for the investigator to give the following testimony?
    a. "Based on my interviews, I conclude that when the race was rehearsed, all the riders stayed on the flat land."
    b. "No one I spoke to said anything about warning the owner that the racing motorcycles would go up the hill."

Written Statements as Hearsay and Non-hearsay

13. Suppose that you parked your car in a shopping center and that after shopping you returned to find that another car had banged into it, crushing one of the doors. If a note on the windshield said, "I saw the accident. The car that hit you had license plate ABC-123," could you introduce that note in a suit against the owner of the car that had that license plate number?

14. Patient sues a surgeon, claiming that medical negligence by the surgeon left him with severely decreased mobility in his hands that weakened them so much that he could no longer use eating utensils or hold a pen or pencil to write. To show that the patient did have the ability to write, the doctor seeks to introduce a note, written by the plaintiff one week

before the trial, that says, "Thank you for your invitation, but I won't be able to come to the party Thursday because I'll be busy with my lawsuit." Is the note hearsay?

Conventional Non-hearsay Situations

15. In a trademark infringement case, a food company claims that an electronics company has marketed a radio with a brand name that is confusingly similar to one of the food company's brand names. The food company seeks to introduce testimony that it has received orders for the radios from many of its customers. Does this testimony include hearsay?

16. Mr. Poor gives some money to Ms. Rich and says, "Here is the repayment of the loan you made to me so I could buy a car." Later, Ms. Rich sues Mr. Poor claiming that the money she received was a gift, and that Mr. Poor still owes her money to repay the car loan. May Mr. Poor quote his own out-of-court statement about the purpose of the payment, or would that be hearsay?

17. A parking lot had a large sign stating "convenient to downtown." If a state consumer affairs department alleged that the lot was really not convenient to downtown and sued the company for false advertising, could the defendant offer testimony that no customer had ever made a complaint about the lot's location or about its advertising claim?

18. To show that Stanley Sportsfan was reckless (in a suit involving a claim that a defendant had been negligent to hire him for work where good judgment was required), the plaintiff seeks to introduce testimony showing that several hours after an important professional football game had been played, Sportsfan saw one of the players in a restaurant; the player was extremely large and strong and had a reputation for committing violent acts against strangers; and Sportsfan said to the player, "I think you're a bum. You play like a little girl." Would testimony including the quotation of what Sportsfan said be defined as hearsay?

Explanations

Underlying Policies

1. The person Walker is quoting is not available for cross-examination. This makes it impossible to find out what the person meant by "light was red." The declarant might not have meant to imply anything at all about whether the light was in the driver's favor or the pedestrian's favor. Without having the speaker present in court, there is no way to determine what the words really meant. Even if it was somehow clear that the declarant meant to express the idea that the light had been red against the driver, there is also no way to assess the declarant's truthfulness. Also,

there is no information about how well the declarant actually saw the accident. Perhaps the declarant arrived at the scene just after it happened and guessed or tried to figure out who had been in the wrong. Having the declarant available at the trial would allow Driver to expose fully the basis for the declarant's beliefs. One of the testimonial infirmities, poor memory, would not be a problem here, since on the facts of the problem very little time had passed between the declarant's perception of the event and the declarant's statement about it.

2. If "What kind of driver just zooms . . . ?" was sought to be introduced to show that the light was red against Driver when Driver entered the intersection, some courts might state that the declarant's words are not hearsay because they are in the form of a question, and questions do not assert anything. A better analysis would be to interpret the out-of-court words as equivalent to the assertion, "Driver had the light against him when he entered the intersection," and treat them therefore as hearsay when they are introduced to support the conclusion that the light was against Driver.

Basic Instances of Hearsay and Non-hearsay

3. Yes. The declarant is the painter. The out-of-court statement is, "This is a Waybright fixture," and it is sought to be introduced to show that the fixture was a Waybright fixture. Thus, the statement's relevance depends on its meaning being true. In terms of the Federal Rules, it is sought to be introduced to prove the truth of the matter it asserts. This makes it hearsay.

4. Yes. The out-of-court statement is the painter's report to Homeowner that the fixture was a Waybright fixture. Note that hearsay can be a direct quotation such as "I said, 'This is a Waybright fixture,'" or an indirect quotation such as "I told her that it was a Waybright fixture." The declarant in this problem is the painter, he made his statement out of court, and it is offered to prove the truth of its contents. The unusual aspect of this example is that he is now repeating the statement in court while he is a witness. Self-quotation, in the opinion of some authorities, ought not to be considered hearsay. However, under the Federal Rules and in most places governed by other rules, even self-quotation can be hearsay.

5. Assuming that this information is relevant, there would be no hearsay problem. The painter in this example, unlike question 4, is telling in court something he *saw*. This is different, for hearsay purposes, from telling what he once *said*.

6. Yes. This testimony gets in, even though testimony by a witness that the insured had once said, "I have arthritis" would be hearsay.[5] The insured's conduct of sitting in a particular waiting room does not fit the Federal Rules definition of assertive conduct. Since it was not a statement and was not conduct meant to convey information, it is outside the scope of the hearsay definition.

7. The testimony does not contain any hearsay. This is an example of out-of-court words that have independent legal significance. They are introduced by the defendant to support the proposition that he was not a trespasser, and they do include words saying that the defendant is not a trespasser. That equivalence of expression is a coincidence that does not make the out-of-court words hearsay. They are introduced by the defendant to prove just that they were said. If they were really spoken, they amount to permission to enter the plaintiff's land. The court and our substantive law will assign a meaning to them such as deciding that they constitute the defense of permission in the trespass case. This effect is provided to the words by our system of property law without regard to what the declarant might have thought, remembered, seen, or meant to say when he said them. The testimonial infirmities do not matter since the words are relevant if a reasonable person who heard them would consider them to constitute permission to enter the land. It doesn't matter, under standard property law, whether the plaintiff meant or did not mean them to have their standard meaning.

8. The out-of-court statement is not exactly equal to the proposition for which it is sought to be introduced — that Mr. Maintainer did bad work. All the declarant said was that she would never have Mr. Maintainer do any work for her. Yet the statement is relevant, if at all, because it conveys the meaning that the inspector thought Mr. Maintainer did bad work. That meaning is so close to the explicit content of the out-of-court statement that the statement should be classified as hearsay. If there was an issue, for example, about whether the inspector had ever heard of Mr. Maintainer or whether Mr. Maintainer had worked on the machine, proof that she said something about Mr. Maintainer would not be hearsay because the ideas that the inspector knew Mr. Maintainer or that Mr. Maintainer had worked on the machine would be unintended implications of the inspector's words.

   On the other hand, it strains the imagination to say that the idea, "Maintainer did bad work," was an *unintended* implication of the

---

5. Remember that many out-of-court statements sought to be introduced to prove the truth of what they assert do escape the standard exclusionary result of the hearsay rules because they fit certain exceptions to the doctrine or because, under the Federal Rules, they fall within specialized exceptions to the definition of hearsay itself. The statement in this example is an admission and would therefore be safe from objection on grounds of hearsay.

statement, "I'd never let that Mr. Maintainer do any work for me." Obviously, there is room for disagreement about whether the inspector's statement should be treated as intending or not intending to assert something about Mr. Maintainer's work. A court would be influenced in deciding whether or not to classify the statement as hearsay by the importance of the statement in the case and by the seriousness of the testimonial infirmities in the specific situation. If the words were ambiguous and they were the proponent's only proof on a crucial issue, there would be a tendency to exclude them.

9. There are three out-of-court statements in this problem:

   1. Hasty to the office manager (words such as "I'd like your office-cleaning business");
   2. Office manager to Clever's worker (words such as "Hasty has been soliciting our business"); and
   3. Clever's worker to Clever (note with words such as "the manager said that Hasty had solicited business").

   Hasty's words would not be hearsay because, whether it was true or not that Hasty wanted Maximum's business, Hasty's saying those words violated Hasty's promise not to contact customers of the office-cleaning business. So if Clever had a witness who could testify that she heard Hasty make his offer to Maximum, that quotation of Hasty's words would not be hearsay.

   Clever does not have a witness to testify that Hasty said the words. Clever has a piece of paper written by his employee. And the piece of paper quotes Maximum's office manager. The manager's words are hearsay since they state that Hasty had done something, and they are relevant only to prove that Hasty had done it (solicit business from Maximum). Similarly, the note from Clever's employee is hearsay. It is an out-of-court statement conveying the idea that Maximum's office manager had said certain things about Hasty to Clever's employee. Unless that information is accurate, the note is not relevant to the trial. It is sought to be introduced to prove that what it asserts is true: that Maximum's manager spoke to Clever's employee and told him that Hasty had solicited business from him.

10. The reference comment ("does excellent work") is not hearsay on the issue of how reasonable it was for the doctor to hire the nurse. Used in connection with that issue, the truthfulness of the reference is not material. All that matters is that the words were communicated to the doctor because, whether or not they were true, a doctor who gets such a reference and then employs the person described in the reference is probably acting reasonably. On the issue of how competent

the nurse really is, the out-of-court words *are* hearsay since they are relevant to that issue only if their assertion ("excellent") is true.

11. The vast majority of courts and scholars agree that this note is not hearsay — it is used just to show that there is a connection between the defendant and the victim. It is not shown to prove what the victim's address is since presumably that will be established in some other way. A minority view is that this note is equivalent to a note in the defendant's handwriting saying, "I know the victim." If the note really did say that, most courts would be more inclined to treat it as hearsay. However, in the recurring instances in which this problem is litigated, the conventional treatment is to call the writing just circumstantial evidence and decide that it raises no hearsay problems.

12. a. The statement that the racers stayed on the flat land when they rehearsed is phrased as a conclusion from the witness's investigation. It is apparent, though, that it is entirely based on what people said to him. Since it is therefore equivalent to a quotation in court of what various people said about the events during the rehearsal, it is hearsay when introduced to support the idea that the rehearsal race did not use the hill.

   b. To prove that no one gave a warning to the owner about use of the hill, the investigator states that no one mentioned warnings in his interviews. Should this be treated as silence that is not hearsay? That analysis fits usually where there is a good reason to think that a certain subject would be mentioned to the person who later testifies about it. Where an investigator is involved, it seems likely that people would answer questions and remain silent about other topics. Their silence ought not logically to be taken as implying anything about their ideas on the non-addressed topic.

   If the investigator had asked, "Did you give warnings?" and people replied to that question, their answers would be hearsay if quoted by the investigator. In this problem, the investigator may not have asked any questions about warnings. If he did not ask about warnings, the lack of mention of warnings in his interviews probably does not prove anything about warnings and is therefore not relevant. If he did ask about warnings, then his reports of nonreplies might best be characterized as reports of assertive conduct (silence in response to a direct question could be the same as a negative shake of the head) or as reports of conversations in which the totality of the speaker's comments added up to a statement that they gave no warnings. For these reasons, the investigator's testimony that no one said anything about warnings should be treated as not relevant (since it is based on conversations in which silence about warnings is not logically related to whether or not warnings were given) or should be treated as hearsay.

Written Statements as Hearsay and Non-hearsay

13. No. The statement is hearsay. Hearsay can be written or spoken. In this instance, you would be seeking to use the written words to establish exactly what they stated: the license plate of the car that hit your car. This makes them hearsay. Another problem is that there is no way of knowing the identity of the declarant (the writer) and showing the source of his or her knowledge.

14. This statement is not hearsay. Written words can be hearsay, just as spoken words can, but only if they are introduced to prove the truth of what they assert. Here the truth of whether the writer will be able to accept the invitation is irrelevant to the issues at trial. But the note is relevant in a non-hearsay way. The fact that it was written shows that the plaintiff did have the ability to do some writing.

Conventional Non-hearsay Situations

15. Information that customers ordered the radio from the food company is relevant because it shows that people who saw the radio and knew its brand name assumed that it was manufactured by the plaintiff food company and not by the defendant electronics company. The standard analysis of this situation is to describe the testimony as non-hearsay. The proponent is not trying to show that the out-of-court statements (the orders) were accurate. The proponent, rather, is using them circumstantially as evidence that some consumers acted in a way that suggests that the defendant's brand name was confusingly similar to the plaintiff's. A contrary result is logically supportable but rarely adopted: If the customers' orders are analyzed as statements that necessarily incorporated the idea, "I believe that you are the manufacturer of the following item," then introducing them to prove that the customers did believe that the food company was the manufacturer of the radio would make them hearsay.[6]

16. Mr. Poor may quote himself in this instance because his out-of-court words are called a verbal act or a verbal part of an act. Without those words being introduced into the trial, the conduct of turning over money would be ambiguous. The reasoning here is similar to the reasoning that permits words of independent legal effect to be introduced without regard to hearsay problems. Some courts use the expression res gestae as a label for defining statements of this kind as non-hearsay since the words are permitted to be introduced as "part of the act" being described.

---

6. Defined as hearsay, this material would still be admissible under a state of mind exception to the hearsay exclusion to prove that the people giving the orders had the belief that the food company made the radios. Alternatively, expert testimony based on a properly conducted survey would be a method of establishing the plaintiff's showing of confusion in the marketplace that would completely avoid the hearsay problem discussed in this example.

17. Yes. Silence by a person (like each of the lot's customers) is not considered to be a statement made out of court. Since there is no statement, there can be no hearsay. Like so many issues in hearsay, this one could reasonably be analyzed to reach an opposite result. The witness is really basing testimony on a report of everything the customers have ever said to show that none of their remarks involved dissatisfaction with the location of the lot or the wording of its sign. This point is logically sound, but courts are satisfied to respond to situations like this one in a conventional way and admit the testimony. Incidentally, this example serves as a reminder that successfully avoiding hearsay objections is not a guarantee that evidence will be admitted. Other requirements, such as relevance, must also be met. Here, to establish that the customers' silence was relevant, the defendant would need to show that it would have been easy for a disappointed customer to find a way to present a complaint.

    Would the words of the sign be hearsay? No. The state consumer affairs department is seeking to introduce them to prove that they were used by the defendant and to show that they are false. There would be a hearsay issue only if the words were used in an effort to state that the meaning they convey is true.

18. This testimony does not fit a sensible definition of hearsay. The words by Sportsfan are relevant regardless of whether they are a true statement of Sportsfan's feelings about the player. The jury can use them to assess Sportsfan's recklessness or good judgment without the jury having to decide whether the words were an accurate representation of Sportsfan's beliefs. Even if the words were false, and Sportsfan did not believe what he was saying, he was probably reckless to say words that the player would likely consider to be insults. The fact that Sportsfan said the words is relevant to deciding if he is a reckless type of person.

Exceptions to the Hearsay Exclusionary Rule

INTRODUCTION

The supreme irony of the hearsay doctrine is that a vast amount of hearsay is admissible at common law and under the Federal Rules. The full analysis of any hearsay problem, therefore, requires considering whether the offered evidence is hearsay and then, if it is hearsay, whether any exception to the rule of exclusion applies to it.

The exceptions give special treatment to recurring instances of hearsay. Many are based on longstanding tradition, while others are newer, justified by a belief that at least one of the testimonial infirmities is unlikely to be a factor in most of the instances they cover. The Federal Rules also permit admission of hearsay as part of an expert's testimony even if no specific hearsay provisions would allow it, under some circumstances.

Some types of hearsay statements are thought to be particularly free from the risk that the maker of the statement intended to lie. Statements of this kind are usually admissible, whether or not the declarant is available to testify. Other types of hearsay are thought to be particularly necessary in special circumstances. These types of statements are usually admissible only if the proponent shows that the declarant is unavailable. Finally, there is a third class of out-of-court statements offered to prove the truth of what they assert that universally is allowed into evidence despite the hearsay rule, even without a belief that the statement is likely to have been truthful when made or that the statement is particularly necessary to a party's case. This class of statements includes statements by an opposing party (sometimes called admissions), which are any statements ever made by a *party* in the current case if introduced against that party, and certain statements made out of court by a person who appears in court as a *witness*. The Federal Rules exceptions to the hearsay exclusion are organized, accordingly, in three categories: (1) hearsay exceptions that apply without regard to whether the declarant is available as a witness, (2) hearsay exceptions that apply only if the declarant is unavailable as a witness, and (3) exemptions from the definition of hearsay for certain out-of-court statements offered for the truth of what they assert. Additionally, a residual or "catch-all" exception allows admission of statements that are outside the coverage of the enumerated exceptions but that seem similarly trustworthy.

Chart 14 shows a suggested order of analysis for evidence that might involve hearsay. It points out that the first inquiry is whether the evidence is a "statement." The next inquiry is whether the statement must be true in order for it to be relevant. The final inquiry is whether the statement is within the definitions of any of the hearsay exclusions or exceptions.

Statements Exempted from the Federal Rules Definition of Hearsay

Opposing Party's Statements (Admissions)

Perhaps the largest loophole in the hearsay doctrine is a category of statements called an *opposing party's statement*. At common law and in the original version of the Federal Rules of Evidence, these statements were called *admissions*. These out-of-court statements are anything a party has ever communicated (in speech, writing, or in any other way) sought to be introduced against that party at trial. At common law these statements are defined as hearsay and admitted under an exception to the hearsay exclusion rule. Under the Federal Rules they are specifically exempted from the definition of hearsay and thus are not barred by the prohibition against introducing hearsay evidence. The statement, at the time the party made it, could have been favorable to some interest of the party, or unfavorable, or neutral. The proponent of an out-of-court statement who seeks to take advantage of the admission or opposing party's statement rationale is required only to show that the statement was once made by the opposing party and that it is relevant in the current trial.

There are two primary rationales for permitting statements by a party opponent to be used in evidence despite the concerns that underlie the hearsay doctrine. First, it seems fair to many that people ought to be forced to live up to their own claims, promises, and statements. Allowing them into evidence when people become involved in lawsuits furthers this goal. Second, because opposing party statements by definition are always statements

Chart 14 Hearsay Flowchart

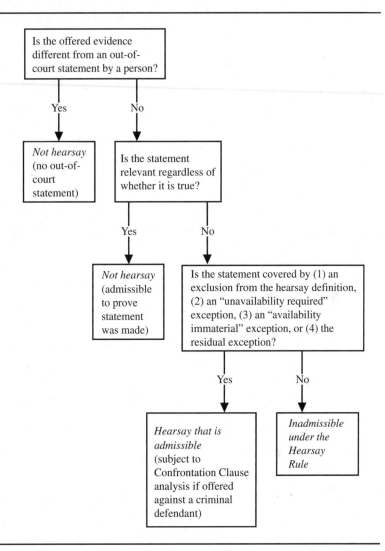

by a party (or someone closely affiliated with a party), many hearsay dangers are obviated. If the statement was false at the time it was made, or if use of the statement at the trial might create a false impression because of discrepancies between the circumstances at the time at which it was made and circumstances at the time of the trial, the party is available to explain what the statement meant at the time it was made.

These justifications for exempting an opposing party's statement from exclusion under the hearsay rule are imperfect at best. They may reflect a basic ambivalence about the hearsay rule. While excluding statements that meet the definition of hearsay seems highly desirable in the abstract, many classes of statements seem too good to ignore. This has led to the current structure of hearsay law with its large number of exceptions rationalized on fairly questionable grounds.

The exemption of opposing party statements (admissions) from the definition of hearsay is accomplished by Rule 801(d)(2):

> *An Opposing Party's Statement.* The statement is offered against an opposing party and:
>
> > **(A)** was made by the party in an individual or representative capacity;
> > **(B)** is one the party manifested that it adopted or believed to be true;
> > **(C)** was made by a person whom the party authorized to make a statement on the subject;
> > **(D)** was made by the party's agent or employee on a matter within the scope of that relationship and while it existed; or
> > **(E)** was made by the party's coconspirator during and in furtherance of the conspiracy.
>
> The statement must be considered but does not by itself establish the declarant's authority under (C); the existence or scope of the relationship under (D); or the existence of the conspiracy or participation in it under (E).

Five types of statements are defined as opposing party's statements by Rule 801(d)(2). The clearest example is a party's own past words, relevant at the time of trial to an issue in the trial. Illustratively, suppose A sues B for damages suffered in a collision allegedly caused by B's bad driving. An issue concerns whether B drove through a red light. If B said after the accident, "I didn't see the traffic light," A would be entitled to introduce evidence of B's statement as a basis for concluding that B did not see the light (which would be relevant to evaluating B's driving).

Related to statements a party makes personally are "adoptive admissions," or "adoptive opposing party statements." An adoptive admission or statement is a party's reaction to a statement or action by another person when it is reasonable to treat the party's reaction as agreement with something stated or implied by the other person. In the automobile collision example, if someone said to B right after the collision, "You didn't stop for the red light," and B answered, "I'm sorry I didn't," B's answer (together with the question to which it was a reply) would be an adoptive opposing party statement (or an adoptive admission). Similarly, there are instances where a party's silence will be treated as an admission or opposing party statement, if that silence occurs after the party heard something that most people would contradict if it was untrue. An example would be someone saying to driver B, "Everyone saw that the light was against you," and B failing to reject that assertion.

Sometimes statements by a person other than a party can be treated as the party's own statement. The statements of a person authorized to speak on behalf of someone who becomes a party to a lawsuit are admissible as an opposing party's statement when offered against the party. A lawyer is the most common example of a person who is authorized to speak on another's behalf.

While a lawyer is a particular kind of agent, employed to provide legal representation, the Federal Rules definition of "opposing party's statement" covers statements made by any type of agent or employee. A statement is usable against a party if it is made by the party's agent or employee concerning something within the scope of agency or employment during the time of the agency or employment. Also, one coconspirator's statements may be introduced against another coconspirator so long as the statements were made during and in furtherance of their conspiracy. So if a truck driver working for a company was involved in a traffic accident and then said something about his or her driving, those words would be admissible in a suit against that company for damages for injuries arising out of the accident. This is true even though the truck driver is probably not authorized by the company to make statements about driving. The Federal Rules would define the driver's words as an opposing party's statement, usable against the company, because they concerned the driver's employment and were made while the driver and the company continued to have an employer-employee relationship.

Some common law jurisdictions are more restrictive than this and would treat quotation of the driver's words as hearsay if used in a suit against the company. Their doctrinal analysis would state that the driver's job is driving, not making statements about driving, and that therefore use of the words against the company would be hearsay because the words were spoken outside the scope of the driver's employment. For these jurisdictions, the authorization to speak on a subject is crucial to deciding whether the speaker's words can be treated as an opposing party's statement against someone other than the speaker.

Parties sometimes dispute whether a declarant was an agent, an employee, or a coconspirator when the declarant made a statement. Some jurisdictions have prohibited a party's use of the contents of a statement to prove a fact required to establish admissibility of the statement, calling this use illogical "bootstrapping." However, in *Bourjaily v. United States*,[1] the United States Supreme Court declined to exclude a statement's contents from the material that its proponent may use to show that it was made by a coconspirator during the course of a conspiracy. Rule 801(d)(2) reflects the

---

1. 483 U.S. 171 (1987).

Bourjaily decision and applies its holding to statements by agents and employees in addition to coconspirators. Significantly, Rule 801(d)(2) resolves a problem *Bourjaily* did not address: Although the trial court can consider the contents of a statement to determine whether it satisfies the requirements of Rule 801(d)(2), the court must exclude the statement if the only evidence that the statement satisfies Rule 801(d)(2) comes from the statement's contents.

Prior Statements by a Witness

The Federal Rules exclude one other group of statements in addition to party opponent statements from the definition of hearsay. These are certain statements made outside of court by a person who then testifies at trial. The need for special treatment arises because under common law and the general Federal Rules definition of hearsay, a witness's own out-of-court words are hearsay even if they are quoted at trial by the witness, if their relevance depends on the truth of what the out-of-court words assert. Despite the applicability of the general definition, it is controversial to treat as hearsay out-of-court statements by a person who appears at a trial and testifies. After all, the fact that the witness and the out-of-court declarant are the same human being makes this situation different from most attempted uses of out-of-court statements. Where the witness's own past statements are involved, a jury would be able to observe the declarant's demeanor and to hear responses to cross-examination about the statements. Since the lack of these opportunities is the basis for excluding hearsay, it has seemed to some authorities that the hearsay rule should be completely withdrawn from past statements of a person who is a witness at the trial.

The Federal Rules mostly adopt the opposing view that a witness's own out-of-court words should be defined as hearsay. Those who believe that the hearsay exclusion can sensibly be applied even to the out-of-court words of a person who is a witness at the trial point out that cross-examination at trial time may be less effective than cross-examination would have been at the time the speaker made the statement. If out-of-court statements by people who become witnesses were generally admissible, well-organized parties would develop a practice of making records of interviews with prospective witnesses. There would be no cross-examination at the time they obtained these statements, and then they would seek to introduce them at a subsequent trial. At the time of the trial, opponents of this practice suggest, the person who gave the interview might be less willing to change or be self-critical of the recollection than he or she might have been if the recollection had been challenged when he or she first expressed it.

4. Exceptions to the Hearsay Exclusionary Rule

In the context of these opposed views, FRE 801(d)(1) treats selected types of statements by witnesses as outside the hearsay definition, under particular circumstances. The Rule states:

> *A Declarant-Witness's Prior Statement.* The declarant testifies and is subject to cross-examination about a prior statement, and the statement:
>
> **(A)** is inconsistent with the declarant's testimony and was given under penalty of perjury at a trial, hearing, or other proceeding or in a deposition;
>
> **(B)** is consistent with the declarant's testimony and is offered:
>
> (i) to rebut an express or implied charge that the declarant recently fabricated it or acted from a recent improper influence or motive in so testifying; or
>
> (ii) to rehabilitate the declarant's credibility as a witness when attacked on another ground; or
>
> **(C)** identifies a person as someone the declarant perceived earlier.

There are three types of out-of-court statements by a witness: prior inconsistent statements, prior consistent statements, and statements identifying a person. For any of them to qualify for exclusion from the hearsay definition, there must be a showing that the declarant is "available for cross-examination" concerning the declarant's out-of-court statement. The "available for cross-examination" requirement may be very easy for the proponent of a witness's out-of-court statement to fulfill. It was satisfied in a case, binding on federal courts and persuasive authority elsewhere, where a witness remembered making a statement but did not remember the events that he had described in his statement and did not remember any circumstances involved in his making the statement.[2] Obviously, the opportunity for realistic cross-examination of such a witness would be very slight.

A prior inconsistent statement is any statement by a witness (1) made out of court (2) before the witness testifies that (3) conflicts with something the witness says in testimony. At common law, these statements may be introduced for impeachment, that is, to support a conclusion that the witness testified falsely. This use does not violate the hearsay rule because, analytically, the out-of-court statement is being introduced to show its *contrast* with the in-court statement, not its *truth*. Prior inconsistent statements may not, at common law, be introduced to support a conclusion that the prior statement was true. Under the Federal Rules, impeachment use of a prior statement is permitted since it raises no hearsay implications. Additionally, if the prior statement was made under oath at a proceeding, it may be introduced as proof of what it asserts.

A prior consistent statement is any statement by a witness made out of court before the witness testified that reinforces or supports the testimony.

---

2. *See* United States v. Owens, 484 U.S. 554 (1988).

Under the Federal Rules, a prior consistent statement does not have to have been made under oath in a proceeding as is required for substantive use of a prior inconsistent statement. A prior consistent statement may be introduced to respond to a claim that the witness's testimony was recently fabricated or was influenced by a recent motive to lie. It might also be introduced to respond to other attacks on a witness's testimony, such as a claim that the witness has a faulty memory or a claim that the testimony has been muddled or internally inconsistent.

To use a prior consistent statement to respond to a claim of recent fabrication or improper motive, the proponent must show that the witness made the prior statement before the time of the alleged fabrication or before the time that he or she was subject to the alleged motive to lie. If a witness who testifies to a certain proposition is accused of lying or of slanting the testimony because of a motive favorable to one side in the trial, proof that the witness has said similar things prior to the trial would support a conclusion that the trial testimony was truthful. This logic is particularly strong if the out-of-court statements were made before a motive to lie arose. For example, Witness A might testify that Defendant D committed a crime. If D shows that the prosecution promised leniency to A in exchange for A's testimony, an implication would arise that A's testimony may have been untruthful in favor of the prosecution. Proof that A had said similar things about D prior to the time of A's deal with the prosecution would support the truthfulness of A's in-court testimony.

Rule 801(d)(1)(B)(i) does not explicitly state anything about the timing of a prior consistent statement offered in response to a claim that the witness was affected by a recent motive to lie. However, the United States Supreme Court has held that in this situation the prior statement must have been made before the witness had a motive to falsify his or her testimony.[3] Thus, a statement made *after* the speaker had a motive to testify falsely but before the witness testified in court would not be eligible for the non-hearsay treatment of Rule 801(d)(1)(B)(i) and would likely be treated as inadmissible for any purpose. In some states, a prior consistent statement made at any time is admissible for whatever weight the trier of fact may give it.

When the proponent of a prior consistent statement offers it to respond to a claim that the witness has a poor memory or to clear up an apparent inconsistency in the witness's testimony, Rule 801(d)(1)(B)(ii) applies and there is no requirement about the timing of the prior statement. The timing requirement for prior consistent statements adopted by the Supreme Court applies only when those statements are introduced to refute claims of recent fabrication or improper motive.

---

3. Tome v. United States, 513 U.S. 150 (1995).

Note that inconsistent statements must have been made under oath in a proceeding to be entitled to substantive treatment, while substantive treatment is accorded for consistent statements however they were made. Greater restrictiveness concerning inconsistent statements may make sense because the proponent of substantive use of a witness's prior *inconsistent* statement asks the jury to reject what it has heard in court and substitute a version of reality drawn from out-of-court statements. In contrast, the proponent of substantive use of a prior *consistent* statement seeks to reinforce a conclusion that what the in-court witness said was true. Belief in the content of the prior consistent statement evidence will lead a jury to conclude that the witness's testimony it heard originally is true. This is a less powerful use of out-of-court words than the use permitted by the Federal Rules for prior inconsistent statements. Because substituting out-of-court words for in-court words with an inconsistent meaning is so drastic, it is not surprising that the Federal Rules place significant requirements on the use of prior inconsistent statements as substantive evidence.

A statement identifying a person previously perceived is covered by Rule 801(d)(1)(C). It provides that a witness's out-of-court statement identifying a person is admissible as substantive evidence of the identification. The rationale of the rule is that identifications of people made prior to trials are likely to be more accurate than identifications made during testimony, and for that reason should be admitted for substantive use. Many courts limit the application of this Rule to situations like a crime victim's statement identifying a person at a lineup or from a photo array. This interpretation is consistent with the intention of the Rule's drafters. It is also supported by the possibility that constitutional safeguards for lineups and photo arrays may enhance the likely accuracy of the declarant's identifying statement. However, the Rule's language does not restrict its coverage to statements made in particular circumstances; on that basis some courts apply the rule broadly.

Examples

1. Plaintiff claims that she was badly hurt by xanadite, an ingredient in a microwave pizza sold by the defendant manufacturer. To support a claim for punitive damages, the plaintiff wants to prove that xanadite is extremely dangerous. Discuss whether the plaintiff may introduce each of the following items of evidence to show that xanadite is dangerous. Remember that admissibility on the issue of *xanadite's dangerousness* is different from admissibility on other issues that might be part of the plaintiff's case, such as the *company's knowledge* about xanadite's dangerousness.
   a. A letter from a university scientist found in the company's files stating that the scientist has discovered that xanadite is very dangerous in microwave pizzas and asking to be hired by the company to do further research about it.

b. A memorandum written by the company's president to the company's chief scientist saying that the president wanted him to start work immediately on a new formula for the company's pizza that would replace the xanadite with another ingredient because the xanadite is extremely dangerous.

c. A note written by the company president to the company's chief of public relations, with an attached copy of a scientific article, saying, "The attached article says that xanadite is dangerous in foods. We use it in our microwave pizza. This shows we've been selling something dangerous."

d. A note like the one in part c, but with the statement, "This shows we may be in serious trouble," instead of the statement, "This shows we've been selling something dangerous."

e. Testimony that a worker in the manufacturer's pizza ingredients warehouse once said to a friend, "If you ever get a job here, be sure you don't get assigned to handling xanadite. That stuff is unbelievably dangerous. Most of the people who work with it lose their hair and get bad rashes."

f. An autobiography by someone who once was the president of the manufacturing company, written after retirement, describing xanadite as a dangerous ingredient.

2. In a variation of Example 1, if it was admitted that xanadite is extremely dangerous, but the manufacturer denied having had that knowledge at the time it made the pizza that hurt the plaintiff, could the evidence offered in parts a to f of Example 1 be introduced to show that the manufacturer did have that knowledge at the relevant time?

3. Manny and Moe are on trial for bank robbery. A witness has testified that she saw them enter the bank together carrying guns. The prosecution seeks to have a police officer testify that after he had been arrested, Manny told the officer that Moe was the other person involved in the robbery. Is this testimony admissible to show that Moe was one of the two robbers?

4. Eagle Enterprises sues Cybernetics Corporation, seeking damages on a claim that a computer program Cybernetics was supposed to produce by January 1, 2015, failed to operate as expected. Fred Micro, an independent computer engineer, testifies for Eagle that he examined the program in February, 2015, and that it did not work. May he testify further to show that the computer program did not work properly, that in February 2015 he told a group of Eagle's employees that the Cybernetics program did not work?

5. Dan Driver left his car to be repaired at a car repair shop. When he picked it up and started to drive away, its brakes failed, causing Driver to hit something in the repair shop's parking lot. A person came up to Driver

right after the accident and said, "I'm the service manager. I'm sorry we forgot to check the brakes." If Driver seeks damages from the operator of the repair shop, could he testify about that statement to show that the repair shop had failed to inspect its work properly?

6. Paula Plaintiff was injured when a large bus she was riding in collided with another vehicle. She sought damages from the transit company that operated the bus. One of her witnesses was an expert at reconstructing accidents. The accident reconstructionist testified that the collision probably occurred because the bus driver did not pay careful attention to oncoming traffic. The transit company contended that a defect in the brakes, for which the bus manufacturer would be responsible, was the cause of the collision. Could the transit company introduce evidence that the expert once testified in a similar case involving a bus collision and stated in the circumstances of that case that brake failure was the most likely cause of the incident? If it is admissible, could proof of the witness's earlier statements be used for any purpose other than impeachment?

7. In a medical malpractice case, a nurse testifies that the defendant doctor followed standard procedures during an operation in which the doctor allegedly harmed the plaintiff. During cross-examination, the nurse admits that since the time of the operation, the defendant doctor has recommended him for several promotions. On redirect examination, may the defendant have the nurse testify that he wrote a letter to a friend a few days after the operation stating that the doctor had followed standard procedures?

8. Someone ran up to Victim on a street and stole his wallet. Victim then hailed a passing police car and drove around in it, looking for the robber. As the police car went by Suspect, Victim pointed at him, started sobbing, and fainted. Suspect is now on trial, accused of stealing Victim's wallet. May a police officer describe how Victim pointed to Suspect?

Explanations

1. a. The letter is hearsay, since the plaintiff seeks to introduce it to prove that what it asserts is true, that xanadite is dangerous. It is not an opponent's statement, since it is not a statement by any employee or agent of the company. Further, it would not be an adoptive opponent's statement, since a company does not indicate agreement with an unsolicited letter just by filing it.

   b. The letter is partly hearsay and partly not hearsay. The portion that is a command to the scientist could be classified as non-hearsay. Yet it might be treated as relevant on the issue of the dangerousness of xanadite since one of the main reasons why a company president might want an ingredient eliminated from a product would be that the ingredient is dangerous. What about the president's statement that xanadite is extremely dangerous? If it is sought to be introduced to prove the danger of xanadite in pizza, it is an out-of-court statement sought to be introduced to prove the truth of what it asserts. This would be hearsay under the common law, but the hearsay rule would not keep it from being introduced since it would be treated as an admissible opponent's statement. It is a party's own statement, sought to be introduced against the party. Under the Federal Rules, the statement fits the description of opponent's statement. Thus, it is exempt from the definition of hearsay.

c. The plaintiff is seeking to introduce the note and the attached article as proof that xanadite is a dangerous ingredient. Therefore, the evidence will be hearsay under common law and will meet the Federal Rules definition of hearsay, too, unless it qualifies under the Federal Rules provision that removes opponents' statements from the definition of hearsay. The evidence is admissible as an adoptive opponent's statement. It is an out-of-court statement by a party (the company president speaks for the company) accepting as true an out-of-court statement by another (the author of the scientific article). The note and the article are both admissible.

d. Changing the president's words from "we've been selling something dangerous" to "we may be in serious trouble" makes it harder to treat the president's note as an adoption of the statements in the scientific article. The trial judge will accept or reject the adoptive opponent's statement rationale depending on what the parties persuade the judge the president may have meant by writing that the article meant the company was "in serious trouble." If that meant the president agreed with the attached scientific article, then the president's statement and the article would all be admissible under the opposing party's adoptive statement rationale. Understood that way, the president's out-of-court statement expresses agreement with (or adopts) the scientist's out-of-court statement. On the other hand, if the president's statement about being "in serious trouble" just meant that the company should anticipate negative publicity about the ingredient, then the trial judge would properly reject the adoptive opponent's statement argument for admissibility. Under Rule 104(a), it is the judge who decides whether the opponent's statement rationale applies.

e. The out-of-court words would be an opponent's statement under the Federal Rules because they were spoken by one of the defendant's employees during the period of the employer-employee relationship, and they concerned something within the scope of the declarant's employment. In some common law jurisdictions, the words would

testimony by someone who knew the speaker and knew that the speaker worked as the service manager or testimony by Driver that the speaker was wearing a uniform and seemed familiar with how the repair shop conducted its business.

6. There are two possible uses the transit company might assert for the evidence of the accident reconstructionist's testimony in the earlier trial. One use is impeachment, where the jury would be permitted to learn that in a similar case the witness had given testimony that conflicts with his testimony in the current case. Where impeachment is the purpose for informing the jury about a witness's earlier statements, no hearsay problems arise because the prior statement is not being used to support a conclusion that it is true. It is used only to suggest to the jury that the witness's current testimony may be false. The second purpose for which the transit company might want to introduce evidence of the accident expert's earlier testimony would be to support a conclusion that bad brakes were the cause of the accident involved in the current trial. This substantive use of the prior statements does involve the use of out-of-court statements to prove the truth of what they assert, but under the Federal Rules, the statements are treated as outside the definition of hearsay. They are prior statements by a witness; in particular, they are prior inconsistent statements given under oath at an earlier proceeding by a witness who is subject to cross-examination in the current trial. Therefore, under the Federal Rules, the testimony by the accident expert at the earlier trial would be admissible for both impeachment and substantive purposes.

7. The nurse's letter is an out-of-court statement that is consistent with the nurse's testimony. Under the Federal Rules, it can qualify for admission to prove the truth of what it asserts only if it meets the requirements of the applicable prior consistent statement portion of the Rules' definition of hearsay. That provision excludes from the definition of hearsay a prior consistent statement of a witness if the witness is available for cross-examination and if there has been an express or implied charge of improper influence or motive. The prior statement must have been made before the witness had a motive to lie in favor of the party whom his or her testimony supports. In this problem the plaintiff has brought out on cross-examination that the defendant, who is supported by the nurse's testimony, has helped the nurse obtain promotions. This suggests a motive for the nurse to slant his testimony in the doctor's favor. It also might suggest that the promotions were made in return for a promise to give favorable testimony. Either of those implications can be rebutted by evidence that the nurse made a statement consistent with his trial testimony, if the trial judge is persuaded that the nurse made the statement before the nurse and doctor had dealings related to the nurse's

interest in being promoted. When a prior consistent statement responds to an impeachment effort different from the improper influence or motive critique illustrated in this example, there is no requirement related to the timing of the consistent statements.

8. The out-of-court conduct by Victim fits the definition of statement, under the Federal Rules, because it is clear that Victim meant it to convey information. (If Victim had only fainted and not pointed to Suspect, an argument could be made that the fainting reaction is relevant to Suspect's guilt and is not a statement by Victim subject to analysis as possible hearsay.) Victim's out-of-court pointing is sought to be introduced to prove the truth of what it asserts, so it will be hearsay (and inadmissible unless an exception applies) unless it qualifies as a prior statement by a witness or as an opposing party statement. It cannot be a statement by an opponent because the declarant is not a party and it is not sought to be introduced against the declarant. It does fit the Rule 801(d)(1)(C) definition of a statement that "identifies a person as someone the declarant perceived earlier." Therefore, so long as the declarant is available for cross-examination, some courts would admit the out-of-court statement is admissible. But many courts would exclude the statement on the theory that Rule 801(d)(1)(C) is best applied only to identification statements made under circumstances that suggest greater reliability, such as statements made at lineups or in response to photo arrays.

Groupings of Hearsay Exceptions Under the Federal Rules

The Federal Rules define 28 specific types of out-of-court statements as *hearsay* that is *admissible* under exceptions to the hearsay exclusion. Additionally, the rules have a "catch-all" exception that allows admission of hearsay in circumstances that are not covered in any of the other 28 exceptions. The exceptions are organized into two groups: exceptions for which the availability of the declarant is immaterial and exceptions that are usable only if the declarant is unavailable. This separation of the exceptions into two classes indicates that the drafters of the Federal Rules believed that the risks inherent in admitting some of the types of hearsay were less than those connected with other types. For situations where the risks are minimal, the material can be used whether or not the declarant is available. For other situations, where the arguments supporting the exceptions are based on the necessity to use the out-of-court statements rather than on the likely truthfulness of the out-of-court declarant, the exception is allowed only if there is proof that the declarant is unavailable.

Statements Defined as Hearsay but Admissible Without Regard to the Declarant's Availability

Twenty-three specific categories of hearsay are admissible under the Federal Rules whether or not the declarant is available. Additionally, there is a "catch-all" provision. Each of these types of hearsay is described in its own subpart of Rule 803. This section discusses the most important ones. Descriptions of *all* the exceptions are in the Appendix "Federal Rules of Evidence," which provides plain language explanations of the significant parts of all of the rules.

Present Sense Impressions

People sometimes describe things as they are seeing them or immediately after seeing them. Statements of this kind are called present sense impressions and are admissible to prove the substance of what they assert. They are defined in Rule 803(1):

> **Present Sense Impression.** A statement describing or explaining an event or condition, made while or immediately after the declarant perceived it.

Problems of memory are extremely slight in these circumstances since the rule requires that the statement be made during or immediately after the event or condition it describes. In most of these statements, there will be some check on the accuracy of the speaker's perception because the speaker may be describing the event to someone else who is seeing it or may be speaking in the hearing of others who know what is going on. In most instances descriptions that are at variance with reality will be repressed by people's fear of seeming to be wrong or will be corrected by others who are present. It should be noted, though, that the rule does not require that the statement be made to anyone who was in a position to correct the statement if it was wrong.

Excited Utterances

Besides narrating descriptions of events that they see, people sometimes speak out of excitement or shock, or in reaction to having been startled. The Federal Rules treat this type of statement slightly differently from present sense impressions. An "excited utterance" is defined in Rule 803(2):

> **Excited Utterance.** A statement relating to a startling event or condition made while the declarant was under the stress of excitement that it caused.

In bar examinations and law school tests, examples of excited utterances are usually statements that begin with the words, "Oh my God," or, "Oh, no." They usually end with an exclamation point. The rationale of this exception is that any motive the declarant might have to lie will be overcome by the shock of the startling event, and that memory is not a problem because the statement must be made close in time to the event.

Present Sense Impression and Excited Utterance Compared

There are small differences between the Federal Rules treatments of the present sense impression and excited utterance exceptions. A statement covered by the present sense impression exception must *describe* or *explain* something, while a statement covered by the excited utterance exception is required only to *relate* to the event that was startling. The present sense impression statement can be made during or immediately after the declarant sees its subject, while the excited utterance must be made while the declarant is under the stress or excitement that justifies the exception. A person who is injured and rendered unconscious may wake up and say something about the cause of the injury. That statement can be treated as an excited utterance despite the passage of a long period of time between the stimulus and the statement since there is no likelihood that the speaker's perception could have been affected by events that occurred while the speaker was unconscious. If a statement about a stress-inducing event is made in response to someone's question, some courts may rule that it was not the product of the speaker's stress.

Statements of Current Mental, Emotional, or Physical Condition

When people say what they think about something or say how they feel physically or emotionally, there are no perception or memory problems likely to diminish the accuracy of what they say. For that reason, the Federal Rules provide a hearsay exception for statements of "then existing mental, emotional, or physical condition." The definition is provided in Rule 803(3):

> **Then-existing Mental, Emotional, or Physical Condition.** A statement of the declarant's then-existing state of mind (such as motive, intent, or plan) or emotional, sensory, or physical condition (such as mental feeling, pain, or bodily health), but not including a statement of memory or belief to prove the fact remembered or believed unless it relates to the validity or terms of the declarant's will.

This exception covers statements about what a person is feeling at the time he or she speaks, including both physical and emotional feelings. A statement like "I feel terrible" would be admissible for its truth — that is, that the speaker was feeling terrible at the time he or she spoke. A person's statements about a fact can show two different things: (1) the fact is something the speaker believes, and (2) the fact is true. The mental state exception allows proof of a person's statement of fact to show that the person believed the fact to be true but prohibits the use of a person's statements of feeling to prove that a remembered fact is true. Thus, proof that a declarant said, "I saw Bill yesterday," would be inadmissible if offered to prove that the declarant did see Bill on the day before he spoke. It would, however, be admissible to show that at the time the declarant said it, the declarant *thought* he had seen Bill on the previous day.

A statement of a person's plan or intention is considered an expression of then-existing mental state. It will be admitted as relevant on two issues: whether the declarant had that plan and whether the declarant carried out the plan. In contrast, a statement about a past act will be hearsay if offered to prove that the past act occurred. For example, to prove that the declarant attended a movie on a Friday, an out-of-court statement on Saturday, "I went to the movies yesterday," would be excludable hearsay if offered to prove that the declarant did go to the movies the day before her statement. It would be a use of a statement of the mental state "memory" to prove the fact remembered and is explicitly prohibited by the Federal Rules. However, a statement on Thursday, "I plan to go to the movies tomorrow," is admissible as relevant to the issue of whether the declarant went to the movies on Friday.

A person's statement that he or she has already done something may seem far more probative on the question of whether he or she did it than the person's earlier statement about having a plan to do it. Yet a statement about a plan is acceptable evidence under this hearsay exception, while the recollection of past conduct is not. One possible rationalization for this choice by the drafters is that both statements are the type of hearsay that incorporates many dangers of error, but that jurors who hear about a person's statement of a plan can be expected to be aware that plans are sometimes not accomplished, so that the risks of having them hear about the statement of plans are not great. If jurors hear that someone said he had actually done something in the past and are permitted to rely on that as support for the conclusion that he had done it, the natural skepticism about whether plans come to fruition would not have any place in the jurors' thinking. There is therefore a greater chance that the jurors would rely on the out-of-court statement as very strong evidence that the declarant actually did do what he said he had done.

The mental state exception permits the introduction of testimony that a declarant stated a plan to meet another person to show that the *other person* went to the location where the declarant said they would meet. This uses the declarant's statement of the declarant's intention as proof of the conduct of another person—to show that the other person acted as the declarant expected. Realizing that this type of proof depends on a large inductive leap, some courts have permitted it only when there is additional evidence suggesting that the declarant's belief about the future actions of the second person was accurate.

The mental state exception provides the practical solution for some of the standard hearsay dilemmas, namely "I'm the King of Mars" and "I think this product was made by Company X." For statements used to support an implication that the speaker was insane, a conclusion that the statement reflected the speaker's belief is all that the proponent seeks. This is permitted under the exception for "then-existing mental condition." Similarly, most survey research is intended to develop information about what people think, not whether what they think is an accurate reflection of reality. Thus, proof that respondents articulated particular beliefs is admissible under the mental state exception.

Statements for Medical Diagnosis or Treatment

This exception, in the Federal Rules, overlaps the exception for statements of physical condition. It is defined in Rule 803(4):

> **Statement Made for Medical Diagnosis or Treatment.** A statement that:
>
> **(A)** is made for — and is reasonably pertinent to — medical diagnosis or treatment; and
>
> **(B)** describes medical history; past or present symptoms or sensations; their inception; or their general cause.

This exception covers more types of statements related to physical condition than are covered in Rule 803(3)'s exception for statements of mental, emotional, or physical condition. Partly on the theory that people have compelling self-interest in speaking truthfully to those who provide medical services, the rule makes admissible statements of past medical history as well as current symptoms if they are made for the purpose of medical diagnosis or treatment. The exception's coverage also extends to descriptions of what caused the patient's problem so long as the descriptions are reasonably pertinent to diagnosis or treatment.

In a break from doctrines applied in some common law jurisdictions, statements made by the declarant to medical personnel involved in treating him or her and statements made by the declarant to medical personnel only involved in diagnosing his or her condition have identical status under this exception. Physicians who only see the declarant to make a diagnosis may be, and often are, physicians whose only purpose for seeing the declarant is to prepare expert testimony for a trial. In some common law jurisdictions, statements to non-treating physicians have no exception from the hearsay exclusion.

The exception does not require that the statements be made by the person who needs medical help since statements of that kind might be made by others on behalf of a sick or injured person. It does not specify that the statements must be made to a doctor; rather it requires that they be for the purpose of medical diagnosis or treatment. This means that many people involved in the delivery of health care could possibly be spoken to in statements that would be within the limits of this exception.

The exception's coverage of statements about the cause of a condition is a significant shift from more limited common law doctrines. Cases in which this portion of the exception has been litigated have typically involved statements made by people who bring an accident victim to an emergency room and say something about the circumstances of the injury. If they say, "He hurt his head diving into a swimming pool," all that information would probably be treated as admissible to show the circumstances of the injury because those details are significant to medical personnel. If the statement was something like, "He hit his head diving into a swimming pool that didn't have any warning signs about which end was the shallow end," the opponent of introduction of that statement would have a strong argument that the information about warnings was not closely enough related to the providing of medical care for it to be covered by the policies supporting this exception.

Past Recollection Recorded

Sometimes a witness at a trial may have no recollection about a relevant fact but may have made written notes about it at an earlier time. Those notes are admissible under the "recorded recollection" exception, provided certain conditions are met. The exception is defined in Rule 803(5):

> **Recorded Recollection.** A record that:
>
> > **(A)** is on a matter the witness once knew about but now cannot recall well enough to testify fully and accurately;
> > **(B)** was made or adopted by the witness when the matter was fresh in the witness's memory; and
> > **(C)** accurately reflects the witness's knowledge.

If admitted, the record may be read into evidence but may be received as an exhibit only if offered by an adverse party.

The proponent of the document (or other type of record) must show that the witness once had knowledge about the subject, that the witness does not have adequate recollection of the subject to testify "fully and accurately," and that the witness made the record (or adopted a record made by someone else) when the witness had a fresh memory of the information. The record will be read to the jury so the jury will be able to make use of the information it contains in exactly the way the jury would have made use of that information if the witness had remembered it and testified about it. The exception does allow the document to be treated as an exhibit at the opponent's option. If the document does become an exhibit, the jury may be allowed to have it with them while they deliberate and may pay more attention to it than they might pay to their memory of the witness's oral testimony.

Past recollection recorded is sometimes confused with a technique for assisting a witness's memory known as present recollection refreshed. Present recollection refreshed is a testimonial process that has no connection with the hearsay doctrine. A party questioning a witness is permitted to try to stimulate the witness's memory in a wide variety of ways. For example, the questioner can show objects to the witness and ask if seeing them helps the witness recall things that the witness once knew. The questioner can also show the witness a document and ask whether it helps the witness come up with a current memory of some topic. If showing the witness a document revives the witness's memory, there is no hearsay issue because the document (which is a written out-of-court statement) is not introduced into evidence. If showing the witness the statement does not enable the witness to say truthfully that his or her memory about some relevant subject has been refreshed, then the witness will not be able to testify about that subject. The document that refreshes the witness's memory does not have to meet the requirements of the hearsay exception for recorded recollection since the proponent is not allowed to have it read to the jury or introduced as an exhibit.

If the document used for refreshing past recollection happens to satisfy the requirements of a hearsay exception, it can, of course, be admitted under that other rationale. It should also be noted that the party against whom the "refreshed memory" witness has testified is entitled to introduce the document the witness used. Rule 612 establishes that right and provides additional safeguards against misleading use of the past recollection refreshed procedure:

(a) **Scope.** This rule gives an adverse party certain options when a witness uses a writing to refresh memory:

(1) while testifying; or

(2) before testifying, if the court decides that justice requires the party to have those options.

(b) **Adverse Party's Options; Deleting Unrelated Matter.** Unless 18 U.S.C. §3500 provides otherwise in a criminal case, an adverse party is entitled to have the writing produced at the hearing, to inspect it, to cross-examine the witness about it, and to introduce in evidence any portion that relates to the witness's testimony. If the producing party claims that the writing includes unrelated matter, the court must examine the writing in camera, delete any unrelated portion, and order that the rest be delivered to the adverse party. Any portion deleted over objection must be preserved for the record.

(c) Failure to Produce or Deliver the Writing. If a writing is not produced or is not delivered as ordered, the court may issue any appropriate order. But if the prosecution does not comply in a criminal case, the court must strike the witness's testimony or — if justice so requires — declare a mistrial.

Business and Public Agency Records

Protecting business records from exclusion on hearsay grounds has been a major reform trend in evidence law. In the Federal Rules, what have often been called "business records" are titled "records of a regularly conducted activity." The exception is defined in Rule 803(6):

> A record of an act, event, condition, opinion, or diagnosis if:
>
> **(A)** the record was made at or near the time by — or from information transmitted by — someone with knowledge;
> **(B)** the record was kept in the course of a regularly conducted activity of a business, organization, occupation, or calling, whether or not for profit;
> **(C)** making the record was a regular practice of that activity;
> **(D)** all these conditions are shown by the testimony of the custodian or another qualified witness, or by a certification that complies with Rule 902(11) or (12) or with a statute permitting certification; and
> **(E)** the opponent does not show that the source of information or the method or circumstances of preparation indicate a lack of trustworthiness.

The policy justification for treating these records as exceptions to the hearsay exclusion is that they are likely to be accurate since they are made for the purpose of running an enterprise rather than for some purpose in litigation. For example, a store has a strong incentive to keep accurate credit records. If they have errors, the store will either lose money or alienate its customers.

To qualify a document for treatment under this exception, the proponent must show that it was made as part of the usual activities of the organization, that a person with knowledge of what the record says made the record or reported the information to the person who made the record, and that the record was made near the time of the occurrence of what it describes. A witness must testify about how the record meets these requirements. A record that meets these explicit requirements may be excluded from the scope of the exception (and thus remain subject to treatment as hearsay) if the opponent shows that the circumstances of its preparation indicate a lack of trustworthiness or that the source of the information similarly seems unreliable.

4. Exceptions to the Hearsay Exclusionary Rule

Business records often involve multiple hearsay or hearsay within hearsay. The general issue of statements that themselves contain or are based on other statements is treated in Rule 805:

> Hearsay within hearsay is not excluded by the rule against hearsay if each part of the combined statements conforms with an exception to the rule.

In order for a business record to be admitted as substantive evidence of all its assertions, each statement it contains must fit the requirements of the business record exception or must avoid the hearsay barrier in some other way. For example, the counter clerk at a tool rental store might make a record stating that a customer had rented a certain tool. The store's manager might use records like those to make a report to the company's top management about what types of tools had been the most popular in a particular month. If monthly variation in the popularity of tools became an issue in a trial, the manager's report would be hearsay. It would involve two levels of hearsay: out-of-court statements by many clerks and the out-of-court statement by the manager.

Note that in this example all the statements satisfy the business records exception since the clerks' statements involved the regular course of business, were made by them about things they knew, and were made at the time they knew the information. The manager's statement was made from information transmitted by others in the enterprise and would also qualify as a business record if it could be shown that reports such as the monthly tool usage report were typically made by managers. Sometimes these problems are treated in a shorthand way by using the concept "duty to report." If all the declarants in a multiple chain of hearsay had a business duty to report the contents of their statements, then the requirements of the business records exception are satisfied. It is also possible to combine various types of hearsay exceptions. For example, a business record might contain an excited utterance by someone who did not have a duty to report.

Related to the business records exception is an explicit provision in the Federal Rules that lack of an entry in a business record is admissible evidence, if relevant, of something's nonoccurrence or nonexistence if its occurrence or existence would normally have been recorded. While it is possible to argue that the absence of an entry is not hearsay because "no statement" is not a "statement," the Federal Rules moot the controversy about whether to call gaps in records hearsay by providing a specific exception. Rule 803(7) provides:

> Evidence that a matter is not included in a record described in paragraph (6) if:
>
> > **(A)** the evidence is admitted to prove that the matter did not occur or exist;

(B) a record was regularly kept for a matter of that kind; and

(C) the opponent does not show that the possible source of the information or other circumstances indicate a lack of trustworthiness.

Government entities, like other enterprises, keep records. The Federal Rules include a complex set of hearsay exceptions that apply only to "public records." Rule 803(8) describes three types of records and varies the power of the hearsay exception according to whether they are sought to be introduced in a civil or criminal case, and according to which party seeks to introduce them:

A record or statement of a public office if:

(A) it sets out:

(i) the office's activities;

(ii) a matter observed while under a legal duty to report, but not including, in a criminal case, a matter observed by law-enforcement personnel; or

(iii) in a civil case or against the government in a criminal case, factual findings from a legally authorized investigation; and

(B) the opponent does not show that the source of information or other circumstances indicate a lack of trustworthiness.

The rule's categories are reports about: the activities of the government entity; matters observed and reported under legal duty by police and law enforcement personnel; matters observed and reported under legal duty by public employees other than police and law enforcement personnel; and factual findings resulting from legally authorized investigations. The theory supporting a hearsay exception for documents of this type is that they are exactly like ordinary business records when their topic is the internal workings of a part of the government and are therefore likely to be reliable because the organization that makes them also uses them in its day-to-day work.

Reports about an agency's own activities, in contrast to the other types of documents covered by the Rule, would be, for example, employment and personnel records. The fact that the office that has maintained them is a government office does not suggest that their accuracy would be any different from the accuracy of similar records in a nongovernmental organization. The Rule provides for their admission in civil and criminal cases. Reports of factual findings from government investigations may not have so exact a parallel in the work of private entities. The Rule allows their admission by any party in civil cases and by the defendant in criminal cases.

Another category of data specified in the Rule is government reports based on observations by workers, including law enforcement personnel or conclusions based on investigations. It is hard to say for such reports that their routine nature is a strong guarantee of their accuracy. Nevertheless, Rule 803(8) exempts them from the hearsay exclusion in civil cases. This exemption does not apply in criminal cases. Observations by law enforcement personnel are excluded from the scope of the exception because the interest those personnel have in obtaining convictions might give them an incentive to falsify records. Even though this reasoning should not logically apply when a defendant seeks to introduce reports of this type, the rule is written to withdraw the exception in criminal cases whether the prosecutor or the defense seeks to introduce the evidence.

Courts have given some varied interpretations to the rule's reference to "law enforcement personnel" for criminal cases. If the worker is a police officer, most courts would rule that the literal meaning of the exception governs the case, so that Rule 803(8)(A)(ii) cannot be used as a basis for admitting the evidence. If the worker is someone like a clerk in a police department property office, the risk of unreliability that is the basis for this subpart of Rule 803(8) might not be as great, and some courts would allow the exception to be used, refusing to define workers like clerks as "law enforcement personnel."

The admissibility of the types of material described in Rule 803(8)(A) is shown in Chart 15. Admissibility is the result under the Federal Rules in 13 of the 16 situations described.

Close attention should be paid to the instances in which a government report is defined as outside the coverage of this exception. In criminal trials, the defendant, but not the prosecution, may introduce findings from official investigations. The Rule treats reports of what law enforcement personnel have observed differently. Neither the prosecution nor the defendant may introduce material of this type. While the rationale for preventing the prosecution from use of this material is obvious, it is highly questionable whether keeping that material out of the defendant's case is supportable on grounds of policy and whether it is constitutionally sound.[4]

Parallel to the Rules' provision on the absence of an entry in business records, there is a provision covering proof that a government report does not say something. This exception is set out in Rule 803(10):

> Testimony — or a certification under Rule 902 — that a diligent search failed to disclose a public record or statement if:
>
> > **(A)** the testimony or certification is admitted to prove that
> > **(i)** the record or statement does not exist; or
> > **(ii)** a matter did not occur or exist, if a public office regularly kept a record or statement for a matter of that kind; and

---

4. See discussion of constitutional controls over evidence admissibility at pages 55-56.

Chart 15   Admissibility of Public Records

	Can It Be Introduced By:			
Type of Report	Civil Plaintiff	Civil Defendant	Criminal Prosecutor	Criminal Defendant
Activities of public office	Yes	Yes	Yes	Yes
Matters observed and reported pursuant to legal duty by public employees except law enforcement personnel	Yes	Yes	Yes	Yes
Findings from official investigations	Yes	Yes	No	Yes
Matters observed and reported pursuant to legal duty by law enforcement personnel	Yes	Yes	No	No*

*This is the Rule's provision, but some decisions allow such evidence, influenced by the criminal defendant's constitutional right to introduce relevant evidence, reinforced by an analogy to the Rules' treatment of statements by a party opponent.

> **(B)** in a criminal case, a prosecutor who intends to offer a certification provides written notice of that intent at least 14 days before trial, and the defendant does not object in writing within 7 days of receiving the notice — unless the court sets a different time for the notice or the objection.

Ancient Documents

An exception with broad reach is the "ancient documents" doctrine. Rule 803(16) defines this exception:

> A statement in a document that was prepared before January 1, 1998, and whose authenticity is established.

Many state versions of this rule do not specify the 1998 date. Instead, they define a document as ancient if was created a specific number of years, such as 20 or 30, before the trial. The policy justification for removing the hearsay bar for "ancient" documents is that it is very unlikely that a declarant would have been lying in a way intended to influence the outcome of a trial that happens to occur a great many years after the declarant made the statement. The ancient documents rule is a good context for remembering that evidence must satisfy a wide variety of requirements to be admissible. Protection from the prohibition of the hearsay rule does not guarantee admissibility. And admissibility does not guarantee that the trier of fact will believe an item of evidence. So even though some "ancient" documents may seem limited in reliability, such as a diary a teenager might have written before 1998, the Federal Rules take the position that the hearsay dangers do not present risks significant enough to reject admissibility.

Miscellaneous Exceptions

A number of other exceptions cover records that are usually highly reliable. They include records of religious organizations (for issues of personal or family history), marriage and baptismal certificates, family records such as tombstones or engravings on urns, market quotations and other information from generally used published material, and learned treatises.

Examples

Availability of Declarant Immaterial

1. Alan Williams was found strangled to death in his apartment. The building's janitor, who was well-known to Williams, is accused of the murder on the theory that he had easy access to Williams's apartment. On the day that Williams was killed he had a phone conversation with a friend of his, Bruce Bender. Williams said to Bender, "I've got to hang up now. Somebody's just come in and he looks really upset. I don't know who he is, but he's got a crazy look on his face." Can the janitor have Bender give testimony quoting Williams?

2. Carl Carter was injured by a hit-and-run driver. While he was being treated in a hospital emergency room, he saw Edward Evers walk in. He started to tremble, and he shouted, "That's the guy who nearly killed me!" Can a nurse who heard Carter's statement quote it at a trial in which Evers is accused of having driven into Carter?

3. A shopping center owner sought damages from a department store corporation, claiming that the store had failed to honor its obligation to operate a store at the center for five years. In defense, the store sought to show that the center had failed in its obligation to manage the shopping center under terms of an agreement describing it as a "first class facility" to be operated with "adequate security provisions." May the store introduce the agreement? May the store introduce a survey of

shoppers at the center showing that many stated that they felt nervous and unsafe at the center?

4. Chris Lender is accused of attacking George Borrower. To show that Lender had a motive, the prosecution seeks to show that Borrower had borrowed money from Lender and had refused to repay it.
   a. The prosecution seeks to have a friend of Borrower's sister testify that two days before the assault, Borrower's sister said to the friend, "Borrower owes Lender a lot of money, but he just keeps stringing her along about it." Is the testimony admissible?
   b. The prosecution seeks to have a friend of Lender's testify that before the assault, Lender said to the friend, "Borrower owes me a lot of money, and he just keeps stringing me along." Is the testimony admissible?

5. Harry Holmby was injured while using a product manufactured by the defendant. In his products liability suit, one issue concerned the seriousness and duration of Holmby's pain from the injury. A few years after the accident, Holmby was treated by Doctor Ina Iliff. May Dr. Iliff testify that Holmby told her he had been suffering from severe back pains since the incident with the product?

6. In a medical malpractice suit, the plaintiff introduces testimony by a doctor who has never treated him but who has examined him as part of preparation for the trial. In her testimony, she states that in her opinion the defendant doctor failed to conform to typical standards of treatment. She states that her opinion is based on what the plaintiff has told her about his symptoms before and after the defendant doctor treated him. Is her testimony based on inadmissible hearsay?

7. A child who could not swim was rescued from a deep swimming pool. The person who pulled him out rode with him in an ambulance and told the receptionist at a hospital emergency room, "This kid just jumped into a pool and he couldn't swim." The child's parents seek damages from the operator of the pool, claiming that their child slipped on a slick walkway near the pool and that this slip made him fall into the water. They contend that more frequent mopping would have prevented the walkway from being so slick. Can the emergency room receptionist testify about what the rescuer said had happened?

8. Louise Levin sought damages for a nuisance inflicted against her property by a neighbor, Marvin Miller. Levin claimed that Miller had a furnace that emitted vast quantities of thick dark smoke and that the smoke drifted into Levin's house. Levin kept a diary, recording her daily observations of the smoke for a two-year period. The diary states hours

and weather conditions on each day that the smoke was noticeable at Levin's house. How might Levin's lawyer make use of that diary at trial?

9. A Buick driven by Mrs. Prince crashed at an intersection into a BMW driven by Mrs. King. In Mrs. King's civil suit, to establish that traffic signals at an intersection were probably working properly at the time of the accident, a witness testifies that she is an office manager at the city's traffic signals department and that she has with her a document that was in the department's regular files. The document was written by Zane Foreman, foreman of one of the department's maintenance crews. It states the following information: On the day of the accident Foreman and William Worker, another traffic signals department employee, went to the intersection to check the lights; while Foreman talked to police officers who were on the scene, Worker examined all the light bulbs and timing devices and found that they were all in good condition. Is the document admissible?

10. Assume that the document from Example 9 also contained this sentence: "Worker said that while he was checking the timing units, the driver of the crashed Buick, Mrs. Prince, came up to him and said that driving is so hard to do nowadays that she knew she really shouldn't do it anymore." Could that information be used at trial against Mrs. Prince to show that she had driven carelessly?

11. Assume that the document from Example 9 also contained this sentence: "Worker said that someone came up to him and said that last week she had seen the traffic lights all go off for about five minutes and that it nearly caused a crash." Could that information be used at trial to support a party's contention that the traffic signals had malfunctioned?

12. Richard Rover was injured in an automobile accident. He seeks damages from the manufacturer of the car, claiming that it had design flaws that intensified his injuries. As a defense, the manufacturer asserts that Rover was speeding at the time of the injury. Rover's hospital record contains the following note made at the time of his admission to the hospital: "Patient says car crash, hit telephone pole at 90 m.p.h." What problems are there with admitting this document to prove that Rover (the patient) was speeding when he was injured?

13. The Libertyville City Library seeks damages in a contract action from the supplier of a checkout and book inventory system. The Library states that the defendant's system was marketed as being capable of cutting down thefts and other losses from the Library's collection. The Library asserts that the number of books unaccounted for during typical months in which it has used the new system has exceeded the number for comparable months in years prior to purchase of the system. May

the Library introduce its own records of books checked out, books found on shelves, and other inventory measures to show that losses have been worse since installation of the defendant's system?

14. To prove that the defendant sold drugs, can the prosecution introduce a videotape that shows the defendant saying, "I've got the stuff. Give me the money," and shows her exchanging drugs for money?

15. In another trial, to prove that the defendant sold drugs, can the prosecution introduce a police officer's notebook with a description in the officer's handwriting stating that he observed the defendant exchanging drugs for money?

16. An issue in a products liability suit is whether a car manufacturer used adequately strong material for the straps of a seatbelt. A federal agency has conducted research on materials that can be used for those straps and has issued a report. The report describes many different tests on various materials and shows that materials usually did well on some tests and less well on others. It also states that certain materials, on the basis of all the test results, will be able to withstand typical crash impacts. Should this report be admissible to show that what it concludes about the material used by the manufacturer is true?

Explanations

Availability of Declarant Immaterial

1. The out-of-court statement is hearsay since it would be introduced to show that a stranger had entered Williams's apartment. The present sense impression exception covers this statement because the declarant was apparently describing something while he was perceiving it. He saw someone come into his apartment, and he described it to Bender. One of the main justifications for this exception is that a false statement will be discovered and corrected. In this problem, Bender would not have had a way to determine the accuracy of Williams's statement, and the stranger would probably not have had any interest in correcting it if it had been false. Usually, hearsay exceptions are given pro-admissibility interpretations. Here, although the underlying policy for the exception is not well-served by admitting the hearsay, the terms of the rule are so clearly met that admissibility would be certain.

2. Yes. Carter's statement is an excited utterance. It is hearsay since it is being introduced to show that Evers is the one who drove a vehicle into him, but the exception covers it. The statement relates to a startling event or condition — either the injury that had happened shortly before

123

the statement or the shock produced by the sight of Evers. The statement explains either of those two possible stimuli.

3. The agreement does not involve any hearsay problems. It is a legal document, which will be given meaning by the legal system, applying doctrines, precedents, and principles of interpretation that do not necessarily depend on the literal meaning of the words in the document. The survey is a method of introducing out-of-court statements by shoppers about how they felt at the time they were interviewed by the survey interviewers. Therefore, since the statements are being introduced to show what the speakers felt and since those statements do describe what the speakers were feeling, the definition of hearsay is satisfied. An exception allows the survey to be admitted: The words are descriptions of the declarants' then-existing mental condition or state of mind.

4. a. The out-of-court words are relevant only if the information they contain is true. That is, they would shed light on Lender's possible motive only if the proposition they assert — Borrower owed Lender money — is true. Therefore, they are hearsay. No exception applies to allow their admission. It is important to recall that evidence can be relevant *and* inadmissible, as in this example, where the evidence is relevant but is kept out by the hearsay rule. The mental state exception does not cover the mental state of memory if the declarant's memory would be relevant only to show that the event happened. Here, the recollection by Borrower's sister that Borrower owed Lender money is relevant not because she possessed that memory but only because what she remembered was true. The rationale would not support admission of the statement by Borrower's sister since she is not a party to the suit.

   b. Lender's out-of-court statement is outside the definition of hearsay since it is an opposing party's statement. It could also be analyzed under the state of mind exception. Whether or not it was true that Borrower owed Lender money, Lender's statement that she believed Borrower owed her money shows a mental state consistent with a motive to attack Borrower. Even if her memory about a debt owed to her by Borrower was false, the fact that she possessed that memory is relevant to her having had a motive to harm Borrower. Statements of belief are outside the scope of the mental state exception if their relevance depends on their use to prove that the fact believed is true. That situation is illustrated in part a of this problem. Statements of belief are covered by the mental state exception if a speaker's possessing that belief is relevant independent of whether the belief is accurate. Part b of this problem illustrates this latter situation.

5. Holmby's out-of-court words to Dr. Iliff are hearsay since they are sought to be introduced to show that since the time of the product-related injury, he has had severe pain. The statement is admissible, however, under the exception for statements for the purpose of medical diagnosis or treatment.

6. The testimony includes hearsay, but it is admissible because the out-of-court words were spoken by the declarant to the doctor for the purpose of medical diagnosis. An expert physician's evaluation of a person is considered to be a diagnosis even if no treatment is expected. This points out the pro-admissibility orientation of the Federal Rules. A person has strong incentives to tell the truth to a doctor who will be performing or prescribing treatment to improve the chances that the treatment will be effective. On the other hand, if a person is speaking to a doctor who will only be giving an opinion in connection with a lawsuit, the incentive is only to say things that will help shape the doctor's opinion in a way that is legally favorable. The Federal Rules do not distinguish, as common law jurisdictions sometimes do, between treating and testifying physicians. Statements to both types of doctors are admissible. It is likely that opposing counsel will be able to alert jurors to the risk of untruthfulness inherent in the situation where a litigant talks to a doctor for the purpose of preparing testimony.

7. The rescuer's out-of-court words are sought to be introduced to prove that their content is true — that the child jumped, rather than fell, into the pool. Used for this reason, they are hearsay. The exceptions for excited utterances and present sense impressions might or might not apply, depending on how soon after the incident the rescuer spoke to the receptionist and on how excited the rescuer was when speaking. If the excited utterance and present sense impression exceptions did not cover the statement, would the exception for statements for medical diagnosis or treatment apply? Statements under that exception do not have to be made to doctors. Any person involved in the providing of health care can be the person to whom the statement is addressed. The receptionist at an emergency room is closely enough connected to the delivery of health services for such statements to be defined as connected with obtaining medical services. It is difficult, however, to extend the reach of this exception to cover the actual out-of-court words that are important to the swimming pool operator's defense. The "jumped into a pool" part of the statement is not easily characterized as intended to facilitate treatment or diagnosis. Certainly a statement that the child had been underwater is fully within the coverage of the exception. But the fact that he got into the water by jumping is hardly something a physician would need to know to treat drowning. Details about causation of a person's health problem are covered by the

exception only if they are reasonably pertinent to the medical worker's task.

8. The information in the diary would be relevant on the issue of the extent of the nuisance. It is hearsay since the written statements are relevant at trial only if what they assert is true. Assuming that Levin does not have the ability to remember the details it contains for many days of a two-year period, Levin's lawyer would attempt to use the hearsay exception for recorded recollection. The exception would apply if testimony by Levin showed that she made entries in the diary at the time she observed the smoke and weather or soon after those times, and that she did not have a good memory of those details at the time of the trial. The diary entries could be read to the jury, but the diary itself would not be admissible as an exhibit unless Miller (the neighbor) offered it. The present sense impression exception might also apply. Its usual rationale for reliability, that the declarant's statements were subject to a contemporaneous check on accuracy, does not exist in this case. Some courts would refuse to apply the exception for that reason. The diary cannot be a business record, because it was not made in the course of a regularly conducted enterprise. Allowing a personal diary to be admitted under the business records exception would ignore the policy behind the doctrine, that a business's own needs for accuracy and its employees' own needs for job security provide fairly strong guarantees that truth, not fiction, will be found in the records of the organization.

9. The document has two levels of hearsay. It is Foreman's written out-of-court statement containing a report of Worker's spoken out-of-court statements about the bulbs and timing devices. Unless Worker's information is true, the document has no relevance to the trial. Further, to establish relevance Foreman's statement must also be true (his statement is that Worker said certain things). The public records exception will cover the document. Worker obtained the information in the document as part of the usual operations of the department for which he works. It can also be said that Foreman wrote his report as part of the department's typical work. There was testimony in court that the document was found in a place where it was supposed to be kept, supporting a finding of reliability. When people are in the workplace, the fact that they want to avoid being fired and want their organizations to work well serves as some guarantee of reliability. Worker's spoken words to Foreman and Foreman's written statement about Worker's spoken words are all admissible under the public records exception, assuming that they related to topics that workers from the traffic signals department were supposed to observe and report.

10. This sentence adds a third level of hearsay to the problem. The document written out of court quotes Worker's statement that quotes Prince's statement. If employees of the traffic signals department are supposed to observe and record information about traffic accidents, then *Worker's* repeating of Prince's statement and *Foreman's* written statement recording what Worker said he had heard Prince say are covered by the public records exception. This treats Foreman's record of what Worker said he heard the same way Example 9 treated Foreman's record of what Worker said he saw. Note, though, that the proponent of the document wants the jury to have more than a basis to believe that Worker said what Prince said. The proponent wants Prince's words to be available to the jury as proof of what they assert. That use would be hearsay, so the portion of the report that sets out Prince's words will be admissible for the truth of what Prince's words assert only if it has its own protection from the hearsay exclusion rule. In this case, Prince's statement will be treated as an opposing party's statement. It is something she said, offered against her at a trial. Therefore, all three out-of-court statements are admissible.

11. The first two levels of hearsay are taken care of by the public records exception. Because the information reported by the stranger is important to the operations of the traffic signal department, Foreman and Worker were probably acting within their duties of employment by listening to it and recording it. The stranger's words fit the definition of hearsay because they are introduced to show that the lights worked badly on a particular occasion (rather than just to show that the stranger said the words, which would avoid the hearsay problem but deprive them of relevance). No exception covers the words. They are not, for example, an excited utterance or a present sense impression. And while the public records exception allows proof of the fact that they were said, it does not allow the words to be introduced to prove the truth of what they assert.

12. There are two out-of-court statements: the hospital worker's written statement and Rover's words about speeding. Rover's words would be an opposing party statement if there was acceptable proof that he ever said them. The offered proof that Rover said those words is the hospital document. Is its written assertion that Rover said the words about speeding admissible to show that Rover said the words? The document is hearsay since its relevance depends on the truth of its statement that Rover said he had been speeding. The business records exception should not defeat the hearsay exclusion on these facts unless hospitals treat car crash victims differently depending on whether they were speeding, driving within the speed limit, or parked in a car that another vehicle crashed into. This shows that the mention of speeding in the

127

hospital record was not necessary for the conduct of the hospital's business. Because it was not important to the hospital, there is an increased chance that it might not have been recorded carefully. Using the business records rule to introduce written material containing information that was not useful for the businesses that made the records would contradict the general rationale for the exception: the idea that business documents are usually accurate because the workers have an incentive to be careful about what they record.

13. Yes. These records are the public agency equivalent of business records in the private context. They are hearsay if introduced to show that what they state about the presence or absence of books is true. However, they are admissible because of the exception, under the Federal Rules, for records setting forth the activities of a public agency.

14. There is only one level of hearsay in this problem: the out-of-court statement by the defendant about having "stuff." It would be admissible under the Federal Rules, defined as a non-hearsay opposing party's statement. The videotape is not an out-of-court statement because it is made by a machine not a person.

15. The notebook is hearsay since it is relevant only to prove that what it asserts — that the defendant sold drugs — is true. To be admitted, its statements must fit within an exception to the hearsay exclusion. They cannot be treated as opposing party's statements since they are not sought to be introduced against the person who made them. They cannot be admitted under the exception for public records and reports because that provision of the Federal Rules cannot be used to admit records of police observations against a criminal defendant. While some courts have been willing to use the standard business records exception to admit some types of documents created by law enforcement personnel in criminal cases, those cases have usually involved documents created in a less adversarial situation than the situation in this example. The past recollection recorded exception might apply if the police officer who wrote the notes testifies at the trial and cannot remember the events described in the notebook.

16. The report is hearsay. Its admissibility depends on how narrowly part of the Federal Rules provision for public records and reports should be read. Rule 803(8)(A)(iii) covers only "factual findings" from investigations. The findings in the report described in this problem are factual, but they are based on interpretations of how performance on various tests can be evaluated in reaching a single conclusion on suitability of materials for typical crashes. The Supreme Court has decided that material of this type is covered by the Federal Rules exception for public

records, Rule 803(8).[5] The decision recognizes that defining a difference between fact and opinion is often impossible. It also may reflect the Federal Rules' general preference for a wide scope for expert testimony and opinion.

Statements Defined as Hearsay but Admissible if the Declarant Is Unavailable

Some hearsay exceptions apply only when the declarant is unavailable. This suggests that they must be thought to be less reliable, generally, than the out-of-court statements covered by exceptions that can be used even if the declarant is available to testify. The exceptions are tolerated, however, because they involve situations where the out-of-court statements have some claim to reliability and there is a strong need for the information they contain. One exception is not based on the probable reliability of the statements it covers. It applies to statements made by a person whom a party wrongfully makes unavailable as a witness and is meant to deter tampering with prospective witnesses. Imposing the requirement of unavailability in connection with certain hearsay exceptions is partly a result of tradition. As will be seen, some of the statements covered by the exceptions for which unavailability is required are probably as reliable as some of the statements covered by the exceptions that can be used regardless of the declarant's availability.

Definition of "Unavailable"

There are a variety of ways in which a party attempting to use one of the unavailability-required exceptions can establish the necessary unavailability of the hearsay declarant. Rule 804(a) establishes the meaning of unavailability:

> **Criteria for Being Unavailable.** A declarant is considered to be unavailable as a witness if the declarant:
>
> **(1)** is exempted from testifying about the subject matter of the declarant's statement because the court rules that a privilege applies;
>
> **(2)** refuses to testify about the subject matter despite a court order to do so;
>
> **(3)** testifies to not remembering the subject matter;
>
> **(4)** cannot be present or testify at the trial or hearing because of death or a then-existing infirmity, physical illness, or mental illness; or

---

5. *See* Beech Aircraft Corp. v. Rainey, 488 U.S. 153 (1988).

> **(5)** is absent from the trial or hearing and the statement's proponent has not been able, by process or other reasonable means, to procure:
>> **(A)** the declarant's attendance, in the case of a hearsay exception under Rule 804(b)(1) or (6); or
>> **(B)** the declarant's attendance or testimony, in the case of a hearsay exception under Rule 804(b)(2), (3), or (4).

But this subdivision (a) does not apply if the statement's proponent procured or wrongfully caused the declarant's unavailability as a witness in order to prevent the declarant from attending or testifying.

Under this rule, a declarant of an out-of-court statement is shown to be unavailable if the declarant has a privilege that permits the declarant to refuse to reveal a communication, refuses to testify about the subject matter of the statement, or cannot remember the subject matter. A declarant is also unavailable if his or her presence is prevented by death or illness. These methods of showing unavailability apply to all the exceptions for which the Federal Rules require unavailability.

Additional options for showing unavailability apply to particular exceptions within the group of unavailability-required exceptions. A showing that the declarant is absent from the proceeding and the proponent of the declarant's out-of-court statement cannot obtain the declarant's presence allows use of the exception for former testimony (discussed later in this chapter). That showing *and* a showing that the proponent of the hearsay could not obtain the declarant's testimony by deposition is an adequate foundation for the other unavailability-required exceptions, which are dying declarations, statements against interest, and family history statements.

The hearsay exception for statements of "recorded recollection," defined in Rule 803(5), is categorized as applicable whether or not the declarant is available. Its use is limited, however, to circumstances where the proponent establishes that the declarant-witness has either no memory or just a slight memory of the previously recorded information. Those findings might constitute unavailability under Rule 804(a)(3).

The wide variety of methods of proving unavailability reflects a pro-admissibility stance by the drafters of the Federal Rules. At common law, requirements for the showing of unavailability may vary from exception to exception. As a counterweight to the general acceptance of many reasons for treating a declarant as unavailable, the Federal Rules also provide that a declarant will not be treated as unavailable if it is shown that the proponent of the hearsay statement is responsible for creating the condition that would otherwise meet one of Rule 804's definitions of unavailability.

Former Testimony

Since the importance of cross-examination is one of the underlying policy groundings for the hearsay rule, it is understandable that there is an exception for testimony given under oath and subject to cross-examination at a proceeding previous to the one at which the past testimony is sought to be introduced. In fact, some consider it odd that this exception is grouped among those for which unavailability of the declarant must be shown, since the reliability of the statements will be virtually identical to the reliability of statements made by a witness in a current trial. Rule 804(b)(1) defines this exception to the hearsay exclusion:

> **Former Testimony.** Testimony that:
>
> **(A)** was given as a witness at a trial, hearing, or lawful deposition, whether given during the current proceeding or a different one; and
>
> **(B)** is now offered against a party who had — or, in a civil case, whose predecessor in interest had — an opportunity and similar motive to develop it by direct, cross-, or redirect examination.

In civil and criminal cases, testimony at an earlier proceeding or deposition is admissible to prove the truth of what its statements assert if the party against whom the testimony is offered had an opportunity to cross-examine the declarant. It is also admissible if that party's motive to cross-examine at the earlier proceeding was similar to the motive the party would have if the witness testified at the current trial. For civil cases there is an additional liberalization: The requirement of opportunity and motive to cross-examine can be satisfied by the presence in the earlier proceeding of a predecessor in interest to the party against whom the testimony is offered in the current trial.

Application of this rule is generally straightforward. One possible complication involves the concept of similar motive to cross-examine. If circumstances at the prior trial were such that the witness's testimony was unimportant or that the whole suit was unimportant to the party, then it would be unfair to permit use of the former testimony by that witness against the party in a new case where the topic of the testimony is important or where the consequences of losing the case are far more costly than in the prior case.

The provision that in civil cases former testimony may be admitted against a party if that party or a predecessor in interest of that party had the required opportunity and motive for cross-examination has been interpreted by federal courts with varied liberality. Some courts have taken a functional approach to interpreting "predecessor in interest" and have not required strict privity so long as the interests of the party opposed to the testimony in the prior case were similar to the interests of the party against whom the testimony is sought to be used in the current case. Other courts have required clear-cut contractual privity or some other type of recognized successor relationship.

Dying Declarations

The common law has recognized a hearsay exception for statements made by a person who believes that his or her death is imminent. The exception is based on the idea that people's religious beliefs make them highly reluctant to lie at the moment of death. A secular argument supporting the exception would be that a person who believes death is near has no motive to make false statements since there is nothing to be gained from them. Contrary to that idea is the possibility that a person might feel particularly free to lie at the time of death because there is no risk of having to suffer worldly consequences for the untruth. The Federal Rules recognize dying declarations as a hearsay exception. The exception is defined in Rule 804(b)(2):

> **Statement Under the Belief of Imminent Death.** In a prosecution for homicide or in a civil case, a statement that the declarant, while believing the declarant's death to be imminent, made about its cause or circumstances.

Dying declarations are protected from the hearsay exclusion only for use on one topic: the declarant's belief about the cause of what the declarant believed to be his or her impending death. The exception applies in all civil cases and in homicide prosecutions. While most examples of dying declarations involve a speaker who dies after making the statement, a speaker can have a reasonable expectation of death but still survive. The words of a speaker who believed death was imminent count as dying declarations even if the speaker recovers. In that event, the proponent will have to establish the speaker's unavailability in any of the variety of methods permitted under Rule 804(a).

Statement Against Interest

Under common law and the Federal Rules, there is a hearsay exception for some statements that were contrary to the declarant's interests when the declarant made them. At common law, the affected interest had to involve monetary or property rights. Under the Federal Rules, the affected interests are monetary or property rights and freedom from criminal liability. The details of the exception are specified in Rule 804(b)(3):

> **Statement Against Interest.** A statement that:
>
> **(A)** a reasonable person in the declarant's position would have made only if the person believed it to be true because, when made, it was so contrary to the declarant's proprietary or pecuniary interest or had so

great a tendency to invalidate the declarant's claim against someone else or to expose the declarant to civil or criminal liability; and

    (B) is supported by corroborating circumstances that clearly indicate its trustworthiness, if it is offered in a criminal case as one that tends to expose the declarant to criminal liability.

Note that this is different from the treatment of statements by an opponent (admissions). An opposing party's statement, or admission, is anything a party to a lawsuit has ever said, if it is relevant against him or her at a trial. The important factors for an opposing party's statement are whether (1) the declarant was someone who is a party to the current suit, and (2) the statement is sought to be introduced as relevant against that party in the current suit. The declarant's unavailability is not a requirement for use of an opposing party's statement. For statements against interest, the declarant need not be a party nor does it matter in whose favor the statement is sought to be introduced. The proponent must show that the declarant is unavailable and must show also that when the declarant made the statement, it had the potential to harm an important interest of the declarant. The rationale for the exception is that when a person says something that is detrimental to a very important interest, it is likely to be true because people rarely say something carelessly or falsely that involves a subject that could be personally harmful. Chart 16 summarizes the distinction between statements by an opposing party and statements against interest.

In applying this exception, a judge must consider what a statement would typically mean to a "reasonable" person, in terms of having an effect on that person's monetary, property, or criminal liability interests. The policy behind the rule could perhaps be served better by a subjective test. In that analysis, a statement would be thought of as trustworthy if, in the

Chart 16 Opposing Party's Statements and Statements Against Interest, Compared		
Points of Comparison	**Opposing Party's Statement**	**Statement Against Interest**
Declarant	Party in current case	Anyone
Declarant's availability	Available or unavailable	Must be unavailable
Subject of statement	Anything adverse to party's interest at trial	Creates financial or criminal risk to declarant when declarant makes statement
Admissible against	Declarant, coconspirator, declarant's employer	Any party

mind of the declarant, it had the potential to harm the declarant even if the vast majority of people would not have considered that type of statement to be one that could harm the specified interests. The problem with a subjective test is that it is hard to administer. Although the language of the Federal Rule is slightly ambiguous, because it refers to a "reasonable person" but also to someone "in the declarant's position," courts use an objective test and ask whether a statement would have seemed risky to a reasonable person rather than specifically to the declarant.

Deciding what interests are important enough to support the inference that a person's statements opposed to them are likely to be true has been controversial. The common law represents the narrowest position on this question, recognizing only pecuniary and proprietary interests. The Federal Rules add penal interest, the interest a person has in being free from criminal liability. Some states expand the list of categories further. For example, California's evidence code treats statements against social interests as admissible hearsay. Social interests are broader but harder to define than penal, pecuniary, or proprietary interests.

When a statement against penal interest is offered by the prosecution or the defendant in a criminal case, Rule 804(b)(3)(B) provides that the statement may be admitted only if corroborating circumstances clearly indicate that the statement is trustworthy. That limitation is withdrawn for civil cases.

Sometimes one part of a statement will be contrary to a speaker's penal interest and another part will relate to a different topic or to possible criminal liability of someone other than the speaker. In *Williamson v. United States*,[6] the Supreme Court held that "non-self-inculpatory" portions of a declarant's statement cannot be admitted under the statement against interest rationale. The Court noted that "[o]ne of the most effective ways to lie is to mix falsehood with truth, especially truth that seems particularly persuasive because of its self-inculpatory nature."

Statement by Person Rendered Unavailable: Forfeiture by Wrongdoing

A party forfeits the right to exclude a hearsay statement if the party was involved in a wrongful act with the purpose and effect of keeping the declarant from being a witness at trial. Rule 804(b)(6) provides an exception to the hearsay exclusion:

> *Statement Offered Against a Party That Wrongfully Caused the Declarant's Unavailability.* A statement offered against a party that wrongfully caused—or acquiesced in wrongfully causing—the declarant's unavailability as a witness, and did so intending that result.

---

6. 512 U.S. 594 (1994).

This rule decreases the incentive a corrupt person might have to bribe, intimidate, or kill a prospective witness. It discourages that type of wrongful conduct by removing the hearsay bar from any statements ever made by a person whom a party has rendered unavailable. Because this rule is not based on the likelihood that those statements will be reliable, it can be used to introduce those statements only against a party whose conduct the rule was meant to deter — a party who was responsible for the absence of the witness.

Residual Exception

The Federal Rules hearsay provisions include a residual or "catch-all" exception, Rule 807, to permit the admission of hearsay evidence not covered by specific exceptions. The residual exception may be invoked regardless of the availability or unavailability of the declarant. It provides:

> **(a) In General.** Under the following circumstances, a hearsay statement is not excluded by the rule against hearsay even if the statement is not specifically covered by a hearsay exception in Rule 803 or 804:
>
> **(1)** the statement has equivalent circumstantial guarantees of trustworthiness;
>
> **(2)** it is offered as evidence of a material fact;
>
> **(3)** it is more probative on the point for which it is offered than any other evidence that the proponent can obtain through reasonable efforts; and
>
> **(4)** admitting it will best serve the purposes of these rules and the interests of justice.
>
> **(b) Notice.** The statement is admissible only if, before the trial or hearing, the proponent gives an adverse party reasonable notice of the intent to offer the statement and its particulars, including the declarant's name and address, so that the party has a fair opportunity to meet it.

To comply with this rule's requirements, the proponent of evidence must compare the reliability of the offered evidence with the typical reliability of evidence covered by the specific exceptions.

Hearsay and the Confrontation Clause

Situations in which out-of-court statements are admitted as proof of what they assert involve an apparent conflict with the Confrontation Clause of the Constitution. The Sixth Amendment states that a criminal defendant "shall enjoy the right . . . to be confronted with the witnesses against him." If this clause were interpreted literally, exemptions and exceptions to the hearsay exclusion rule would be unconstitutional because they allow statements by absent "unconfronted" declarants to be introduced at criminal trials. As a matter of constitutional law, however, the Supreme Court has determined that the Confrontation Clause applies only to *testimonial* out-of-court statements. In 2004, *Crawford v. Washington*[7] held that testimonial hearsay statements must be excluded unless (1) the declarant is available at the trial for cross-examination, or (2) the declarant is unavailable and the defendant against whom the statement is sought to be introduced had an earlier opportunity to cross-examine the declarant.

Crawford did not define "testimonial," but the opinion provided examples of statements that the term includes: preliminary hearing testimony, grand jury testimony, former trial testimony, and statements made in police interrogations. The reference to interrogations was elaborated in *Davis v. Washington*,[8] with the Supreme Court holding that statements made in a 911 call are non-testimonial when the objective circumstances indicate that the primary purpose of the questioning was to enable the police to respond to an ongoing emergency. On the other hand, statements to the police will be testimonial when the objective circumstances show that there was no emergency and that the primary purpose of the questioning was to establish past events potentially relevant to criminal prosecution.

In 2011, a closely divided court in *Michigan v. Bryant*[9] considered statements a shooting victim made to police while he was waiting for an ambulance. He named the person who had shot him and described how it happened. The majority characterized those statements as non-testimonial on a variety of theories, including the suggestion that the police had questioned the victim to gain information to protect the public and themselves from further violence, rather than primarily to learn the name of the person who had shot the victim. And in 2015, over strong dissents, the Court furthered narrowed the likely scope of Confrontation Clause protections in *Ohio v. Clark*.[10] A child's vague statement to a pre-school teacher possibly naming an assailant was found to be non-testimonial, with the concept of ongoing emergency expanded to include a belief that the child might be harmed at home in the future, and with the majority stating that a declarant of the child's young age would not understand that his words could be used in prosecuting a crime. The majority also rejected the argument that because a state statute required the teacher to report the child's statement to state authorities, the teacher should be characterized as part of the state's law enforcement system.

---

7. 541 U.S. 36 (2004).
8. 547 U.S. 8123 (2006).
9. 131 S. Ct. 1143 (2011).
10. 135 S.Ct. 2173 (2015).

Applying the Confrontation Clause to documentary evidence has led to other significant disputes among the Justices. In *Melendez-Diaz v. Massachusetts*[11] and *Bullcoming v. New Mexico*,[12] majorities held that the Clause applies to documents reporting the results of tests about the composition and weight of drugs and blood alcohol volumes. Dissenters urged that cross-examination in these circumstances is unlikely to be helpful to defendants and that interpreting the Confrontation Clause to require it will burden the criminal justice system too heavily. Perhaps reaching a contrary result a year after *Bullcoming*, in *Williams v. Illinois*[13] the Court declined to apply the Clause to testimony that was based on out-of-court statements by workers in a DNA laboratory.

The unsettled nature of current Confrontation Clause jurisprudence may make it worthwhile to consider its earlier treatment. Prior to *Crawford*, constitutional law established that hearsay statements of all kinds were admissible against criminal defendants if they fit within firmly rooted exceptions to the hearsay exclusionary rule or if they had indicia of reliability or particularized guarantees of trustworthiness. *Crawford* rejected that approach for testimonial hearsay, but some Justices may be interested in returning to it.

Since the Confrontation Clause's exclusionary effect applies only when a hearsay declarant fails to testify at the trial, criminals have an incentive to prevent witnesses from testifying. That might deprive the trial of whatever the witness would have said in court *and* also cause the exclusion of statements that witness might have made to investigators prior to trial. The Supreme Court held in *Giles v. California*[14] that the rule of forfeiture by wrongdoing withdraws a person's Confrontation Clause protections if the person caused a declarant's unavailability at trial by acting in a way that was intended to accomplish that result. This loss of Confrontation Clause rights occurs only if the defendant's conduct related to the declarant was specifically intended to prevent the declarant from being a witness.

The forfeiture by wrongdoing doctrine applied in *Giles* and Rule 804(b)(6) address the same kind of conduct by a defendant. The *Giles* holding takes away a defendant's Confrontation Clause objection to admission of the absent declarant's statements. Rule 804(b)(6) takes away the defendant's possible hearsay objections to those same statements. (In a state that does not have a rule parallel to Federal Rule 804(b)(6), even if Confrontation Clause rights are forfeited, hearsay objections to the absent declarant's statements might still be permitted.)

---

11. 558 U.S. 305 (2009).
12. 131 S. Ct. 2705 (2011).
13. 132 S. Ct. 2221 (2012).
14. 554 U.S. 353 (2008).

Examples

1. Horace Homer has sued Delta Pharmaceutical Corporation, claiming that it failed to provide an adequate warning that one of its drugs was habit-forming. Delta's defense, in part, is that Homer was extraordinarily predisposed to abuse drugs. Two years prior to instituting his suit against Delta, Homer sought Workers' Compensation benefits, claiming that hazardous conditions at his workplace had harmed him. At the Workers' Compensation hearing, Homer's employer introduced testimony by a psychiatrist who had treated Homer. The psychiatrist testified that Homer was addicted to a number of drugs. Under applicable substantive law, this testimony, if believed, would have led to drastic reduction of Homer's compensation benefits. If the psychiatrist is now deceased, can Delta introduce a transcript of his testimony?

2. Seeking damages for asbestos-related disease, John James sued Giant Asbestos Corporation, claiming that it had made some of the asbestos-containing products that James had worked with in a career as a pipefitter. May James introduce testimony given by a witness at another plaintiff's trial against Giant if that witness is now unavailable and the testimony concerned a general issue of the degree to which Giant's products did or did not contain asbestos?

3. What if the testimony sought to be introduced in Example 2 against Giant Asbestos Corporation had been given in a trial involving similar products produced by Medium-Sized Asbestos Corporation, a company that merged with Giant a week before Homer sued Giant?

4. What if the testimony sought to be introduced in Example 2 against Giant Asbestos Corporation had been given in a trial involving similar products produced by Enormous Asbestos Corporation, Giant's main competitor?

5. An insurance company seeks to avoid paying the beneficiary of a life insurance policy, Paula Pillgiver, claiming that Pillgiver caused the insured's death by intentionally giving him an overdose of a prescription drug. Pillgiver concedes that the decedent took an overdose but contends that it was by mistake. A doctor from the hospital emergency room at which the decedent died heard him say, "I know I'm dying, and it must be the pills. I told Pillgiver not to make me take so many of them." Can the doctor quote that statement in testimony in a lawsuit between the insurance company and Pillgiver?

6. Quentin Quire worked for 30 years as a billboard painter. He became ill with cancer and suspected that the disease had been caused by some of the paint products he used at work. One year before he died, he told his

son that he thought one product in particular, "Super Smooth Brush Cleaner," had been the most harmful and that he had used that brand of brush cleaner exclusively for the past 20 years. In a wrongful death suit against the maker of "Super Smooth Brush Cleaner," if there is a dispute about whether Quire ever used that brand of brush cleaner, may the son testify that his late father had told him "Super Smooth" was the brand he had used for 20 years?

7. Rex Riley was on trial for selling drugs to high school students. When a witness testified that he had seen Riley sell drugs in the school gym, Riley shouted out in the courtroom, "You liar, it was the lunchroom." If the school board fired the lunchroom supervisor, could Riley's words be introduced in a suit challenging the firing?

8. The state has condemned Lucy Lowin's small shopping center to obtain land for a highway project. In a suit contesting the amount the state must pay Lowin, the state contends that the center's value is $1.5 million. Lowin argues that its value is $4 million. The state seeks to introduce evidence that one year prior to the condemnation, a county real estate assessor had valued a very similar shopping center one block away at $1.5 million. Its owner, Max Miller, testified in a hearing that in his opinion the center was worth no more than $1 million. If Miller is now unavailable to testify, can Miller's words be used against Lowin in the current case?

9. Nancy Neville sues a former friend, Oscar Ordway, claiming that she contracted a sexually transmitted disease from him and that he negligently failed to inform her that he was infected at the time she and he had sexual relations. Ordway claims that Neville probably contracted the disease from a third person, Steve Stoner, with whom she had a sexual relationship prior to meeting Ordway. Stoner is unavailable to testify at the time of trial of the Neville-Ordway suit. However, at a party about a year after Stoner's relationship with Neville had ended, Stoner said, "I had a sexually transmitted disease when I was going out with Neville, but I never let it bother me." Can someone who was at the party and heard Stoner admit that he had been infected testify to Stoner's statements at the Neville-Ordway trial?

10. A newspaper reporter wrote a series of articles exposing unsanitary practices at various restaurants. The articles gave hypothetical names for the restaurants, but they were based on observations the writer made after having been hired as a dishwasher under an assumed name at the restaurants. A food poisoning victim seeks damages against a particular restaurant at which she claims she was given unwholesome food. To bolster her case, she seeks to introduce one of the newspaper articles, along with notes the reporter made that give the real names of the

restaurants. Putting the notes and the article together, the plaintiff claims, provides a basis for allowing the jury to consider the reporter's observations about sanitary practices at the defendant restaurant. Assume the following facts: the reporter has died since writing the articles, and the articles were written only two years prior to the suit. Does the hearsay rule bar admission of the article and the reporter's notes?

11. A police officer, William Wilson, may have used excessive force against Vincent Vining, an individual he had arrested. On the occasion in question, Carl Carlson called 911 and told the operator, "I just saw a police officer stop his police car, pull a guy out of it, and hit him on the head with a hammer. Some other police cars drove up, and he stopped. The situation is over, but I wanted to report what I saw the first officer doing." There is an adequate basis for believing that Carlson was describing conduct involving Wilson and Vining. If Carlson is unavailable to testify, could Carlson's statements be introduced to show that Wilson hit Vining with a hammer in a civil case in which Vining seeks damages from Wilson for battery? Could the statements be introduced in a criminal case in which Wilson is charged with attempted murder?

Explanations

1. The transcript is hearsay because it represents a method of bringing the out-of-court statements of the psychiatrist into the current trial to support the proponent's case by having the jury believe the conclusions the psychiatrist asserted in the Workers' Compensation proceeding. The former testimony exception will permit the hearsay to be admitted. To use it, the proponent must first establish that the declarant is unavailable. Death is the ultimate unavailability. Next, the rule's requirement that the testimony had been under oath must be satisfied. Finally, the proponent must establish that the party against whom the former testimony is sought to be introduced (or a predecessor in interest to that party) had a motive and opportunity to cross-examine that were similar to the motive that would be present in the current case if the declarant were to testify. To do that, Delta would have to show that under the circumstances of the Workers' Compensation case, resisting the import of the psychiatrist's testimony was important to Homer. Since the testimony, if believed, would have severely limited Homer's recovery, Homer would have had a strong motive to discredit it. This makes admission of the former testimony correct in the current tort case.

2. Yes. The testimony is hearsay, but it is sought to be introduced against the same party who opposed it at the earlier trial. Giant had an opportunity to cross-examine the witness at the earlier trial and had the same

motive there that it would have had at the current trial if the witness had appeared in person.

3. Medium-Sized Asbestos Corporation would be a predecessor in interest to Giant Asbestos Corporation, so these facts fit the Federal Rules description of testimony that was exposed to cross-examination by a predecessor in interest of the party against which the former testimony is sought to be introduced. Medium-Sized's motives in the case would have been similar to the motives Giant would have had if Giant had been the defendant, so the testimony would be admissible.

4. Enormous Asbestos Corporation would have had a strong motive to cross-examine the expert, and it presumably would have been the same motive that Giant would have had if Giant had been the defendant in the former suit. For a minority of courts interpreting the Federal Rules, this similarity of motive is adequate to permit use of the former testimony exception. Most courts continue to pay separate attention to the requirements of "similar motive" and "predecessor in interest" and would refuse to treat a party's competitor as a predecessor in interest to the party.

5. Yes. The out-of-court words are hearsay because they are sought to be introduced to show that what they assert is true — that Pillgiver intentionally gave the decedent a drug overdose. The statement fits the definition of dying declaration, however, and could therefore be admitted. The speaker was aware of his impending death, the subject of the statement was the cause of his death, and the case in which the statement is sought to be used is a civil case. Recall that dying declarations are permitted in homicide cases and all civil cases.

6. Identifying the out-of-court statement as hearsay is simple. The point to be proved is that Quire used "Super Smooth," and Quire's out-of-court statement was exactly to that effect. The only hearsay exception that might cover the statement is the dying declarations exception. However, the doctrine requires that the declarant have the belief that death is imminent. How broadly should a court define "imminent"? Since it relates to the notion that people will be likely to tell the truth when they anticipate prompt consequences in the afterlife, applying a definition of "imminent" that would let Quire's statement in would be too great a stretch. In a sense, everyone knows that death will occur in the future and might be motivated by that knowledge to speak truthfully and act morally. The dying declarations doctrine, however, is based on the idea that those motivations are particularly strong when a declarant expects to die soon after making a statement.

7. Riley's words would certainly meet the definition of a statement that exposes the declarant to criminal liability. For that reason, they would

be admissible as a statement against interest in the suit between the school board and the lunchroom supervisor.

8. Offered for the truth of its meaning that the nearby shopping center was worth only $1 million, Miller's statement is hearsay. The former testimony exception will not apply because there was no opportunity for Lowin or a predecessor of Lowin's to cross-examine Miller in the real estate assessment hearing. For the statement against interest exception to apply, the proponent of Miller's statement must show that the statement was contrary to Miller's pecuniary interest at the time he made it. Did it hurt Miller to state that his property was worth less than the real estate assessor said it was worth? A superficial response would be that it always harms an owner's interests to minimize the value of an asset. However, it is well-known that owners seek to have their real estate assessments reduced to improve their financial status. Thus, it cannot fairly be said that Miller's claims at the assessment hearing were contrary to his financial interests. The words, therefore, do not qualify for admission under the statements against interest exception.

9. The out-of-court words by Stoner are relevant only if their content is true. Therefore, they are hearsay. Their admissibility would be governed by the jurisdiction's position on statements against interest. Under the Federal Rules, the words would be kept out since they did not expose Stoner to monetary or criminal liability (assuming there was no statute prohibiting sexual conduct by one who was infected with a sexually transmitted disease). In a jurisdiction that recognizes social interests as among those that can be a basis for invoking the statements against interest exception, an admission that the declarant has a sexually transmitted disease would be a statement against interest.

10. The article and notes are relevant only if their contents are taken as true, so the proponent must find a way around the hearsay bar. The ancient documents exception will not work because the material is too new. Calling the article and the notes business records has some superficial appeal, but there may not be any evidence about how much time elapsed between the observations and the reporter's recording of them in his diary. Also, the business records exception cannot apply if circumstances indicate a lack of trustworthiness. Many courts might hold that allowing a reporter's notes to be treated as business records would avoid most of the protections that are the basis for special treatment of those records: No one in the enterprise but the reporter relies on the notes, and there is no way of knowing whether the reporter even considered all of them accurate.

Rule 807, the residual exception, might work here. The proponent would have to give notice of the intention to introduce the notes and article and would have to establish that their circumstantial guarantees of trustworthiness are equivalent to those of the specific exceptions. Reporters have an incentive to be accurate because their careers may depend on their reputations for accuracy and honesty. Their notes are likely to be accurate for the same reason. These items come so close to the descriptions of business records that their reliability might be equal to that of some business records. Another requirement would be harder for the proponent to meet. The evidence must be more probative on its point than other evidence that could be procured through reasonable efforts. Depending on what the article and notes taken together seem to say about the defendant restaurant, and depending on the availability of information from current and former employees of the restaurant, the article and notes might or might not satisfy that requirement.

11. The tape is proper evidence of Carlson's out-of-court statements. The statements are hearsay since they are offered to show that the conduct they describe actually did occur. However, they satisfy the requirements for the present sense impression exception to the hearsay exclusion. For that reason the statements are admissible in the civil case.

In the criminal case, however, the Confrontation Clause requires that the statements be excluded because they are testimonial. Carlson made them to the police and they described events that had concluded when an emergency was over. When the declarant does not testify, testimonial hearsay can be admitted in a criminal case only if the declarant is unavailable and the defendant had an opportunity to cross-examine the declarant. Wilson had no opportunity to cross-examine Carlson when Carlson made his 911 call, so the Confrontation Clause forbids the use of Carlson's statements.

CHAPTER 5

Examination and Impeachment

INTRODUCTION

Under the Federal Rules almost anyone can be a witness. This is a change from common law doctrines that placed a variety of limits on competency to testify. The proponent of a witness shows that the witness has personal or expert knowledge about a disputed issue and asks that person questions about it in "direct examination." The main constraints on direct examination are the general requirement of relevance, the exclusionary rules, and the prohibition against "leading questions." When a witness testifies, parties are entitled to counteract the force of the testimony through cross-examination and by introducing other evidence that might make the witness seem less credible. These efforts are known as *impeachment*.

Impeachment generally involves showing that the witness lied intentionally, had questionable perception or memory of the subject of the testimony, or made statements that are factually incorrect. To use the method of impeachment that relies on suggesting that the witness has purposely told lies, the opponent usually introduces evidence of the witness's propensity to lie or evidence of a bias that could lead the witness to testify in a particular way regardless of the truth. Impeachment that focuses on faulty memory or perception involves evidence showing how the witness saw or learned what the witness thinks he or she knows. Either intentional lying or poor memory can be shown with evidence of statements made by the witness before the trial that are inconsistent with the witness's testimony during the trial. A witness may also be impeached by contradiction, with evidence showing that the witness has made incorrect statements.

145

General Competency Rules

At common law, a potential witness had to be characterized as "competent" in order to testify. In a number of recurring situations, potential witnesses were defined as not competent. Parties to a dispute were not competent to testify. Similarly, people who had been convicted of crimes were barred, as were people who did not believe in God. Young children were often treated as not competent.

Under the Rules, the competency of witnesses is controlled by state law when they testify in connection with substantive issues that are controlled by state law. In all other situations, the Rules reject the common law approach and define all people as competent to testify, subject to a few exceptions. Rule 601 makes this explicit:

> Every person is competent to be a witness unless these rules provide otherwise. But in a civil case, state law governs the witness's competency regarding a claim or defense for which state law supplies the rule of decision.

The pro-competency position of Rule 601 does not extend to permitting a judge to testify in a trial the judge is conducting. Rule 605 states:

> The presiding judge may not testify as a witness at the trial. A party need not object to preserve the issue.

Note that the prohibition related to judges is absolute and can be enforced even if a party prejudiced by a violation of the rule chooses not to object to the violation (the objection would have to be made, obviously, to the judge who was in the process of violating the rule by testifying while presiding).

The possibility that jurors might testify occurs in two different contexts: a juror might have information about the facts in dispute in a case for which the person is a juror; and a losing party might hope to have a result reversed by having a juror testify about improper conduct by the jury. Rule 606 covers these two possibilities:

> **(a) At the Trial.** A juror may not testify as a witness before the other jurors at the trial. If a juror is called to testify, the court must give a party an opportunity to object outside the jury's presence.
>
> **(b) During an Inquiry into the Validity of a Verdict or Indictment.**
> **(1) Prohibited Testimony or Other Evidence.** During an inquiry into the validity of a verdict or indictment, a juror may not testify about any statement made or incident that occurred during the jury's deliberations; the effect of anything on that juror's or another juror's vote; or any juror's mental processes concerning the verdict or indictment. The court may not

receive a juror's affidavit or evidence of a juror's statement on these matters.

   (2) Exceptions. A juror may testify about whether:

   (A) extraneous prejudicial information was improperly brought to the jury's attention;

   (B) an outside influence was improperly brought to bear on any juror; or

   (C) a mistake was made in entering the verdict on the verdict form.

This Rule states clearly that a person may not serve as both a witness and a juror in a trial. This Rule also covers a more complicated topic, testimony by a juror about how a jury reached its verdict or indictment. With regard to testimony about a jury's conduct, the Rule allows testimony about "extraneous" information or "outside influence" on the theory that it will describe events that will be clear and easy to establish and will not involve an inquiry into how a juror evaluated various arguments during deliberations. Similarly, if there is a mistake in a verdict form, such as the word "guilty" written down instead of the words "not guilty," the Rule allows testimony about that error.

In contrast, the Rule prohibits testimony about "mental processes," to encourage jurors to speak freely in their deliberations. This limitation has blocked testimony, for example, about (1) widespread drug and alcohol use by jurors[1] and (2) a juror's statements during deliberations that showed she had lied during voir dire about being willing to give fair treatment to personal injury plaintiffs.[2] But a closely divided U.S. Supreme Court declined to apply the limitation and thus allowed testimony about a juror's statements of racial bigotry made during deliberations, because participation in deliberations by a juror with racial bigotry would violate a defendant's due process rights.[3]

For witnesses whose competency is not treated specifically in the rules, the trial judge can apply Rules 401, 402, and 403 to control whether they will be permitted to testify.

In addition to being competent, a person must satisfy an oath or affirmation requirement to be permitted to testify. Rule 603 states:

> Before testifying, a witness must give an oath or affirmation to testify truthfully. It must be in a form designed to impress that duty on the witness's conscience.

If a witness chooses not to swear an oath but rather uses the secular "affirmation," that witness may not be impeached with references to his or her

---

1. Tanner v. United States, 483 U.S. 107 (1987).
2. Warger v. Shauers, 135 S. Ct. 521 (2014).
3. Pena-Rodriguez v. Colorado, 137 S. Ct. 855 (2017).

lack of religious belief. Rule 610, discussed later in this chapter, prohibits that type of impeachment.

Personal Knowledge

Analytically related to the concept of competency to testify is a requirement that a witness must have personal knowledge of the subject of his or her testimony (unless the witness is an expert allowed to base testimony on information obtained in other ways). Rule 602 states:

> A witness may testify to a matter only if evidence is introduced sufficient to support a finding that the witness has personal knowledge of the matter. Evidence to prove personal knowledge may consist of the witness's own testimony. This rule does not apply to a witness's expert testimony under Rule 703.

To satisfy the personal knowledge requirement, the proponent of the witness must introduce evidence that provides a basis on which a jury or a judge sitting as trier-of-fact could reasonably conclude that the witness has personal knowledge of the subject matter of his or her testimony. This evidence can be incorporated in the witness's own testimony or can be provided in other forms. For example, a witness has personal knowledge that a street was slippery on a certain day if the witness saw the street or experienced its slipperiness in any way. In contrast, a witness who thinks a street was slippery because someone else saw it and told him or her about it does not have personal knowledge of the condition of the street. All that witness has is personal knowledge of the fact that someone else thought the street was slippery.

Children

At common law, testimony by children was closely controlled and was barred if the judge thought the child did not understand the concept of truthfulness. The Federal Rules do not include any express provision allowing this inquiry and seem to reject it, given the explicit provision that all people are competent to testify. A statute[4] separate from the Federal Rules applies to children who are witnesses to crimes or who are alleged to be victims of physical abuse, sexual abuse, or exploitation. It provides that the judge, in response to an offer of compelling proof that a prospective child witness is incompetent, may have a competency examination on the record focused on questioning the child to determine whether the child can understand and answer simple questions. The statute states that a child's age alone is not a compelling reason to have such a competency examination.

---

4. 18 U.S.C. §3509.

Even under the Federal Rules and parallel state codes, where a proposed witness is a child, courts can exclude the testimony under the general authority of Rule 403 if it seems that the probative value of the testimony will be very weak because of the child's inability to tell truth from falsehood. This treatment of children's testimony is supported by the oath and personal knowledge requirements as well. A judge might rule that a child does not have the ability to understand and give the required oath or affirmation related to truth-telling. The judge might also rule that the child's ability to recall events or to distinguish between reality and fantasy is so slight that no reasonable juror could find that the child has "personal knowledge" of the topics of the testimony. These rulings would keep the child off the stand, a result identical to that reached under the explicit federal statute and under common law doctrines that allowed the judge to determine competency of a child witness.

Hypnosis

A witness who has been hypnotized after experiencing something he or she will testify about presents special problems. Will the witness testify about his or her own personal knowledge of the event, or will the witness bring to the trial ideas and information implanted by the hypnotist? Will the effect of the hypnosis on the witness detract from the jury's ability to use the witness's demeanor as a guide to the witness's certainty about the testimony? The witness may seem highly certain that his or her memory is accurate because it has been reinforced by the process of hypnosis. That extra confidence may or may not be correct, but it would be difficult for a jury to estimate how much confidence the witness would have shown in the absence of hypnosis.

No provision of the Federal Rules refers specifically to hypnosis, and the rule stating that all people are competent to testify would seem to preclude a general prohibition against testimony from previously hypnotized witnesses. Nevertheless, many federal courts have imposed restrictions on this type of testimony using the authority of FRE 403 to balance probative value against the risk of improper prejudice. In criminal cases restrictions on this type of testimony can be based additionally on constitutional prohibitions against the state's use of impermissibly suggestive processes to identify the perpetrator of a crime. Where it is the defendant who seeks to introduce such testimony, another constitutional principle (the defendant's right to introduce relevant defense evidence) has led to a holding that the state may not rely on the fact that a witness has been hypnotized to exclude that witness from testifying.

The majority view prohibits the admission of hypnotically enhanced testimony either on the theory (at common law) that a witness who has been hypnotized is not competent or on the theory (under the Federal Rules) that the risk of the jury giving improper weight to the testimony is too great since the jury will not have a basis for evaluating credibility.

However, it is also part of the majority position that a witness who has been hypnotized may still give testimony that is limited to the witness's pre-hypnosis knowledge. Effecting this limitation requires significant procedural safeguards so that a record will exist showing the extent of the person's knowledge prior to the hypnosis. Some courts also require that the proponent of the testimony establish that the hypnosis itself was not suggestive.

Spousal Testimony in Criminal Cases

A vestige of the special common law competency rules continues to be important in criminal law. Under federal practice, a defendant's spouse has a privilege to refuse to testify at the trial of his or her spouse. At common law and under federal practice prior to 1980, this "spousal incompetency" doctrine allowed *either spouse* to prevent the testimony of a spouse so that in a husband's criminal trial, for example, the wife could not testify if either she or her husband chose to invoke spousal incompetency. The modern reform incorporated in federal practice allows only the *prospective witness spouse* to exercise the incompetency right.[5]

Claims Involving Decedents ("Dead Man's Statutes")

In some states, a "dead man's statute" prevents witnesses from testifying about transactions with a person involved in the litigated claim if the person has died prior to the trial. The origin of the dead man's rule is an older and now completely rejected competency rule that prohibited testimony by plaintiffs in their own behalf and gave defendants a privilege to refrain from testifying. These older doctrines were based on the assumption that people with a strong interest in a case could not be trusted to tell the truth. The dead man's statutes are typically the product of reform efforts that abolished the general rule of parties' incompetency but retained it in the small category of cases involving claims by or against an estate.

The general reason for abolishing the broad incompetency doctrine is a belief that juries are likely to recognize and consider a witness's self-interest, so that bringing in a party's testimony can add to the available information without creating an opportunity for successful perjury. In line with this analysis, the Federal Rules completely reject the position represented by the dead man's statutes. Many states have also abrogated or restricted their dead man's statutes. Where they apply, it is usually said that the witness is not competent to testify about statements or events covered by the statute.

There are many variations in the language of state dead man's statutes and in judicial interpretations of them. Most courts seek to construe the

---

5. A decision by the United States Supreme Court effected this change in competency doctrine for federal courts. *See* Trammel v. United States, 445 U.S. 40 (1980).

statutes narrowly to favor the admission of testimony. Depending on the statute, a party may be prohibited only from testifying about his or her own statements to a decedent or may be prohibited from giving any testimony at all concerning a transaction. Courts also differ on how they define "transaction." For example, in some states an automobile collision is a transaction for the purpose of the dead man's statute, and a surviving participant may not testify in a suit against the estate of a driver killed in the accident. A position adopted in some states allows a witness to testify about his or her own statements to a decedent, but simultaneously eliminates any possible hearsay objection that might otherwise have prevented the quotation of the decedent's words.

Scope and Style of Examination

Rule 611(a) makes explicit that the trial judge controls the mode and order of presentation of each party's case:

> **(a) Control by the Court; Purposes.** The court should exercise reasonable control over the mode and order of examining witnesses and presenting evidence so as to:
> **(1)** make those procedures effective for determining the truth;
> **(2)** avoid wasting time; and
> **(3)** protect witnesses from harassment or undue embarrassment.

In direct examination, a party asks its witness questions about relevant issues, and the witness answers the questions. Cross-examination is the questioning of an opponent's witnesses after direct examination. In addition, the trial judge may question witnesses. While judges have considerable discretion in controlling the style and order of examination, some additional rules apply.

Leading Questions

The primary consideration of form for direct examination is that the Federal Rules restrict the use of leading questions. A leading question is one that suggests its answer. Rule 611(c) provides:

> **(c) Leading Questions.** Leading questions should not be used on direct examination except as necessary to develop the witness's testimony. Ordinarily, the court should allow leading questions:
> **(1)** on cross-examination; and
> **(2)** when a party calls a hostile witness, an adverse party, or a witness identified with an adverse party.

The question, "Is it true that you locked the door when you left the house?" would be defined as leading, while, "What did you do, if anything, when you left the house?" would be totally immune from an objection on grounds that it was a leading question. This doctrine is based on the belief that a witness is more likely to testify truthfully if the witness does not know what answer the questioner wants the witness to give. Obviously, characterizing a question as leading or not leading may be a matter of degree, subject to differences in judgment. Typically, judges permit leading questions freely when they involve topics that are not controversial or are really only preliminary to the main points of a witness's testimony.

Scope of Cross-examination

After a witness has testified on direct examination, the opposing party is entitled to cross-examine the witness. Cross-examination is limited to two areas of inquiry: (1) topics involved in the witness's direct examination and (2) topics concerning the witness's credibility. This is the "scope of direct" rule for controlling the coverage of cross-examination, adopted by Rule 611(b), subject to the judge's discretion to allow questions on other topics:

> **(b) Scope of Cross-examination.** Cross-examination should not go beyond the subject matter of the direct examination and matters affecting the witness's credibility. The court may allow inquiry into additional matters as if on direct examination.

The Federal Rules reject an opposite idea, the "wide-open" rule. Under the wide-open rule, a cross-examiner is entitled to ask a witness anything that is relevant to an issue at trial. The scope-of-direct rule entitles the cross-examiner to ask questions only related to topics raised in direct examination. If a witness has information on a topic outside the scope of the witness's direct examination, a party who would like the trier of fact to learn that information must use that witness as part of his or her own direct case and question the witness about that topic on direct examination.

The "scope of direct" rule thus allows a party a great deal of control over the order in which the trier of fact learns relevant information. Even if a witness has information on a variety of relevant topics, the rule allows a party to organize the presentation of his or her case by using that witness just to supply information on topics the party chooses to develop through that witness. The opposing party cannot use cross-examination of the witness to direct the jury's attention to other aspects of the case that might be within that witness's knowledge if the party presenting that witness has chosen to ignore them. The rule is flexible, however, and grants discretion to the trial judge to allow a cross-examiner to expand the scope of examination beyond the topics covered in direct examination.

Form for Cross-examination Questions

Leading questions are permitted on cross-examination, in contrast to direct examination. Additionally, a cross-examiner is permitted to make repeated efforts to obtain an answer by asking questions more than once, or by rephrasing questions to get at a single idea in more than one way. Balanced against this traditional freedom is the trial court's ability to protect witnesses from, in the words of Rule 611(a), "harassment or undue embarrassment."

Questions by the Judge

Judges may question witnesses, but they are supposed to be very sparing in using this right. Parties have primary responsibility for their own cases and should not be helped or hurt by the court. Additionally, questions from the bench may assume more significance to jurors than their substance would justify merely because the person asking the questions is the trial judge. While appellate courts are highly deferential to trial courts on an issue like the timing and extent of judicial questioning of witnesses, occasional remands for new trial are ordered where judicial questioning is excessive. The most acceptable occasions for questions from the bench are instances when a witness has accidentally used a word improperly and the judge, noticing it, can give the witness a chance to make the testimony clearer. In general, the judge's motive for questioning should always be to increase the clarity of the testimony rather than to influence the result in the case.

Statements of Opinion

Rule 701 limits the expression of opinions by witnesses. It provides:

> If a witness is not testifying as an expert, testimony in the form of an opinion is limited to one that is:
>
> **(a)** rationally based on the witness's perception;
> **(b)** helpful to clearly understanding the witness's testimony or to determining a fact in issue; and
> **(c)** not based on scientific, technical, or other specialized knowledge within the scope of Rule 702.

The theory behind the rule is that juries can find facts better if witnesses report concrete information and allow the juries' members to analyze the information. The rule provides that unless a witness is testifying as an expert, statements of opinion or inferences are allowed only if they help provide a clear understanding of the testimony or of a fact in issue. It must also be shown that the opinion or inference is based on some perception by the witness. This rule rejects a controversial common law position that attempted to distinguish clearly between factual and opinion statements and was supposed to exclude statements of opinion by any witnesses other than expert witnesses. A witness may state, for example, that a person seemed drunk, or that a driver seemed to be in control of a vehicle so long as those statements (which could be characterized as reporting conclusions, inferences, or opinions) have some support in actual perceptions of the witness.

Rule 701 refers to Rule 702 to reinforce the distinction between expert witnesses and non-expert witnesses (sometimes called "lay" witnesses). Rule 702, discussed in Chapter 6, treats expert testimony. Rule 701 prevents a "non-expert" from giving testimony of the types that Rule 702 defines. This insures that a witness whose testimony is based on scientific or technical knowledge will be subject to certain detailed requirements specified in Rule 702.

Physical Location of Witnesses and Parties

A judge ordinarily controls the locations of witnesses and attorneys in the courtroom. An issue of current importance is whether a judge, in a case involving alleged assault against a child, may prevent a complaining witness and a defendant from seeing each other in the courtroom. Decisions of the United States Supreme Court suggest that the confrontation clause does not prohibit arrangements such as a physical barrier or the use of television for testimony from a location other than the courtroom so long as an individualized finding is made in each case that standard arrangements could traumatize the child due to the child's awareness of the defendant's presence.

The statute[6] providing detailed procedures for considering the competency of a child witness also sets up procedures for allowing a child to testify in a room separate from the defendant in a criminal case. If the trial judge believes that style of testimony is needed, the statute requires that television equipment be used to allow the child and defendant to see each other's faces.

At the request of any party, a witness may be sequestered, that is, barred from presence in the courtroom except during that witness's testimony. Rule 615 states:

> At a party's request, the court must order witnesses excluded so that they cannot hear other witnesses' testimony. Or the court may do so on its own. But this rule does not authorize excluding:
>
> **(a)** a party who is a natural person;
> **(b)** an officer or employee of a party that is not a natural person, after being designated as the party's representative by its attorney;
> **(c)** a person whose presence a party shows to be essential to presenting the party's claim or defense; or
> **(d)** a person authorized by statute to be present.

---

6. 18 U.S.C. §3509.

Note that a person may not be sequestered if his or her presence when not testifying is shown to be necessary to a party's representation. For example, a person who is expected to testify as an expert may be essential as an assistant to a lawyer for a party so that the lawyer can understand and counter testimony by experts for the opposing side. There is also a general limitation on the right of parties to require sequestration: A party cannot personally be required to be absent from the trial even if that party will be a witness. Where a party is an entity rather than a person, a representative of that entity is treated as equivalent to a person who is a party and is protected from sequestration as well.

General Right to Impeach

Any party may impeach any witness. Rule 607 states, "Any party, including the party that called the witness, may attack the witness's credibility." This rejects a common law doctrine that required a party who presented a witness to "vouch" for the witness's credibility and prohibited the party from showing that the witness might have testified untruthfully. In modern practice, where parties may have to rely on testimony from individuals whose reliability they may question, allowing any party the freedom to use impeachment techniques has seemed reasonable.

Various provisions of evidence law allow the admission of "impeachment-only" information; that is, information about a witness that can be considered by the trier of fact only for the light it may shed on whether the witness has testified truthfully. Material of this type may not be used by the trier of fact to prove any substantive part of a party's case. This distinction between information that is admissible only for impeachment and information that can be relied upon for substantive purposes leads to a limitation on parties' general ability to impeach all witnesses. Some courts have prohibited a party from impeaching its own witness when it seems that the party has used the witness only as part of a plan to impeach that witness with material that would be inadmissible for other purposes. In that setting, what purported to be a defensive use of impeachment material would really be an effort to bring that material into the trial so that the fact finder might improperly use it as a substantive basis for judgment rather than just as information that reflects on the witness's truthfulness.

Impeachment by Showing the Witness Lied Intentionally

Convictions of Crimes

If a witness has been convicted of a crime, evidence of the conviction is often admissible to support the following linked inferences: (1) the witness does not respect our society's rules of conduct; (2) the witness is a person who has a propensity to lie; and (3) because of that propensity, the witness may have lied while testifying. This general rule permits jurors to base a conclusion about the witness's conduct in court (the witness lied or spoke truthfully) on information about the witness's past conduct out of court. It is an exception to the general prohibition against propensity evidence. Under that general rule, for example, evidence of a person's past bad driving would be kept out if offered to support an inference about the person's driving on a later occasion. In connection with the conduct of testifying in court, however, evidence of a witness's past lying or other past conduct in disrespect of law is admitted to support an inference about the person's later conduct as a testifying witness.

There are a number of reasons why the standard bar against propensity inferences is modified for the issue of impeachment. Some think that there is a particularly strong logical link between past lying and current lying. Others justify allowing jurors to make propensity-based inferences about a witness's truthfulness because the veracity of witnesses is a highly important issue or because they believe the types of data on which these propensity inferences are allowed to be based are likely to be accurate and subject to quick and clear proof. Finally, it may have seemed anomalous at common law and to the drafters of the Federal Rules for a person who had been convicted of serious crimes in the past to appear before a jury and benefit from the jury's likely assumption that the person did not have a criminal record. Obviously, the fact that a jury may learn about a witness's past wrongdoing will deter many defendants from testifying in their own defense, since if they refrain from testifying, evidence of their past convictions will be admissible only on other rationales that are harder for the opponent to establish.

Admissibility of evidence of prior convictions is often determined in pretrial proceedings. If the court rules that this type of impeachment will be allowed, the defendant will only be allowed to challenge that ruling if he or she decides to testify and is then impeached with the controversial evidence. This means, in practice, that defendants are deterred from testifying in cases where a proper application of the rule would expose them to impeachment based on proof of past convictions *and* are also deterred in cases where a ruling allowing that type of impeachment might well be wrong. The deterrence occurs in the latter type of case because a defendant will only be able to challenge the ruling allowing that impeachment by testifying and allowing the jury to hear it. The gamble this presents may lead many defendants to refrain from testifying.

The arguments against allowing past convictions to be the basis for inferences about the credibility of witnesses are the same arguments that have led to strict limitations on this type of propensity evidence in other contexts. This may explain why common law judges and the Federal Rules have imposed detailed and complicated restrictions on the process even though they take the general position that the propensity inference can properly have some role in determining witness's credibility. Rules 609(a) and (b) set out the main controls on this process:

(a) **In General.** The following rules apply to attacking a witness's character for truthfulness by evidence of a criminal conviction:

(1) for a crime that, in the convicting jurisdiction, was punishable by death or by imprisonment for more than one year, the evidence:

(A) must be admitted, subject to Rule 403, in a civil case or in a criminal case in which the witness is not a defendant; and

(B) must be admitted in a criminal case in which the witness is a defendant, if the probative value of the evidence outweighs its prejudicial effect to that defendant; and

(2) for any crime regardless of the punishment, the evidence must be admitted if the court can readily determine that establishing the elements of the crime required proving — or the witness's admitting — a dishonest act or false statement.

(b) **Limit on Using the Evidence After 10 Years.** This subdivision (b) applies if more than ten years have passed since the witness's conviction or release from confinement for it, whichever is later. Evidence of the conviction is admissible only if:

(1) its probative value, supported by specific facts and circumstances, substantially outweighs its prejudicial effect; and

(2) the proponent gives an adverse party reasonable written notice of the intent to use it so that the party has a fair opportunity to contest its use.

The Rule varies the availability of proof of past convictions for impeaching the credibility of a witness in accordance with factors such as: whether the witness sought to be impeached is a criminal defendant; the type of crime committed (its seriousness and its connection with false statements); and the likely balance between probative value and prejudice, including the effect of the length of time between the trial and the conviction.

Crimes of dishonesty or false statement. If a crime's elements require proof (or admission) of a "dishonest act or false statement" to support conviction, evidence that any witness (whether or not a criminal defendant) was convicted of it is usually admissible to impeach that witness's credibility in the current trial. Crimes that involve dishonesty or false statement include perjury, criminal fraud, and embezzlement. For the conviction to meet the requirements of this rule, the ultimate criminal act must involve deceit. For example, this provision would not cover bank robbery, even if the robber had lied to gain admission to a particular room in the bank.

For convictions of dishonesty or false statement crimes, there is ordinarily no comparison of probative and possible prejudicial effects. Even the usual Rule 403 balancing test is withdrawn for this particular question of admissibility. The only time admission of this evidence is not automatic is when a ten-year period has elapsed since the date of conviction or the witness's release from confinement related to the conviction (whichever date is later). In that circumstance, the evidence is subject to a balancing test under Rule 609(b).

Crimes that do not involve a "dishonest act or false statement." Proof of conviction of crimes that do not involve a "dishonest act or false statement" is also admissible, subject to two important qualifications. First, the crime must have been punishable by death or imprisonment in excess of one year. Misdemeanors are thus not bad enough to be relevant for impeachment. Second, the evidence must pass a balancing test comparing its probative value to certain risks of misuse. If the witness is a criminal defendant, the evidence must be excluded if the court determines that its probative value is outweighed by its prejudicial effect to that person, the criminal defendant who testifies in his or her own trial. If the witness is anyone other than the defendant in a criminal trial, the evidence is excluded only if its probative value is *substantially* outweighed by its prejudicial effects. The balancing test for criminal defendants is unique to this issue; the balancing test for witnesses other than criminal defendants is the test set out in the general "unfair prejudice" rule, Rule 403. Trial court decisions on admissibility of this type of evidence are usually affirmed as within the court's discretion. It is considered good practice, however, for a trial court to make explicit findings about the balancing of probative force and possible prejudice.

Probative value of past convictions of crimes that do not involve a "dishonest act or false statement." If a person who is a witness in a current trial was once convicted of a crime that did not involve dishonesty or false statement, how does that fact relate to the likelihood that the witness gave truthful testimony in the current trial? The rationale for relevancy of a conviction such as assault, for example, must be that a person who breaks any law (in circumstances that make the conduct punishable by at least a year's imprisonment) has so little respect for propriety and the legal system that he or she is more likely to lie in court than an otherwise similar person who had not committed that type of crime. It is important to identify the probative value of past convictions because trial courts are required to balance that probative value against risks of prejudice or misuse of the evidence. Also, that balancing must involve an evaluation of the probative force of the evidence. Rule 609 explicitly treats non-truth-telling offenses as related to a witness's likely truthfulness while testifying. Therefore in evaluating the probative value of that type of conviction, courts usually focus on whether the witness's credibility is particularly important in the trial and on whether there are other means to give the jury a basis for assessing that credibility.

Prejudice related to past convictions of crimes that do not involve a "dishonest act or false statement." The risk of prejudice or jury misuse will depend on the nature of the past crime. If the witness is not a party, the only risk of jury misuse of the past crimes information will be that jurors may assume that the party on whose behalf the witness testified is to be disfavored because that party is associated with a witness who has previously committed a serious crime. While this "birds of a feather flock together" analysis may reflect reality in some instances, it is a fairly attenuated theory. In most cases, there is only a small risk that a jury will misuse information about the past of a nonparty witness. This is why Rule 609 applies the balancing test of FRE 403 to past convictions of a non-defendant witness: They can be admitted even if the risk of prejudice outweighs their probative force (so long as that risk does not *substantially* outweigh their probative value).

Where the witness is a criminal defendant, Rule 609 uses a balancing test that limits the admission of evidence about his or her past non-truth-telling convictions. They may be admitted only if their probative value outweighs the risks of prejudice. In the situation of a criminal defendant who testifies, the strongest likelihood of prejudicial misuse of information about the defendant's past convictions arises where they involve an offense that is the same as or similar to the offense being adjudicated in the current trial. For example, evidence that an alleged bank robber has robbed a bank in the past would be barred by the propensity rule if offered to show that because the defendant robbed a bank once he or she is more likely to have robbed a bank another time. If an alleged bank robber testified at trial and was then impeached with evidence that he or she had robbed a bank in the past, the explicit theory of admissibility would be that information about the past robbery would help jurors decide whether the defendant acted truthfully on the witness stand.

There is a significant risk, however, that the jury would use the information about the past bank robbery to decide how the defendant acted on the day of the bank robbery. Jurors might ignore the permitted use of the evidence as a basis for evaluating the witness's credibility and might use it as a basis for deciding that having robbed a bank in the past, he or she probably committed the bank robbery that is the subject of the current prosecution. The risk of prejudice is extremely high in this situation. However, if credibility is a crucial issue, and other evidence about credibility is not available, courts will sometimes permit this type of information about a defendant's past to be used under the impeachment rationale. This strongly deters a criminal defendant who has been convicted in the past of any crime from testifying in his or her own defense.

Staleness, pardons, juvenile adjudications, appeals. The ten-year staleness provision of Rule 609(b), discussed above in the context of crimes involving dishonesty or false statement, also applies to other crimes covered by the impeachment rules. Where a conviction has been the subject of a pardon or was the result of a juvenile adjudication, the Rules restrict introduction of evidence about it. Those limitations are in Rule 609(c) and (d):

(c) Effect of a Pardon, Annulment, or Certificate of Rehabilitation. Evidence of a conviction is not admissible if:

    (1) the conviction has been the subject of a pardon, annulment, certificate of rehabilitation, or other equivalent procedure based on a finding that the person has been rehabilitated, and the person has not been convicted of a later crime punishable by death or by imprisonment for more than one year; or

    (2) the conviction has been the subject of a pardon, annulment, or other equivalent procedure based on a finding of innocence.

(d) Juvenile Adjudications. Evidence of a juvenile adjudication is admissible under this rule only if:

    (1) it is offered in a criminal case;

    (2) the adjudication was of a witness other than the defendant;

    (3) an adult's conviction for that offense would be admissible to attack the adult's credibility; and

    (4) admitting the evidence is necessary to fairly determine guilt or innocence.

If a pardon was based on a finding of innocence, evidence of the conviction for which the pardon was granted is inadmissible. If a pardon was based on factors such as rehabilitation, evidence of the conviction is similarly inadmissible unless the person has subsequently been convicted of a serious crime. Juvenile adjudications are ordinarily excluded from evidence, but trial courts have discretion to admit them if necessary for fair evaluation of a witness's testimony with regard to guilt or innocence of a criminal defendant.

Impeachment uses of past convictions involve four different possible descriptions of the relationship between the probative value of the information and the risks of prejudice. Rule 609 relates admissibility to the type of past conviction and the identity of the individual witness against whom the information is sought to be used. Chart 17 illustrates the choices incorporated in Rule 609. Notice that for evidence of past convictions to be admitted, the Rule sets the required balance between probativeness and prejudicial potential increasingly towards probativeness as the likelihood of fair and accurate use of the information decreases either because the conviction is old or because it involved the current criminal defendant.

Past Bad Acts That Did Not Lead to Criminal Convictions

The same theory of logical relevance that supports admission of evidence of a witness's conviction of crimes also applies to the relevance of information that a witness committed bad acts that did not lead to criminal convictions. A person who has been seriously disrespectful of law may likely be a person who would not testify truthfully in a judicial proceeding. However, because proving that a person committed any particular act in the past is so much

Chart 17 — Is Evidence of a Witness's Past Conviction Admissible?

Balance Between Probative Value and Risk of Prejudice

Type of Conviction and Type of Witness	Substantially More Probative than Prejudicial	More Probative than Prejudicial	Less Probative than Prejudicial	Substantially Less Probative than Prejudicial
Crime involved truth-telling; any witness	Yes	Yes	Yes	Yes
Crime did not involve truth-telling; any witness *except* a criminal defendant	Yes	Yes	Yes	No
Crime did not involve truth-telling; criminal defendant witness	Yes	Yes	No	No
Any crime more than ten years old; any witness	Yes	No	No	No

more difficult than proving he or she was convicted of a crime, extrinsic evidence of past bad acts is not permitted when their only relevance is to impeach a witness's credibility. Rule 608(b) states:

> **(b) Specific Instances of Conduct.** Except for a criminal conviction under Rule 609, extrinsic evidence is not admissible to prove specific instances of a witness's conduct in order to attack or support the witness's character for truthfulness. But the court may, on cross-examination, allow them to be inquired into if they are probative of the character for truthfulness or untruthfulness of:
>
> **(1)** the witness; or
>
> **(2)** another witness whose character the witness being cross-examined has testified about.
>
> By testifying on another matter, a witness does not waive any privilege against self-incrimination for testimony that relates only to the witness's character for truthfulness.

Thus, a witness may be questioned about past acts that did not lead to a conviction if they are relevant to the witness's character for truthfulness, but proof other than this testimony is prohibited.

There are three important controls on the use of information about a witness's past acts that did not lead to a criminal conviction. The questioner must have a good faith belief that the event actually occurred or else may not ask questions about it. Also, the questions must be asked during cross-examination, not during direct examination. Finally, the questioner may not introduce other proof about the alleged past act by testimony from other witnesses or by any other method. This is why it is sometimes said that the examiner must "take the witness's answer." The examiner is allowed to ask about the past acts, but all the examiner can do if witness denies having committed the acts is to ask about them again (subject to limits on harassment of a witness).

The rationale for allowing inquiry but not extrinsic proof is that proving the occurrence of past acts by particular witnesses would be time-consuming since it might entail the equivalent of a trial within the current trial. Of course, the fact that a process is costly is significant only in comparison to the results it can be expected to accomplish. In this case the benefit from establishing the truth about a witness's past conduct would be that the jury could use the information to make an inference about the witness's character for truthfulness and then make an inference from its opinion about that character to a belief about how the witness acted while testifying (in conformity with that character or not in conformity with that character). Since character inferences are generally disfavored, it is sensible to give up the chance to let juries make them on the basis of information about the past bad acts of witnesses if it would be difficult to provide juries with clear information about those acts. In contrast, where the past acts have become the subject of a criminal conviction, it is easy to give juries clear information about them. It is also true that a conviction means that guilt was established under the beyond a reasonable doubt standard. These are the primary reasons for treating past convictions differently from past acts of witnesses. Convictions, subject to Rule 609's detailed provisions, may be proved with extrinsic evidence. Past acts of a witness, if relevant only to credibility, are treated only with the process in which an examiner asks about them and the witness gives a reply.

Evidence of Character for Truth-telling: A Permitted Propensity Inference

When a person testifies, evidence may be introduced about his or her character traits related to truth-telling. A party seeking to impeach the credibility of a witness may introduce evidence showing that the witness is the type of person who is likely to lie. Rule 608(a) allows this type of evidence and specifies the form in which it must be introduced:

> **(a) Reputation or Opinion Evidence.** A witness's credibility may be attacked or supported by testimony about the witness's reputation for having a character for truthfulness or untruthfulness, or by testimony in the form of an opinion about that character. But evidence of truthful character is admissible only after the witness's character for truthfulness has been attacked.

Evidence attacking a witness's character for truth-telling is introduced by testimony from other witnesses. For clarity, they can be called "testifying witnesses" and "impeaching witnesses," although both testifying and impeaching witnesses, of course, give testimony. An impeaching witness is allowed to provide the fact finder with negative information about the testifying witness's untruthful nature in either of two ways: by describing the testifying witness's reputation for truth-telling or by giving an opinion about the testifying witness's typical truthfulness. This is another instance in which the usual rule against propensity evidence is modified where the issue at stake is whether a witness has given truthful testimony.

After a witness's character for truthfulness has been attacked with evidence in the form of reputation or opinion evidence, it can be rehabilitated. Other witnesses may testify about the testifying witness's positive character traits for truthfulness. These rehabilitating witnesses are limited to reporting the reputation of the testifying witness or to stating their own opinions about the testifying witness's character for speaking the truth. It is important to remember that no witness is allowed to give reputation or opinion evidence showing that another witness has probably testified truthfully unless character evidence has already been introduced to show that that witness probably gave false testimony. In criminal cases there may be an exception to the usual requirement that evidence about truthfulness is not permitted until there has been an attack on a witness's credibility: A defendant may comment on his or her own truthfulness if truthfulness is a trait pertinent to the charged crime, whether or not there has been a character-based attack on the defendant's truthfulness.

Timing for Proof of Crimes, Acts, and Character

The rules controlling proof about a witness's past convictions, past acts, and character related to truthfulness impose some restrictions on the timing of these kinds of proof. Some of these can be used only on cross-examination. Also, some kinds can be used only after a witness's credibility has been attacked.

Chart 18 — When May Character Evidence on Credibility Be Admitted?

	Occasions for Use of Proof		
Type of Proof	Prior to Other Credibility Evidence	During Direct Examination	During Cross-Examination
Convictions showing untruthfulness	Yes	Yes	Yes
Opinion or reputation showing untruthfulness	Yes	Yes	Yes
Past acts showing untruthfulness	Yes	No	Yes
Opinion or reputation showing truthfulness	No	Yes	Yes
Past acts showing truthfulness	No	No	Yes

Convictions can be used at any time if they satisfy the requirements of Rule 609. Character evidence that satisfies the requirements of Rule 608 and *attacks* a witness's credibility can be used at any time, but if it *supports* a witness's credibility it can be used only after that credibility has been attacked in some way. Past acts may be inquired about only on cross-examination. Chart 18 summarizes these requirements.

Proof of Bias

If a witness is biased either against or in favor of a party at a trial, proof of that bias is permitted on the theory that the witness may have shaded his or her testimony in line with it. A cross-examiner is entitled to ask questions that will show possible sources of bias. Other types of evidence of bias may also be introduced.

Common sources of bias involve family ties, financial ties, and membership in organizations. Information about links of this sort may suggest that a witness has slanted testimony in favor of a party with whom he or she is related. This type of proof may also support an inference that the witness has distorted his or her testimony to be unfavorable to an opponent of the party with whom the witness is related. Similarly, if a witness has been paid by a party, proof of that fact may help a jury evaluate the likely honesty of the witness's statements. In criminal cases, prosecution witnesses sometimes have made deals with the prosecution. If the prosecution is in a position to reduce the degree of a charged crime or to make a sentencing recommendation in a pending case involving a witness, that witness may be influenced to testify favorably to the prosecution in that case or some other case. Information concerning this type of relationship is usually admissible, although some courts will exclude it if the witness's arrangement with the prosecutor did not involve an obligation to testify.

Inquiry into Religious Beliefs Prohibited

While learning about a witness's religious beliefs might influence some jurors to form an opinion about whether the witness has testified truthfully, just how that influence would work would probably vary among jurors and according to the type of religious beliefs the witness did or did not have. There is an explicit rule prohibiting this type of reference to religious beliefs. Rule 610 provides:

> Evidence of a witness's religious beliefs or opinions is not admissible to attack or support the witness's credibility.

If a witness's religious beliefs or membership in a religious organization could be a basis for bias toward or against a party, then proof related to religion would be proper because kinship or antipathy would be the basis for the claim of relevance. In such a bias theory the nature of the witness's religious beliefs is not offered as a basis for believing or disbelieving the witness. Rather, the evidence is offered to show a motive that could affect the truthfulness of the witness. This use would not be prohibited by Rule 610.

Impeachment by Proof of Poor Perception or Memory

Because a person's ability to perceive things is so strongly related to the likelihood that what a person says about those things is accurate, cross-examiners are permitted to ask witnesses questions about how well they can see or hear and about the circumstances in which they observed or heard things that are the subjects of their testimony. Independent evidence on these topics is also admissible.

Impeachment by Contradiction

If some of a witness's testimony is factually incorrect, proof that those portions were wrong could support a conclusion that the other parts of the testimony were also false. It is logical that a person who remembers or describes some things incorrectly might give incorrect testimony about other things also. Regardless of whether the falsehoods are intentional or accidental, the fact that the witness claimed to believe things that are actually false could decrease a juror's belief in the credibility of the witness. Evidence law recognizes the logical relevance of factual errors to general credibility. However, a party may not introduce extrinsic proof that particular details of a witness's testimony are false unless those details involve a topic that could be subject to proof even if the witness had not referred to them. In other words, the topic on which a party seeks to introduce evidence in contradiction to a witness's testimony must be a topic that would be relevant in the trial whether or not a witness had earlier given testimony about it. If it has no independent significance, the topic is called *collateral*. Evidence that will only show a mistake or false statement in something a witness has said about a collateral topic is prohibited from being introduced extrinsically.

This limitation is based on the belief that allowing impeachment by contradiction would cost our litigation system too much for benefits that would probably be slight. A party seeking to impeach a witness by contradiction would introduce lots of evidence that was unrelated to the main issues at trial but did relate to the alleged error in the witness's testimony. A jury would have to deliberate not only about the factual issues related to the parties' claims and defenses but also about factual issues that would show whether minor portions of a witness's testimony were accurate. Of necessity, parties would spend large amounts of time and resources pursuing these factual questions. In contrast, the benefit a jury would derive from a full-fledged scrutiny of the factual accuracy of every part of a witness's testimony might be very slight. It might be worth far less than the expenditures of time and attention it would require.

For example, a witness might testify, "I was at the corner of Main and Broadway, and I saw the defendant run out of the National Bank carrying a gun and a bag of money." If the bank at that corner is really "Continental Bank," how much value would there be to having the jury find out that the witness had been mistaken in what he called the bank? It does not show very much about the witness's accuracy on the topics of identity, the gun, and the money that the witness remembered the name of the bank incorrectly. If a witness makes an error on some aspect of his testimony that has relevance to the disputed issues at trial, contrary evidence may always be introduced. For example, a defense witness in a bank robbery trial might testify, "I saw the defendant the afternoon of the robbery and he had a full beard." If eyewitnesses had testified that the robber was clean-shaven, this defense witness's testimony would help the defendant. A witness for the prosecution would be allowed to testify that he had seen the defendant on the same day and that the defendant did not have a beard. The prosecution's witness would be contradicting a point in the defense witness's testimony, but the testimony would be admissible. The physical appearance of the defendant on the day of the robbery would be relevant to an issue at trial (identity of the robber) and would not be called a collateral part of the defense witness's testimony. In contrast, suppose the defense witness stated, "I saw the defendant at a Burger King on the afternoon of the robbery and he had a beard," and suppose the prosecution knew that the restaurant was McDonald's, not a Burger King. Proof that the witness had used the wrong name for the restaurant would not be permitted.

The limitation on impeachment by contradiction only prevents the introduction of extrinsic evidence (extrinsic proof is proof in any style other than statements by the witness being questioned). During cross-examination a witness can be asked about any part of his or her direct examination. The defense witness could be asked, for example, "Wasn't it a McDonald's, not a Burger King?" but no matter what answer the witness gave to that inquiry, additional evidence from a source other than the witness would be prohibited.

Prior Statements by a Witness

When a witness says something in testimony but has also written or said something earlier that conflicts with that testimony, what the witness said or wrote at the earlier time is called a "prior inconsistent statement." On the theory that a person who says one thing one time and another thing another time has probably lied or has suffered from memory deficiencies on one of the two occasions, proof of prior inconsistent statements is permitted as a type of impeachment. Rule 613(a) states:

> **Showing or Disclosing the Statement During Examination.** When examining a witness about the witness's prior statement, a party need not show it or disclose its contents to the witness. But the party must, on request, show it or disclose its contents to an adverse party's attorney.

Except in limited circumstances, the jury or judge may not rely on the past statement as proof of what it asserts (because of the hearsay bar), but the fact finder may rely on it to disbelieve what the witness has said in court.

A cross-examiner may ask a witness about a prior statement without showing it to the witness, if the statement was written, and without saying in advance what the details of that prior statement might have been. However, the Rules require that the contents of the prior statement be disclosed to opposing counsel on request. The cross-examiner may accept the witness's denial or explanation of the prior statement but is also given the right to introduce extrinsic evidence of the prior statement. Extrinsic evidence of the statement could be a document or testimony by another person who knows about the statement. If extrinsic evidence of a past statement is introduced, the witness who made the current and past statements must be given an opportunity to explain the past statement. That opportunity may come either before or after extrinsic evidence of the statement is introduced. Use of extrinsic evidence is controlled by Rule 613(b):

> **Extrinsic Evidence of a Prior Inconsistent Statement.** Extrinsic evidence of a witness's prior inconsistent statement is admissible only if the witness is given an opportunity to explain or deny the statement and an adverse party is given an opportunity to examine the witness about it, or if justice so requires. This subdivision (b) does not apply to an opposing party's statement under Rule 801(d)(2).

There are a few situations in which prior statements by a witness, in addition to their use to scrutinize a witness's credibility, can have substantive use. These situations are explained in Chapter 4 and summarized below in Chart 19 "Summary: Prior Statements by a Witness." The chart covers Past Recollection Recorded, Prior Inconsistent Statements for Substantive Use, Prior Consistent Statements, and statements used in the Present Recollection Refreshed process.

Impeaching a Hearsay Declarant

When hearsay evidence is admitted, any party is permitted to impeach the credibility of the hearsay declarant. This process is controlled by Rule 806:

> When a hearsay statement — or a statement described in Rule 801(d)(2)(C), (D), or (E) — has been admitted in evidence, the declarant's credibility may be attacked, and then supported, by any evidence that would be admissible for those purposes if the declarant had testified as a witness. The court may admit evidence of the declarant's inconsistent statement or conduct, regardless of when it occurred or whether the declarant had an opportunity to explain or deny it. If the party against whom the statement was admitted calls the declarant as a witness, the party may examine the declarant on the statement as if on cross-examination.

The methods allowed for this impeachment are parallel to those permitted when a witness testifies in person during a trial. Evidence is admissible that the declarant was convicted of a crime, with the same restrictions that apply to an in-court witness's impeachment. Similarly, evidence is admissible showing that the declarant had a bias that could have affected the statement as well as evidence relating to the declarant's ability to have perceived what he spoke about. Evidence can be introduced showing the character of the declarant for untruthfulness, and also for truthfulness, in instances where evidence of character for untruthfulness is first introduced.

When a witness testifies in person, inquiry is permitted during cross-examination about past bad acts that did not lead to criminal conviction but

Chart 19 Summary: Prior Statements by a Witness

Purpose and Type of Statement	Does witness testify about past facts?	Can jury rely on witness's testimony about past facts?	Can jury rely on record or past statement about past facts?
Substitute for Testimony Past Recollection Recorded – FRE 803(5)	No (has impaired memory)	No	Yes
Substitute for Testimony Prior Inconsistent Statement for Substantive Use – FRE 801(d)(1)(A)	Yes	Yes	Yes
Substitute for, or Supplement to Testimony Prior Statement Identifying a Person – FRE 801(d)(1)(C)	Yes or No	Yes	Yes
Supplement to Testimony Prior Consistent Statement – FRE 801(d)(2)(B)	Yes	Yes	Yes
To Scrutinize Testimony Prior Inconsistent Statement for Impeachment Use – FRE 613(b)	Yes	Yes	No
To Stimulate Testimony Present Recollection Refreshed (with a writing) – FRE 612	Yes (after memory is refreshed)	Yes	No

that might still reflect on the witness's truthfulness. No parallel procedure is possible for hearsay declarants since they are not present in court and cannot be asked about their past conduct. If, however, the declarant is available and can be a witness, then impeachment with inquiries about past bad acts would be possible.

Rule 806 also covers the use of inconsistent statements. Usually, they may be introduced only if the witness is given an opportunity at some time in the trial to explain or deny them. In the case of a hearsay declarant who had made a statement out of court that was inconsistent with the hearsay statement that was introduced, evidence of the inconsistent statement is admissible without regard to the usual rule that requires an opportunity for the speaker to explain the earlier statement. According to the literal words of the rule, there is no requirement that the additional statement have been made earlier than the time of the already introduced hearsay statement.

Examples

1. The losing party in a civil case seeks to have a new trial ordered on the ground of jury misconduct. He has found out that at the start of deliberations, the jurors agreed to have a brief period of silent prayer. A juror would be willing to testify that the foreman had recommended that the jurors "seek Divine guidance" in their work. Should the trial judge permit this testimony?

2. In a suit seeking damages for personal injury, the plaintiff testified that she was hurt in the lobby of a bank when someone entering the bank pushed a door open, toward the inside of the lobby, and banged it into her. At the close of direct examination, the judge said to the witness, "I use that bank all the time, and it's got revolving doors into the lobby, no regular doors that you push open. Are you sure you're remembering this right?" What evidentiary problems are raised by the judge's conduct?

3. The defendant, accused of embezzling money from a church at which he worked, testified in his own defense. Prior to testifying, he affirmed his intention to tell the truth but did not swear an oath of truthfulness. Is "Tell us why you wouldn't swear on the Bible to tell the truth" a permissible inquiry on cross-examination?

4. A defendant is accused of attacking a victim with a baseball bat. A prosecution witness testifies, "The defendant beat up the victim with a baseball bat. I know that because everyone in the neighborhood has heard about it." Is there a reasonable objection to this testimony?

5. In an assault and battery trial, a prosecution witness testifies, "I know the defendant beat up the victim. I saw them go into a small storeroom together, and then I saw the defendant run out. Then I went in and found the victim all bruised and bloody." Is this testimony admissible?

6. A janitor is accused of thefts from a nursery school. The prosecution seeks to introduce testimony by a five-year-old child. If permitted to testify, the child will say that about a year ago he saw the janitor take a computer from a classroom. If the defense was aware that the child has a vivid imagination and has told numerous lies to playmates, how might it attempt to keep the child from testifying?

7. Assume that someone who has seen a crime committed is going to be hypnotized by the police in an effort to help the person remember more details. Why would it help that person's potential availability as a witness at a trial involving the crime if a tape recording had been made of his or her answers to questions about the event prior to the hypnosis and of the hypnosis session itself?

8. Allan Anders and Ellen Anders are husband and wife. Allan is on trial for robbery. The prosecution seeks to compel testimony by Ellen about vehicles she might have seen parked outside her and Allan's house on the day of the robbery. Can Allan prevent her from testifying on the grounds of spousal incompetency? Can Ellen refuse to testify on that theory? Could the prosecution refute a claim of spousal incompetency with evidence showing that the Allan and Ellen's marriage was unstable and that they had been separated from time to time during recent years?

9. In a robbery trial, a defense witness testifies about the defendant's whereabouts on the date of the crime. On cross-examination, the prosecution asks whether the defendant had experienced a sudden need for a large sum of money on the day prior to the robbery. Is that question permissible on cross-examination?

10. In a prosecution involving a tax return with false statements, the government is seeking to convict the tax preparer, claiming that he listed charitable contributions on his client's return even though the client never told him he had made any. If a witness for the prosecution was the defendant tax preparer's client, could the prosecutor ask: "Did you tell the defendant you had made no charitable contributions?"

11. Prosecutors believe that a defendant committed a sexual assault on a young child on a certain date in a certain location. They have evidence that the child and the defendant were seen on that date in that location. A few days after that date, the child told law enforcement officials that there had been a sexual assault. A year later the child recanted and said that there had never been an assault. What issues are raised if the prosecution has the child testify in its case against the defendant, knowing that the child will say no sexual assault took place and planning to then impeach the child with evidence of the earlier report of an assault?

12. In a rape trial, the alleged victim testifies that on the night of the alleged attack:
    a. she spent some time with the defendant at a bar;
    b. the bar was very crowded and had a band playing loud music;
    c. she was wearing a dress she had bought at Kmart two years earlier; and

   d. the defendant surprised her by attacking her in the bar's parking lot and forcing her to have sexual intercourse.

  The defendant testifies that the plaintiff's recollection is incorrect and that they had consensual sexual intercourse in the parking lot. The defendant has other witnesses available who would testify that:

   e. there was no band at the bar that night; and

   f. Kmart had stopped selling dresses of the type worn by the alleged victim at least four years before the night of the alleged attack. Should testimony by these other defense witnesses be admitted?

13. Vilma Vane is a criminal defendant charged with the crime of extortion (threatening an alleged victim with violence to obtain something of value).

   a. If she does not testify in her defense, can she put on a witness to testify that she has a reputation for being respectful of other people's property?

   b. If she does not testify in her defense, can she put on a witness to testify that she has a reputation for truthfulness?

   c. If Vane does testify, can she then put on a witness to testify that she has a reputation for truthfulness?

   d. If Vane testifies and the prosecution cross-examines her, showing that she has been convicted in the past of perjury, can Vane then put on a witness to testify that she has a reputation for truthfulness?

14. William Worsted is on trial for car theft. He testifies that he did not commit the crime. The prosecution has evidence that he was convicted in the past of car theft and was released from a prison sentence for that crime nine years before the trial. Can the prosecution introduce this evidence?

15. How would it affect the analysis in Example 14 if the trial court thought Worsted's testimony was crucial to the defense and also knew that the prosecution had no means to discredit it other than the evidence of the past car theft conviction?

16. In a breach of contract case, the plaintiff testifies that machinery supplied by the defendant failed to operate as well as the defendant had claimed it would.

   a. If the defendant knows that the plaintiff was once fired from work as a security guard because he was caught stealing merchandise from a warehouse, would questions about that past theft be proper on cross-examination?

   b. To impeach the plaintiff's credibility, can the defendant introduce testimony by the plaintiff's former employers stating that he had stolen merchandise from them?

17. Frank First testifies at a trial. During cross-examination, he is impeached with evidence that he has been convicted of perjury. Another witness, Sandra Second, then testifies that in recent years First has had a reputation in his community as a truthful person.
    a. In cross-examining Second, can the cross-examiner ask whether she has heard about conduct by First, such as cheating on his income taxes, that is inconsistent with truth-telling?
    b. In cross-examining Second, can the cross-examiner ask whether she knows that First was convicted 20 years ago of embezzlement?

18. A witness who testifies about another witness's character for truthfulness is permitted to use two different bases for testimony: what the witness knows about the first witness's reputation for truthfulness and what the witness thinks personally about the first witness's character for truthfulness. If a cross-examiner of a character witness knew that the witness about whom the character witness had testified once was seen stealing money from a church collection box, could the cross-examiner ask a question about that conduct no matter what type of character evidence the witness had given, or would the choice of reputation or opinion testimony affect the availability of cross-examination about the stealing?

19. In a shoplifting prosecution, the state produces two witnesses. One says she thinks she saw the defendant stealing something from a store but that she's not sure whether it was the defendant or someone else. Another witness testifies that he is sure the shoplifter was not the defendant. May the prosecution impeach that second witness with evidence of a written statement by him saying that he had figured out that the defendant had been shoplifting?

20. If the only evidence introduced by the state in Example 19 (shoplifting) is the testimony by the two witnesses and whatever use is allowed for the prior statement, should the judge let the case go to the jury?

21. Alice Anders sought damages from the seller of a condominium apartment, contending that the apartment was smaller than the seller had represented it to be and that it had a terrible odor. She testified that she had bought the apartment without inspecting it and that the defendant had concealed its true size and smell. The defendant has a copy of a letter Anders wrote to a friend a few months after buying the apartment: It says, "I'm living in my new apartment now. It's smaller than I thought it would be, but I like it anyhow." Might the defendant want to introduce that letter, and if so, should it be admitted?

Explanations

1. Testimony by jurors about their deliberations is forbidden unless it relates to "extraneous" or "outside" influences brought to bear on their work. No inquiry is permitted into the mental processes of a juror, and no testimony about those thoughts is allowed. In this problem, the jurors themselves might consider the divine guidance to originate outside the jury room. However, because it only involves individual thoughts and feelings of jurors, it would not be the type of outside information or influence allowed to be a subject of testimony by a juror.

2. The judge should not ask this type of question since the opposing party will have an opportunity to bring in a variety of evidence about what kinds of doors the bank has in its lobby. The justification for judicial questioning that is the strongest, a need to clarify the record or make a witness's testimony as clear as possible, does not apply here because the judge's effort was to contradict, not to clarify. Additionally, the judge's remarks are equivalent to testifying. He has brought factual information to the jury's attention, but the rules prohibit the judge from being a witness in a case over which he is presiding.

3. No. First of all, witnesses are allowed, under the Federal Rules, to swear or affirm that they will testify truthfully. To allow a negative implication from the choice of one of the two explicitly provided options would functionally eliminate the availability of the option to affirm rather than to give an oath. Secondly, FRE 610 precludes references to a witness's religious beliefs with respect to credibility.

4. The testimony should be stricken. The witness does not have personal knowledge of the defendant's conduct. The witness only has personal knowledge of what people in the neighborhood think happened. Additionally, if offered to prove that what the neighborhood people say happened actually is what happened, the testimony would be inadmissible on hearsay grounds as well.

5. This testimony is acceptable. With regard to the requirement of personal knowledge, all the Federal Rules require is that there be evidence adequate to support a jury finding that the witness has personal knowledge of the subject of his or her testimony. In this problem, even though the witness did not see the beating, the witness did personally see everything that the testimony states about who was present, where they went, and what happened. The statement, "I know the defendant beat up the victim," is arguably an opinion rather than a report of clear-cut information. It would, however, probably be allowed as a natural summary of what the witness really did observe.

6. The defense could argue that the child's testimony will fail to fulfill the personal knowledge requirement on the ground that because of the child's past inability to separate fact from fiction, it cannot provide a basis for a belief that she has knowledge about the subject of her testimony. It is possible that the defense could also be persuasive in arguing that the child cannot satisfy the obligation of affirming or swearing to tell the truth if it appears that the child does not know what truth is. The past lies would not be particularly helpful to the defense because there is no general bar to testimony from frequent liars. Rather, the defense would have to rely on the child's proven imagination and difficulty (if any) in separating truth from fantasy to suggest that the requirements of personal knowledge and a promise to tell the truth are not satisfied.

7. Most courts reject testimony by a witness who has been hypnotized on the theory that the hypnosis creates a risk that the witness will think he or she knows something that was really only suggested during the hypnosis. For this reason the testimony can be rejected on grounds of lack of personal knowledge or on the ground in criminal cases, related to the constitution, that the prosecution has impermissibly facilitated the witness's identification of an individual. It is common, however, for courts to allow testimony by a person who had been hypnotized if the proponent of the witness can show that the testimony only repeats information the witness believed prior to the hypnosis and that the hypnosis session was not itself suggestive with regard to the topic of the witness's testimony. For these reasons, the tape recordings of what the witness knew in advance of the hypnosis and what went on during the hypnosis session would be valuable as a means of showing the court that the requirements for limited use of testimony by a formerly hypnotized witness had been met.

8. Under federal practice Allan has no power to keep his wife off the witness stand. In some states spousal incompetency may be invoked by either spouse. Under federal practice the witness-spouse is in control of whether or not to testify. Thus, in this problem, Ellen's assertion of spousal incompetency would be binding on the court. The prosecution's attempt to avoid the spousal incompetency would fail because the underlying policy of the doctrine is to avoid putting stress on marriages. Presumably a weak marriage is as deserving of state-sponsored assistance as is a strong marriage.

9. Questions on cross-examination are generally limited to topics covered in a witness's direct testimony. Since this defense witness only gave information about where the defendant was on a particular day, a question about the defendant's financial status would likely be treated

as beyond the scope of cross-examination. The "scope-of-direct" rule is subject to the judge's discretion, so the prosecutor would have to argue for relaxing the rule on these facts. If showing a motive was an important part of the prosecution case, the prosecutor should have located witnesses who could provide information relevant to that theory and should have included them in the state's direct case. If the court is persuaded that the prosecutor has acted in good faith, seeking witnesses on this issue, it might allow the question.

10. This is an improper leading question. The legitimate form for bringing out this information is a question like, "What did you tell the defendant, if anything, about charitable contributions?"

11. The Federal Rules allow any party to impeach any witness, rejecting the common law doctrine that a party must support its own witness's testimony. In this case, it is clear that the only reason the prosecution has for using the child as a witness is its plan to impeach the child's testimony with the child's earlier out-of-court statement. If that statement would otherwise be inadmissible (because of the bar against hearsay evidence), most courts would refuse to permit the prosecution to use the statement as impeachment material. Despite the literal requirements of the Federal Rule, most courts would hold that the prosecution in this case is only using the witness as part of a plan to avoid the restrictions of the hearsay doctrine. The freedom to impeach a party's own witness, courts usually hold, is meant to allow parties to use witnesses of unreliable truthfulness who have information on many topics; they can use those witnesses as sources for their information but can also try to control how the jury deals with the information. Where it is clear to the prosecution that the totality of a witness's testimony will be false, most courts prefer to rule in a way that leads the prosecution to keep the witness off the stand.

12. This problem requires an analysis of impeachment by contradiction, collateral matters, and impeachment by evidence related to the witness's ability to have perceived the things about which the witness has testified. The witness has testified that there was a band playing loudly at the bar and that the dress she had been wearing had been bought two years earlier at Kmart. Testimony by other witnesses that there was no band and that Kmart had sold those dresses four years earlier would contradict the complainant witness's testimony. A first step in analyzing the admissibility of the testimony is to apply the rule that prohibits extrinsic evidence of contradictory material if it is collateral. Would evidence about a band or about the date of a dress purchase be admissible in this trial, even if the complainant witness had not brought up those topics? Answering that question determines

whether the inquiries are "collateral." In this case, presence of a band and age of a dress are not relevant to prosecution for the crime of rape so they would properly be classified as collateral matters. This analysis provides a complete treatment of the offered testimony about the age of the dress. There is another aspect to the testimony about the presence or absence of a band, however. If a witness's mistakes of fact involve collateral matters, extrinsic evidence about them is not admissible unless a theory of relevance other than impeachment by contradiction is available. The witness's possible mistake about whether a band was playing might be relevant to show that her ability to perceive events that night was weak or impaired in some way. That would be a theory different from showing contradiction to imply bad memory or intentional lying. Proof of error about the band could also support a finding that the witness was unable to comprehend reality well at the time. For this reason, it would probably be admissible through the extrinsic evidence of the witness who would testify that no band was playing.

13. a. Yes. Under FRE 404(a)(2), a criminal defendant is permitted to introduce character evidence of a trait that is relevant to the charged offense. That rule would authorize her use of a witness to testify that she has a reputation for being respectful of people's property since that attitude towards property would be a trait "pertinent" to the charged offense.

   b. No. Evidence showing that she is likely to tell the truth would be relevant to her credibility in her role as a witness. Since Vane has not taken the stand, her credibility is not in issue, and a witness's testimony that Vane has a reputation for truthfulness would not be admissible. Her truthfulness is not pertinent to a crime of violence.

   c. No. A witness to bolster the credibility of another witness may not testify unless that other witness's credibility has been attacked.

   d. Yes. Once Vane has been impeached, as in this case by evidence of her past criminal conviction of a crime related to truth-telling, rehabilitating testimony in the form of reputation or opinion may be introduced to show that she has a character consistent with giving truthful testimony.

14. The prosecution's effort must be analyzed under the terms of Rule 609. The past crime is not one involving truth-telling. This means that its admissibility involves a balancing test. Under the rule, where the person sought to be impeached is a criminal defendant, evidence of the past conviction is only allowable if it will be more probative than prejudicial. If the conviction or date of release from confinement related to the conviction was ten years ago or more, then evidence about it can be introduced only if it is substantially more probative than prejudicial. Would a judge find that evidence of car theft is more probative than

prejudicial on the issue of truth-telling as a witness in court? The fact that the conviction's timing approaches the ten-year period that triggers the "substantially more probative" requirement would also be an element in the judge's thinking. Because the past offense is identical to the charged offense, the risk of prejudice is extremely high; a juror might well use the information about the prior conviction not to test the credibility of the defendant's particular testimony but rather to decide that since he's committed car theft before, he likely did it on the occasion involved in the current trial, too. Rule 609 clearly adopts the position that past felonies are related to current truth-telling, so it must be acknowledged that the car theft conviction has relevance to truth-telling at trial. However, the risk of prejudice is quite high and the conviction was a relatively long time prior to the current trial. These reasons suggest that the stronger argument favors rejecting the evidence.

15. Except for past convictions of crimes involving truth-telling, all treatment of a witness's past convictions in connection with the witness's credibility involves balancing tests relating the probative value and the risks of prejudice. If the witness's testimony is crucial, then discrediting it becomes highly important. Thus, the probative value of impeachment material increases. Similarly, if a challenged item of evidence is the only type of evidence its proponent has that speaks to a particular issue at trial, the probative value of that item is thought to be high. In this version of the car theft example, the probative value of impeaching the witness with evidence of his past car theft conviction would be quite high, and the evidence might properly be admitted. The trial judge can require that some of the details of the past crime be "sanitized" so that a limited description of the conviction is all that the jury hears.

16. a. Yes. Past bad acts, if they are relevant to a witness's truthfulness, can be inquired into on cross-examination. Stealing merchandise while in a position of trust such as security guard seems relevant to character for truthfulness, so questions about it would be proper.

    b. No. Extrinsic evidence of past bad acts is not permitted if their relevance is only to support an implication about the witness's character for truthfulness.

17. a. Yes. A witness who supports the credibility of another witness can be asked about knowledge of past conduct by the first witness if there is good faith basis for believing that the past conduct did occur and if that past conduct would contradict or modify the witness's description of the first witness's reputation for honesty.

    b. If Second's testimony was clearly limited to recent reputation, then the question would be improper. Events 20 years prior to the trial cannot be logically related to Second's reports of First's current reputation. If Second's testimony was not clearly limited to a recent time period, then the question about the old conviction would be allowable. Note that extrinsic evidence of this conviction would probably not be permitted since it is much more than ten years old and may not be substantially more probative than prejudicial. However, there is no time limit in the rules concerning inquiries about past bad conduct.

18. Most courts would allow the question in both situations. It can be argued, though, that if the character witness used reputation as the basis for testimony, a question about the stealing from a church collection box might not be proper. The most legitimate probings on cross-examination of a witness who reports someone's reputation are questions that confront the witness with contrary descriptions of the primary witness's reputation. Referring to particular conduct by the primary witness might not be allowed unless there was a good faith basis for the questioner to believe that knowledge of the conduct had become part of the person's reputation in the community. If, on the other hand, the character witness has used his or her own opinion about the primary witness as a basis for stating a belief about the primary witness's likely truth-telling, then questions about specific conduct of the primary witness would be proper. They show either that the witness does not really have a thorough basis for forming an opinion, or that the witness knows about the past conduct but has not reacted to it in a way that diminished his estimation of the likely truth-telling of the primary witness.

19. The prosecution may ask the witness about his prior contradictory statement, under the rules for prior inconsistent statements. If the prosecution wants to introduce the document, it must give the witness an opportunity to explain it at some time during the trial.

20. The judge should dismiss the case. The prior statement is admissible only as impeachment evidence; this means it is not an allowable basis for a substantive conclusion but can only be used to discredit the witness's statements. If the second witness's testimony is completely wiped out — the strongest allowable benefit to the prosecution from the impeachment evidence — the case for the prosecution would be too weak to support a conviction since it would consist only of a self-criticized eyewitness identification.

21. The theory for admissibility would be that it is a prior inconsistent statement. Its explicit content supports part of Anders's testimony. On the other hand, its silence on the subject of the apartment's odor might be deemed equivalent to a statement that size, not odor, was the problem with the apartment. Proof that a person said nothing about a

topic on an occasion when a comment would naturally have been expected can be treated identically to proof of a statement. In this case, the lack of a mention of a bad smell in the letter is contradictory to Anders's statement in court that the apartment had a bad smell. It could be inquired about in cross-examination, and the letter could be admitted without any hearsay problem because it is a statement by a party offered against that party.

6

Expert Testimony

INTRODUCTION

When resolving a disputed issue involves information or analysis beyond the knowledge or capabilities of a typical juror, parties are allowed to present testimony by expert witnesses. Unlike eyewitnesses or participants in events that are the subject of litigation, expert witnesses give testimony based on their own general experience and knowledge and are allowed to apply their expertise to the facts of the case.

The important issues connected with expert testimony involve determining (1) what *topics* are appropriate for this type of testimony, (2) *who* should be permitted to testify as an expert, (3) probable *reliability* of the testimony, (4) what types of *data* an expert may rely on to form an opinion, and (5) whether the *style* or form of the testimony should be restricted. As this chapter will discuss in detail, the Rules cover all these issues. A subject is appropriate for expert testimony if an expert's opinion on it would assist the trier of fact. A person can qualify as an expert witness by a showing of knowledge or experience. An expert's opinion can be based on any data that experts in the field ordinarily use, but it must apply reliable principles to sufficient data related to the case. An expert may state an opinion or conclusion based on the facts the expert believes to be true or may answer a hypothetical question that asks the expert to make assumptions. In criminal cases, an expert's freedom to state conclusions is narrowed: An expert may not testify specifically that a defendant did or did not have a mental state that is an element of a crime.

Topics for Expert Testimony

Using an expert witness involves costs and risks. For example, the testimony will take time, and jurors may give great deference to the observations of someone with significant professional qualifications. For these reasons, parties are permitted to introduce expert testimony only when the trial court is persuaded that jurors (or the court personally in a non-jury trial) will benefit from help on the topic for which the expert testimony is proposed. Rule 702 states:

> A witness who is qualified as an expert by knowledge, skill, experience, training, or education may testify in the form of an opinion or otherwise if:
>
> (a) the expert's scientific, technical, or other specialized knowledge will help the trier of fact to understand the evidence or to determine a fact in issue;
>
> (b) the testimony is based on sufficient facts or data;
>
> (c) the testimony is the product of reliable principles and methods; and
>
> (d) the expert has reliably applied the principles and methods to the facts of the case.

Sometimes the substantive law underlying a dispute makes it clear that expert testimony will be required, as in medical malpractice suits where a plaintiff must establish that the defendant's treatment fell below a professional standard of care. In other instances, reasonable assumptions about the common knowledge of jurors make it clear that without information from an expert, jurors would be unable to reach conclusions. Experts' knowledge would be necessary to prove whether something found in a defendant's possession was an illegal drug or to establish that a product's design was likely to facilitate misuse.

There are some topics on which there is a dispute about whether expert testimony should be admissible. Some social scientists have conducted research on the reliability of eyewitness observations. They believe that crime victims or witnesses to crimes are likely to overestimate their certainty when they think they have identified an individual as a person who committed the crime. Where the identification is of a person whose race is different from the race of the person who does the identifying, some social scientists believe that the rate of incorrect identification is high. Defense lawyers in cases where identification of an individual is crucial often seek to introduce testimony by experts familiar with this research. A court faced with this issue must decide whether jurors can evaluate the risks of incorrect identification by eyewitnesses on the basis of their own knowledge and experience, or whether information from experts would help them reach a better conclusion about the reliability of an identification. Trial courts have been affirmed for either admitting or rejecting offered testimony of this type.

Courts uniformly reject offers of expert testimony on the issue of whether a witness in a case has testified truthfully. Deciding the credibility of witnesses is usually described as the "province of the jury," and that province is typically protected from being "invaded." Nonetheless, there is a trend to admit expert testimony about various syndromes in ways that may be close to the traditionally forbidden expert commentary on truthfulness. For example, "rape trauma syndrome" is widely considered to be a subject on which expert testimony may be admitted. An expert may testify that the statements or behavior of the alleged victim of rape are consistent with those of other rape victims. A common position courts take on this type of testimony is to admit it to provide an explanation for delayed reporting of the rape, where delayed reporting is suggested by the defense to indicate that the claimed sexual intercourse did not occur. Courts have stated that jurors can benefit from scientific explanations of the significance or prevalence of delayed reports of sex crimes, and that without such expert information jurors might be less able to evaluate what they learn about the alleged victim's delay in reporting the crime. This type of expert testimony may come close to being a statement by the expert that the expert believes the complainant. However, if it were characterized that way, virtually all courts would exclude it.

Cases involving alleged assaults against children also involve syndrome testimony. Experts may testify that a child's statements are consistent with those of children who have been abused. This testimony would be kept out if the rationale for its admission was that it supports the credibility of the alleged victim's testimony. However, it often is admitted on the theory that it provides a scientific assessment of the likelihood that an assault took place, based in part on the victim's own words and their believability and in part on the comparison of those words with the patterns of past cases involving other children.

Qualification as an Expert

The Federal Rules are extremely broad in their definition of how a person may qualify as an expert witness. Rule 702 refers to education, experience, and other attributes that can justify treating a witness as an expert. At one extreme, in a case where a crucial issue was whether a particular sample of marijuana had been grown inside or outside of the United States, an "expert" was permitted to testify that it was foreign-grown, based on his frequent experience in smoking Colombian marijuana and in selling that and other types of marijuana.[1] More conventionally, witnesses qualify as

---

1. United States v. Johnson, 575 F.2d 1347 (5th Cir. 1979).

expert witnesses on the basis of their education and legitimate work experience.

Just how specifically a person's experience and training must relate to the topic of testimony is an issue on which trial courts have great discretion. In products liability cases, for example, a manufacturer will often contend that the only truly appropriate witness to testify about safety aspects of its product is someone who has designed that particular type of product. A plaintiff in such a case will often seek to qualify a person with general experience in product design as an expert. Obviously, if courts held that an expert must be someone who has worked on the specific type of product that allegedly harmed the plaintiff, the supply of experts would be reduced. On the other hand, if courts are extremely permissive in allowing generalists to testify as experts, or in allowing witnesses with expertise in one field to generalize and apply it to other fields, the value of the expert testimony will be considerably weakened. Courts often favor the admissibility of expert testimony, particularly because the opponent of a party who uses that type of testimony is free to counter it with opinions from rival experts.

Reliability

Even if a person is qualified as an "expert," his or her testimony must satisfy another requirement in order to be admissible. The testimony must have a certain degree of reliability. Courts have struggled with the tension between protecting the legal system from phony science and allowing litigants and jurors free access to all potentially helpful information.

Beginning in the 1920s, courts had applied a rule known as the *Frye* test, requiring the proponent of testimony based on scientific procedures to show that the procedures were generally accepted in their field.[2] In the *Frye* analysis, the consensus of scientists in the expert's field controlled the admissibility of the testimony. Testimony based on theories that were on the cutting edge of knowledge was rejected. This imposed a lag on the availability of current technical knowledge in trials, but it protected the process against using evidence that might later be discredited. The *Frye* test also made it relatively easy for opponents of scientific evidence to obtain rival experts to interpret and critique any scientific testimony that was admitted.

Current practice expands on the *Frye* test, on the basis of two U.S. Supreme Court decisions, *Daubert v. Merrell Dow Pharmaceuticals, Inc.*,[3] and *Kumho Tire Co. v. Carmichael.*[4] In a case involving scientific evidence (testimony

---

2. The test was originated in Frye v. United States, 293 F. 1013 (D.C. Cir. 1923).
3. 509 U.S. 579 (1993).
4. 526 U.S. 137 (1999).

of an epidemiologist about claimed harmful effects of a drug), the *Daubert* court established new requirements for admission of scientific evidence.

Under *Daubert*, a court must determine the admissibility of scientific evidence by evaluating the validity of two separate aspects of the evidence: (1) its scientific method and (2) the application of that method to the factual inquiry under consideration. Experimental or scientific testimony must be based on a principle that supports what the testimony purports to show. Also, another type of validity is required, the production of consistent results from repeated applications of the principle. The *Daubert* court provided a nonexclusive checklist for these inquiries. A court may analyze the following aspects of an expert's theory or technique:

1. Can it be tested, and if it can be tested, has that testing taken place?
2. Has it been described in scientific publications subject to peer review?
3. What are its known or potential error rates?
4. Are there standards that can control its operation, and if so, were they used in developing the expert's testimony?
5. Has it achieved some degree of acceptance in a relevant community?

In *Kumho Tire*, the court held that *Daubert* applies to all expert testimony, not just expert testimony based on science. It also reiterated that not all of the factors set out in *Daubert* need be applied in every case and that factors other than those can also be used by a trial court in assessing reliability of expert testimony.

The language in Rule 702 that refers to reliable principles and methods and the reliable application of those principles and methods became effective after the decisions in *Daubert* and *Kumho Tire*. It specifies that the trial judge must apply gatekeeping inquiries of three types to all expert testimony based on scientific principles or other kinds of technical expertise. The trial court must assess the sufficiency of the expert's underlying data, the reliability of the expert's methods, and the reliability of the expert's application of those methods to the facts of the case. Decisions on the admissibility of expert testimony are reviewed under the "abuse of discretion" standard,[5] so they will rarely be reversed.

Opponents of expert testimony that they characterize as based on "fringe" or "junk" science can argue against its admissibility in terms of its topic, the training of the proposed expert, and the reliability of the expert's methods and application of those methods. For example, if an accused bank robber sought to introduce testimony by a psychic that a person with an appearance different from his had committed the crime, a court would reject that testimony. Applying Rule 702, it might say that the

---

5. *General Elec. Co. v. Joiner*, 522 U.S. 136 (1997).

topic of the proposed witness's testimony is not one on which specialized knowledge can assist the trier of fact in determining whether the defendant committed the crime. The basis for this would be a belief that psychics are frauds. The court might say that the proposed psychic is not an expert psychic, since there is no legitimate field in which people can obtain training or recognition as psychics.

Finally, the court might say that the proposed expert's basis for having an opinion — psychic feelings — is not reliable enough. Using the *Daubert* factors, a court would likely conclude that psychic feelings cannot be tested, have not been documented in publications subject to peer review, do not have known error rates, are not used with controls, and have not gained acceptance in some significant community. This would support a ruling that the testimony is not based on sufficient facts or data, that it is not the product of reliable principles and methods, and that it is not based on a reliable application of reliable principles to the facts of the case.

Thus, testimony from a psychic about who robbed a bank would be rejected on three bases: Psychic evaluation of robbers' identities is not a field of knowledge that can help a jury decide who robbed a bank; the proposed witness is not a qualified psychic because there can be no such thing as a qualified psychic; and the witness's testimony would not be the product of reliable methods that the witness applied reliably to the facts of the case.

Type of Data

Rule 702 requires an expert's testimony to be based on "sufficient facts or data." In attempting to satisfy that requirement, an expert may rely on information from a variety of sources, including material that would not be admissible in evidence. Rule 703 provides:

> An expert may base an opinion on facts or data in the case that the expert has been made aware of or personally observed. If experts in the particular field would reasonably rely on those kinds of facts or data in forming an opinion on the subject, they need not be admissible for the opinion to be admitted. But if the facts or data would otherwise be inadmissible, the proponent of the opinion may disclose them to the jury only if their probative value in helping the jury evaluate the opinion substantially outweighs their prejudicial effect.

The expert is entitled to state an opinion based on facts he or she believes to be true because of what the expert has seen or heard at the current trial or based on facts the expert believes to be true because of observations outside the trial. Rule 705 allows the court to require disclosure of the data relied on by the expert.

With regard to testimony that is based on information the expert obtains other than by observing the trial, the rule makes it clear that there is no requirement that this information be admissible in evidence so long as it is the type of data that experts in the field reasonably rely on in forming opinions. A medical expert, for example, could base testimony on X-rays that the expert had seen outside of court even if technical rules would preclude admission of the X-ray films as evidence, if the trial court had a basis for believing that experts typically consider that type of X-ray reliable. An assessor of real estate could testify about the value of a house even if the testimony was based in part on hearsay statements by people who lived in the neighborhood where the house is located, if relying on statements of that kind is reasonable conduct in the field of real estate appraising.

Rule 703 is written to avoid a situation where a litigant might seek to have an expert rely on inadmissible facts or data mainly for the purpose of bringing that otherwise inadmissible evidence to the attention of the jury. The rule assumes that an expert can usually state his or her opinion without revealing the underlying information. It controls the disclosure of otherwise inadmissible information that is a basis for an expert's opinion with a balancing test administered by the court. An expert will be allowed to disclose otherwise inadmissible facts or data if their value in assisting the jury to evaluate the expert's opinion substantially outweighs their prejudicial effect on the opponent's case.

Style of Testimony

Expert witnesses may state their opinions and conclusions in any way they choose, subject only to a limitation in criminal cases that prevents them from saying explicitly whether a defendant possessed a specific mental state that is an element of a charged crime. Rule 704, "Opinion on an Ultimate Issue," provides:

> **(a) In General — Not Automatically Objectionable.** An opinion is not objectionable just because it embraces an ultimate issue.
> **(b) Exception.** In a criminal case, an expert witness must not state an opinion about whether the defendant did or did not have a mental state or condition that constitutes an element of the crime charged or of a defense. Those matters are for the trier of fact alone.

The basis of the expert's opinion does not have to be stated when the expert gives it, but when the expert is cross-examined, he or she must reveal the underlying data if asked about it. In prior practice, experts were sometimes required to give testimony in the form of answers to hypothetical questions. The questioner would state a long series of hypothetical conditions and then ask the expert for an opinion about the consequences of those conditions. If it later turned out that supporting evidence was deficient for any element of the hypothetical question, the jury would be prohibited from relying on the expert's opinion.

Hypothetical questions were used to prevent the jury from believing that the facts treated by the expert as true were really true just because the expert believed them. However, appellate courts were sometimes required to order new trials because a careful analysis of a long hypothetical question and the whole trial record showed that some minor premise in the question had not been supported by evidence. Also, use of these long questions may have made it hard for the jury to understand fully what the expert really believed. The drafters of the Federal Rules chose to reject the requirement of hypothetical questions to avoid unnecessary appellate reversals, and because they believed jurors could themselves decide whether an expert's opinion was well enough related to established facts to be persuasive.

An expert is permitted to state an opinion on an ultimate issue in a case with the exception of issues of mental state in criminal cases. Some common law jurisdictions prohibit statements on ultimate issues, but it is difficult to define "ultimate issues." The Rules generally avoid the complications that a limitation can present. The criminal case exception in Rule 704(b) was added in 1984 following John Hinckley's acquittal of the charge of attempted assassination of President Ronald Reagan. It apparently is an effort to reduce the potential impact of psychiatric testimony in criminal cases. An expert on mental health can testify about definitions of mental states, symptoms, and methodologies for making diagnoses and can describe "facts." However, the testimony is improper if it crosses a vague line to make a specific statement about the crucial mental state of the defendant that is at issue in the criminal prosecution.

Examples

1. The seller of a house is sued for fraud on the claim that she intentionally failed to disclose that the house had suffered severe termite damage a few years before the sale. The seller is 75 years old. Should the trial judge allow the seller to introduce testimony from a psychologist to show that as people get older, their memories become weaker?

2. A plaintiff seeks damages for personal injury from the owner of an amusement park ride that stopped suddenly and threw him out of his seat. The plaintiff's theory is that a part of the ride's drive motor suddenly broke, causing the motor to stop. The plaintiff seeks to introduce testimony about the motor from a person who has worked as an elevator mechanic for 20 years but never graduated from college or from any technical training program. How should the court analyze an objection to

this testimony made on the ground that the person is not qualified to testify as an expert?

3. In a tort action, the plaintiff accuses the defendant of having punched him and kicked him in the parking lot of a bar. The defendant denies that any contact occurred. On cross-examination of the plaintiff, the defendant's lawyer establishes that the plaintiff told no one about being harmed until several weeks after the attack allegedly had taken place. The plaintiff seeks to have a psychologist who has studied war veterans testify that the plaintiff, a war veteran, suffers from posttraumatic shock syndrome. The psychologist would also testify that a consequence of posttraumatic stress is a reluctance to talk about violence and a fear that reporting violence will lead to additional harm. Should the testimony be admitted?

4. A passenger in a private plane was injured when the plane crashed during an attempted landing, and later files suit against the manufacturer of the plane. To establish the cause of the crash, the passenger offers testimony by a former Federal Aviation Administration crash investigator who studied the crash using the methods he had used in his prior work for the government. The witness will testify that the pilot flew the plane properly and that the crash must have therefore been due to a mechanical malfunction. The witness will base that conclusion on interviews he conducted with airport personnel who saw the crash and on his general experience in aviation. Statements by the airline personnel who saw the crash would be hearsay if they were quoted at trial by a witness. Is it permissible for the expert to base conclusions on those same statements?

5. Can a medical expert witness state an opinion that a defendant doctor's conduct fell below the standard of care typically exercised by practitioners in the defendant's specialty, or must the expert describe the typical standard of care, describe what the defendant did, and leave it to the jury to analyze those facts to reach a conclusion?

6. Can a medical expert state an opinion that a criminal defendant who admits the conduct for which he or she is charged lacked the capacity to intend the conduct and its consequences and therefore did not have the intentionality required by the relevant statute as an element of the charged crime?

7. A disputed issue at a trial is whether paint applied to the exterior of a building 20 years ago caused deterioration in the building's brick walls. All parties agree that the walls are deteriorated, but they dispute the cause of the problem. What issues are raised by efforts to introduce each of the following types of testimony?
   a. A professor of materials science who has worked in the field of building materials and their durability for 20 years seeks to testify that the

type of damage found in the building is caused by internal flaws in the bricks and not by coatings applied to bricks.

b. An artist who makes ceramic sculptures and has experience in painting them and applying other coatings to them seeks to testify that paint does not harm surfaces in the way that the building has been damaged.

c. An expert in public opinion polling who conducted a survey of people who work near the damaged building seeks to testify that the majority of them believe that the paint caused the damage.

d. A chemist who specializes in analyzing bricks and paint seeks to testify that she performed widely used standard tests on the bricks. The witness seeks to testify that the tests show that the paint had no effect on the bricks.

e. A physicist is an expert in the use of high energy particle accelerators to conduct biochemical medical research. He has examined a brick from the building in the accelerator and is prepared to testify that although no other physicist has ever conducted such an experiment, the response of the brick in the accelerator can reasonably be evaluated in comparison to the results of biochemistry experiments. The physicist will state that the results show that the brick itself was flawed regardless of any effect the paint may have had.

f. An anthropologist who has studied witchcraft seeks to testify that she brought a live chicken to the building site, spoke to it about the problem, and then saw the chicken turn away from the building repeatedly. In the cultures the anthropologist has studied, this type of conduct by the chicken indicates that the bricks, not the paint, were bad.

Explanations

1. Probably not. Jurors can understand themselves that people suffer from weakened memories as they age. The offer of an expert witness must involve a subject on which expertise will be helpful to the jurors. If the defendant in this case claimed that a disease had impaired her memory, that claim would be different from reliance on the general effects of aging. Jurors could properly be given help from an expert witness about a specific disease even though information about what happens to people when they get old would likely be thought of as too well-known to be a permissible subject of expert testimony.

2. The witness's lack of technical training or a college degree is not dispositive since the Federal Rules recognize that a person can obtain expertise through "experience" and "skill" as well as by education. The court should focus on how closely the witness's knowledge relates to the

type of issue on which he is being offered as a witness. For example, the court would need to know whether elevator motors are the same type, generally, as the motor on the amusement ride. Also, the court would need to know whether control devices and electrical components are similar in rides and elevators. If there are substantial similarities, the court should qualify the witness as an expert. If a court held that a person must have experience on amusement park rides specifically to be allowed to testify about them, this would impose a severe limitation on the number of potential witnesses. There is no reason to impose that significant a bar so long as knowledge about elevators, in this example, is related to the type of malfunction alleged in the case.

3. Yes. Jurors might ordinarily assume that someone who had been beaten up in a bar's parking lot would complain about it to friends or others immediately. If there is a reason for silence, such as the effects of armed forces experience, that a typical juror would not know about in the absence of information from an expert, testimony by the expert should be admitted. Note that the expert's testimony will contradict the implication that because the victim did not complain promptly, no attack was committed against the victim. This supports the victim's testimony but is different from an expert's statement that the victim is a truthful person in general.

4. Yes. An expert is allowed to rely on information in his or her testimony whether or not that information would ordinarily be admissible in evidence. The information must, however, be a type of information usually relied on by people in the expert's field. In this case, if the expert could persuade the court that air crash investigators reasonably rely on statements from people who work at airports, the testimony would be admissible. Ordinary eyewitness statements are not permitted to be used as a basis for expert testimony, according to the legislative history of the rule, but airport personnel would probably be treated differently from casual observers.

5. An expert may state a conclusion even if it is an "ultimate issue" in the case. This allows the expert to speak more naturally and to give a description of his or her opinion in a manner that might closely resemble a lecture or a discussion. If the expert were prohibited from stating a conclusion on whatever were defined as ultimate issues, the testimony might be interrupted more frequently by objections and would likely be artificially constrained in how its ideas were expressed.

6. No. Unlike the medical expert referred to in Example 5, the expert witness in a criminal case is prohibited from stating conclusions about the defendant's mental state in connection with any required element of the charged crime. Recall that this limitation is explicit in Rule 704(b).

7. a. Because of his or her experience, the professor is qualified to form and state an opinion about the source of the damage.

   b. Admissibility of testimony by the artist is a closer question than admissibility of the professor's testimony. The judge would need to consider evidence, perhaps from the artist personally or from other witnesses, about the similarities between bricks and the ceramics with which the artist is experienced. If the field of sculpture was related enough to the topic of brick degradation so that information from the first field could make conclusions about the second field more likely than they would have been without the information based on experience with sculptures, a relevancy test would be satisfied, and the artist's expert opinion would be admissible.

   c. This evidence must be kept out. No matter how accurate the poll is, it still reflects only the opinions of non-experts about the bricks and the paint. Ideas possessed by people in the neighborhood about the cause of the problem have no relevance to determining the cause of the problem. Therefore, even if the ideas are collected and organized with good social science techniques, they must be kept out of the trial.

   d. All courts would admit this testimony. A person whose expertise is squarely consistent with the subject matter at trial seeks to testify on the basis of a generally accepted test. This satisfies Rule 702's requirements that a witness use reliable methods and that the witness apply the methods reliably to the facts of the case. To show that the testimony is based on sufficient facts or data, the chemist would likely testify that she performed the tests on actual bricks that were involved in the lawsuit.

   e. The physicist seeks to use a scientific technique that has been established in biochemistry in a field to which it has not previously been applied — brick and paint interactions. The proponent of the physicist's testimony would have to show that the particle accelerator method is itself reliable, and would have to provide a basis for the court to conclude that the technique can be applied to the analysis of bricks and paint with some degree of reliability, even though the technique is ordinarily used for other purposes. Rule 702's requirement that testimony be based on adequate facts or data is intertwined with the question of reliability of the experiment. If a court concludes that the experiment is too unrelated to analysis of bricks and paint to permit the testimony, then it would not have to consider whether the experiment had produced enough data. If a court concludes that the physicist's medical techniques could reliably be used on questions about bricks and paint, then the court would have to be persuaded that it had produced adequate data in this specific instance to be helpful to the trier of fact.

f. The methodology employed by the anthropologist is too far outside the current culture of the United States, both in terms of popular culture and scientific culture, to be acceptable. It illustrates the difference between a "far-out" adaptation of recognized techniques, on the one hand, and techniques that are themselves "far-out" on the other.

Privileges

INTRODUCTION

Privileges give special treatment — a cloak of secrecy — to a variety of confidential communications such as those made in the relationships of lawyer and client, husband and wife, or priest and penitent. The Federal Rules include a general rule on this subject. Rule 501 states:

> The common law — as interpreted by United States courts in the light of reason and experience — governs a claim of privilege unless any of the following provides otherwise:
>
> - the United States Constitution;
> - a federal statute; or
> - rules prescribed by the Supreme Court.
>
> But in a civil case, state law governs privilege regarding a claim or defense for which state law supplies the rule of decision.

As originally drafted, the Rules contained detailed privilege definitions. Congress rejected that approach in part because of controversy that had arisen over executive privilege in the context of the then recent Watergate crisis.

Information conveyed in a privileged communication cannot be brought into a trial and cannot be a subject for discovery even though the statement may be relevant to a disputed issue. In the lawyer-client context, for example, a client can refuse to answer a question like, "What did you tell your lawyer?" The client is also entitled to prevent the lawyer from revealing what the client said. Similarly, a letter written by the client to the lawyer will not be admissible.

Only the actual statements made in confidential relationships are kept secret by privileges. Suppose that a client had said to his lawyer, "I knocked down a telephone pole while I was driving my red car." The client could not be asked (at a trial), "What did you tell your lawyer about the telephone pole and your car?" However, the lawyer-client privilege would not block questions like, "Did you knock down a telephone pole?" or "What color is your car?" The privilege protects against revealing the *statements* that a person makes privately to his or her lawyer. It does not protect against revealing the *information* a client knows, whether or not the client may have communicated that information in privileged conversations. The privilege prohibits questions that would call for answers like, "My client told me his car is red," or "I told my lawyer my car is red." The privilege permits a question that calls for the answer, "My car is red." If information can be developed in ways that do not involve reliance on a communication made in a confidential relationship, privilege doctrines have no effect. They keep secret the fact that the information was discussed but they do not make the information itself a secret.

Like the special relevance rules for character or subsequent remedial measures, privileges represent a social choice that particular goals should overcome the general premise that relevant evidence is admissible. The most widely accepted rationale for evidentiary privileges is a utilitarian analysis, that the communications are socially desirable and that people would be less likely to make them if they were not privileged. In the lawyer-client case, the utilitarian argument would be that the society as a whole benefits when the frequency of people's consultation with lawyers increases. Also, people who need advice about complicated transactions or other events might decline to seek it if they thought that the words they spoke to lawyers could be used against them sometime later at trials. Besides the utilitarian point of view, two other explanations are sometimes given. One is that privileges reflect a recognition that the state should not intrude in certain personal relationships. In contrast, another theory argues that rather than showing government's sensitivity to privacy, privileges show government's interest in corrupting the search for truth to benefit powerful social groups such as lawyers.

Although there are many different privileges, they all involve certain basic issues. Did the communication take place within the relationship required for the privilege? Was it confidential? Who is entitled to claim the privilege? Has the proponent of the privilege waived its benefit by acting in ways that destroyed the confidentiality it is meant to provide? Does the communication involve a topic for which the protection of the privilege is removed to serve other social interests? This chapter discusses the general issues in connection with the details of the lawyer-client privilege. The chapter then covers significant aspects of other privileges such as those for communications between husband and wife, doctor and patient, psychotherapist and patient, priest and penitent, and informer and the government.

Attorney-Client Privilege

When a client talks or writes to a lawyer, the client's communications are protected by the lawyer-client privilege, provided that certain conditions related to the basic utilitarian justifications for the privilege are met. There must be a genuine lawyer-client relationship, the client must have a reasonable expectation of privacy in the communication, the client must have preserved the confidentiality of the communication after making it, the topic of the communication must be connected with obtaining legal counsel, and the topic must not involve planning a crime.

Defining "Communication"

An initial question in some privilege claims is whether the client actually made a communication to the lawyer. Easy cases involve words spoken in person or by telephone or letters written to the lawyer. More complex are instances where a lawyer might be asked to describe whether a client seemed drunk or sober on a particular occasion or whether the client has a scar or other physical attribute. Courts faced with these problems have not reached uniform results, although the majority support requiring disclosure of aspects of the client's appearance that were visible to the lawyer and would have been visible to others who saw the client.

Testimony is sometimes sought from lawyers on the questions of the identity of their clients or of the source of payment for services on behalf of a particular client. Courts generally allow such inquiries on the theory that the identity of a client or the source of payment is not so closely related to the actual providing of legal services that requiring these disclosures would counter the overall goals of the lawyer-client privilege. However, where there are public policy reasons for keeping a client's identity secret, or where information on the client's identity or the source of funds for representation would provide a "last link" in an evidentiary chain that could incriminate the individual named, many courts retreat from the usual identity exception and allow the privilege to shield the information.

When clients give documents to their lawyers, another problem of defining communications arises. A letter from a client to a lawyer would clearly be treated as a communication for the purpose of obtaining legal services. It could not, therefore, be discovered in pretrial procedures, and neither the client nor the lawyer could be required to answer questions about it. On the other hand, clients sometimes give their lawyers documents that were created outside of the lawyer-client relationship so that their lawyers can read them and use them in providing legal advice. When this happens, the fact that the client gave a document to his or her lawyer would be privileged.

Despite the lawyer-client privilege, if a document would have been discoverable in the client's possession, it would not be shielded from discovery because the client had given it to his or her lawyer. Since the document cannot be kept secret, it might be supposed that the privilege should not prevent questioning a lawyer about the document's contents—for example, if there is suspicion that the document was altered at some time after it had been returned to the client. A court has nonetheless applied the privilege in circumstances like these, reasoning that to require a lawyer to disclose the identity of records he or she had looked at could inhibit some clients from seeking legal counsel.[1] If responses to questions regarding the contents of a document a client had given a lawyer might lead to inferences concerning the issues the client had sought advice about, the overall policy basis for the lawyer-client privilege supports applying the privilege to allow the lawyer to refuse to answer the questions.

Existence of the Lawyer-Client Relationship

Doubt about the existence of a lawyer-client relationship arises in a number of recurring circumstances. Sometimes a person has a conversation with a lawyer to explore the possibility of hiring the lawyer. While it could be argued that the statements made in such a conversation do not meet the definitional requirement of having been made during the lawyer-client relationship, courts will ordinarily apply the privilege, bearing in mind that one purpose of the privilege is to facilitate individuals' search for legal advice. Another occasional problem involves communications by a would-be client with someone who seems to be, but is not in fact, a lawyer. As long as the "client" has a reasonable basis for believing that he or she is speaking with a lawyer, the policies supporting the privilege suggest that it should cover the client's communications. Finally, clients sometimes employ lawyers for work that does not involve legal representation or legal counseling. A lawyer might study investment opportunities for a client and evaluate them in terms of economics or might collect rent for a landlord. Communications by the "client" to the lawyer in connection with these types of non-legal work are outside the protection of the privilege.

---

1. United States v. Hankins, 631 F.2d 360 (5th Cir. 1980).

There has been considerable controversy over identifying the "client" and shaping the lawyer-client privilege where a lawyer provides legal services to a corporation. Since a corporation is not a human being, some of the ideas that support the privilege cannot logically apply: It has no sense of propriety and indeed cannot even possess "personal" information. The profit motive might be strong enough to establish links between corporations and lawyers whether or not there was a guarantee of privacy for communications made in that relationship.

Although a number of factors cut against applying a privilege where a client is a corporation, all jurisdictions extend some form of privilege, with variations as to which corporate employees are covered. Some jurisdictions grant the privilege for communications made by those in the "control group." They define those individuals as the people who are able to direct the company's acquisition of legal advice and are able to take actions in response to legal advice. In *Upjohn Company v. United States*,[2] the Supreme Court ruled against limiting the privilege this way. Thus, in cases in which federal law applies, and in cases governed by the law of states that have adopted the *Upjohn* position, communications between a corporate employee and the corporation's lawyer are privileged if their topic relates to the employee's work, if the purpose of the communication is to facilitate the providing of legal services to the corporation, and if the communications are confidential. Under *Upjohn* the privilege determination does not depend on the employee's ability to direct litigation.

Required Confidentiality

If a client acts without caring whether communications to the lawyer are private or not, the utilitarian justification for the privilege is weakened. This has two consequences. If the client takes inadequate precautions to insure privacy when he or she makes a communication, there will be no privilege. In earlier days, an eavesdropper to a conversation between a client and a lawyer would be permitted to testify about the conversation on the theory that a client who did not protect against eavesdropping had not done enough to insure the confidentiality of the communications. Modern courts will apply a reasonableness analysis to preserve the privilege in situations where it would be unrealistic to believe that a client could have avoided being overheard.

The presence of a known third party when a client communicates to a lawyer will sometimes destroy the confidentiality required for the privilege. For example, if a client's friend is present while the client talks to a lawyer, the client's communications to the lawyer will not be considered confidential enough to be covered by the privilege. On the other hand, if an interpreter, a secretary, or someone else necessary to the providing of legal advice

---

2. 449 U.S. 383 (1981).

is present along with the client and the lawyer, the privilege will still protect the client's words.

Defining confidentiality in the context of corporate clients can involve complications. If a corporate employee sends a memo to the corporation's lawyer, no special problem arises. However, if a corporate employee sends a memo to another corporate employee and also sends a copy of it to the lawyer, the fact that another person besides the memo writer and the lawyer has seen the memo might be thought to eliminate the type of confidentiality required for the lawyer-client privilege. Lawyer-client privilege is not defined so broadly that corporate employees can shield all their memos from discovery just by including their lawyers among the people to whom they circulate their memos. There would be no privilege if it were apparent that sending the memo to the lawyer was not reasonably related to obtaining legal advice or keeping the lawyer well enough informed so that the lawyer could give legal advice.

One response to this situation is to look at the dominant purpose of the memo and to examine the exact breadth of its distribution. If the primary purpose of the memo was to facilitate legal work, and if the people other than the writer and the lawyer who receive copies of the memo need to have its information to carry out their ordinary work for the corporation, privilege will probably apply. However, if the "extra" people who receive copies of the memorandum do not have a strong need for it, or if its functions could have been satisfied with some other kind of document, then their having received the memo will probably destroy the possibility of protecting it with the privilege.

Besides letting other people know that he or she had communicated certain information to a lawyer, a client might just disclose the information to others. This would indicate that secrecy about the information was not vital to the client. Yet the fact that the client had communicated with a lawyer about the information might still be something the client wished to conceal. Courts have not clearly resolved whether telling additional people about facts already communicated to a lawyer should waive the lawyer-client privilege and legitimize questions to the lawyer about the information. However, since courts are often antagonistic to the information-concealing consequences of privileges, it is sometimes said that any disclosure of the substance of a lawyer-client communication waives the privilege.

Purpose of the Communication

To be covered by the privilege, the client's communication with the lawyer must be for the purpose of obtaining legal advice about past lawful or unlawful conduct or about future conduct that the client wants to carry out lawfully. When a person seeks legal advice about any past events, no matter what their lawfulness, evidence law places the privilege shield over the communications in line with the social policy of facilitating access to legal representation. Since the conduct has already taken place, denying the privilege to discussions about it could not keep it from happening. There is a doctrinal shift, however, for communications made for the purpose of planning future events. If the client intends to obey the law, the consultation is privileged. If the client intends to break the law, then the privilege does not apply because there is no social benefit to facilitating the planning of illegal acts. Also, denying the privilege might have the socially desirable result of hampering the intended misconduct. This distinction between the treatment of planning consultations for the purpose of obeying the law and consultations for the purpose of breaking the law is theoretically sound but difficult to apply in practice. In some cases it depends on information about the subjective intent of the client. A judge may hold an *in camera* hearing (a hearing kept secret from the jury and the public) to determine whether future illegal acts were the subject of a client's conversation with his or her lawyer. As a practical matter, the fact that a client was in touch with a lawyer to plan a crime is not likely to be known to prosecutors or civil plaintiffs, so the issue of applying the privilege is not likely to arise.

Allowable Privilege Claimants

The privilege prevents disclosure of confidential communications in all parts of the trial process, including pretrial discovery. It can be claimed by the client, the client's lawyer (acting on behalf of the client), or by others who represent the client (such as a guardian or conservator). In the case of corporate clients, the claim must be made by the business's current lawyer, the lawyer with whom the privileged communication was made, or by other representatives of the business.

The privilege continues to operate after the death of the client if it is claimed by the decedent's executor or other representative. This aspect of the privilege has been recognized by many common law decisions over a long period of time. In 1998 the Supreme Court considered this issue and reversed a lower court holding that modified the privilege for a deceased client by balancing the need for information in a criminal case against the values served by applying the privilege.[3] Relying on Rule 501's requirement that privileges should be governed by principles of common law, the Supreme Court retained the traditional rule that the privilege outlives the client.

In one circumstance, the privilege is withdrawn after the client's death. When there is a dispute in which rival parties each make a claim based on actions of a deceased client, then no privilege will be permitted, and the attorney will be required to reveal the substance of his or her communications with the client.

---

3. Swidler & Berlin v. United States, 524 U.S. 399 (1998).

Waiver

When a client intentionally reveals a significant portion of a privileged communication, the privilege is waived and the client loses its protection. For example, the owner of a business charged with bringing baseless lawsuits against a competitor might use an "advice of counsel" defense by showing that he or she decided to sue after consultations with counsel. To do this, the defendant would have to reveal some of his or her communications with that lawyer. The competitor would then be permitted to ask questions about the whole range of communications between the defendant and the lawyer on the theory that the defendant's disclosure of some of the communications breached the confidentiality required for application of the privilege.

Sometimes a client reveals a confidential lawyer-client communication by accident. This kind of inadvertent disclosure may be particularly likely in litigation where discovery involves huge numbers of documents or computer files. As a matter of common law, some courts had held that any disclosure eliminated a privilege, and other courts had held that accidental disclosure never had that effect. The majority position determines whether to treat an inadvertent disclosure as a waiver by considering whether the privilege holder acted reasonably to prevent the disclosure and took prompt remedial steps after learning about it. Rule 502(b) adopts this position for federal courts:

> **Inadvertent Disclosure.** When made in a federal proceeding or to a federal office or agency, the disclosure does not operate as a waiver in a federal or state proceeding if:
>
> (1) the disclosure is inadvertent;
> (2) the holder of the privilege or protection took reasonable steps to prevent disclosure; and
> (3) the holder promptly took reasonable steps to rectify the error, including (if applicable) following Federal Rule of Civil Procedure 26(b)(5)(B).

Issues Unique to Lawyer-Client Communications

For the lawyer-client privilege there are some particularized doctrines about loss of the privilege that reflect recurring aspects of legal practice. When there is a dispute between a lawyer and a client over the payment of fees or the quality of representation, for example, the lawyer-client privilege does not apply. Also, where two or more individuals have consulted a lawyer for advice on a matter that concerned all of the individuals, they will be characterized as joint clients. If the joint clients later sue each other, their communications to their lawyer will not be privileged if relevant to the dispute.

Work Product

A doctrine separate from attorney-client privilege also provides confidentiality to some material attorneys may possess in connection with their representation of clients. Announced by the Supreme Court in *Hickman v. Taylor*,[4] the work product doctrine protects from discovery any records of interviews and statements, for example, or tangible items collected in connection with serving a client to further the same principles that underlie the attorney-client privilege (facilitation of the use of legal services). The doctrine is conditional in most cases: A party who seeks material from an opponent's lawyer can obtain it (if it is not subject to the attorney-client privilege) by demonstrating a strong need for the material. A lawyer might interview someone who saw an incident and might take a statement from that person or might write down a summary of the person's information. Those documents are not covered by the attorney-client privilege because they do not involve communications between the attorney and the client. The work product doctrine, however, does shield them unless the opponent makes a showing that it would be very difficult to obtain the information in any other way than from the lawyer. An example of strong need might be the death or disappearance of the person who talked with the lawyer about the incident. The portions of a lawyer's work product that reflect the lawyer's own thinking are given almost total protection under the doctrine, and courts order their production only when there is an extremely compelling showing of need.

Examples

1. Defendant is accused of fraud in the sale of a business, and the plaintiff seeks damages. The plaintiff claims that at the time defendant sold the business, defendant knew that it was in very weak shape financially. At the trial, could the plaintiff's lawyer ask the defendant the following question: "At the time you and the plaintiff were negotiating for the sale of the business, did you consult Alan Able [a lawyer who specializes in bankruptcy] to find out how your business might use the bankruptcy laws?"

2. In the case described in Example 1, could the plaintiff's lawyer ask the defendant this question: "At the time you and the plaintiff were negotiating, did you buy a book *Fundamentals of Bankruptcy Law* and charge its cost to your business?"

3. Lawyer James Fielding wrote a letter to a regulatory agency urging it to investigate bribe soliciting by some of its inspectors. The letter stated that

---

4. 329 U.S. 495 (1947).

one of Fielding's clients had been a victim of the inspectors' illegal conduct. The agency sought to compel testimony by Fielding on the issue of the identity of his client. Should the client's identity be privileged?

4. A restaurant is sued by an alleged victim of food poisoning who claims that her illness was caused by some of the restaurant's food. The restaurant denies that the plaintiff's illness was related to its food. At trial, can the restaurant's lawyer be required to respond to any of these questions:

   a. Did the restaurant owner tell you that he fired a cook the day after the incident because he found that the cook did not follow proper sanitary practices in his work?

   b. Did the restaurant owner write to you about this case and enclose a document reporting on a food safety inspection carried out at the restaurant by a private consulting firm *two weeks before* the plaintiff's alleged injury? If the owner did, what did the report say?

   c. Did the restaurant owner write to you about this case and quote from a report of a food safety inspection that had been conducted at the restaurant two weeks before the plaintiff's alleged injury? If the owner did, what did his letter say the report said?

5. John Wilson, an accountant employed by a company that operates a group of movie theaters, was at one of his company's theaters one night to see a movie. While he was waiting to buy a ticket, he saw another customer slip and fall. He later sent the company's lawyer a memo describing what he had seen. If the person who fell sues the company, can the lawyer be required to give the plaintiff a copy of the accountant's memo?

6. While Harry Lang was talking with his lawyer in her office, painters were working there, preparing the walls before applying new paint. In a lawsuit filed by Lang against a business competitor, can the competitor seek to have Lang or Lang's lawyer state what Lang said to the lawyer during that consultation?

7. Rex Riley was on trial for selling drugs in a high school. When a witness testified that she had seen Riley selling the drugs in the gym, the client turned to his lawyer at the defendant's table in the courtroom and shouted, "It was in the cafeteria, not the gym." He sought a mistrial on the ground that his shouted statement was probably heard by the jury and that their use of its information would violate attorney-client privilege. Does Riley have a valid claim of privilege?

8. A car manufactured by ABC Automobile Company was involved in an accident. The company's lawyer asked its vice president for product safety to investigate the accident, and the vice president wrote a memo describing her conclusions. She addressed it to the company's

lawyer and sent copies to the company's president and about 50 members of the company's engineering staff. Would lawyer-client privilege prevent someone who was injured in the accident from getting a copy of the memo from the vice president or the lawyer?

Explanations

1. The question seeks to develop information that would be relevant to the disputed issues. If the defendant did try to get information on how the bankruptcy laws would have affected his business, it suggests that the business was in weak shape financially at that time. However, establishing relevance does not guarantee the admissibility of evidence. In this problem, lawyer-client privilege would prohibit a response to the question. As long as the consultation with the lawyer was private, and a lawyer-client relationship did exist when it took place, the lawyer-client privilege provides secrecy for the communications for the purpose of encouraging people to obtain legal advice free from the fear that their statements or questions to their lawyers might someday be used against them.

2. The defendant's purchase of a book, *Fundamentals of Bankruptcy Law*, would be relevant because it tends to show that he was concerned about the financial strength of his business at the time he bought it. Even though the topic of the book relates to law, the lawyer-client privilege would not prevent the asking and answering of this question. The privilege does not cover everything a person does with respect to law but covers only communications between a client and a lawyer. A book on bankruptcy is not, obviously, a lawyer.

3. Traditionally, the identity of a client has not been protected by the lawyer-client privilege. However, if public policy reasons suggest that confidentiality would be valuable, some courts are now willing to extend the privilege to cover the issue of the client's name. On the facts of this problem, there are policy arguments both for and against revealing the client's name. If the agency learns the name of the client who complained about the inspectors' solicitation of bribes, it may be able to do a better investigation than if it only has an anonymous tip. On the other hand, if the client's name is revealed, there is a risk that it will become known to the allegedly corrupt inspectors. That could lead to retaliation by the inspectors. It would certainly be contrary to public policy to expose a whistleblower to the risk of harm at the hands of those whose conduct the whistleblower has exposed. Finally, even if this particular client was not harmed by the people he or she named, there is a risk that a practice of obtaining the names of those who give investigatory leads to law enforcement agencies could have a general effect of making people less likely

to give those leads to agencies than they otherwise would be. In a famous case involving facts similar to those of the problem, the court struck this balance in favor of confidentiality.[5]

4. a. The lawyer cannot be asked to state what the restaurant owner said about firing a cook the day after the incident. This is an example of the kind of information a client would reasonably give a lawyer while trying to obtain legal advice about a past problem. It should be remembered that lawyer-client privilege does not apply if a lawyer is consulted for advice in non-legal matters such as general business management. This kind of conversation, though, is clearly relevant to anticipated legal problems and could not reasonably be treated as merely a business consultation.

    b. The lawyer is being asked a two-part question about a document that had nothing to do with the current litigation when it was created since it was created two weeks before the food poisoning incident. The first part asks if the client gave the lawyer a document. The second part asks what the document said. Because giving a lawyer a document does not protect it from being disclosed in future litigation, the plaintiff in this example could have obtained a copy of the document in discovery. If the document had not been obtained before trial, a balance would have to be drawn between protecting the confidentiality of the lawyer-client consultation and protecting the right of litigants to have access to relevant documents possessed by their opponents.

        If the lawyer had to state whether the client gave him or her a safety inspection report, this could reveal to the fact finder something regarding the nature of the topics about which the lawyer and client communicated. A careful judge would press the parties to resolve the question of the document and its contents before the trial. If the client no longer has a copy of the document, and the lawyer does have a copy of it, production from the lawyer would be compelled. If the client has lost it, and the lawyer has lost it, then testimony from either of them about its contents would be proper, and the question in the example, "What did it say?" would be proper.

        If sought to be introduced to show that the information about the restaurant was true, the documents would be hearsay; they might be admissible as government reports under Rule 803(8) or might be treated as non-hearsay adoptive admissions under Rule 801(d)(2).

    c. This part of the example is identical to part b, except that in part b the client enclosed an actual copy of the inspection report to the lawyer as part of a letter seeking legal advice, and in this part the client quotes the inspection report in a letter seeking legal advice. Should it make a

---

5. *See* In re Kaplan, 8 N.Y.2d 214, 203 N.Y.S.2d 836, 168 N.E.2d 660 (1960).

difference that in one case the document was enclosed and in another case the document was quoted? The privacy of the lawyer-client communications would be easier to maintain if the actual inspection report was given to the plaintiff. The report could be divulged without revealing anything about the lawyer-client communication. Where the lawyer received the defendant's letter quoting the report, revealing the entire letter would totally conflict with the usual operation of the lawyer-client privilege. If the client's letter included a direct quotation of the report, and that quotation could be extracted from the letter without revealing the rest of the letter's contents, a strong argument could be made that the quotes from the safety inspection report should not be privileged. It would be logical to treat them as equivalent to the attached copy of the report discussed in part b.

5. Wilson, the accountant, has no responsibilities in the theater company concerning safety and maintenance to prevent patrons' injuries. He also is not employed in a function that requires him to direct litigation or obtain legal advice on matters such as the plaintiff's injury. For these reasons, no attorney-client privilege would attach to the report he gave the company's lawyer. The company's lawyer would be required to produce a copy of the memo. For the purposes of privilege, Wilson is identical to a bystander who was not a company employee who might nonetheless have given a written report to the company's lawyer.

6. The privilege for *confidential* lawyer-client communications will be lost if nonessential individuals are allowed to overhear the client's or the lawyer's words. The painter cannot be classified rationally as someone whose presence was required for the providing of legal services (as the presence of secretaries and interpreters sometimes may be). In contrast, statements by a client to a doctor during an examination arranged by the client's lawyer are usually covered by the lawyer-client privilege on the theory that the doctor is serving as a necessary intermediary between the client and lawyer.

7. There can be no privilege on these facts because the client could not reasonably have considered his communication confidential. He said it in a room where other people were present and said it loudly enough so that they were able to hear it. (This problem was also used in connection with the former testimony hearsay exception in Chapter 2.)

8. The vice president's memo was circulated widely within ABC Automobile Company. Since the lawyer-client privilege will only be applied in situations where there is a *confidential* communication between the lawyer and the client, having lots of people see the memo makes this problem harder than it would be if the vice president had written the memo just

for the lawyer and had sent it only to the lawyer. In *Upjohn*, the company's employees made communications directly to the company's lawyer, and although he made a report to corporate officers about the information contained in those communications, he did not disclose their precise substance to others. The Supreme Court characterized the communications as having been kept confidential.

The Supreme Court's *Upjohn* decision was meant to expand the application of privilege to more cases than the "control group" test would permit. Therefore it is reasonable to assume that the lawyer-client privilege would not be lost if a company's lawyer shared memos from employees with the company's officers who are in a position to direct litigation or respond to legal advice. On the other hand, if the vice president had sent her memo to a newspaper as well as to the company's officers and engineers, no one would make a claim that it could be treated as a privileged communication. In this example, the hard issue is deciding whether there was adequate confidentiality to support lawyer-client privilege when the document in question was shared with 50 members of the engineering department. Since learning about the cause of a vehicle's bad performance would clearly be within the scope of the engineers' responsibilities, giving the memo to those people would probably not vitiate the privilege. This area of the law is unsettled. Certainly the argument for keeping the privilege intact would be stronger if the engineering department employees needed the information for a law-related purpose.

Notice the broad scope of privilege under *Upjohn*. In this problem, the accident study would probably be unobtainable by parties suing ABC Company. If the vice president had decided to do the study without having had a request from the lawyer and had addressed the study to the engineers, even sending a copy to the lawyer would probably not entitle the company to claim lawyer-client privilege and avoid disclosing the study.

Spousal Communications

One of the most revered and widely accepted privileges is the spousal communications privilege protecting communications between spouses. This privilege keeps information about statements made in confidence between spouses secret when a spouse or anyone else testifies. This is distinct from spousal disqualification, which prevents a spouse from being a witness (discussed in the section on competency of witnesses at page 148). When a spouse is prohibited from being a witness, none of his or her knowledge is available to the trial in the form of testimony from the spouse. Other people who know the same things as the spouse are allowed to testify about them. When the spousal communications privilege is invoked, the occurrence or the contents of confidential communications between a husband and wife may not be the subject of testimony by the husband, wife, or anyone else. Chart 20 shows the main comparisons between the two concepts.

It is usually stated that our society respects the institution of marriage and helps make marriages happier and more enduring by providing a privilege to keep confidential marital communications out of trials. The empirical accuracy of this rationale might be questioned by asking whether those who know the most about the existence of the privilege — lawyers — have happier marriages than those others in society who meet, fall in love, marry, and live their lives without knowledge of how evidence law shields their private statements. Nevertheless, the privilege is deeply entrenched.

For the privilege to apply, the spouses must have been married when the communication was made. This is a question of state law. For example, there is great variation among states on the issue of common law marriage. People living together in identical arrangements might be treated as married in some states and as not married in others. That issue of family law would control application of the spousal communications privilege.

The privilege is ordinarily described as shielding marital communications. This can lead to problem cases where a husband, for example, learns something about his wife from her conduct at home, but where she did not have any intent to convey the information. If the privilege is strictly limited

Chart 20 Spousal Communication Privilege and Disqualification, Compared

Points of Comparison	Spousal Communication Privilege	Spousal Disqualification
Topics covered	Confidential communications	Everything spouse knows
Proceedings covered	All	Proceedings brought against other spouse
May someone other than the spouse testify about the covered topics?	No	Yes
Duration	Forever	During marriage

to communications and meant to foster communications between husbands and wives, then no protection should apply and the husband should be allowed to testify about what he learned. An illustration would be a wife hiding stolen property at home, her husband seeing it, and an effort by the wife to prevent the husband's testimony about the stolen property by stating that she kept it at home relying on the confidential relationship that inheres in marriage. Deciding whether to sustain the wife's objection would depend on whether a jurisdiction characterizes the privilege as meant to protect marriages through fostering communications or as meant to protect marriages through fostering a zone of privacy and freedom from fear of disclosures. The zone of privacy idea would protect far more information than would be covered by the communications theory. Since many courts are hostile to privileges and seek to curtail the circumstances in which they deprive the legal system of relevant information, there may be a trend towards limiting the definition of "communication" to verbal and non-verbal acts meant to convey information.

The topic of the communication must have some relationship to the spouses' marriage. Meeting this requirement in attempting to claim application of the privilege is ordinarily easy since virtually all things that husbands and wives may say or indicate to each other may have some significance for their marital relationship. However, there may be instances where spouses have a business relationship as well as a marital relationship, and their communications about how their business operates might be characterized as outside the range of coverage of the marital communications privilege.

Even after a marriage has ended by death of a spouse or by divorce, the privilege applies to prevent testimony about confidential communications between the spouses during the marriage. Clearly this approach cannot be justified as being intended to increase the future happiness of the married couple who communicated with each other. The common law belief that privacy is essential to the relationship between a husband and wife supports the idea of extending the privilege beyond the life of the marriage. Spouses might not feel the freedom and intimacy the privacy is supposed to encourage if they knew that after death or dissolution of the marriage their statements and communicative conduct could be revealed in court.

The marital communications privilege is subject to important exceptions. Spouses' communications are no longer shielded when they litigate against each other. The privilege is also removed in criminal proceedings that involve a charge of intra-familial wrongdoing such as assault on a spouse or a child. It is straightforward to justify removal of the privilege for criminal cases because society's need to deter and punish criminal conduct in marriages exceeds the need to foster privacy in a relationship that is marked by violence.

Physician-Patient

Out of respect for the intimacy of the typical relationships between doctors and patients, common law treats statements made by patients to their doctors as privileged. On utilitarian grounds, however, this is hard to support since people who are sick have a strong motivation to speak to doctors regardless of whether evidence law will shield their words with a privilege. The fact that its practical underpinnings are weak may explain why the privilege, though widely recognized, has a great number of exceptions. The exceptions are so broad that some have argued that no physician-patient privilege should be recognized at all.

The most significant exception to application of the privilege is for cases where the holder of the privilege has put his or her own physical condition into dispute in litigation. Statements by a litigant-patient to a doctor are not protected from being revealed. Also, in most jurisdictions, the privilege does not apply in criminal cases.

Therapist-Patient

Related to the physician-patient privilege is the psychotherapist-patient privilege, recognized in all states and under the Federal Rules. This privilege has broader application than the physician-patient privilege because it covers statements made to therapists who are not physicians as well as to physician-therapists. The privilege has been adopted by judicial decision and by legislation because of beliefs that psychotherapy is valuable to individuals and society, and that it cannot be performed effectively unless a patient is assured that statements to the therapist will be confidential.

A small number of states limit the privilege to statements made to psychiatrists and psychologists. In most states, the privilege also covers communications to social workers. In *Jaffee v. Redmond*,[6] the United States Supreme Court adopted this privilege for federal courts, holding that it should extend to licensed social workers performing psychotherapy, and that it should be an absolute privilege applied without any balancing of the public's need for information against the social value of encouraging psychotherapy.

Priest-Penitent

All jurisdictions recognize a privilege for confessional statements to Catholic priests. Additionally, this privilege extends in many jurisdictions to

---

6. 518 U.S. 1 (1996).

statements made to ministers, rabbis, and practitioners of other religions to whom similar communications might be made. In the narrowest form, the privilege is limited to statements made in confidence due to the requirements of a religion to a person authorized within the applicable religion to receive such statements. It is often extended to cover statements made to members of the clergy for purposes of counseling (even including draft counseling, in a case[7] that provided a notably broad application of the "priest-penitent" notion).

Governmental Executives and Informers

Privileges protect certain types of governmental communications thought to have high societal value. One privilege allows the government, in the criminal justice process, to keep secret the identity of informers in many circumstances. This "informer's privilege" is intended to encourage people to give information to police about criminal conduct without fear that they will be identified and thus put at risk of injury by the person about whom they give information. The possessor of the privilege is the government. The claim of privilege will be rejected if the criminal defendant makes a showing that revealing the contents of an informer's communications will not reveal the identity of the informer, or shows clearly that knowledge of the informer's identity is critical for his or her defense.

There are also privileges for "state secrets" and "executive communications." These privileges prevent disclosure of communications that could impair national security and of communications made by those in the executive branch of government as part of their decision-making process. This "executive privilege" is based on the idea that people in high office require frank advice from their governmental associates, and that their conversations would not be free and open if there was a risk that what they said could be disclosed in judicial proceedings. Where executive privilege is claimed, courts usually require a statement from the head of the relevant agency that disclosure would be harmful, and courts often conduct an *in camera* examination of the material sought to be protected. If a claim is made involving military secrets or national security information, courts are likely to uphold the privilege even without examining the material if the surrounding circumstances make the claim plausible.

---

7. In re Verplank, 329 F. Supp. 433 (C.D. Cal. 1971).

Examples

1. The wife of a defendant accused of bank robbery is willing to testify for the prosecution. One evening, after the robbery and before the trial, she said to her husband at home, "You never make any money, and you waste all your time." Hearing that, her husband then silently opened a desk drawer so that she could see lots of large denomination bills wrapped in bands with the name of the bank that had been robbed. Can the defendant prevent his wife from testifying about what she saw?

2. Someone accused of a crime discussed it with her spouse and then had a discussion with her lawyer in which she revealed that she had discussed it with her spouse. Should her multiple revelations destroy her claim of privilege with respect to either of the conversations? How would it affect your analysis if the spouse and lawyer were both present with the accused and had a group conversation?

3. A theater owner sues a musician for fraud, alleging that at the time the musician agreed to appear in a series of performances at the theater, the musician knew he was very ill and was unlikely to fulfill the contract. The day the musician signed the contract, he had been examined by his doctor. Can the theater owner have the doctor testify concerning (a) what the musician said to the doctor about his physical condition or (b) what the doctor believed the musician's condition was, based on the doctor's physical examination of the musician?

4. An actor sues a theater owner for negligence, claiming that he was scratched by a sharp piece of metal backstage and suffered a serious infection as a consequence of the injury. May the theater owner question the actor's doctor about (a) things the actor said and things the doctor observed during a checkup prior to the alleged injury or (b) the actor's statements and the doctor's observations during an examination conducted by the doctor after the alleged injury?

5. A defendant in a tax evasion case is charged with making false statements in connection with claims of charitable deductions for contributions to a foundation she had established to benefit musical groups. The defendant claims that she had no intent to make false claims of charitable deductions. May the prosecution introduce testimony by the defendant's minister that the defendant had talked privately with the minister about setting up a charitable foundation to benefit the church, and that the defendant had said the foundation could receive money from the defendant and then secretly repay a portion of that money to the defendant to reduce the defendant's tax liability?

6. Edward Elbert sues the United States claiming that he is owed back pay for work in foreign countries on behalf of the C.I.A. Can the plaintiff be barred from introducing evidence about the agency's methods of operation in foreign countries and about the identity of those individuals whom it employs?

7. A police department obtained a copy of a prisoner's diary and address book. When she sought an injunction barring allegedly unconstitutional surveillance, the police department claimed that it had obtained the copy from an informant but that it had not asked the informant to make the copy and was therefore not responsible for any misconduct that might have been involved in the informant's actions. The prisoner sought the name of the informant. How should the court rule?

Explanations

1. The defendant-husband will base his claim on the marital communications privilege. He must show a valid marriage and a communication made in confidence during that marriage. Assuming that the marriage was legitimate and that no one else was present when he opened the drawer, the remaining issue is whether the conduct involved in showing the bank's money should be characterized as a communication. Since the husband acted as he did in response to a verbal statement by the wife, there is a strong argument that the conduct was the equivalent of a verbal reply to the wife's accusation. Seen that way, it ought to be considered a statement and ought, therefore, to be covered by the privilege.

2. If a person voluntarily reveals details of a communication that is ordinarily privileged, the privilege is abolished. This Example poses the situation in which the possessor of the marital communications privilege disclosed her privileged marital communications in a conversation that is itself subject to the lawyer-client privilege. It would not make sense to have disclosure of one privileged communication in another privileged communication work to eliminate the privilege for the first communication. The overriding policy behind the privileges is to encourage the conversations so long as they are kept secret.

    When the wife told her lawyer about what she had earlier told her husband in confidence, she did expand the number of people who knew the information. But the expansion included only one person, the lawyer, and posed no risk of further communication of the information because the lawyer was obligated to keep it confidential. Since sharing the information with the lawyer is so different from sharing it with a person who would be permitted to repeat it, mentioning the spousal communication in the attorney-client communication should not be treated as waiving the confidentiality ordinarily applied to marital communications.

The fact that part of the conversation with the attorney involved revealing something that had been said before would not in any way impair the client's ability to invoke attorney-client privilege to prevent testimony that she had actually told the attorney what she had said to her husband.

If the husband and lawyer were both present, the better view is that both privileges are intact. Communications by the wife to the "extra" people present (the husband in the context of the attorney-client privilege, and the attorney in the context of the marital communications privilege) are themselves privileged, so it makes sense to treat the simultaneous disclosure of information to the husband and lawyer equivalently to sequential individual disclosures to them.

3. Communications from the musician to the doctor are covered by the physician-patient privilege. None of the many exceptions to the privilege are operative here, mainly because the musician is not the party who has raised an issue about his physical condition. Clearly, words spoken by the musician to the doctor are protected from disclosure by the privilege.

   Things the doctor observed about the musician during the examination are also protected by the privilege. One of the ways people communicate with their doctors about their symptoms and physical condition is by allowing doctors to look at them and touch them. For this reason, *communication* is usually defined broadly for purposes of applying the physician-patient privilege.

4. The defendant is entitled to both types of testimony: descriptions by the doctor of what the actor said and of what the doctor observed. The reason the physician-patient privilege does not apply is that the plaintiff-actor has put his own physical condition into issue by alleging that the defendant had caused him harm. Depriving the defendant of information about the plaintiff's physical condition before and after the alleged injury would place too heavy a burden on the defendant's ability to present a defense. If the plaintiff values privacy, he can preserve it by declining to sue for damages.

5. The evidence would be relevant because it shows the defendant's knowledge of charitable contribution law and shows that the alleged improprieties in the musical foundation were probably not due to inadvertence. The conversation with the minister would not be privileged because it was not for the purpose of confession or religious counseling.

6. Information about C.I.A. activities would clearly be protected by the state secrets privilege. If the plaintiff is unable to establish a prima facie case on his contract claim without disclosing details of how the agency operates, his claim must be dismissed.

7. In applying the informant's privilege, a court must balance the need for secrecy against the need described by the party seeking the informant's identity. In this case, without knowing the identity of the informant, the prisoner will be unable to verify the police department's claim that the informant supplied the material acting on his own and that the police department had not asked him to make the copy. On these facts, the court should reject the claim of privilege.

Authentication and the Original Writing Rule

INTRODUCTION

This chapter covers two related topics: authentication and the original writing rule. Authentication is a requirement that the proponent of evidence provide a basis for the fact finder to believe that the evidence is what the proponent claims it is. The rule applies to documents, records, or other physical things described in testimony or offered into evidence. It also applies to references to human beings as having been seen by a witness or as having spoken to a witness.

The original writing rule, also known as the best evidence rule, applies to documents, photographs, and recordings. If their contents are the subject of testimony, the party offering the testimony must provide the original of the writing, document, or recording. This rule is applied far less strictly under the Federal Rules than it was at common law, so that the requirement of an original can usually be satisfied by introducing a copy or by providing an excuse for failure to have the original. Issues in these areas do not arise frequently at modern trials because pretrial discovery and the use of stipulations usually sort out the problems and avoid the dangers the rules are meant to avert.

Authentication

The requirement of authentication is ordinarily very easy to satisfy under the Federal Rules. Rule 901(a) sets out the general rule:

> To satisfy the requirement of authenticating or identifying an item of evidence, the proponent must produce evidence sufficient to support a finding that the item is what the proponent claims it is.

The proponent must introduce evidence adequate to support a jury finding (or a finding by the court if there is no jury) that the matter is what its proponent claims it is. The rule offers as examples a group of frequently used methods for authentication, but a party is not limited to the methods used in the examples. The authentication requirement is essentially a refinement of the requirement of relevancy because testimony about objects or conversations can be relevant only if it refers to objects or conversations that really did involve the people or things the witness claims were involved. Authentication is an example of conditional relevance, discussed in Chapter 1. Testimony that satisfies the authentication requirements is often called "foundation testimony."

Witness with Knowledge

Rule 901(b) provides examples of methods parties may use to satisfy the authentication requirement. Its first illustration makes it plain that parties are entitled to use a wide variety of methods to supply the necessary information. It states:

> **(b)** The following are examples only — not a complete list — of evidence that satisfies the requirement:
>
> **(1) Testimony of a Witness with Knowledge.** Testimony that an item is what it is claimed to be.

This type of testimony could be as simple as a witness saying that he knows the person he talked to on a certain day was the defendant because he has known the defendant for many years and is always able to recognize him. It could be more complex "chain of custody" testimony in which various witnesses state that some object was the same object obtained from another person by stating how, at what time, and from whom each one obtained the item.

In criminal cases involving a claim that a substance possessed by the defendant was an illegal drug, a witness (usually a police officer) will testify about taking the substance from the defendant, sealing it in a container, and marking it. That witness will state what he or she did next with the substance. Then, another witness will describe having obtained the marked container from the first witness and will say what he or she did with it. In this way, a number of witnesses will provide a basis for a jury conclusion that testimony the last witness in the chain may give, such as a report of a chemical analysis of the substance, is really testimony about the actual substance that was taken from the defendant.

Handwriting

Rule 901 provides examples concerning the identification of handwriting. If a party claims that a document was written by a particular person, the authentication rule requires that evidence be introduced adequate to support a finding that the document really was written by that individual. Laypersons who are familiar with someone's handwriting may testify that handwriting on a document offered into evidence is by that person. An example of this would be someone identifying his or her spouse's handwriting. An expert on handwriting analysis may testify that a document was written by a particular person if the expert can base that opinion on samples of the person's handwriting that are themselves authenticated. Those examples would have to have been authenticated in some way other than by the handwriting expert who uses them for comparison. Where authenticated examples of someone's handwriting are available, they can also be used by the trier of fact to decide whether a challenged writing was made by the person who wrote the authenticated examples.

Distinctive Characteristics

The uniqueness of an object or an object's appearance, along with the circumstances of how it was found, can provide adequate evidence to satisfy the authentication requirement. For example, under a doctrine known as the "reply doctrine," if a party introduces evidence that a communication was made to another party, that evidence is treated as adequate authentication of another communication that seems to have been a reply to the first communication.

Voices and Telephone Conversations

A witness may authenticate a voice by testifying about familiarity with it if the witness has a reasonable basis for recognizing and identifying the speaker. That type of familiarity may be obtained in circumstances that provided a connection between that voice and the identity of the person whose voice the witness testifies that it was. That method of authentication is allowed for voices heard in telephone calls or in other ways. For telephone calls, other methods of authentication are also outlined in the rule when there is testimony that a call was made to a number assigned by the telephone company to a person or a business. If a call was made to a business, it can be authenticated with testimony that the conversation was about business reasonably transacted by phone. For other phone calls, authentication is permitted by testimony that the person who answered the call was the person who was called. This testimony can describe the circumstances of the call, including self-identification by the person who was called.

Public Records

For documents required or authorized to be recorded or filed in a public office, or any other records or "data compilation" from a public office, one of the rule's examples states that authentication can be provided by evidence that the writing or data compilation came from the office where items of that type are kept. The proponent of the evidence may have to produce a witness who knows and can testify about the source of the exhibit. This is a kind of chain of custody method of establishing that a document is what it is claimed to be. The reference to data compilations extends the example to computerized records and various forms of computer output.

Ancient Documents

Another of the rule's examples relates to "ancient" documents, defined as documents or data compilations 20 years old or older at the time they are offered, that are found in a place where they would likely be if they were authentic and in a condition that does not create suspicion about their authenticity. Satisfying the criteria in the example is adequate compliance with the authentication rule. Recall that there is a hearsay exception covering the statements made in these documents.

Process or System

Where an item of evidence has been produced with a process or system, such as a computer system or a scientific device, testimony describing the process or system can serve to authenticate the evidence. For example, a computer-generated listing of information could be authenticated with testimony about the way in which data were assembled and the program used to organize and extract the data.

Self-authentication

The fairly straightforward methods of authentication sometimes burden litigants. For a specific class of documents called self-authenticating, litigants may satisfy the authentication requirement simply by presenting the documents themselves. These documents are described in Rule 902 as exceptions to the ordinary requirement of "extrinsic evidence of authenticity in order to be admitted." They include certain certified documents, where the certification takes the place of a witness who could state where the document had been found and establish that it is legitimate, and other items such as newspapers and "trade inscriptions" where the chance of forgery or mistake is remote.

Self-authentication categories. Self-authentication is controlled by Rule 902. That rule withdraws the requirement of extrinsic authenticating evidence for certain specific types of documents, defined in subparts of the rule. This differs from the structure of Rule 901, which sets up the general requirement of authentication and provides examples illustrating possible ways of satisfying it. The examples in Rule 901 are not exclusive but are merely suggestive. The categories established in Rule 902 are limiting definitions of the types of documents that qualify for self-authentication. They are: a domestic public document bearing a seal of a governmental entity; a domestic public document not bearing a seal but containing a signature of an official and accompanied by a document under seal attesting to the official's signature; certain foreign public documents bearing certified signatures; certified copies of public records, official publications, newspapers and periodicals, trade inscriptions, acknowledged documents, commercial paper and related documents, certified domestic records of a regularly conducted activity, and certified foreign records of a regularly conducted activity. Also within the rule's definitions are documents or other items declared by federal statutes to be prima facie genuine or authentic.

The significance of self-authentication can be illustrated with respect to one of its categories: trade inscriptions. If a party wished to introduce a package allegedly marketed by a defendant for the purpose of establishing what types of directions for use the defendant had provided in the product's labeling, the package would be self-authenticating.[1] If self-authentication were not allowed, the proponent would be required to introduce testimony from a witness with knowledge about the way in which the label's words got on the package and about how the manufacturer and the package were linked. Self-authentication saves the proponent those steps on the theory that items in the specified classes are virtually never forgeries. Protection against phony exhibits is still available since the party against which a self-authenticating item is introduced is free to introduce evidence casting doubt on its legitimacy.

---

1. It is important to remember that evidence must satisfy more requirements than merely authentication to gain admission. For example, depending on the purpose for which the package's labeling was sought to be introduced, hearsay problems might arise. Also, the original writing rule could apply.

Examples

1. The plaintiff in a products liability case was injured when a screwdriver slipped out of his hand and cut him. Claiming that the product's design was defective, he seeks to introduce a screwdriver as an exhibit, asserting it is the actual screwdriver that hurt him. If the plaintiff testifies that the screwdriver has been in his control since the accident and that the screwdriver offered in evidence is the actual one that was involved in his injury, would the plaintiff's testimony be adequate to satisfy the authentication requirement?

2. In the same case as Example 1, the plaintiff seeks to introduce a screwdriver into evidence, testifying that:
   a. after the accident he threw the screwdriver down into a pile of hammers, screwdrivers, and other tools on his workbench;
   b. several weeks later, the plaintiff picked up the screwdriver sought to be introduced into evidence from that pile of tools;
   c. the plaintiff saw a number of screwdrivers in that pile and does not know if this screwdriver is the one that he was using at the time of his injury; and
   d. this screwdriver looks like it probably is the one that hurt him.

   Is this testimony adequate to authenticate the screwdriver sought to be introduced into evidence?

3. To authenticate a surveillance videotape showing that there was no activity at a certain door to a building during certain hours, the prosecution introduces testimony of a technician who states the location of the camera and the time at which the videotape was made. Would that be an adequate basis for a finding that the videotape was in fact made as the technician claimed?

4. To support a claim that a neighbor made harassing phone calls, the plaintiff states that she received several calls from someone who identified herself as the neighbor late at night. If this was all the plaintiff stated, would there be adequate authentication of the calls?

5. In a suit about adverse possession of real property, a party claims that a letter written 25 years ago granted permission for use of a portion of a driveway and that because permission had been granted, no adverse possession was possible. The letter was found in a real estate company's files in a folder marked "driveway permissions" in a group of similar letters. With respect only to authentication, what ruling should the judge make if the judge believes that the letter is not 20 years old or more but also believes that a jury could reasonably conclude that in fact the letter is 25 years old?

6. Has the proponent provided adequate authentication that a can of a soft drink was manufactured by the "CBE Bottling Group" if the proponent introduces a can with that statement printed on it?

7. A cigarette company seeks to establish that the health risks of smoking were commonly known in the 1950s. What would the company need to do to authenticate copies of *Life* magazine and the *Readers' Digest* published during that decade containing articles about smoking and health?

Explanations

1. Yes. All that the authentication rules require is that the proponent of evidence supply an adequate basis for a finding that the evidence is what the proponent claims it to be. Here, the offered evidence is a screwdriver that the proponent claims is the screwdriver that hurt him. His own testimony is an adequate basis for a finding that the screwdriver is the tool he claims it to be.

2. No. In this version of the screwdriver example, the proponent claims that the screwdriver he is seeking to introduce is the same one that was involved in his injury. The plaintiff's statements are too weak to support a finding that this screwdriver really is the particular one he was using when he was hurt. Therefore, the screwdriver would not be properly authenticated. It would be excluded from evidence. However, on another theory, the screwdriver could be admitted. If it were helpful to his case, the plaintiff could describe the screwdriver as very similar to the one with which he got hurt. It could then be admitted for the limited purpose of serving as an illustrative example for purposes of clarifying the plaintiff's testimony.

3. Yes. The technician has knowledge that the tape was made in the way she stated. Additional evidence might be required to rule out possible tampering. It could be supplied by witnesses who testify as to the chain of custody so that opportunities for tampering could be explored, or it could be supplied by internal evidence from the videotape itself such as superimposed time and date markings.

4. No. To authenticate these calls, the plaintiff could testify that she recognized the voice. If she did not recognize the voice, all she can say is that an unknown person claimed to be the neighbor. This example shows a distinction in Rule 901 between incoming and outgoing telephone calls: Outgoing calls can be authenticated by testimony that a witness called a certain number and that a person at that number to whom the number was assigned either identified herself or seemed through other circumstances to be that person. Incoming calls require more because the

witness received the call and did not make it, and there is no way to know from what number the call was made. The witness can still testify about the calls but would be precluded from identifying the speaker as her neighbor.

5. The judge should rule that the letter is adequately authenticated. The proponent need only introduce evidence adequate to support a finding that the item is what the proponent claims it to be. Here, the judge personally believes that the document is less than 20 years old, but that is not a valid reason for ruling that it has not been authenticated. Because the judge believes that the opposite finding would be supportable, and because the rule requires only that the proponent introduce evidence adequate to support such a finding, the correct ruling would be that the document was authenticated. Recall that authentication is only one aspect of admissibility. In the example, there might be issues of hearsay and the original writing rule as well.

6. Yes. Printing on a commercially produced can would qualify as a self-authenticating "trade inscription" under Rule 902. Because it is self-authenticating, extrinsic evidence that could provide additional authentication is not required.

7. The company would need only to introduce the magazines themselves. Periodicals and newspapers are treated as self-authenticating. Note that relevancy, original writing rule, and hearsay issues might also need to be considered.

Original Writing Rule

The original writing rule applies only to writings, recordings, and photographs. Rule 1002 states its basic requirement:

> An original writing, recording, or photograph is required in order to prove its content unless these rules or a federal statute provides otherwise.

If a party seeks to introduce testimony specifically about what such an item says, the party must produce the original of the item or satisfy the requirement with a method authorized by other rules related to this issue. Rule 1003 provides an easy way to avoid introducing the original:

> A duplicate is admissible to the same extent as the original unless a genuine question is raised about the original's authenticity or the circumstances make it unfair to admit the duplicate.

If a duplicate is not available, a party can offer an excuse, instead, under Rule 1004:

> An original is not required and other evidence of the content of a writing, recording, or photograph is admissible if:
>
> > **(a)** all the originals are lost or destroyed, and not by the proponent acting in bad faith;
> >
> > **(b)** an original cannot be obtained by any available judicial process;
> >
> > **(c)** the party against whom the original would be offered had control of the original; was at that time put on notice, by pleadings or otherwise, that the original would be a subject of proof at the trial or hearing; and fails to produce it at the trial or hearing; or
> >
> > **(d)** the writing, recording, or photograph is not closely related to a controlling issue.

The rule derives from the "best evidence rule" that once, in abstract theory, prohibited testimony about the contents of any document unless the original of the document was itself introduced. The policy basis for the rule is that having a document physically present at trial will increase the chances of discovering any forgery or tampering. Also, details in documents are sometimes hard to remember so that it is unfair to allow testimony about a document without having the actual document available as a check on memory lapses. At present, pretrial discovery gives parties ample opportunity to judge the accuracy of copies. As ways of transacting business have changed, the concept of an "original" document has reflected actual business practices less and less.

The original writing rule does not necessarily affect testimony about every aspect of a past event or condition that was a subject of a writing, recording, or photograph. If the witness has a means of knowing about that past reality that does not depend on having obtained the knowledge from the writing, recording, or photograph, he or she is allowed to testify from personal knowledge, and the fact that a tangible record of the event or condition exists has no bearing on the testimony.

Illustratively, whether the plaintiff had given a dress to a tailor for alterations might be an issue at a trial. The original writing rule would not prevent the plaintiff from testifying that she did leave the dress with the tailor even if the tailor had given her a receipt that said she had left the dress. Her statement about leaving the dress would not be testimony about the contents of a writing (the receipt) even though the existence of the receipt is consistent with her testimony. If the plaintiff sought to testify that the receipt had specific words written on it, then her testimony would properly be characterized as within the scope of the original writing rule, and its requirement of an original, a copy, or an excuse would have to be met.

The rule's text and history make it clear that its main targets are documents and things like computer tapes that are equivalent to documents. In this sense, a document is a medium meant primarily for containing data and making it accessible. When an object has writing on it but is not really like a document, the rule's role is less clear. There might, for example, be a serial number on a huge piece of industrial equipment or a sign painted on the wall of a building. Dealing with "inscribed chattels" such as the machine or the building, courts will assess the benefit to be obtained from applying the rule (in terms of protection from fraud or mistake). They will also consider the inconvenience or impossibility of producing the "original." One solution is to require introduction of a photograph of the item. Another solution is to define the item as something other than a "writing, recording or photograph" covered by Rule 1002.

Definition of "Original"

According to Rule 1001, an original of a document or recording is the document or recording itself or any "counterpart" meant to be an original by the parties who created the first version of the document or recording. For example, if parties to a contract prepare two copies of the agreement and sign each copy, each of the signed contracts is an "original." The rule defines the original of a photograph as the negative and any print made from the negative. Any output from a computer that is readable by sight is defined as an original.

Definition and Use of "Duplicate" Writings and Recordings

Rule 1001 defines a duplicate as a "counterpart" produced at the same time as the original or produced through other processes such as photocopying. The word counterpart is apparently synonymous with "copy" for the purpose of this rule. The original writing rule is technically a rule requiring the production of originals where it applies. Under Rule 1003 duplicates are admissible to the same extent as originals unless there is a genuine question about the authenticity of the original or there are circumstances that would make the use of a duplicate unfair. If a reasonable claim of forgery were made, for example, a court would require production of the original document so that experts could evaluate it.

Excuses for Non-production of Original or Duplicate

The fairly weak requirements of the original writing rule are revoked entirely by Rule 1004 in a variety of circumstances so that a witness is allowed to testify about the contents of documents without the production of an original or a duplicate. These circumstances are: when the original has been lost or destroyed by someone other than the proponent of the testimony; when the original cannot be obtained through judicial procedures; when the opponent has control of the original and has failed to produce it despite notice that there would be testimony about it; and when the writing, recording, or photograph is "not closely related to a controlling issue."

Summaries

Sometimes materials covered by the original writing rule are so voluminous that it would be inconvenient to use them in court. Rule 1006 authorizes the use of summaries:

> The proponent may use a summary, chart, or calculation to prove the content of voluminous writings, recordings, or photographs that cannot be conveniently examined in court. The proponent must make the originals or duplicates available for examination or copying, or both, by other parties at a reasonable time and place. And the court may order the proponent to produce them in court.

With respect to the risks that justify the original writing rule, Rule 1006 reflects those concerns by its provisions that the originals or duplicates must be made available for the opposing party, and that the court can order their production at trial.

Examples

1. An undercover police officer secretly tape-recorded a conversation with Alice Andrews. Andrews is now on trial, charged with selling illegal drugs to the officer. The officer seeks to testify about what Andrews said to her during the alleged sale. Does the original writing rule require that the prosecution introduce the tape recording in order for the officer to testify about what Andrews said?

2. After being arrested and given the *Miranda* warnings, Bruce Blair told a police officer that he had stolen a car. He then wrote down his confession and signed it. May a police officer testify: "Blair told me he stole it, and then we wrote out a confession that gave all the details," if the prosecution fails to introduce the written confession?

3. To prove that Carl Classen was knowledgeable about Corvettes, a party seeks to introduce testimony by the publisher of a newsletter for Corvette owners that Classen had written to him describing an unusual problem with a particular Corvette and suggesting some ways to solve it. Would the proponent of testimony by the publisher need to satisfy the original writing rule? Are there issues of authentication and hearsay as well?

4. For a witness to testify that an application for an insurance policy contained no statement by the applicant that she had been hospitalized for a particular disease, must the proponent satisfy the original writing rule?

5. Can a witness testify that a defendant hit a victim on the head with a "Louisville Slugger" baseball bat without introducing the bat?

Explanations

1. The officer may testify without the prosecution being required to introduce the tape recording. The original writing rule would require introduction of the tape only if the officer's testimony stated that the tape contained certain words by Andrews. Since the officer knows herself what she and Andrews said, the officer is permitted to testify about those statements. The existence of the tape provides an additional means of proof, but its introduction is not required.

2. Yes and no. The existence of the writing is independent of the information that the police officer learned in some way other than by reading the written confession, so the officer is entitled to testify what Blair "confessed" without the prosecution introducing the written confession. Proof of what Blair said is not proof of the contents of the written confession even if — coincidentally — the written document's contents are equivalent to what Blair said. On the other hand, the testimony that Blair wrote a confession with "all the details" should be characterized as testimony about the contents of a document; that part of the officer's testimony is inadmissible unless the prosecution complies with the original writing rule.

3. Since the publisher's testimony is that a letter written by Classen contained certain statements, the only fair way to characterize the testimony is that its subject is the contents of the writing by Classen. For that reason, the original writing rule applies. The proponent would need to introduce the original of the letter, a duplicate, or would have to explain that one of the excuses for non-production applied. It might be, for example, that the letter had been lost or destroyed in good faith. Additionally, the Rule 901 authentication requirement would have to be met with regard to testimony about the letter or introduction of the letter or a copy of the letter. The proponent might have testimony that the signature was known to a witness, that the stationery was printed with Classen's name, that the letter was a reply to a communication from the publisher, or there might be an admission by Classen that he had written it.

   With regard to hearsay, if Classen is a party and the letter was sought to be introduced against Classen, it would be a statement by an opposing party (or admission) under Rule 801(d)(1). If Classen is not a party, his statements about the Corvette could be treated as non-hearsay because they would be introduced not to show their primary meaning (that a particular problem with Corvettes could be solved in a certain way) but rather for their implication that Classen knew about Corvettes.

4. This testimony could be analyzed as literally outside the scope of the original writing rule since it is about a lack of information in a document rather than about the "contents" of a document. The policy reasons for the original writing rule, however, would support applying it because introduction of the document would assist the trier of fact in knowing how accurately its contents were being described by the witness.

5. Yes. The bat is not a writing, recording, or photograph. The policy justifications for the original writing rule are that mistakes and forgeries will be easier to discover if the actual writing or its equivalent is introduced. On these facts, the likelihood of forgery or confusion is minuscule. This would support a court's refusal to apply the original writing rule. Even if a court felt that the inscription on the bat did qualify the bat as a writing, the brand name is a collateral matter, so Rule 1004(d) would excuse compliance with the rule.

Presumptions

INTRODUCTION

Parties ordinarily introduce testimony or exhibits to support conclusions about the facts they seek to prove. Evidence law also offers two shortcut techniques for establishing facts. These are presumptions and judicial notice. With a presumption, a party is allowed to establish its position about a disputed fact by introducing evidence on some other fact. The party does not have to introduce evidence that is explicitly about the disputed issue. Judicial notice, discussed in Chapter 10, is another technique for quick and efficient proof of some types of facts. Where it applies, the court will treat certain facts as true without any requirement that they be supported by admissible evidence.

Presumptions

A presumption is a procedural device that relates two factual propositions, so that proof of the first fact (called the basic fact) is sometimes treated as proof of the second fact (the presumed fact). Rule 301 defines the function of presumptions:

> In a civil case, unless a federal statute or these rules provide otherwise, the party against whom a presumption is directed has the burden of producing evidence to rebut the presumption. But this rule does not shift the burden of persuasion, which remains on the party who had it originally.

Additionally, Rule 302 states:

In a civil case, state law governs the effect of a presumption regarding a claim or defense for which state law supplies the rule of decision.

Presumptions have developed for a variety of reasons. Many of them reflect common experience, such as a presumption that a person driving a car is driving it with the authorization of the owner, or that a letter properly mailed will be received by its addressee. Some presumptions are established by statute to further social policies, such as a presumption that a child born to a married woman is the child of that woman and her husband.

Using the mailed letter presumption as an example, the basic fact is the proper mailing of a letter, and the presumed fact is the addressee's having received the letter. Under the Rules, a presumption shifts the "burden of going forward with evidence to rebut or meet the presumption." Assume that in the mailed letter example, a party wanted to establish that the addressee of a letter had received it. That party could introduce evidence of the basic fact — that he or she had mailed the letter. If the evidence of the basic fact was adequate to support a finding that the basic fact was true, then unless the addressee presented evidence about not having received the letter, the judge would instruct the jury to find that the addressee had received the letter.

The Federal Rules Choice

Rule 301 represents a choice by the drafters with respect to a crucial and controversial issue about presumptions: how much benefit the proponent of a presumption should receive for introducing evidence that could support a finding that the basic fact is true. Rule 301 incorporates a shift only in the production burden and does not affect the persuasion burden. Understanding the rule involves analyzing the differences between the burdens of production and persuasion.

Production and Persuasion Burdens Defined and Compared

The burdens of production and persuasion are procedural concepts. A party who bears the burden of production on an issue loses if the party does not produce some evidence on it. When a party bearing the production burden does not produce some evidence on the issue, the party's opponent will be entitled to a directed verdict. The burden of persuasion (sometimes called the risk of non-persuasion) works differently. A party who bears the burden of persuasion on an issue loses on that issue if the party does not persuade the finder of fact that the proposition has been established by the preponderance of evidence or some other applicable standard. If the party bearing the persuasion burden fails to produce evidence that could support a jury verdict on the issue, the opponent will be entitled to a directed verdict. More importantly, the jury will be instructed that it feels that the evidence on an issue is evenly balanced, it must decide against the party who bore the burden of persuasion.

In many states and under Rule 301, presumptions affect only the production burden. This means that the proponent of a presumption is entitled to a directed verdict on the presumed fact if (1) the proponent introduces evidence adequate to support a finding that the basic fact is true, and (2) the opponent fails to produce evidence showing that the presumed fact is not true. On the other hand, if the opponent of the presumption does introduce some evidence about the existence of the presumed fact, that evidence (whether or not believed by the jury) stops the presumption from having any effect in the case. The jury will decide about the existence of the fact the proponent of the presumption wanted to establish by thinking about it in the same way the jury considers any other disputed fact. The jury will weigh all the evidence in the case to see if the proponent has established the fact's existence by a preponderance of the evidence or by whatever other standard of proof applies to the case.

A presumption affects the persuasion burden under some state evidence rules. In those situations, there are stronger benefits to the proponent of the presumption. First, the proponent must prove the basic fact or introduce evidence adequate to support a finding that the basic fact is true. Then, even if the opponent of the presumed fact introduces evidence about the presumed fact, the presumption continues to affect the case. The court will instruct the jury to find that the presumed fact is true unless the jury is persuaded by the opponent of the presumed fact that the presumed fact does not exist. This shifts the burden of persuasion, taking it away from the party who would ordinarily have borne it and placing it instead on the party who opposed the operation of the presumption.

Using the mailed letter presumption as an example, if a plaintiff had the burden of persuasion on the issue of whether the addressee of a letter had actually received the letter, the plaintiff might seek to satisfy that burden without using a presumption at all. The plaintiff could introduce direct evidence of the proposition such as testimony of an eyewitness who saw the defendant read the letter. If the plaintiff did want to use the presumption, the plaintiff would have to introduce evidence that could support a finding of the basic fact, that the plaintiff mailed the letter. In a jurisdiction that follows Rule 301, the plaintiff would then be entitled to a directed verdict on that issue unless the defendant introduced some evidence related to

233

non-receipt of the letter. If the defendant did introduce some evidence contradicting the existence of the presumed fact, that the defendant had received the letter, then the presumption would no longer have any power in the case. The judge would instruct the jury to decide the letter issue in the plaintiff's favor only if the jury was persuaded under the applicable standard that the letter was received.

In a jurisdiction that allows presumptions to shift the persuasion burden, once the plaintiff introduces evidence establishing the basic fact or providing a basis on which a jury could decide that the basic fact exists, the plaintiff would then be entitled to a directed verdict on that issue unless the defendant introduced some evidence related to non-receipt of the letter. This is the same as in a Rule 301 jurisdiction. The difference between Rule 301's production burden shift and the other approach that shifts the persuasion burden shows up if the defendant introduces some evidence contradicting the existence of the presumed fact. In that circumstance, Rule 301 requires that the presumption be ignored as a matter of procedure. In contrast, in jurisdictions where the persuasion burden is shifted, the judge would instruct the jury to decide the letter issue in the plaintiff's favor unless the jury was persuaded under the applicable standard that the letter was not received. If the jury is in doubt, the party who originally has the production burden (usually the plaintiff) wins in a persuasion-shift jurisdiction, while the party who originally has the production burden loses in a Rule 301 jurisdiction since the burden of persuasion stays where it was originally located.

The two positions on the possible effects of presumptions are identified by the names of evidence scholars who advocated them. Thayer's position, also known as the bursting bubble theory, advocated shifting only the production burden. For Thayer (and the Rules), when the opponent of a presumption introduces evidence that contradicts the existence of the presumed fact, the bubble of the presumption bursts and the presumption disappears.

The point of view that would shift the persuasion burden is identified with the scholar Morgan. This view is more complex. Morgan emphasized that many presumptions reflect common experience about the likely link between the basic fact and the presumed fact. Because of this, Morgan argued that once a party introduced evidence adequate to support a finding that the basic fact was true, the burden of persuasion should be placed on the opponent of the presumption. This point of view was rejected in the Rules.

When a presumption related to a particular issue has no effect in a case as a matter of procedure, the party who sought its benefit may still win on that issue. Referring again to the mailed letter presumption, a jury that hears testimony that a plaintiff had mailed a letter and also hears testimony that the defendant did not receive the letter could well be entitled to decide that the defendant did, in fact, receive it. In reaching that conclusion, the jury members would be relying on their own experience of life, even though they might never know that a presumption about mailed letters (based on similar conclusions about typical consequences of events) is part of our legal system's doctrines.

Chart 21 illustrates the consequences under Rule 301 for various combinations of proof by proponents and opponents with regard to basic and presumed facts.

Criminal Cases

Presumptions can cause constitutional problems in criminal cases if they are seen as foreclosing the jury's fact-finding function too much. Instructions about permitted inferences pose no difficulty because they leave a jury free to disregard the possible conclusion suggested by the inference. If using a presumption, however, would require a jury to treat proof of a basic fact as equivalent to proof of a presumed fact, then the constitutional guarantee of a jury trial may be impaired.

Chart 21 Consequences of Opponent's Responses When Proponent Introduces Evidence That Could Support a Finding That a Presumption's Basic Fact Exists (Rule 301 and Morgan Theory Compared)

Opponent's Response	Rule 301	Morgan Theory
No evidence on basic or presumed fact	Proponent entitled to directed verdict on the presumed fact	Same as Rule 301
Evidence that could support a finding that the basic fact does not exist	Jury instructed to find the presumed fact if it finds the basic fact	Same as Rule 301
Evidence that contradicts the existence of the presumed fact	No jury instruction requiring a finding; possible instruction on allowable inference from the plaintiff's evidence	Jury instructed to find the presumed fact unless it is persuaded that the presumed fact does not exist

Examples

1. A common presumption is that a death that appears to be from unnatural causes was the result of an accident rather than of suicide. This presumption may be important in claims against insurance companies where policies may exclude recovery for suicide and may provide double recovery for accidental death. Assume that a plaintiff's decedent died as a result of a fall from a high window. No one knows if he jumped intentionally or fell by accident. The decedent's estate seeks double benefits under an insurance policy, and the defendant insurance company claims that no benefits are due because the insured committed suicide. Neither party introduces any evidence about the cause of death other than evidence that would support a finding of the facts stated in this example. If the jurisdiction recognizes the accidental death presumption and treats presumptions as Rule 301 provides, how should the court rule if the plaintiff seeks a directed verdict on the insurance company's liability?

2. Another common presumption is that a person who has been absent from home without explanation for at least seven years prior to the time of trial is dead. Assume that a plaintiff seeks life insurance proceeds claiming that the insured is dead and offers evidence that the insured left home one evening eight years ago, saying he would return, and has never been seen again. The defendant insurance company introduces evidence that the insured was hospitalized and treated successfully for an illness only four years prior to the trial. The jurisdiction recognizes the seven years unexplained absence presumption and treats presumptions as Rule 301 provides. If the plaintiff presents only the evidence set out in this example, is the defendant entitled to a directed verdict?

3. In a jurisdiction that follows Rule 301, there is a presumption that if goods are given to a bailee in good condition but are returned by the bailee to the owner in damaged condition, the damage was caused by the bailee's negligence. A plaintiff owned a valuable antique automobile in excellent condition. The defendant company agreed to store the car outdoors for two years. When the defendant returned the car after that time to the plaintiff, the car showed signs of body damage. The plaintiff seeks damages from the storage company on a negligence theory, with no evidence other than testimony about the condition of the car when he dropped it off and when he picked it up. If the defendant shows that an unprecedented hailstorm had occurred, causing body damage to many cars on the defendant's property, what effect would the presumption have in the case? Would a Morgan jurisdiction treat the case differently?

Explanations

1. The plaintiff has introduced evidence adequate to support a finding of the basic fact, an unnatural death. This places the burden of producing evidence related to the nature of the death to the defendant under Rule 301. Since the defendant has failed to produce any evidence on the subject, the plaintiff is entitled to a directed verdict.

2. The plaintiff has introduced evidence adequate to support a finding of the basic fact, absence from usual whereabouts without explanation for at least seven years. The defendant has introduced evidence contradicting the existence of the basic fact. This means that there is a jury question as to the existence of the basic fact. The judge should charge the jury that if it believes that the plaintiff has established the basic fact, it must find that the insured is dead. This result is required because in a circumstance where the jury believes the basic fact has been established, Rule 301 states that the presumed fact will be taken as true unless the opponent of the presumption produces some evidence about the presumed fact. In this case, the defendant has failed to produce any evidence about whether the insured is dead or alive at the time of trial. The defendant's only evidence relates to the insured's being alive at an earlier date. That evidence might be adequate to prevent a finding of the basic fact, but it does not counter the fact sought to be presumed (that the insured is dead at the time of trial).

3. Under Rule 301, this is a case in which the plaintiff has gained the benefit of the presumption by providing evidence on which it could be concluded that the basic facts were true. There was credible evidence that the car was bailed in good condition and was returned with damage. The effect of the presumption was to require the defendant to produce evidence related to the presumed fact. The defendant has done that, by showing that the harm to the car could have been caused non-negligently (by an unpredictable hail storm). Under Rule 301, the jury instructions would make no reference to the presumption, and it would have no effect on the outcome of the case. In a Morgan jurisdiction, the jury would be instructed to decide whether the plaintiff had established the basic facts. If the jury believed that the basic facts were established, it would be required to find negligence *unless* the defendant proved it had exercised reasonable care. This is in contrast to the standard approach in negligence cases, which requires the plaintiff to show that the defendant was unreasonable. Morgan's view would shift the persuasion burden in a case like this, while the Federal Rules treat it as one in which the "bubble" of the presumption has burst.

CHAPTER 10

Judicial Notice

INTRODUCTION

The Federal Rules regulate judicial notice of "adjudicative" facts. Those are facts that are unique to the parties in the litigation in contrast to other facts, called "legislative" facts, that are related to background ideas about reality or law. These legislative facts are so unavoidably a part of the judicial process that they operate without any controls from the law of evidence. For this reason, the judicial notice provisions of the Rules apply only to adjudicative facts. The necessary definitions and procedures are set out in Rule 201:

> **(a) Scope.** This rule governs judicial notice of an adjudicative fact only, not a legislative fact.
>
> **(b) Kinds of Facts That May Be Judicially Noticed.** The court may judicially notice a fact that is not subject to reasonable dispute because it:
>
> **(1)** is generally known within the trial court's territorial jurisdiction; or
>
> **(2)** can be accurately and readily determined from sources whose accuracy cannot reasonably be questioned.
>
> **(c) Taking Notice.** The court:
>
> **(1)** may take judicial notice on its own; or
>
> **(2)** must take judicial notice if a party requests it and the court is supplied with the necessary information.
>
> **(d) Timing.** The court may take judicial notice at any stage of the proceeding.

(e) Opportunity to Be Heard. On timely request, a party is entitled to be heard on the propriety of taking judicial notice and the nature of the fact to be noticed. If the court takes judicial notice before notifying a party, the party, on request, is still entitled to be heard.

(f) Instructing the Jury. In a civil case, the court must instruct the jury to accept the noticed fact as conclusive. In a criminal case, the court must instruct the jury that it may or may not accept the noticed fact as conclusive.

Adjudicative and Legislative Facts Distinguished

When a witness uses a word like *chair*, no one requires that it be defined because we assume that everyone knows what the witness means. If a case involves bad driving and a witness wants to testify that the driver seemed extremely tired just before he started to drive, a judge will decide the relevancy of that testimony on the basis of the judge's own knowledge about driving and tiredness. Judges will not require a witness to define *chair* because they assume we all know what it is. They base that assumption not on evidence introduced by any party but on what they know of our society and culture. Similarly, when a judge uses his or her perceptions of how our civilization works to decide whether tiredness is relevant to poor driving, the judge is permitted to decide the relevancy question without any evidence being admitted on just how tiredness and driving may really be related.

Adjudicative facts are usually more specific than legislative facts. They include such matters as the identity of people or companies involved in a dispute, what they might have done, where they did it, when they did it, and why and how they have acted. Parties usually seek to establish this type of fact through witnesses and physical evidence. With judicial notice, however, a party can be excused from presenting any proof at all. The doctrine applies only to facts that are generally known in the trial court's jurisdiction or that can be determined easily from sources whose accuracy cannot reasonably be questioned. The location of a large hotel, the residential character of a neighborhood, typical fees charged by attorneys, typical costs of staying in a hotel and buying meals in local restaurants, and frequent occurrences of icy driving conditions in an area would all be types of facts that could be subject to judicial notice as well-known in the court's jurisdiction. The other basis for judicial notice, that a fact can be ascertained from a standard trustworthy source, supports judicial notice, for example, of times of sunrise and sunset found in an almanac, the incubation period for measles found in a medical text, and a person's past conviction of a crime found in court records.

Procedures for Judicial Notice

Any party may request the court to take judicial notice of a fact, and argument is permitted on that motion. A court may also take judicial notice on its own motion. It is significant that the party opposed to the use of judicial notice is entitled to argue that the process should not be used, because once judicial notice is taken of a fact, the jury will be instructed in a civil case that it must take that fact as true. In criminal cases, the instruction will be that the jury may treat the judicially noticed fact as true because a mandatory instruction might impinge on the constitutionally protected right to jury consideration. Since judicial notice may completely or partially foreclose the jury's decision on an issue, the ability to argue against it is important. Evidence that would be relevant in an effort to persuade a jury about the issue will be presented instead to the judge in the effort to keep the decision as one for the jury and to prevent it from being made personally by the judge.

Examples

1. Masterful Detergent Corporation has sued a competitor, Kenmore Cleansers Corporation, claiming that its advertisements falsely represent that Kenmore's detergent is better for the environment than brands sold by Masterful. Assuming that an advertisement is actionable only if its claims involve a topic that is important to buyers, could Masterful successfully seek to have a court judicially notice the fact that concern about the environment is common among consumers of household products?

2. In Example 1, if the defendant claimed that the main ingredient in the plaintiff's detergents is poisonous to fish, how should a court respond to a request that it take judicial notice of that fact?

3. In a negligence suit, the plaintiff sought to establish that the defendant was on notice that some consumers had problems with its products because it had been the defendant in several suits alleging injuries from the products. Could the court take judicial notice of the judgments in those suits?

4. In a suit involving alleged negligent driving, the plaintiff sought judicial notice of the fact that a street where an accident occurred is in a residential neighborhood. Since that fact was well-known in the jurisdiction, the court ruled that it would take judicial notice of it. If a defense witness stated in testimony that the neighborhood has a lot of stores and gas stations, is the defendant entitled to a jury instruction that leaves to the jury the question of whether the street is in a residential neighborhood?

Explanations

1. Judicial notice would be wrong for this claimed fact. A court would probably consider this fact to be "legislative" since it is a general fact about the society, rather than a specific fact about one of the party's products. The idea that people generally care about health or the environment is something that a court could assume itself in its own interpretation of legal standards. On the other hand, if the *degree* to which consumers care about the environment is at issue in the current trial, the court would not consider it suitable for judicial notice since it is not ascertainable from well-regarded reference books and it might be hard to describe it as generally known in the court's jurisdiction.

2. If the poisonous nature of the chemical in the plaintiff's detergent is described in standard reference books, the court could properly take judicial notice of that fact.

3. Because court records of judgments are likely to be highly reliable, the requested judicial notice should be taken. Note that the plaintiff's theory of relevancy does not require that hearsay issues be considered because whether the claims were true or not, they would support a showing of the defendant's awareness of consumers' dissatisfaction with the products.

4. Once judicial notice has been taken, the fact noticed is properly made the subject of a conclusive jury instruction. In this case the jury would be told that as a factual matter, it must hold that the street is in a residential neighborhood. Despite the contrary statement made by one of the defendant's witnesses, if the court has decided to judicially notice a fact, the jury must treat that fact as conclusively established.

Analyzing Exam Questions: Multi-Issue Essay and Multiple-Choice Questions

INTRODUCTION

The examples in the previous chapters are meant to help you understand and apply the rules and doctrines for specific issues in evidence law. Because each chapter covers a particular topic, figuring out the focus of each example is ordinarily straightforward. Similarly, in practice and in many law school exams the topics of evidence problems can be easy to identify.

But law school exams may have essay questions that raise multiple evidence issues in the context of a single fact pattern. And with multiple-choice questions, it may not always be easy to identify to rule or doctrine being tested. For review, this chapter offers some practice exam questions and explanations of the issues they raise.

Techniques for Analyzing Essay Questions

Several approaches can help you write an excellent analysis of an evidence issue. First, be sure to be clear about exactly what evidence is being considered and the exact purpose for which it is offered. Second, be explicit about the details of any rule that you apply, because that will help you notice and treat all the ways in which the rule applies to your issue. Finally, accept the fact that evidence problems can have more than one right answer. For some items of evidence, a trial judge might reasonably choose either admission or exclusion. Trial judges are accorded broad discretion. And many evidence decisions require weighing of amounts of probative value and amounts of potential prejudice, in a necessarily imprecise balancing. A thoughtful analysis will explain this, and explain why a particular evidence issue may be "too close to call."

Examples

1. Victor Victim was beaten by an assailant who hit him many times with a lead pipe. David Defendant is charged with this crime and is being tried in federal court.

   The prosecution's case is fairly weak. There is no forensic evidence. Two somewhat unreliable witnesses testified that they saw Defendant commit the crime.

   Defendant testified that he did not commit the crime, and that he has a gentle and non-aggressive disposition. Frank Friend, a friend of Defendant's, testified for Defendant. Friend stated that he was present at the scene of Victim's beating, and that the person who beat Victim did not look like Defendant.

   Defendant had been convicted of two felonies prior to the current trial. Six years ago he was convicted of assault with a deadly weapon. Four years ago he was convicted of stealing a car. Friend is also a felon. Seven years ago he was convicted of assault with a deadly weapon.

   A. Discuss what use the prosecution may make, if any, of Defendant's convictions to show that he committed the charged crime.

   B. Discuss what use the prosecution may make, if any, of Defendant's convictions to impeach his testimony, assuming that the judge believes each conviction has low probative value with regard to truth-telling.

   C. Discuss what use the prosecution may make, if any, of Friend's conviction to impeach Friend's testimony, assuming that the judge believes the conviction has low probative value with regard to truth-telling.

2. Sam Shopper was injured in Bigstore, a home improvement store, when a heavy box fell from the top of a very tall display and hit him in the head. Shopper has sued Bigstore for damages, claiming that it acted negligently in setting up the display. As part of its defense, Bigstore will seek to establish that careless conduct by Shopper played a major role in the incident.

   Assume that you represent Shopper. You have investigated the event and found the following facts:

   • Whenever there is an injury at Bigstore, the manager on duty prepares an "incident report" about it. Each year, managers prepare about fifty such reports. After Shopper's injury, Max Manager, the manager who was on duty at the time, talked to some people who had seen it and then wrote a report. The report says, in part, "About ten minutes after the accident, a customer named Walter Watcher told me that he saw the whole thing and that Shopper was running around like crazy and ran right into the display and made the box fall on him."

- Manager has a reputation among Bigstore employees for lying about conditions in the workplace and about how well workers do their jobs.
- Manager once told a friend of his that "Bigstore's been a great employer for me — I hope it stays in business for a hundred years and keeps on getting more and more successful."
- Two years ago, Manager lied about his age to get a discount ticket for a movie.
- Watcher was convicted five years ago of selling stolen goods and sentenced to a two-year prison term.

Discuss the following aspects of the case.

A. Could Manager testify that Shopper was running around before he was hurt, if Manager's only knowledge of that comes from what Watcher told Manager?

B. If Manager is allowed to testify about what Watcher said, must Bigstore introduce the incident report that contains a record of his words?

C. Is the incident report likely admissible to prove that Shopper was running around before he was hurt?

D. Can Shopper make any use of the information about Manager's reputation, his feelings for Bigstore, and his lying to get a discount if Manager testifies?

E. If the incident report is introduced, can Shopper make any use of the information about Watcher's conviction, Manager's reputation, Manager's feelings for Bigstore, and Manager's lying to get a discount?

3. Dan Driver was sued by the estate of Walt Walker, on the theory that negligent driving by Driver caused Walker's death. Last year, Driver was driving an SUV on a busy street in the business district of a large city. At a point in the middle of a block, Walker walked into the street from between two parked cars. There was a collision between Walker and Driver's vehicle.

Walker was hospitalized after the incident for treatment of serious injuries. Four days after the collision, Walker said to Frank Friend in the hospital:

"I don't know if I'm ever going to recover, but I can tell you one thing I've learned from this. It's really stupid to try to drive an SUV and read a newspaper at the same time."

About a week later, Walker died as a result of his injuries.

A. To show that Driver had been reading a newspaper while driving, Walker's estate sought to introduce testimony by Friend quoting the statement Walker made in the hospital. Discuss whether this testimony should be permitted.

B. To show that Walker had darted out in front of the vehicle suddenly, without looking around to see if any vehicles were coming, the estate sought to introduce testimony that Walker had been fired from a factory job for being careless around machinery and that Walker had been hit by cars while crossing streets on two prior occasions during the previous twenty-five years. Discuss whether this testimony should be permitted.

Explanations

1. This example raises issues about character evidence and the propensity inference in two contexts, substantive uses (to show that the defendant acted within the law) and impeachment uses (to show that Defendant and Friend may have lied while testifying).

   A. The prosecution would ordinarily be prohibited from using Defendant's convictions to show that he committed the charged crime, because Rule 404(a)(1) states that evidence about a person's character may not be used to show that he or she acted in conformity with that character at a particular time. However, this example brings Rule 404(a)(2)(A) into play. That provision authorizes a criminal defendant to use proof of his or her character to support a positive propensity inference and also authorizes the prosecution to respond to such an effort with opposite character evidence.

      In this example, Defendant has introduced evidence of his own character by testifying that he has a gentle and non-aggressive disposition. This makes it allowable for the prosecution to introduce rival character evidence about the same trait. The past conviction for assault with a deadly weapon could support a conclusion that Defendant has a violent and aggressive disposition, so it would likely be admissible in response to Defendant's character evidence. Defendant's other conviction, for car theft, would likely be kept out, since it does not involve the character traits that Defendant raised.

   B. When someone is a witness, that person may be impeached with evidence of prior convictions, under the terms of Rule 609. Applying this rule requires identifying whether the witness is a criminal defendant or any other witness, and whether the crime involved truth-telling or was a felony of some other kind.

In this example, the witness to be impeached is Defendant, a criminal defendant, and the past convictions are for crimes other than truth-telling crimes. Rule 609(a)(1)(B) states that evidence of those convictions may be admitted if its probative value outweighs the prejudicial effect to the defendant. The example tells us that the trial judge believes the convictions have low probative value with regard to truth-telling, which is the correct context for evaluating probative value of a conviction offered for impeachment. What risk of prejudice would these convictions have? The assault with a deadly weapon conviction would have high prejudice risk, since the current crime for which Defendant is on trial is assault with a lead pipe. The similarity between the two offenses makes it likely that a jury might use information about the past crime to conclude that Defendant is a violent person and therefore committed the charged crime. The Rule 609(a)(1)(B) balancing test would likely require exclusion of this conviction. On the other hand, Defendant's conviction for car theft has low probative value and also has low risk of prejudice. It would likely be within the trial judge's discretion to admit evidence of that conviction.

C. Friend is subject to impeachment with evidence of convictions. For Friend, the balancing test would be the one in Rule 609(a)(1)(A) for a witness other than a criminal defendant. This test is the Rule 403 balancing test. Evidence is excludable under that test only if its probative value is substantially outweighed by risks of unfair prejudice. Friend's past conviction has low probative value with regard to truthfulness, but it presents only a small risk of unfair prejudice. Perhaps a jury would conclude that because Defendant has a friend with a violent past, Defendant is also a violent person. But that risk is somewhat remote, and the Rule 403 standard incorporated in Rule 609(a)(1)(A) is a pro-admissibility standard. The trial judge would likely allow the prosecution to introduce evidence of Friend's conviction.

2. This example raises issues of hearsay, personal knowledge, the original writing rule, and impeachment. The hearsay issues require careful analysis of multiple levels of hearsay, with careful identification of the individual declarants.

A. Manager has no personal knowledge of how Shopper was acting at the time of the injury, since he did not perceive it. On the other hand, Manager does have personal knowledge of Watcher's statements, since Watcher spoke to Manager when Manager was investigating the incident. Manager would be allowed to testify that Watcher said certain words to him (words expressing the idea that Shopper was running around like crazy). Watcher's words would be hearsay if introduced to support the idea that Shopper was running around in the store. A likely hearsay exception that would cover them is the present sense impression exception, although the report says that Watcher spoke about ten minutes after the accident. Ten minutes might be too long a lapse in time, in the view of some courts, for applying the exception. Rule 803(1) requires that the statement be made "while or immediately after" the speaker perceived what the statement describes.

B. If Manager testifies about what Watcher said, Manager's testimony will presumably be identical to what Manager wrote about Watcher's words in the incident report. Does the original writing rule, Rule 1002, require that the report be introduced, on the theory that Manager's testimony is proof of the contents of that document? The correct analysis of this issue is that Manager would be allowed to testify regardless of whether the report was introduced. Manager's testimony would be based on Manager's own memory of his conversation with Watcher. It would not be based on the contents of the report, even though the report is an additional record of what Watcher said. As long as a witness is testifying about an event from his or her personal knowledge, the fact that there is also a writing or recording that contains information about that event does not require compliance with the original writing rule.

C. If it were introduced to show that Shopper was running around, the report would be hearsay. Its admissibility depends on whether hearsay exceptions apply. The report has two declarants and therefore two levels of hearsay. One declarant is Watcher, who is quoted as having said Shopper was running around. The second declarant is Manager, who wrote the entire report including the quotation of Shopper.

To prove that Shopper was running around, Watcher's words must be used for their truth. Therefore, they are hearsay. They might, or might not, be covered by the present sense impression exception, as discussed above in Part A.

Manager is the other declarant. His statement is the written incident report that quotes Watcher. In order for the report to be relevant, its contents must be true. Therefore it's hearsay, and must be covered by an exception in order to be admissible. The exception that is likely to apply is the business records exception (the "records of a regularly conducted activity" exception). Some courts have been reluctant to admit accident reports under this exception, on the theory that they are prepared with litigation in mind and not in connection with the regular activities of the enterprises that make them. On the other hand, modern businesses probably do try to acquire and analyze information about injuries, and the facts of this example state that Bigstore prepares about 50 of these reports every year. They are certainly a regular occurrence in the operation of the business.

A court would likely be within its discretion if it admitted the report, although there are legitimate grounds for rejecting both the present sense impression and business records exceptions. If either one was rejected, that would require exclusion of the entire report.

D. If Manager testifies, he is subject to impeachment. His reputation for truthfulness, proved by testimony about his reputation in the workplace, would be admissible under Rule 608(a). Manager's feelings for Bigstore would be a proper subject for testimony, since they are indicative of bias. Bias may always be proved by extrinsic testimony. When Manager testifies, he may be asked on cross-examination about lying to get a discount at the movies. This is allowed by Rule 608(b), although the questioner is permitted only to ask about the act and is not allowed to prove it with other evidence.

E. If the incident report is admitted, each declarant will be subject to impeachment, under Rule 806. Watcher's conviction could be proven under Rule 609 if Watcher had testified in person, so it may be proved when Watcher is a hearsay declarant. The crime has some probative value with regard to truth-telling, and it would impose no prejudice on Bigstore, since Bigstore and Watcher are apparently not connected in any way. Regarding Manager, his reputation and bias may be proved, as discussed above in Part D. (Asking about Manager's past lying at the movies would be possible if Manager testifies, but if his words were brought into the trial only by means of the incident report, the Rule 608(b) method of impeachment might not be available.)

3. This example covers relevance, the hearsay treatment of unintended assertions, and the distinction between character and habit.

A. Walker's out-of-court words are sought to be introduced to show that Driver was reading while driving. They don't say that explicitly, and for that reason they might not be classified as hearsay. Under the Federal Rules, a statement that is relevant for an idea different from the one the speaker intended to convey can be introduced to prove that "different" idea. Walker's statement is not something like "Driver was reading." Instead, it is a statement about the stupidity of driving and reading at the same time. The statement does not even name Driver. If a judge considers it relevant, then it might be treated as outside the definition of hearsay. The decision on relevance would be easier, of course, if the statement did name Driver. Because the statement is vague, it may avoid being characterized as hearsay. However, that vagueness could possibly prevent its being characterized as relevant.

If the statement is relevant, which is a likely outcome under the pro-relevance test of Rule 401, then it may be admissible as non-hearsay. If it were defined as hearsay, then the Rule 804(b)(2) dying declarations exception could cover it, since the speaker anticipated death, the statement is about the cause of the death, and the trial in which it is being introduced is a civil trial.

B. Proof that Walker was fired from a factory job for carelessness could relate to how he crossed the street when he was hit by the SUV only if a jury inferred from the firing that Walker is a careless person. This is the type of propensity inference from character that Rule 404(a)(1) prohibits.

Proof that Walker had been hit by cars while crossing streets twice in the past could show that he is characteristically careless, but that use of this information would be barred by Rule 404(a)(1). Rule 406 allows proof of habit to prove conduct in conformity with that habit. Walker's instances of being hit ought to be treated as outside the definition of habit. A habit is a kind of conduct that is almost automatic in response to a particular stimulus. To have been hit by cars three times in twenty-five years is clearly different from a habit. Walker must have crossed streets many times in that many years and Walker was hit only three times. Since the evidence would be barred by Rule 404 and is outside the coverage of Rule 406, it should be kept out.

Techniques for Analyzing Multiple-Choice Questions

The obvious key to success in a multiple-choice test is to know the subject matter really well. But a few techniques can help you to make sure that the test format does not prevent you from showing the knowledge you actually have.

First, pay careful attention to the call of each question. A question may ask which of the possible answers is best, least likely, or most likely, for example. If you're tempted to read the question very quickly to save time, remember that no matter how much time you have to use in considering your answer, you can make a correct selection only if you understand the question.

Before you read the possible answers, it's a good idea to try to answer the question on your own. That thought process will help you identify the best choice. It will position you to evaluate the various choices critically.

Of course, any suggested answer that contains an erroneous description of a rule or doctrine is an answer to reject. Also, when answers contain words like all, none, always, or never, they may well be incorrect (because life and the law are complex, lots of times unqualified statements will be wrong). Finally, it may help you to evaluate the offered answers if you do a rough "true/false" estimate for each of them.

Examples

1. Harry Helper pleaded guilty to conspiring to rob a bank. At the proceeding in which his plea was accepted, Helper admitted in open court that he agreed with Bruce Boss to rob a bank. Helper died one week later. Later, at a trial of Boss for the same bank robbery, the prosecution seeks to introduce evidence of what Helper said when he made his plea of guilty, to show that Helper agreed with Boss to rob the bank. What ruling is best?
   A. Exclude it.
   B. Admit it as a statement against penal interest.
   C. Admit it as a prior statement made under oath at a proceeding.
   D. Admit it as a coconspirator's statement.

2. The estate of Victor Victim has brought a products liability suit against FruitCo, a manufacturer of diet supplements, claiming that Victim was killed by contaminants in a FruitCo product. The estate seeks to introduce a hospital record with the following notation: "Victim's wife says Victim told her he had two glasses of FruitCo supplements a few hours ago." The number of out-of-court statements in this evidence is:
   A. One.
   B. Two.
   C. Three.
   D. Four.

3. Paul Plaintiff was hurt in an accident involving a truck driven by Tess Trucker for her employer, XYZ Company. Plaintiff sought damages from XYZ. To show that XYZ had failed to maintain the truck properly, Plaintiff seeks to introduce evidence that a week after the accident, after having been fired by XYZ, Trucker told someone that the truck's steering wheel did not work properly when the accident occurred. With regard to hearsay, what ruling is best?
   A. Not hearsay, under Rules 801(a), (b), and (c).
   B. Not hearsay, under Rule 801(d).
   C. Hearsay under Rules 801(a), (b), and (c), but admissible under Rule 803 or Rule 804.
   D. Inadmissible hearsay.

4. Sally Sleuth, an accident investigator, interviewed many people who had seen an accident, and made notes of their statements. On the basis of that information Sleuth reached a conclusion about what caused the accident. Sleuth seeks to testify about her conclusion. What ruling is best?
   A. If Sleuth is qualified as an expert, the testimony is admissible.
   B. If Sleuth is qualified as an expert and experts in this field typically rely on interviews with eyewitnesses, the testimony is admissible.
   C. Because the testimony is based on hearsay statements, it should be excluded.

251

    D. The testimony is admissible only if its proponent also introduces Sleuth's interview notes, or copies of those notes, or an explanation for the unavailability of those notes.

5. Tom Talker testifies for the plaintiff in a consumer fraud case against a local car dealer. The defendant seeks to discredit Talker's testimony. Which of the following methods would be *forbidden*?

    A. Introducing testimony by a witness that Talker has a poor reputation for truthfulness in his home town.

    B. Introducing testimony by a witness that Talker has made many calls to radio talk shows in which he called car dealers as "the worst thieves in history."

    C. Asking Talker whether Talker has been involved in fights in his workplace (assuming the defendant has a good faith basis for believing that Talker has been involved in fights at his workplace).

    D. Asking Talker whether Talker was once fired from a job for lying to customers (assuming the defendant has a good faith basis for believing that Talker was fired from a job for lying to customers).

Explanations

1. Choice A is the best answer. How would you reach that choice? A starting point would be to notice that this question involves a trial in which a party is seeking to introduce a statement made out of court, to prove the truth of what it asserted. The declarant of that statement is Helper, and he made the statement in a courtroom in a proceeding different from the one in which Boss is being tried.

    It is important to notice that Boss is a criminal defendant. When there is an out-of-court statement and a criminal trial, there can be Confrontation Clause issues. Testimonial hearsay is prohibited by the Confrontation Clause but non-testimonial hearsay may be admitted if it is covered by an exception to the usual rule that bars hearsay.

    Is this hearsay testimonial? It was made in a formal context where criminal prosecution would have been in the mind of the speaker and those to whom he spoke. There was no on-going emergency requiring communication to law enforcement or anyone else. So, this is a clear example of testimonial hearsay that must be excluded, unless the declarant is unavailable and the defendant against whom it is sought to be admitted had a chance to cross-examine the declarant when the declarant made the statement. There is no cross-examination when a defendant enters a plea, and Boss would not have been involved in Helper's plea proceeding.

    Choices B, C, and D are all possible ways that some out-of-court statements may be admitted to prove the truth of what they assert. But the Confrontation Clause supersedes these considerations. If it requires exclusion of a statement, the statement must be kept out. This leads to the conclusion that Choice A is the correct answer.

By the way, if it weren't for the Confrontation Clause, Choice B could be a good answer. The statement was clearly against the declarant's penal interest, and the declarant is unavailable because he has died. Choice C would be wrong no matter what, since Helper's words are neither consistent nor consistent with trial testimony (Helper is not giving any testimony against Boss) and Boss did not have an opportunity to cross-examine Helper. Choice D is wrong because a statement admitting guilt cannot be a statement that furthers the goals of a conspiracy.

2. Choice C is correct. This is an example of a multiple-choice question where the best approach is to answer it before reading the answers that are offered. To analyze a hearsay within hearsay problem, it's a good idea to identify each declarant and each declarant's statement. Here, Victim said something to Victim's wife about taking supplements. Victim's wife said something to a hospital worker about Victim having made a statement concerning supplements. The hospital worker made a written statement saying that Victim's wife said Victim had said some words. Thus, Victim, Victim's wife, and a hospital worker were all declarants — making a total of three declarants.

3. Choice D is the best answer. A quick reading of this question shows that it involves an out-of-court statement. The available answers do not suggest any analytical approaches, since they just identify four kinds of out-of-court statements (out-of-court statements not admitted for their truth, out-of-court statements that are opponent's statements or certain declarant-witness statements, out-of-court statements that are covered by enumerated exceptions, and out-of court statements that are inadmissible hearsay).

The question tells us that the out-of-court statement by Trucker is sought to be admitted for a purpose that requires it to be used for its truth. This means it will be excluded unless it is exempt from the definition of hearsay or is covered by an exception to the hearsay exclusion rule. The likeliest provisions that *might* allow the words to be admitted are the rules for opponents' statements, excited utterances, and present sense impressions. The statement is outside the coverage of the provision for an employee's statement offered against an employer, since Trucker was not working for XYZ when she made it. It is not an excited utterance or a present sense impression, since there is no indication she was upset when she spoke and the problem says that Trucker made the statement a week after the accident, not during or immediately after the event the statement described. This reasoning leads to the conclusion that the statement is inadmissible hearsay, Choice D.

4. The best answer is Choice B. This question illustrates an important technique for multiple choice tests: it's possible to identify a choice as wrong, and then to consider only the remaining possibilities. Choice D represents a misunderstanding of the Original Writing Rule. That rule comes into action when a witness seeks to testify about the contents of a document; it has no application is a witness testifies about things the witness knows personally even if those things happen also to be recorded in a document. Sleuth's knowledge of her interviews derives from her having conducted the interviews, not from having read written records of those interviews.

   Having eliminated Choice D, the next step is to consider the other possible answers. This problem involves testimony based on out-of-court statements. Usually that kind of testimony would be subject to a hearsay objection. That makes Choice C seem like a plausible answer, but it's really too broad. Lots of times hearsay is admissible. And one of the other two possible answers represents exactly that situation. When a person testifies as an expert witness, he or she may rely on any sources of information that experts in his or her field typically use. This is what Choice B describes. Comparing Choice A with Choice B shows another aspect of multiple choice questions that's important to notice. The idea in Choice A is partly correct, but it leaves out an important idea — experts may use otherwise inadmissible material in formulating their opinions, but they may do so only if other experts typically would use that kind of material. Because Choice B gives a full explanation of this concept, Choice B is the best response.

5. Choice C is the correct answer. This question does not ask for a "right" answer, instead it asks you to identify which of four possibilities would be forbidden. This means that three of the four choices will be accurate applications of evidence rules or doctrines, and one will be erroneous. The correct answer will be the single example of a wrong application of evidence law.

   Since the question states that a party will be trying to discredit a witness's testimony, it might be helpful to remember the various kinds of impeachment that parties are allowed to use. One can prove a witness's bad character for truthfulness with reputation or opinion testimony. Evidence that shows a witness's bias is permitted. Proving specific instances of a witness's past conduct with extrinsic testimony is prohibited, but a cross-examiner can ask about them if they are relevant to the witness's character for truthfulness.

   With those ideas in mind, it's clear that Choice A describes a standard permitted style of impeachment, presenting testimony about a witness's reputation related to truthfulness. Choice B is an example of evidence that could show the bias of a witness. A person who thinks car dealers are the worst thieves in history may be influenced by that feeling when testifying against a particular car dealer in a particular case. Choices C and D are similar. In each one, a cross-examiner would ask the witness about a particular incident in his past. In Choice C, the past conduct has nothing to do with truthfulness (fights in a workplace), so the question would be prohibited. In Choice D, the past conduct is closely related to truthfulness (lying to customers), so a cross-examiner would be allowed to inquire about it.

Federal Rules of Evidence

This appendix provides the full text of the Federal Rules of Evidence. Explanations are provided for most of the rules, clarifying their meaning and providing reminders of important issues in their application. The paragraphs bordered by vertical lines that begin with the word "Explanation" are *not* part of the text of the Rules.

ARTICLE I. GENERAL PROVISIONS

Rule 101. Scope; Definitions

(a) **Scope.** These rules apply to proceedings in United States courts. The specific courts and proceedings to which the rules apply, along with exceptions, are set out in Rule 1101.

> **Explanation:** The Federal Rules of Evidence apply in the federal proceedings described in the rule. They also have been copied in a large majority of states, with some variation among states in specific provisions.

(b) **Definitions.** In these rules:
　(1) "civil case" means a civil action or proceeding;
　(2) "criminal case" includes a criminal proceeding;
　(3) "public office" includes a public agency;

(**4**) "record" includes a memorandum, report, or data compilation;

(**5**) a "rule prescribed by the Supreme Court" means a rule adopted by the Supreme Court under statutory authority; and

(**6**) a reference to any kind of written material or any other medium includes electronically stored information.

Rule 102. Purpose

These rules should be construed so as to administer every proceeding fairly, eliminate unjustifiable expense and delay, and promote the development of evidence law, to the end of ascertaining the truth and securing a just determination.

> **Explanation:** In cases requiring interpretation of these Rules, the United States Supreme Court has generally adopted a "plain meaning" approach and applied a literal analysis.

Rule 103. Rulings on Evidence

(**a**) **Preserving a Claim of Error.** A party may claim error in a ruling to admit or exclude evidence only if the error affects a substantial right of the party and:

(**1**) if the ruling admits evidence, a party, on the record:

(**A**) timely objects or moves to strike; and

(**B**) states the specific ground, unless it was apparent from the context; or

(**2**) if the ruling excludes evidence, a party informs the court of its substance by an offer of proof, unless the substance was apparent from the context.

> **Explanation:** To preserve an evidentiary issue for appeal, a party must object to the court's ruling. This protects the system against wasteful circumstances in which a party might tolerate an incorrect ruling in the hope of obtaining a favorable trial result, but then seek reversal on the evidentiary ground if the result was unfavorable. The offer of proof requirement is intended to assist trial courts in making evidentiary rulings, since it guarantees that the trial court will have a clear idea of the offered evidence.

(b) Not Needing to Renew an Objection or Offer of Proof. Once the court rules definitively on the record — either before or at trial — a party need not renew an objection or offer of proof to preserve a claim of error for appeal.

(c) Court's Statement About the Ruling; Directing an Offer of Proof. The court may make any statement about the character or form of the evidence, the objection made, and the ruling. The court may direct that an offer of proof be made in question-and-answer form.

(d) Preventing the Jury from Hearing Inadmissible Evidence. To the extent practicable, the court must conduct a jury trial so that inadmissible evidence is not suggested to the jury by any means.

(e) Taking Notice of Plain Error. A court may take notice of a plain error affecting a substantial right, even if the claim of error was not properly preserved.

Rule 104. Preliminary Questions

(a) In General. The court must decide any preliminary question about whether a witness is qualified, a privilege exists, or evidence is admissible. In so deciding, the court is not bound by evidence rules, except those on privilege.

> **Explanation:** The trial judge, not the jury, decides whether evidence is admissible. For almost every possible objection to admission, the judge rules. There is only one specific type of objection that is left for the jury to rule on, "conditional relevance," described in the next part of this rule. See page **4**.

(b) Relevance That Depends on a Fact. When the relevance of evidence depends on whether a fact exists, proof must be introduced sufficient to support a finding that the fact does exist. The court may admit the proposed evidence on the condition that the proof be introduced later.

> **Explanation:** This is the one type of objection to admissibility that the jury decides itself (and is not, therefore, something ruled on by the judge). If the party seeking to introduce an item of evidence agrees that it is not relevant by itself but states that it will be relevant when some other fact is established that provides a context for it, the situation is defined as "relevancy conditioned on fact." In this situation, the evidence is required to be admitted. The jury will hear it. If the proponent then

> fails to produce information about the supporting context that is required to make the challenged evidence relevant, the jury can be depended on to notice that the challenged evidence has no relevancy to the case. The jury will thus disregard it easily, since there will be no temptation to use a nonrelevant item of evidence in deliberations. See pages **9-10**.

(c) Conducting a Hearing So That the Jury Cannot Hear It. The court must conduct any hearing on a preliminary question so that the jury cannot hear it if:

> **(1)** the hearing involves the admissibility of a confession;
>
> **(2)** a defendant in a criminal case is a witness and so requests; or
>
> **(3)** justice so requires.

(d) Cross-Examining a Defendant in a Criminal Case. By testifying on a preliminary question, a defendant in a criminal case does not become subject to cross-examination on other issues in the case.

(e) Evidence Relevant to Weight and Credibility. This rule does not limit a party's right to introduce before the jury evidence that is relevant to the weight or credibility of other evidence.

> **Explanation:** When evidence is admitted because of a ruling by the judge that it is relevant or otherwise suitable for admission, that finding by the judge does not prevent the opponent of the evidence from attempting to show that it is not relevant or that in some other way its admission was based on an incorrect finding. For example, a confession may be introduced after a finding by the judge that it was given voluntarily, but the opponent of that evidence is still entitled to introduce evidence and argue to the jury that the confession was coerced.

Rule 105. Limiting Evidence That Is Not Admissible Against Other Parties or for Other Purposes

If the court admits evidence that is admissible against a party or for a purpose — but not against another party or for another purpose — the court, on timely request, must restrict the evidence to its proper scope and instruct the jury accordingly.

> **Explanation:** Sometimes there is a legitimate basis for bringing evidence into a trial even though the same evidence would have to be excluded if its proponent

sought to have it admitted on another basis. In this situation, a rule could state that the evidence must stay out, but the drafters of the Federal Rules decided that it was better to bring the worthwhile information into the trial, and take the chance that a jury would be able to obey an instruction telling it that certain evidence could influence their deliberations only with respect to a certain party or with respect to a certain issue. See page **9**.

Rule 106. Remainder of or Related Writings or Recorded Statements

If a party introduces all or part of a writing or recorded statement, an adverse party may require the introduction, at that time, of any other part — or any other writing or recorded statement — that in fairness ought to be considered at the same time.

Explanation: When a writing or recording is introduced, any other parts of it or any related statements selected by the opposing party must be admitted if the judge thinks they provide a fair context for understanding the portions already admitted.

ARTICLE II. JUDICIAL NOTICE

Rule 201. Judicial Notice of Adjudicative Facts

(a) Scope. This rule governs judicial notice of an adjudicative fact only, not a legislative fact.

Explanation: "Adjudicative facts" are facts that are specific to a particular litigation, such as whether a certain street is in a business or residential district. A related term, "legislative facts" refers to more general facts about society and human nature that are not available for judicial notice, such as whether business districts usually have more pedestrian traffic than residential districts do. See page **240**.

(b) Kinds of Facts That May Be Judicially Noticed. The court may judicially notice a fact that is not subject to reasonable dispute because it:

(1) is generally known within the trial court's territorial jurisdiction; or

(2) can be accurately and readily determined from sources whose accuracy cannot reasonably be questioned.

> **Explanation:** Examples of facts suitable for judicial notice are the time of sunset on a particular day, found in an almanac, or the location of a well-known building in a city. See page **240**.

(c) Taking Notice. The court:

(1) may take judicial notice on its own; or

(2) must take judicial notice if a party requests it and the court is supplied with the necessary information.

(d) Timing. The court may take judicial notice at any stage of the proceeding.

(e) Opportunity to Be Heard. On timely request, a party is entitled to be heard on the propriety of taking judicial notice and the nature of the fact to be noticed. If the court takes judicial notice before notifying a party, the party, on request, is still entitled to be heard.

> **Explanation:** A party seeking to have a court judicially notice a fact is entitled to present arguments in favor of judicial notice, and the opponent may counter those arguments. If a court announces it is taking judicial notice of a fact and there has been no argument in advance about it, an opposed party is entitled to present arguments to show that the fact is not appropriate for judicial notice. See page **241**.

(f) Instructing the Jury. In a civil case, the court must instruct the jury to accept the noticed fact as conclusive. In a criminal case, the court must instruct the jury that it may or may not accept the noticed fact as conclusive.

> **Explanation:** The special provision for criminal cases reflects the constitutional right to a jury trial and a belief that requiring the jury to accept as true a fact that the judge had accepted as true would be an unconstitutional invasion of that right. See page **241**.

ARTICLE III. PRESUMPTIONS IN CIVIL ACTIONS AND PROCEEDINGS

Rule 301. Presumptions in Civil Cases Generally

In a civil case, unless a federal statute or these rules provide otherwise, the party against whom a presumption is directed has the burden of producing evidence to rebut the presumption. But this rule does not shift the burden of persuasion, which remains on the party who had it originally.

> **Explanation:** A presumption is a procedural device involving a relationship between a specific "basic" fact and a "presumed" fact. Under the federal rules, when a party introduces evidence that could support a finding that a basic fact is true, the consequences vary according to how the opponent responds. If the opponent introduces no evidence about the presumed fact, the jury will be instructed to treat the presumed fact as true if it believes that the basic fact is true. If the opponent introduces evidence about the presumed fact that is too weak to support a conclusion that the presumed fact is not true, the result will be the same as if the opponent had introduced no evidence about the presumed fact. If the opponent introduces evidence strong enough to support a finding that the presumed fact is not true, then the trier of fact will decide about the existence of the presumed fact in the same way it decides about the existence of any other fact without regard to presumptions. See pages **231-235**.

Rule 302. Applicability of State Law in Civil Actions and Proceedings

In a civil case, state law governs the effect of a presumption regarding a claim or defense for which state law supplies the rule of decision.

> **Explanation:** State law may grant the proponent of a presumption greater benefits than the standard treatment set out in Rule 301 for presumptions that are

not a matter of state law; in those situations, state law controls. See pages **231-235**.

ARTICLE IV. RELEVANCE AND ITS LIMITS

Rule 401. Test for Relevant Evidence

Evidence is relevant if:

> **(a)** it has any tendency to make a fact more or less probable than it would be without the evidence; and
> **(b)** the fact is of consequence in determining the action.

> **Explanation:** This crucial definition of relevancy sets up a pro-admissibility standard: evidence is relevant if it has any effect on the likelihood that a disputed fact is true. Relevant evidence can make it more likely or less likely that a disputed fact is true, but no piece of evidence will make a fact more *and* less likely to be true. See pages **2-4**.

Rule 402. General Admissibility of Relevant Evidence

Relevant evidence is admissible unless any of the following provides otherwise:

- the United States Constitution;
- a federal statute;
- these rules; or
- other rules prescribed by the Supreme Court.

Irrelevant evidence is not admissible.

> **Explanation:** In order to be admitted, evidence must satisfy Rule 401's definition of relevancy. However, some evidence that would satisfy that definition is still excluded, for various reasons of policy. For example, privileges and the rules about character evidence exclude material that meets the definition of relevance.

Rule 403. Excluding Relevant Evidence for Prejudice, Confusion, Waste of Time, or Other Reasons

The court may exclude relevant evidence if its probative value is substantially outweighed by a danger of one or more of the following: unfair prejudice, confusing the issues, misleading the jury, undue delay, wasting time, or needlessly presenting cumulative evidence.

> **Explanation:** This balancing test allows trial courts to exclude relevant evidence where its admission would harm the judicial process through delay, confusion, or unfair prejudice. All evidence is intended to be prejudicial to the party against which it is introduced (a party ordinarily avoids introducing evidence that is favorable to the opposing side). For prejudicial effect to be significant under this rule, the effect must be one of *unfair* prejudice. See pages **4-7**.

Rule 404. Character Evidence Not Admissible to Prove Conduct; Exceptions; Other Crimes

(a) Character Evidence.

(1) **Prohibited Uses.** Evidence of a person's character or character trait is not admissible to prove that on a particular occasion the person acted in accordance with the character or trait.

> **Explanation:** Evidence may not be admitted, generally, if its only relevance is to support an inference that because a person has a certain type of character the person acted in a way typical of that character at a particular time. This is the rule against "propensity" evidence. See pages **32-36**.

(2) *Exceptions for a Defendant or Victim in a Criminal Case.* The following exceptions apply in a criminal case:

(A) a defendant may offer evidence of the defendant's pertinent trait, and if the evidence is admitted, the prosecutor may offer evidence to rebut it;

> **Explanation:** Despite the general rule against the propensity inference, a criminal defendant may introduce evidence of "good" character related to the type of

offense for which the defendant is being tried. If the defendant takes advantage of this opportunity, the prosecution is entitled to introduce opposing character evidence. If the defendant takes advantage of a different opportunity to offer character evidence, the provision in Rule 404(a)(2) about character evidence concerning an alleged victim, then the prosecution may offer similar character evidence about the defendant. See pages **49-53**.

(B) subject to the limitations in Rule 412, a defendant may offer evidence of an alleged victim's pertinent trait, and if the evidence is admitted, the prosecutor may:

(i) offer evidence to rebut it; and

(ii) offer evidence of the defendant's same trait; and

(C) in a homicide case, the prosecutor may offer evidence of the alleged victim's trait of peacefulness to rebut evidence that the victim was the first aggressor.

Explanation: To establish the defense of self-defense in criminal cases involving an attack by the defendant on another person, the defendant is entitled to introduce evidence that the victim had a violent character. The prosecution may respond to this with contradictory evidence about the victim's character and with evidence about the defendant's character. And in homicide cases, when the defendant introduces any kind of evidence to show that the victim was the aggressor, the prosecution may respond with evidence about the victim's peaceful character. See pages **49-53**.

(3) Exceptions for a Witness. Evidence of a witness's character may be admitted under Rules 607, 608, and 609.

Explanation: Character evidence that would otherwise be prohibited due to the general bar against propensity evidence is admissible for impeachment purposes under Rules 607, 608, and 609. See pages **155-164**.

(b) Crimes, Wrongs, or Other Acts.

(1) Prohibited Uses. Evidence of a crime, wrong, or other act is not admissible to prove a person's character in order to show that on a particular occasion the person acted in accordance with the character.

(2) Permitted Uses; Notice in a Criminal Case. This evidence may be admissible for another purpose, such as proving motive, opportunity, intent, preparation, plan, knowledge, identity, absence of mistake, or lack of accident. On request by a defendant in a criminal case, the prosecutor must:

      (A) provide reasonable notice of the general nature of any such evidence that the prosecutor intends to offer at trial; and

      (B) do so before trial — or during trial if the court, for good cause, excuses lack of pretrial notice.

> **Explanation:** The general bar against propensity evidence excludes evidence when the only rationale for admission is to support inferences about a person's character and the person's having acted in conformity with that character. This rule confirms that information about a person's past conduct that would naturally lead to inferences about the person's character may be introduced for different, and therefore allowable, purposes. It provides examples of typical allowable rationales such as proving that the person had special knowledge or a particular motive. See pages **36-40**.

Rule 405. Methods of Proving Character

    (a) By Reputation or Opinion. When evidence of a person's character or character trait is admissible, it may be proved by testimony about the person's reputation or by testimony in the form of an opinion. On cross-examination of the character witness, the court may allow an inquiry into relevant specific instances of the person's conduct.

> **Explanation:** Character evidence requires a two-step analysis. The first step, treated in Rule 404, is determining *whether* any information related to character is allowed to be introduced. The second step, treated in this rule, is determining *how* that character information may be proved. In every situation where character information is admissible, it may be shown with opinion or reputation testimony. Information about specific past acts relevant to establishing a person's character may be asked about on cross-examination. See pages **43-44**.

    (b) By Specific Instances of Conduct. When a person's character or character trait is an essential element of a charge, claim, or defense, the character or trait may also be proved by relevant specific instances of the person's conduct.

> **Explanation:** Information about specific things a person has done can support conclusions about that person's character. Proof of this type of information about character is permitted only when character itself is an issue required to be resolved in a case, as it may be in defamation or negligent entrustment cases or cases where a criminal defendant seeks to establish entrapment. See pages **43-44**.

Rule 406. Habit; Routine Practice

Evidence of a person's habit or an organization's routine practice may be admitted to prove that on a particular occasion the person or organization acted in accordance with the habit or routine practice. The court may admit this evidence regardless of whether it is corroborated or whether there was an eyewitness.

> **Explanation:** A habit or custom is a routine way of doing something that a person or organization accomplishes in a uniform way, free from individual thought or judgment about how to do it. Proof that a person has a habit is admissible, since it is different from proof that a person has a particular character trait. For example, always parking in a certain space in an office building's parking lot would be treated as a habit, while always driving carefully would be treated as a character trait. See pages **42-43**.

Rule 407. Subsequent Remedial Measures

When measures are taken that would have made an earlier injury or harm less likely to occur, evidence of the subsequent measures is not admissible to prove:

- negligence;
- culpable conduct;
- a defect in a product or its design; or
- a need for a warning or instruction.

But the court may admit this evidence for another purpose, such as impeachment or — if disputed — proving ownership, control, or the feasibility of precautionary measures.

> **Explanation:** Evidence that a defendant changed or repaired something after it was allegedly involved in an injury is not admissible to establish a defendant's negligence or a product's defectiveness. If there is a rationale for proving the change to establish something other than negligence or product defect, proof of the change may be admitted. The rule lists examples of such other uses, such as to prove ownership or control. See pages **20-22**.

Rule 408. Compromise and Offers to Compromise

(a) Prohibited Uses. Evidence of the following is not admissible — on behalf of any party — either to prove or disprove the validity or amount of a disputed claim or to impeach by a prior inconsistent statement or a contradiction:

(1) furnishing, promising, or offering — or accepting, promising to accept, or offering to accept — a valuable consideration in compromising or attempting to compromise the claim; and

(2) conduct or a statement made during compromise negotiations about the claim — except when offered in a criminal case and when the negotiations related to a claim by a public office in the exercise of its regulatory, investigative, or enforcement authority.

(b) Exceptions. The court may admit this evidence for another purpose, such as proving a witness's bias or prejudice, negating a contention of undue delay, or proving an effort to obstruct a criminal investigation or prosecution.

> **Explanation:** Evidence that a settlement was offered or accepted may not be admitted with respect to the validity of the claim involved in the settlement or settlement negotiations, and it may not be used to impeach by prior inconsistent statement or contradiction. Evidence of statements and conduct in settlement negotiations is similarly barred, except in criminal cases if a party to the negotiations was a governmental unit. The evidence may, however, be admitted on any other rationale such as those the rule lists as examples. See pages **22-24**.

Rule 409. Offers to Pay Medical and Similar Expenses

Evidence of furnishing, promising to pay, or offering to pay medical, hospital, or similar expenses resulting from an injury is not admissible to prove liability for the injury.

> **Explanation:** Information about medical payments and promises of medical payments is not admissible to show liability for the injury. Statements made while paying or promising can be admitted, in contrast to the Rule 408 treatment of statements made in settlement negotiations. See pages **24-25**.

Rule 410. Pleas, Plea Discussions, and Related Statements

(a) **Prohibited Uses.** In a civil or criminal case, evidence of the following is not admissible against the defendant who made the plea or participated in the plea discussions:

(1) a guilty plea that was later withdrawn;

(2) a nolo contendere plea;

(3) a statement made during a proceeding on either of those pleas under Federal Rule of Criminal Procedure 11 or a comparable state procedure; or

(4) a statement made during plea discussions with an attorney for the prosecuting authority if the discussions did not result in a guilty plea or they resulted in a later-withdrawn guilty plea.

(b) **Exceptions.** The court may admit a statement described in Rule 410(a)(3) or (4):

(1) in any proceeding in which another statement made during the same plea or plea discussions has been introduced, if in fairness the statements ought to be considered together; or

(2) in a criminal proceeding for perjury or false statement, if the defendant made the statement under oath, on the record, and with counsel present.

> **Explanation:** Certain pleas and plea bargaining statements are inadmissible except to provide a full context for partial revelation of plea bargaining statements or where a case involves perjury. See pages **25-27**.

Rule 411. Liability Insurance

Evidence that a person was or was not insured against liability is not admissible to prove whether the person acted negligently or otherwise wrongfully. But the court may admit this evidence for another purpose, such as proving a witness's bias or prejudice or proving agency, ownership, or control.

> **Explanation:** Evidence of insurance may not be admitted to show liability for negligence or other wrongful action, but other rationales, such as those given as examples, can provide a basis for admission. See pages **19-20**.

Rule 412. Sex Offense Cases: The Victim's Sexual Behavior or Predisposition

(a) **Prohibited Uses.** The following evidence is not admissible in a civil or criminal proceeding involving alleged sexual misconduct:

(1) evidence offered to prove that a victim engaged in other sexual behavior; or

(2) evidence offered to prove a victim's sexual predisposition.

> **Explanation:** This rule is sometimes called the "rape shield" provision, but it applies to all types of sexual misconduct cases. Evidence about a person's past sexual conduct and sexual traits may not be admitted to show how he or she acted in a situation that is the basis for a sex offense charge. See pages **53-55**.

(b) **Exceptions.**

(1) *Criminal Cases.* The court may admit the following evidence in a criminal case:

(A) evidence of specific instances of a victim's sexual behavior, if offered to prove that someone other than the defendant was the source of semen, injury, or other physical evidence;

(B) evidence of specific instances of a victim's sexual behavior with respect to the person accused of the sexual misconduct, if offered by the defendant to prove consent or if offered by the prosecutor; and

(C) evidence whose exclusion would violate the defendant's constitutional rights.

> **Explanation:** In criminal cases, the rule's general prohibition does not apply to evidence of the alleged victim's sexual behavior that (a) supports a claim that someone other than the defendant was the source of semen or other physical evidence, (b) occurred with the defendant and supports a claim of consent, or (c) is so crucial that exclusion would be unconstitutional.

(2) Civil Cases. In a civil case, the court may admit evidence offered to prove a victim's sexual behavior or sexual predisposition if its probative value substantially outweighs the danger of harm to any victim and of unfair prejudice to any party. The court may admit evidence of a victim's reputation only if the victim has placed it in controversy.

> **Explanation:** In civil cases, this rule's general prohibition does not apply if evidence of the alleged victim's sexual behavior or sexual traits passes a balancing test. Where the balance between probative value and risk of unfair prejudice is very close, the evidence will be excluded, even though under Rule 403 evidence will be admitted when the balance between that rule's factors is very close. Note that harm to a victim is included in this rule's list of factors to be balanced.

(c) Procedure to Determine Admissibility.

(1) Motion. If a party intends to offer evidence under Rule 412(b), the party must:

(A) file a motion that specifically describes the evidence and states the purpose for which it is to be offered;

(B) do so at least 14 days before trial unless the court, for good cause, sets a different time;

(C) serve the motion on all parties; and

(D) notify the victim or, when appropriate, the victim's guardian or representative.

(2) Hearing. Before admitting evidence under this rule, the court must conduct an in camera hearing and give the victim and parties a right to attend and be heard. Unless the court orders otherwise, the motion, related materials, and the record of the hearing must be and remain sealed.

(d) Definition of "Victim." In this rule, "victim" includes an alleged victim.

> **Explanation:** Evidence covered by this rule must be the subject of an in camera hearing on its admissibility. This protects an alleged victim from emotional trauma and invasion of privacy that otherwise might occur if implications about his or her sexual behavior were made in open court. If a judge believes that information about an instance of an alleged victim's past sexual conduct would be admissible if the past event really did occur, this would be treated as a question of conditional relevancy to be resolved by the jury on the basis of evidence and testimony presented in open court.

Rule 413. Similar Crimes in Sexual-Assault Cases

(a) **Permitted Uses.** In a criminal case in which a defendant is accused of a sexual assault, the court may admit evidence that the defendant committed any other sexual assault. The evidence may be considered on any matter to which it is relevant.

> **Explanation:** Evidence of a defendant's past sexual offense is admissible to support an inference that his or her commission of such an act in the past increases the likelihood that he or she committed the charged offense. See pages **35-36**.

(b) **Disclosure to the Defendant.** If the prosecutor intends to offer this evidence, the prosecutor must disclose it to the defendant, including witnesses' statements or a summary of the expected testimony. The prosecutor must do so at least 15 days before trial or at a later time that the court allows for good cause.

> **Explanation:** Because evidence of past sexual offenses is so prejudicial, a notice provision requires that the defendant have warning prior to its introduction.

(c) **Effect on Other Rules.** This rule does not limit the admission or consideration of evidence under any other rule.

(d) **Definition of "Sexual Assault."** In this rule and Rule 415, "sexual assault" means a crime under federal law or under state law (as "state" is defined in 18 U.S.C. §513) involving:

(1) any conduct prohibited by 18 U.S.C. chapter 109A;

(2) contact, without consent, between any part of the defendant's body — or an object — and another person's genitals or anus;

(3) contact, without consent, between the defendant's genitals or anus and any part of another person's body;

(4) deriving sexual pleasure or gratification from inflicting death, bodily injury, or physical pain on another person; or

(5) an attempt or conspiracy to engage in conduct described in subparagraphs (1)–(4).

Rule 414. Similar Crimes in Child-Molestation Cases

(a) **Permitted Uses.** In a criminal case in which a defendant is accused of child molestation, the court may admit evidence that the defendant committed any other child molestation. The evidence may be considered on any matter to which it is relevant.

> **Explanation:** Evidence of a defendant's past sexual offense is admissible to support an inference that his or her commission of such an act in the past increases the likelihood that he or she committed the charged offense. This rule is parallel to Rule 413, except that it deals with child molestation cases rather than "sexual assault" cases. See pages **35-36**.

(b) **Disclosure to the Defendant.** If the prosecutor intends to offer this evidence, the prosecutor must disclose it to the defendant, including witnesses' statements or a summary of the expected testimony. The prosecutor must do so at least 15 days before trial or at a later time that the court allows for good cause.

(c) **Effect on Other Rules.** This rule does not limit the admission or consideration of evidence under any other rule.

(d) **Definition of "Child" and "Child Molestation."** In this rule and Rule 415:

(1) "child" means a person below the age of 14; and

(2) "child molestation" means a crime under federal law or under state law (as "state" is defined in 18 U.S.C. §513) involving:

(A) any conduct prohibited by 18 U.S.C. chapter 109A and committed with a child;

(B) any conduct prohibited by 18 U.S.C. chapter 110;

(C) contact between any part of the defendant's body — or an object — and a child's genitals or anus;

(D) contact between the defendant's genitals or anus and any part of a child's body;

(E) deriving sexual pleasure or gratification from inflicting death, bodily injury, or physical pain on a child; or

(F) an attempt or conspiracy to engage in conduct described in subparagraphs (A)–(E).

Rule 415. Similar Acts in Civil Cases Involving Sexual Assault or Child Molestation

(a) **Permitted Uses.** In a civil case involving a claim for relief based on a party's alleged sexual assault or child molestation, the court may admit evidence that the party committed any other sexual assault or child molestation. The evidence may be considered as provided in Rules 413 and 414.

> **Explanation:** This is the only provision in the Federal Rules that allows character evidence to be introduced in a civil case as relevant to the issue of someone's out-of-court conduct. It allows introduction of evidence of a party's past sexual offense or child molestation to support an inference that his or her commission of such an act in the past increases the likelihood that he or she committed the conduct charged in the civil suit. See pages **35-36**.

(b) **Disclosure to the Opponent.** If a party intends to offer this evidence, the party must disclose it to the party against whom it will be offered, including witnesses' statements or a summary of the expected testimony. The party must do so at least 15 days before trial or at a later time that the court allows for good cause.

(c) **Effect on Other Rules.** This rule does not limit the admission or consideration of evidence under any other rule.

ARTICLE V. PRIVILEGES

Rule 501. Privilege in General

The common law — as interpreted by United States courts in the light of reason and experience — governs a claim of privilege unless any of the following provides otherwise:

- the United States Constitution;
- a federal statute; or
- rules prescribed by the Supreme Court.

But in a civil case, state law governs privilege regarding a claim or defense for which state law supplies the rule of decision.

> **Explanation:** No specific privilege provisions have been adopted as part of the federal rules, although detailed provisions had been proposed by the drafters. Privilege law, therefore, under the federal rules, is open to traditional common law development. In civil cases, state privilege law governs where an issue is governed by state law. See pages **195-203, 208-212**.

Rule 502. Attorney-Client Privilege and Work-Product; Limitations on Waiver

The following provisions apply, in the circumstances set out, to disclosure of a communication or information covered by the attorney-client privilege or work-product protection.

(a) **Disclosure made in a Federal proceeding or to a Federal office or agency; scope of a waiver.** When the disclosure is made in a Federal proceeding or to a Federal office or agency and waives the attorney-client privilege or work-product protection, the waiver extends to an undisclosed communication or information in a Federal or State proceeding only if:

(1) the waiver is intentional;

(2) the disclosed and undisclosed communications or information concern the same subject matter; and

(3) they ought in fairness to be considered together.

(b) **Inadvertent disclosure.** When made in a Federal proceeding or to a Federal office or agency, the disclosure does not operate as a waiver in a Federal or State proceeding if:

(1) the disclosure is inadvertent;

(2) the holder of the privilege or protection took reasonable steps to prevent disclosure; and

(3) the holder promptly took reasonable steps to rectify the error, including (if applicable) following Federal Rule of Civil Procedure 26(b)(5)(B).

(c) **Disclosure made in a State proceeding.** When the disclosure is made in a State proceeding and is not the subject of a State-court order concerning waiver, the disclosure does not operate as a waiver in a Federal proceeding if the disclosure:

(1) would not be a waiver under this rule if it had been made in a Federal proceeding; or

(2) is not a waiver under the law of the State where the disclosure occurred.

(d) **Controlling effect of a court order.** A Federal court may order that the privilege or protection is not waived by disclosure connected with the litigation pending before the court—in which event the disclosure is also not a waiver in any other Federal or State proceeding.

(e) **Controlling effect of a party agreement.** An agreement on the effect of disclosure in a Federal proceeding is binding only on the parties to the agreement, unless it is incorporated into a court order.

(f) **Controlling effect of this rule.** Notwithstanding Rules 101 and 1101, this rule applies to State proceedings and to Federal court-annexed and Federal court-mandated arbitration proceedings, in the circumstances set out in the rule. And notwithstanding Rule 501, this rule applies even if State law provides the rule of decision.

(g) **Definitions. In this rule:**

(1) "attorney-client privilege" means the protection that applicable law provides for confidential attorney-client communications; and

(2) "work-product protection" means the protection that applicable law provides for tangible material (or its intangible equivalent) prepared in anticipation of litigation or for trial.

> **Explanation:** Inadvertent disclosure of privileged information in connection with federal litigation does not create a waiver if the holder acted reasonably to prevent it and to retrieve the information. A waiver, if found, applies only to the information disclosed unless a subject matter waiver is necessary to prevent intentional and misleading use of privileged information. State courts must apply Rule 502 if there is a disclosure of privileged material at the federal level. If there is a disclosure of privileged material in a state proceeding, in a federal trial the court must determine admissibility of that material in accordance with the most protective of either state or federal law. Also, a federal court order providing that a disclosure did not constitute a waiver is enforceable in both federal and state proceedings. See page **202**.

ARTICLE VI. WITNESSES

Rule 601. Competency to Testify in General

Every person is competent to be a witness unless these rules provide otherwise. But in a civil case, state law governs the witness's competency regarding a claim or defense for which state law supplies the rule of decision.

> **Explanation:** In contrast to the common law, virtually all people are competent as witnesses, under the federal rules. Where state law governs a claim, state competency law applies. See pages **146-150**.

Rule 602. Need for Personal Knowledge

A witness may testify to a matter only if evidence is introduced sufficient to support a finding that the witness has personal knowledge of the matter. Evidence to prove personal knowledge may consist of the witness's own testimony. This rule does not apply to a witness's expert testimony under Rule 703.

> **Explanation:** If someone testifies as a lay, not an expert, witness, evidence must be introduced that could support a jury finding that the witness has direct knowledge of the subject of his or her testimony. That evidence may be introduced as part of the witness's own testimony. See pages **147-148**.

Rule 603. Oath or Affirmation

Before testifying, a witness must give an oath or affirmation to testify truthfully. It must be in a form designed to impress that duty on the witness's conscience.

> **Explanation:** The requirement of an oath or affirmation to tell the truth must be understood in the context of Rule 610 which prohibits references to religion if relevant only to attack or bolster a witness's credibility. See page **147**.

Rule 604. Interpreter

An interpreter must be qualified and must give an oath or affirmation to make a true translation.

Rule 605. Judge's Competency as a Witness

The presiding judge may not testify as a witness at the trial. A party need not object to preserve the issue.

> **Explanation:** A judge may not testify at a trial over which he or she presides. The rule protects a litigant from the futile effort of asking a judge who violates this rule to sustain an objection to his or her testimony. See page **146**.

Rule 606. Juror's Competency as a Witness

(a) At the Trial. A juror may not testify as a witness before the other jurors at the trial. If a juror is called to testify, the court must give a party an opportunity to object outside the jury's presence.

> **Explanation:** A juror cannot testify in a case he or she will be deciding. In contrast to the provision related to judges as witnesses (Rule 605), an objection is required to be made, but it can be made without the jury's knowledge. See pages **146-147**.

(b) During an Inquiry into the Validity of a Verdict or Indictment.

(1) Prohibited Testimony or Other Evidence. During an inquiry into the validity of a verdict or indictment, a juror may not testify about any statement made or incident that occurred during the jury's deliberations; the effect of anything on that juror's or another juror's vote; or any juror's mental processes concerning the verdict or indictment. The court may not receive a juror's affidavit or evidence of a juror's statement on these matters.

(2) Exceptions. A juror may testify about whether:

(A) extraneous prejudicial information was improperly brought to the jury's attention;

(B) an outside influence was improperly brought to bear on any juror; or

(C) a mistake was made in entering the verdict on the verdict form.

> **Explanation:** Jurors may not testify nor may affidavits from jurors be accepted on the subject of any juror's mental processes, statements, or anything else

> concerning how the jury reached its conclusion, except that testimony and affidavits are allowed about extraneous prejudicial information, outside influences, and mistakes on the verdict form. See pages **146-147**.

Rule 607. Who May Impeach a Witness

Any party, including the party that called the witness, may attack the witness's credibility.

> **Explanation:** This rejects the common law requirement that an offering party vouch for the honesty of its witness. All parties may impeach all witnesses. See page **155**.

Rule 608. A Witness's Character for Truthfulness or Untruthfulness

(a) **Reputation or Opinion Evidence**. A witness's credibility may be attacked or supported by testimony about the witness's reputation for having a character for truthfulness or untruthfulness, or by testimony in the form of an opinion about that character. But evidence of truthful character is admissible only after the witness's character for truthfulness has been attacked.

> **Explanation:** Opinion and reputation evidence may always be introduced to detract from the credibility of any witness. These types of evidence may also be introduced to support the credibility of any witness whose credibility has been attacked in any way. See pages **162-163**.

(b) **Specific Instances of Conduct.** Except for a criminal conviction under Rule 609, extrinsic evidence is not admissible to prove specific instances of a witness's conduct in order to attack or support the witness's character for truthfulness. But the court may, on cross-examination, allow them to be inquired into if they are probative of the character for truthfulness or untruthfulness of:

(1) the witness; or

(2) another witness whose character the witness being cross-examined has testified about.

By testifying on another matter, a witness does not waive any privilege against self-incrimination for testimony that relates only to the witness's character for truthfulness.

> **Explanation:** Past conduct of a witness, relevant to the character trait of truthfulness, may be asked about in cross-examination of the witness or in cross-examination of another witness who has testified in support of the witness's credibility. The past conduct may only be the subject of extrinsic proof if it is a crime for which the witness was convicted or if it is relevant in some way other than to show the witness's character with regard to truthfulness. See pages **160-162**.

Rule 609. Impeachment by Evidence of a Criminal Conviction

(a) In General. The following rules apply to attacking a witness's character for truthfulness by evidence of a criminal conviction:

(1) for a crime that, in the convicting jurisdiction, was punishable by death or by imprisonment for more than one year, the evidence:

(A) must be admitted, subject to Rule 403, in a civil case or in a criminal case in which the witness is not a defendant; and

(B) must be admitted in a criminal case in which the witness is a defendant, if the probative value of the evidence outweighs its prejudicial effect to that defendant; and

> **Explanation:** If a witness other than a criminal defendant has been convicted of a felony, evidence of the conviction shall be admitted unless its probative value on the topic of the witness's credibility is substantially outweighed by the risk of prejudicial effect on the defendant. If a witness is a criminal defendant, such evidence shall be admitted only if its probative value outweighs in any degree the risk of prejudice. See pages **155-161**.

(2) for any crime regardless of the punishment, the evidence must be admitted if the court can readily determine that establishing the elements of the crime required proving — or the witness's admitting — a dishonest act or false statement.

> **Explanation:** If any witness has been convicted of a crime involving dishonesty or false statements, such as perjury, evidence of the conviction shall be admitted with no balancing of probative and prejudicial impact. See page **157**.

(b) Limit on Using the Evidence After 10 Years. This subdivision (b) applies if more than ten years have passed since the witness's conviction or release from confinement for it, whichever is later. Evidence of the conviction is admissible only if:

(**1**) its probative value, supported by specific facts and circumstances, substantially outweighs its prejudicial effect; and

(**2**) the proponent gives an adverse party reasonable written notice of the intent to use it so that the party has a fair opportunity to contest its use.

> **Explanation:** If a conviction or a release from confinement related to a conviction (whichever occurred later) took place ten years or more before the trial, evidence of the conviction is admissible only if its probative value substantially outweighs its prejudicial effect. Advance notice is required. See pages **157–160**.

(c) Effect of a Pardon, Annulment, or Certificate of Rehabilitation. Evidence of a conviction is not admissible if:

(**1**) the conviction has been the subject of a pardon, annulment, certificate of rehabilitation, or other equivalent procedure based on a finding that the person has been rehabilitated, and the person has not been convicted of a later crime punishable by death or by imprisonment for more than one year; or

(**2**) the conviction has been the subject of a pardon, annulment, or other equivalent procedure based on a finding of innocence.

(d) Juvenile Adjudications. Evidence of a juvenile adjudication is admissible under this rule only if:

(**1**) it is offered in a criminal case;

(**2**) the adjudication was of a witness other than the defendant;

(**3**) an adult's conviction for that offense would be admissible to attack the adult's credibility; and

(**4**) admitting the evidence is necessary to fairly determine guilt or innocence.

(e) Pendency of an Appeal. A conviction that satisfies this rule is admissible even if an appeal is pending. Evidence of the pendency is also admissible.

Rule 610. Religious Beliefs or Opinions

Evidence of a witness's religious beliefs or opinions is not admissible to attack or support the witness's credibility.

> **Explanation:** A witness's religious beliefs or views may not be the subject of evidence introduced as relevant to credibility. This rule relates to Rule 603 that allows a witness to swear or affirm to tell the truth. See page **165**.

Rule 611. Mode and Order of Examining Witnesses and Presenting Evidence

(a) Control by the Court; Purposes. The court should exercise reasonable control over the mode and order of examining witnesses and presenting evidence so as to:
   (1) make those procedures effective for determining the truth;
   (2) avoid wasting time; and
   (3) protect witnesses from harassment or undue embarrassment.

> **Explanation:** The judge controls the order and style of testimony. See page **151**.

(b) Scope of Cross-Examination. Cross-examination should not go beyond the subject matter of the direct examination and matters affecting the witness's credibility. The court may allow inquiry into additional matters as if on direct examination.

> **Explanation:** Cross-examination may cover only the topics raised in direct examination, unless the judge allows a broader scope. See page **152**.

(c) Leading Questions. Leading questions should not be used on direct examination except as necessary to develop the witness's testimony. Ordinarily, the court should allow leading questions:
   (1) on cross-examination; and
   (2) when a party calls a hostile witness, an adverse party, or a witness identified with an adverse party.

> **Explanation:** Leading questions are allowed on cross-examination and in examining an opposing party or a hostile witness. In direct examination of a party's own witness, they are only allowed "to develop" the testimony. See page **151**.

Rule 612. Writing Used to Refresh a Witness's Memory

(a) Scope. This rule gives an adverse party certain options when a witness uses a writing to refresh memory:

(1) while testifying; or

(2) before testifying, if the court decides that justice requires the party to have those options.

(b) Adverse Party's Options; Deleting Unrelated Matter. Unless 18 U.S.C. §3500 provides otherwise in a criminal case, an adverse party is entitled to have the writing produced at the hearing, to inspect it, to cross-examine the witness about it, and to introduce in evidence any portion that relates to the witness's testimony. If the producing party claims that the writing includes unrelated matter, the court must examine the writing in camera, delete any unrelated portion, and order that the rest be delivered to the adverse party. Any portion deleted over objection must be preserved for the record.

(c) Failure to Produce or Deliver the Writing. If a writing is not produced or is not delivered as ordered, the court may issue any appropriate order. But if the prosecution does not comply in a criminal case, the court must strike the witness's testimony or — if justice so requires — declare a mistrial.

> **Explanation:** When a witness uses a document to refresh his or her recollection and then testifies from "present recollection refreshed," the opposing party is entitled to see the document, cross-examine the witness about it, and introduce parts of it that are relevant to the testimony. See pages **114-115, 169**.

Rule 613. Witness's Prior Statement

(a) Showing or Disclosing the Statement During Examination. When examining a witness about the witness's prior statement, a party need not show it or disclose its contents to the witness. But the party must, on request, show it or disclose its contents to an adverse party's attorney.

> **Explanation:** A common impeachment technique is to show that something a witness said or wrote before the trial conflicted with the witness's testimony at trial. This rule allows a questioner to use this technique without being required to produce the document or describe the statement in advance. See pages **167-170**.

(b) Extrinsic Evidence of a Prior Inconsistent Statement. Extrinsic evidence of a witness's prior inconsistent statement is admissible only if the witness is given an opportunity to explain or deny the statement and an adverse party is given an opportunity to examine the witness about it, or if justice so requires. This subdivision (b) does not apply to an opposing party's statement under Rule 801(d)(2).

> **Explanation:** Ordinarily, if a party wants to introduce a witness's past statement, rather than just ask the witness about it, the witness must be given an opportunity to comment specifically on that past statement, and the opposing party must also have an opportunity to question the witness about it. See pages **167-168**.

Rule 614. Court's Calling or Examining a Witness

(a) Calling. The court may call a witness on its own or at a party's request. Each party is entitled to cross-examine the witness.

(b) Examining. The court may examine a witness regardless of who calls the witness.

(c) Objections. A party may object to the court's calling or examining a witness either at that time or at the next opportunity when the jury is not present.

Rule 615. Excluding Witnesses

At a party's request, the court must order witnesses excluded so that they cannot hear other witnesses' testimony. Or the court may do so on its own. But this rule does not authorize excluding:

(a) a party who is a natural person;

(b) an officer or employee of a party that is not a natural person, after being designated as the party's representative by its attorney;

(c) a person whose presence a party shows to be essential to presenting the party's claim or defense; or

(d) a person authorized by statute to be present.

> **Explanation:** Someone who is a witness may be excluded from the courtroom, so that he or she cannot hear the testimony of other witnesses. Witnesses who are exempt from this treatment are people who are parties themselves or are designated representatives of

entities like corporations. Also exempt is anyone a lawyer in the case persuades the court is essential as an assistant to the lawyer. See pages **154-155**.

ARTICLE VII. OPINIONS AND EXPERT TESTIMONY

Rule 701. Opinion Testimony by Lay Witnesses

If a witness is not testifying as an expert, testimony in the form of an opinion is limited to one that is:

(**a**) rationally based on the witness's perception;

(**b**) helpful to clearly understanding the witness's testimony or to determining a fact in issue; and

(**c**) not based on scientific, technical, or other specialized knowledge within the scope of Rule 702.

> **Explanation:** A witness may speak in terms of opinions if that style of narration makes the testimony clearer. The opinions must be based on actual perceptions by the witness. See pages **153-154**.

Rule 702. Testimony by Expert Witnesses

A witness who is qualified as an expert by knowledge, skill, experience, training, or education may testify in the form of an opinion or otherwise if:

(**a**) the expert's scientific, technical, or other specialized knowledge will help the trier of fact to understand the evidence or to determine a fact in issue;

(**b**) the testimony is based on sufficient facts or data;

(**c**) the testimony is the product of reliable principles and methods; and

(**d**) the expert has reliably applied the principles and methods to the facts of the case.

> **Explanation:** Where expertise from an identifiable field will assist the finder of fact, opinion testimony by an expert in the field is permitted. The trial court must determine whether the witness's science or technology is "reliable" and whether the witness has applied that expertise "reliably." See pages **182-184**.

Rule 703. Bases of an Expert's Opinion Testimony

An expert may base an opinion on facts or data in the case that the expert has been made aware of or personally observed. If experts in the particular field would reasonably rely on those kinds of facts or data in forming an opinion on the subject, they need not be admissible for the opinion to be admitted. But if the facts or data would otherwise be inadmissible, the proponent of the opinion may disclose them to the jury only if their probative value in helping the jury evaluate the opinion substantially outweighs their prejudicial effect.

> **Explanation:** An expert can base testimony on anything the expert has heard at the trial. The testimony can also be based on anything else experts in the field reasonably rely on, such as hearsay, whether or not that material is admissible. The expert can reveal otherwise inadmissible information that was the basis of his or her testimony only if the judge concludes that its probative value outweighs any prejudicial effect it may have. See pages **186-187**.

Rule 704. Opinion on Ultimate Issue

(a) In General — Not Automatically Objectionable. An opinion is not objectionable just because it embraces an ultimate issue.

> **Explanation:** Testimony may contain conclusions on issues that the trier of fact must decide. See pages **187-188**.

(b) Exception. In a criminal case, an expert witness must not state an opinion about whether the defendant did or did not have a mental state or condition that constitutes an element of the crime charged or of a defense. Those matters are for the trier of fact alone.

> **Explanation:** Experts in criminal cases are prohibited from expressing an opinion on the specific issue of a defendant's possession of a mental state that is an element of a crime. See pages **187-188**.

Rule 705. Disclosing the Facts or Data Underlying an Expert's Opinion

Unless the court orders otherwise, an expert may state an opinion — and give the reasons for it — without first testifying to the underlying facts or data. But the expert may be required to disclose those facts or data on cross-examination.

> **Explanation:** An expert's testimony does not have to include the basis for the opinion it states, but that basis must be given on cross-examination if it is requested. See pages **186–187**.

Rule 706. Court Appointed Expert Witnesses

(a) Appointment Process. On a party's motion or on its own, the court may order the parties to show cause why expert witnesses should not be appointed and may ask the parties to submit nominations. The court may appoint any expert that the parties agree on and any of its own choosing. But the court may only appoint someone who consents to act.

> **Explanation:** Allowing the court to appoint an expert is a response to the "battle of the experts" problem in which rivals are hired by opposing sides; the provision is rarely used, however, and carries the risk that a jury will give improperly significant weight to the expert's opinion on the theory that because the judge has appointed the expert, the opinions must be respected.

(b) Expert's Role. The court must inform the expert of the expert's duties. The court may do so in writing and have a copy filed with the clerk or may do so orally at a conference in which the parties have an opportunity to participate. The expert:

(1) must advise the parties of any findings the expert makes;

(2) may be deposed by any party;

(3) may be called to testify by the court or any party; and

(4) may be cross-examined by any party, including the party that called the expert.

(c) Compensation. The expert is entitled to a reasonable compensation, as set by the court. The compensation is payable as follows:

(1) in a criminal case or in a civil case involving just compensation under the Fifth Amendment, from any funds that are provided by law; and

(2) in any other civil case, by the parties in the proportion and at the time that the court directs — and the compensation is then charged like other costs.

(d) Disclosing the Appointment to the Jury. The court may authorize disclosure to the jury that the court appointed the expert.

(e) Parties' Choice of Their Own Experts. This rule does not limit a party in calling its own experts.

ARTICLE VIII. HEARSAY

Rule 801. Definitions That Apply to This Article; Exclusions from Hearsay

(a) Statement. "Statement" means a person's oral assertion, written assertion, or nonverbal conduct, if the person intended it as an assertion.

> **Explanation:** A person's words in speech or writing and a person's conduct can all be statements under the hearsay rule, if the person intended them to convey an idea or information. See pages **73-77**.

(b) Declarant. "Declarant" means the person who made the statement.

> **Explanation:** Note that only people, not machines, can make "statements," so that a print-out from a measuring device, for example, does not involve any hearsay considerations. See pages **81-82**.

(c) Hearsay. "Hearsay" means a statement that:

(1) the declarant does not make while testifying at the current trial or hearing; and

(2) a party offers in evidence to prove the truth of the matter asserted in the statement.

> **Explanation:** A statement made by anyone (including a person who testifies as a witness at a trial) out of court is "hearsay" if the proponent seeks to introduce it to support a conclusion that the idea or information it asserts is true. See pages **68-73**.

(d) Statements That Are Not Hearsay. A statement that meets the following conditions is not hearsay:

(1) *A Declarant-Witness's Prior Statement.* The declarant testifies and is subject to cross-examination about a prior statement, and the statement:

(A) is inconsistent with the declarant's testimony and was given under penalty of perjury at a trial, hearing, or other proceeding or in a deposition;

(B) is consistent with the declarant's testimony and is offered:

(i) to rebut an express or implied charge that the declarant recently fabricated it or acted from a recent improper influence or motive in so testifying; or

(ii) to rehabilitate the declarant's credibility as a witness when attacked on another ground; or

(C) identifies a person as someone the declarant perceived earlier.

> **Explanation:** These specified situations are exceptions from the usual rule that a witness's own out-of-court words can be hearsay if introduced to support the conclusion that their assertions are true. Note that prior inconsistent statements must have been made under oath, but that prior consistent statements do not have that requirement. See pages **98-101, 167-168**.

(2) An Opposing Party's Statement. The statement is offered against an opposing party and:

(A) was made by the party in an individual or representative capacity;

(B) is one the party manifested that it adopted or believed to be true;

(C) was made by a person whom the party authorized to make a statement on the subject;

(D) was made by the party's agent or employee on a matter within the scope of that relationship and while it existed; or

(E) was made by the party's coconspirator during and in furtherance of the conspiracy.

The statement must be considered but does not by itself establish the declarant's authority under (C); the existence or scope of the relationship under (D); or the existence of the conspiracy or participation in it under (E).

> **Explanation:** At common law, statements by an opposing party, known as admissions, were an exception to the general rule of excluding hearsay. Under the Federal Rules, these statements are treated as outside the definition of hearsay. An "opposing party's statement" (formerly called an admission) is any statement a party ever made out of court that is relevant for use against the party. The rule classifies a variety of types of opponent's statements, ranging from an opponent's own statement to statements made by the opponent's agent, employee, or coconspirator. See pages **94-98**.

Rule 802. The Rule Against Hearsay

Hearsay is not admissible unless any of the following provides otherwise:

- a federal statute;
- these rules; or
- other rules prescribed by the Supreme Court.

> **Explanation:** Evidence that fits the definition of hearsay may not be admitted. Although the rule is written in absolute terms, there may be circumstances where excluding evidence on grounds of hearsay would violate a criminal defendant's constitutional right to present evidence.

Rule 803. Exceptions to the Rule Against Hearsay–Regardless of Whether the Declarant Is Available as a Witness

The following are not excluded by the rule against hearsay, regardless of whether the declarant is available as a witness:

> **Explanation:** This rule sets out a large group of hearsay exceptions, usable without regard to the availability or unavailability of the declarant.

    (1) Present Sense Impression. A statement describing or explaining an event or condition, made while or immediately after the declarant perceived it.

> **Explanation:** Note that the statement must describe or explain something while it is going on or immediately after it was going on. See page **109**.

    (2) Excited Utterance. A statement relating to a startling event or condition, made while the declarant was under the stress of excitement that it caused.

> **Explanation:** The statement stimulated by something startling must relate to (but need not describe) the startling experience. It must be made when the stress is

present, although that condition may be satisfied where a long period of time has passed if the circumstances (such as awakening from unconsciousness) support the idea that the stress could still be having an impact on the declarant. See pages **109-110**.

(**3**) **Then-Existing Mental, Emotional, or Physical Condition.** A statement of the declarant's then-existing state of mind (such as motive, intent, or plan) or emotional, sensory, or physical condition (such as mental feeling, pain, or bodily health), but not including a statement of memory or belief to prove the fact remembered or believed unless it relates to the validity or terms of the declarant's will.

> **Explanation:** This exception lets in statements like "I am the King of Mars" when introduced to show that the declarant believed he was the King when he spoke. It does not let in statements of belief about past facts. The mental state of intent is covered by the exception, as in a declarant's statement, "I plan to go to the restaurant tomorrow," introduced to show that the declarant had that plan. See pages **110-112**.

(**4**) **Statement Made for Medical Diagnosis or Treatment.** A statement that:

(**A**) is made for — and is reasonably pertinent to — medical diagnosis or treatment; and

(**B**) describes medical history; past or present symptoms or sensations; their inception; or their general cause.

> **Explanation:** Statements about physical condition, medical history, and symptoms are covered. The declarant may make the statements to either treating or diagnosing medical personnel. Statements about the cause of a condition are within the coverage of this exception only if they involve topics that reasonably relate to diagnosis or treatment. See pages **112-113**.

(**5**) **Recorded Recollection.** A record that:

(**A**) is on a matter the witness once knew about but now cannot recall well enough to testify fully and accurately;

(**B**) was made or adopted by the witness when the matter was fresh in the witness's memory; and

(**C**) accurately reflects the witness's knowledge.

If admitted, the record may be read into evidence but may be received as an exhibit only if offered by an adverse party.

> **Explanation:** Note that the witness must be shown to have either slight or no memory of the information recorded in the document, but must have known it when he or she made the record or accepted the record as accurate. See pages **113-115, 169**.

(6) *Records of a Regularly Conducted Activity*. A record of an act, event, condition, opinion, or diagnosis if:

    (A) the record was made at or near the time by — or from information transmitted by — someone with knowledge;

    (B) the record was kept in the course of a regularly conducted activity of a business, organization, occupation, or calling, whether or not for profit;

    (C) making the record was a regular practice of that activity;

    (D) all these conditions are shown by the testimony of the custodian or another qualified witness, or by a certification that complies with Rule 902(11) or (12) or with a statute permitting certification; and

    (E) the opponent does not show that the source of information or the method or circumstances of preparation indicate a lack of trustworthiness.

> **Explanation:** This "business records" exception is widely used. The declarant who is the originating source of the information in the record has a duty within the organization to provide the information. The information must be of a type that the organization usually records. If someone with no duty to report provides information that is the type of information usually kept by the organization, the document will serve as proof that the words were communicated, but the words will be admissible for their truth only if some other exception applies to them. See pages **115-116**.

(7) *Absence of a Record of a Regularly Conducted Activity*. Evidence that a matter is not included in a record described in paragraph (6) if:

    (A) the evidence is admitted to prove that the matter did not occur or exist;

    (B) a record was regularly kept for a matter of that kind; and

    (C) the opponent does not show that the possible source of the information or other circumstances indicate a lack of trustworthiness.

> **Explanation:** This is the mirror image of the business records exception, allowing evidence that information is lacking in a place where it would normally be

recorded. An argument could be made that this type of omission is not hearsay, but the presence of this exception moots that controversy. See pages **116-117**.

(8) Public Records. A record or statement of a public office if:
   (A) it sets out:
      (i) the office's activities;
      (ii) a matter observed while under a legal duty to report, but not including, in a criminal case, a matter observed by law-enforcement personnel; or
      (iii) in a civil case or against the government in a criminal case, factual findings from a legally authorized investigation; and
   (B) the opponent does not show that the source of information or other circumstances indicate a lack of trustworthiness.

Explanation: This exception applies the basic idea of business records to public entities. Note that it treats criminal and civil cases differently in some instances. The expression "factual findings resulting from an investigation" means both statements of observed facts and statements of conclusions developed from observed facts. See pages **117-119**.

(9) Public Records of Vital Statistics. A record of a birth, death, or marriage, if reported to a public office in accordance with a legal duty.

Explanation: These documents are usually made by people with an obligation to report and with no motive to lie. Also, their information may be difficult to obtain from any other sources. Unlike the business records exception, this exception does not require testimony from a custodian of the records. The authentication provision of Rule 902(4) would require the proponent to offer a certified copy of the record.

(10) Absence of a Public Record. Testimony — or a certification under Rule 902 — that a diligent search failed to disclose a public record or statement if:
   (A) the testimony or certification is admitted to prove that
      (i) the record or statement does not exist; or
      (ii) a matter did not occur or exist, if a public office regularly kept a record or statement for a matter of that kind; and
   (B) in a criminal case, a prosecutor who intends to offer a certification provides written notice of that intent at least 14 days before trial, and the defendant does not object in writing within

7 days of receiving the notice—unless the court sets a different time for the notice or the objection.

> **Explanation:** This is the mirror image of the public record or entry exception, and is based on the same rationale. See pages **118-119**.

(11) *Records of Religious Organizations Concerning Personal or Family History.* A statement of birth, legitimacy, ancestry, marriage, divorce, death, relationship by blood or marriage, or similar facts of personal or family history, contained in a regularly kept record of a religious organization.

> **Explanation:** The information treated in this exception does not need to have been provided to the religious organization by someone with a duty to report it. Nevertheless, the circumstances in which religious organizations usually make notes in their records provide fairly strong guarantees of accuracy.

(12) *Certificates of Marriage, Baptism, and Similar Ceremonies.* A statement of fact contained in a certificate:

(A) made by a person who is authorized by a religious organization or by law to perform the act certified;

(B) attesting that the person performed a marriage or similar ceremony or administered a sacrament; and

(C) purporting to have been issued at the time of the act or within a reasonable time after it.

> **Explanation:** This exception covers topics additional to those in the public records exception, Rule 803(9), with no requirement that a certified copy of the record be provided.

(13) *Family Records.* A statement of fact about personal or family history contained in a family record, such as a Bible, genealogy, chart, engraving on a ring, inscription on a portrait, or engraving on an urn or burial marker.

> **Explanation:** Yes, even engravings on urns have their own hearsay exception. The theory behind this exception is that statements about family history are likely to be either accurate or corrected when they are made in places that are subject to inspection and are regarded as important.

(14) *Records of Documents That Affect an Interest in Property.* The record of a document that purports to establish or affect an interest in property if:

(A) the record is admitted to prove the content of the original recorded document, along with its signing and its delivery by each person who purports to have signed it;

(B) the record is kept in a public office; and

(C) a statute authorizes recording documents of that kind in that office.

> **Explanation:** Under this exception a title document can serve as proof of the detailed information recorded in another document, only if local statutes set up a recording system that includes documents such as records of title documents.

(15) *Statements in Documents That Affect an Interest in Property.* A statement contained in a document that purports to establish or affect an interest in property if the matter stated was relevant to the document's purpose — unless later dealings with the property are inconsistent with the truth of the statement or the purport of the document.

> **Explanation:** This exception provides a means of proving information stated in documents involved in the transfer of property interests, such as descriptions of the grantors.

(16) *Statements in Ancient Documents.* A statement in a document that was prepared before January 1, 1998, and whose authenticity is established.

> **Explanation:** A document that was prepared in 1997 or earlier, found in a place where it would likely have been kept, is admissible to prove the truth of its assertions. See pages **119-120**.

(17) *Market Reports and Similar Commercial Publications.* Market quotations, lists, directories, or other compilations that are generally relied on by the public or by persons in particular occupations.

> **Explanation:** Information like published weather reports, stock prices, commodity prices, or telephone directories is covered by this exception. They are compiled by people with no motive to lie, and because they are used by the public, errors are likely to be discouraged.

(18) *Statements in Learned Treatises, Periodicals, or Pamphlets.* A statement contained in a treatise, periodical, or pamphlet if:

(A) the statement is called to the attention of an expert witness on cross-examination or relied on by the expert on direct examination; and

(B) the publication is established as a reliable authority by the expert's admission or testimony, by another expert's testimony, or by judicial notice.

If admitted, the statement may be read into evidence but not received as an exhibit.

> **Explanation:** If the judge under Rule 104(a) concludes that published material is considered reliable by professionals in a field, statements in such material are admissible for their truth, if they are used in direct or cross-examination of an expert witness. To avoid the risk that the jury will rely too heavily on these items, the rule prohibits their use as exhibits.

(19) *Reputation Concerning Personal or Family History.* A reputation among a person's family by blood, adoption, or marriage — or among a person's associates or in the community — concerning the person's birth, adoption, legitimacy, ancestry, marriage, divorce, death, relationship by blood, adoption, or marriage, or similar facts of personal or family history.

> **Explanation:** It is likely that the only way people will have knowledge of issues of kinship such as birth, marriage, and the other specified family relationships is through hearsay statements by others. This rule allows testimony about such statements, on the basis that the need for this type of information is likely to be great, and that statements on these subjects are likely to be careful and therefore accurate. The rule does not limit its coverage to statements made prior to disputes or to statements made in any specified community.

(20) *Reputation Concerning Boundaries or General History.* A reputation in a community — arising before the controversy — concerning boundaries of land in the community or customs that affect the land, or concerning general historical events important to that community, state, or nation.

> **Explanation:** Note that for reputation in a community concerning land use must have arisen prior to the

dispute in which the statements are sought to be introduced. No such requirement is imposed for statements connected with general history.

(21) Reputation Concerning Character. A reputation among a person's associates or in the community concerning the person's character.

> **Explanation:** This Rule is related to the provisions in Rule 405(a) and Rule 608(a) which detail how character may be proved when its admission is proper. This rule protects the uses of reputation allowed by those other rules from being barred by the hearsay doctrine.

(22) Judgment of a Previous Conviction. Evidence of a final judgment of conviction if:

(A) the judgment was entered after a trial or guilty plea, but not a nolo contendere plea;

(B) the conviction was for a crime punishable by death or by imprisonment for more than a year;

(C) the evidence is admitted to prove any fact essential to the judgment; and

(D) when offered by the prosecutor in a criminal case for a purpose other than impeachment, the judgment was against the defendant.

The pendency of an appeal may be shown but does not affect admissibility.

> **Explanation:** Conviction of a serious crime may be used in other proceedings as proof of any fact that was essential support for the judgment. Note that in criminal cases, this exception may not be used against a person different from the person who was found guilty.

(23) Judgments Involving Personal, Family, or General History, or a Boundary. A judgment that is admitted to prove a matter of personal, family, or general history, or boundaries, if the matter:

(A) was essential to the judgment; and

(B) could be proved by evidence of reputation.

> **Explanation:** This exception is parallel to the exceptions for proof by reputation in property disputes. Judgments are at least as reliable as reputation, so this exception permits their substantive use.

(24) [Other Exceptions.] [Transferred to Rule 807.]

Rule 804. Exceptions to the Rule Against Hearsay–When the Declarant is Unavailable as a Witness

(a) Criteria for Being Unavailable. A declarant is considered to be unavailable as a witness if the declarant:

> **Explanation:** Rule 804 provides additional exceptions to the hearsay exclusion, allowed only if the declarant meets any of its definitions of "unavailability." See pages **129-130**.

(1) is exempted from testifying about the subject matter of the declarant's statement because the court rules that a privilege applies;

> **Explanation:** A declarant is unavailable if an order of the court excuses him or her from testifying.

(2) refuses to testify about the subject matter despite a court order to do so;

> **Explanation:** A declarant who refuses to testify is unavailable.

(3) testifies to not remembering the subject matter;

> **Explanation:** People state that they have no memory in many instances, sometimes truly and sometimes because they do not want to testify. In either circumstance, such a witness is unavailable.

(4) cannot be present or testify at the trial or hearing because of death or a then-existing infirmity, physical illness, or mental illness; or

> **Explanation:** Death is the ultimate unavailability to testify. Serious illness also receives treatment as establishing unavailability.

(5) is absent from the trial or hearing and the statement's proponent has not been able, by process or other reasonable means, to procure:
    (A) the declarant's attendance, in the case of a hearsay exception under Rule 804(b)(1) or (6); or
    (B) the declarant's attendance or testimony, in the case of a hearsay exception under Rule 804(b)(2), (3), or (4).

> **Explanation:** This alternative for showing unavailability states that unavailability for Rule 804(b)(1) is established by a showing that the presence of the declarant cannot be obtained. To establish unavailability under this alternative for Rules 804(b)2, 804(b)(3) and 804(b)(4), the proponent must show inability to obtain both the declarant's presence and the declarant's testimony (for example, by deposition). See pages **129-130**.

But this subdivision (a) does not apply if the statement's proponent procured or wrongfully caused the declarant's unavailability as a witness in order to prevent the declarant from attending or testifying.

> **Explanation:** The hearsay exceptions in this rule may not be used by a party who intentionally prevents the declarant from being present.

(b) The Exceptions. The following are not excluded by the rule against hearsay if the declarant is unavailable as a witness:

(1) Former Testimony. Testimony that:

(A) was given as a witness at a trial, hearing, or lawful deposition, whether given during the current proceeding or a different one; and

(B) is now offered against a party who had — or, in a civil case, whose predecessor in interest had — an opportunity and similar motive to develop it by direct, cross-, or redirect examination.

> **Explanation:** Testimony or deposition statements are admissible if at the time they were made the party against whom they are currently sought to be introduced had an opportunity to develop the testimony by questioning. In addition to the opportunity, that party's motivation at the time of the testimony must have been similar to its motivation in the current trial. In civil cases a predecessor in interest is treated as equivalent to the current party. See pages **131-132**.

(2) Statement Under the Belief of Imminent Death. In a prosecution for homicide or in a civil case, a statement that the declarant, while believing the declarant's death to be imminent, made about its cause or circumstances.

> **Explanation:** In murder cases (not all criminal cases) and in all civil cases, a statement made by a person who believed he or she was about to die that relates to the cause of the expected death is admissible. This is the classic dying declarations exception. See page **132**.

(3) Statement Against Interest. A statement that:

(A) a reasonable person in the declarant's position would have made only if the person believed it to be true because, when made, it was so contrary to the declarant's proprietary or pecuniary interest or had so great a tendency to invalidate the declarant's claim against someone else or to expose the declarant to civil or criminal liability; and

(B) is supported by corroborating circumstances that clearly indicate its trustworthiness, if it is offered in a criminal case as one that tends to expose the declarant to criminal liability.

> **Explanation:** Because people do not usually say things that could harm them, it is likely that when a person does say such a thing, it is true. Statements that could hurt a person in the contexts of money, property, or criminal liability are covered by this exception, provided that a reasonable person would have understood the risks involved in making the statement. If the statement is made to exculpate an accused, it can qualify only if it is corroborated. See pages **132-134**.

(4) Statement of Personal or Family History. A statement about:

(A) the declarant's own birth, adoption, legitimacy, ancestry, marriage, divorce, relationship by blood, adoption, or marriage, or similar facts of personal or family history, even though the declarant had no way of acquiring personal knowledge about that fact; or

(B) another person concerning any of these facts, as well as death, if the declarant was related to the person by blood, adoption, or marriage or was so intimately associated with the person's family that the declarant's information is likely to be accurate.

> **Explanation:** Statements by the declarant about himself or herself, about the declarant's relatives or about people with whom the declarant had intimate associations are admissible to show kinship and similar family history.

(5) [Other Exceptions.] [Transferred to Rule 807.]

(6) *Statement Offered Against a Party That Wrongfully Caused the Declarant's Unavailability.* A statement offered against a party that wrongfully caused — or acquiesced in wrongfully causing — the declarant's unavailability as a witness, and did so intending that result.

> **Explanation:** If a party wrongly prevents a person from testifying, for example by being involved in bribing, intimidating, or killing that person, any statement that person ever made can be introduced against the party. See pages **134–135**.

Rule 805. Hearsay Within Hearsay

Hearsay within hearsay is not excluded by the rule against hearsay if each part of the combined statements conforms with an exception to the rule.

> **Explanation:** Out-of-court statements that themselves contain additional statements may be admitted, so long as each statement can overcome a hearsay objection. A police officer's notebook might contain a quote from someone who claimed to have seen a vehicular accident. To introduce the eyewitness's statement, two levels of hearsay would have to be overcome. The first hearsay statement is the words of the eyewitness. The second is the written words of the police officer. The eyewitness's statement might have fit the present sense impression exception, and the police officer's notes might fit the public records exception. See page **116**.

Rule 806. Attacking and Supporting Credibility of Declarant

When a hearsay statement — or a statement described in Rule 801(d)(2)(C), (D), or (E) — has been admitted in evidence, the declarant's credibility may be attacked, and then supported, by any evidence that would be admissible for those purposes if the declarant had testified as a witness. The court may admit evidence of the declarant's inconsistent statement or conduct, regardless of when it occurred or whether the declarant had an opportunity to explain or deny it. If the party against whom the statement was admitted calls the declarant as a witness, the party may examine the declarant on the statement as if on cross-examination.

> **Explanation:** Hearsay declarants and the people whose statements are admissible as statements of a party opponent (admissions) may be impeached with any technique that would have been available if they had made their statements in testimony. The provisions for allowing a declarant to deny or explain inconsistent statements do not apply, since the declarant may not be available at trial. See pages **168-170**.

Rule 807. Residual Exception

(a) **In General.** Under the following circumstances, a hearsay statement is not excluded by the rule against hearsay even if the statement is not specifically covered by a hearsay exception in Rule 803 or 804:

(1) the statement has equivalent circumstantial guarantees of trustworthiness;

(2) it is offered as evidence of a material fact;

(3) it is more probative on the point for which it is offered than any other evidence that the proponent can obtain through reasonable efforts; and

(4) admitting it will best serve the purposes of these rules and the interests of justice.

(b) **Notice.** The statement is admissible only if, before the trial or hearing, the proponent gives an adverse party reasonable notice of the intent to offer the statement and its particulars, including the declarant's name and address, so that the party has a fair opportunity to meet it.

> **Explanation:** Note the five main requirements under this "catch-all" exception. First, the statement offered must have equivalent trustworthiness, in comparison to statements treated in the specific exceptions. Second, the statement must be relevant. Third, strong necessity must be shown. Fourth, justice and the purposes of the rules of evidence must be served by admission. And fifth, the proponent must have given notice of intention to use the rule. This exception has been used to admit types of statements that have significant reliability but are not provided for in the detailed exceptions. A controversial example is the use of grand jury testimony, given under oath. See page **135**.

ARTICLE IX. AUTHENTICATION AND IDENTIFICATION

Rule 901. Authenticating or Identifying

(a) In General. To satisfy the requirement of authenticating or identifying an item of evidence, the proponent must produce evidence sufficient to support a finding that the item is what the proponent claims it is.

> **Explanation:** When a party seeks to introduce a document or any object or thing, the party must also provide a basis for a finding that the document or object really is what the proponent claims it is. This requirement also applies to testimony about conversations. It is important to remember that authentication is only one requirement that must be satisfied for admission of an item of evidence. For example, an authenticated document may still need to satisfy the rules concerning hearsay and original writings. See page **218**.

(b) Examples. The following are examples only — not a complete list — of evidence that satisfies the requirement:

> **Explanation:** It is extremely easy to satisfy the authentication requirement. The examples provided in this part of the rule are typical methods litigants use, but any proof that could support the required finding is allowed. See pages **218-221**.

(1) *Testimony of a Witness with Knowledge.* Testimony that an item is what it is claimed to be.

(2) *Nonexpert Opinion About Handwriting.* A nonexpert's opinion that handwriting is genuine, based on a familiarity with it that was not acquired for the current litigation.

(3) *Comparison by an Expert Witness or the Trier of Fact.* A comparison with an authenticated specimen by an expert witness or the trier of fact.

> **Explanation:** The specimen with which the trier of fact compares the item sought to be authenticated must itself be authenticated. The specimen can satisfy that requirement in a variety of ways, such as circumstantial evidence or through testimony by a witness who can state that the specimen is what it is claimed to be. See page **219**.

(4) Certified Copies of Public Records. A copy of an official record — or a copy of a document that was recorded or filed in a public office as authorized by law — if the copy is certified as correct by:

(A) the custodian or another person authorized to make the certification; or

(B) a certificate that complies with Rule 902(1), (2), or (3), a federal statute, or a rule prescribed by the Supreme Court.

(5) *Official Publications.* A book, pamphlet, or other publication purporting to be issued by a public authority.

(6) *Newspapers and Periodicals.* Printed material purporting to be a newspaper or periodical.

(7) *Trade Inscriptions and the Like.* An inscription, sign, tag, or label purporting to have been affixed in the course of business and indicating origin, ownership, or control.

(8) *Acknowledged Documents.* A document accompanied by a certificate of acknowledgment that is lawfully executed by a notary public or another officer who is authorized to take acknowledgments.

(9) *Commercial Paper and Related Documents.* Commercial paper, a signature on it, and related documents, to the extent allowed by general commercial law.

(10) *Presumptions Under a Federal Statute.* A signature, document, or anything else that a federal statute declares to be presumptively or prima facie genuine or authentic.

(11) *Certified Domestic Records of a Regularly Conducted Activity.* The original or a copy of a domestic record that meets the requirements of Rule 803(6)(A)-(C), as shown by a certification of the custodian or another qualified person that complies with a federal statute or a rule prescribed by the Supreme Court. Before the trial or hearing, the proponent must give an adverse party reasonable written notice of the intent to offer the record — and must make the record and certification available for inspection — so that the party has a fair opportunity to challenge them.

> **Explanation:** This provision is cited in Rule 803(6) as a way of excusing the proponent of a record of regularly conducted activity from the obligation of presenting a witness to testify about the creation and maintenance of the record.

(12) *Certified Foreign Records of a Regularly Conducted Activity.* In a civil case, the original or a copy of a foreign record that meets the requirements of Rule 902(11), modified as follows: the certification, rather than complying with a federal statute or Supreme Court rule, must be signed in a manner that, if falsely made, would subject the maker to a criminal penalty in the country where the certification is signed. The proponent must also meet the notice requirements of Rule 902(11).

> **Explanation:** This provision is cited in Rule 803(6) as a way of excusing the proponent of a record of regularly conducted activity from the obligation of presenting a witness to testify about the creation and maintenance of the record.

(13) Certified Records Generated by an Electronic Process or System. A record generated by an electronic process or system that produces an accurate result, as shown by a certification of a qualified person that complies with the certification requirements of Rule 902(11) or (12). The proponent must also meet the notice requirements of Rule 902(11).

(14) Certified Data Copied from an Electronic Device, Storage Medium, or File. Data copied from an electronic device, storage medium, or file, if authenticated by a process of digital identification, as shown by a certification of a qualified person that complies with the certification requirements of Rule 902(11) or (12). The proponent also must meet the notice requirements of Rule 902(11).

Rule 903. Subscribing Witness's Testimony Unnecessary

A subscribing witness's testimony is necessary to authenticate a writing only if required by the law of the jurisdiction that governs its validity.

ARTICLE X. CONTENTS OF WRITINGS, RECORDINGS, AND PHOTOGRAPHS

Rule 1001. Definitions That Apply to This Article

In this article:

(a) A "writing" consists of letters, words, numbers, or their equivalent set down in any form.

(b) A "recording" consists of letters, words, numbers, or their equivalent recorded in any manner.

(c) A "photograph" means a photographic image or its equivalent stored in any form.

(d) An "original" of a writing or recording means the writing or recording itself or any counterpart intended to have the same effect by the person who executed or issued it. For electronically stored information, "original" means any printout — or other output readable by sight — if it accurately reflects the information. An "original" of a photograph includes the negative or a print from it.

(e) A "duplicate" means a counterpart produced by a mechanical, photographic, chemical, electronic, or other equivalent process or technique that accurately reproduces the original.

> **Explanation:** These definitions are used to establish the Federal Rules' version of the "best evidence" rule. The rule applies only to items defined as writings, recordings, or photographs. It does not require "best" evidence of their contents, but rather sets up a specific requirement about production of originals rather than copies. See pages **224-226**.

Rule 1002. Requirement of Original

An original writing, recording, or photograph is required in order to prove its content unless these rules or a federal statute provides otherwise.

> **Explanation:** The requirement of the original applies only when the proponent seeks to prove the contents of the writing, recording, or photograph. A party may provide evidence of a fact without regard to the original writing rule if the proof does not depend on a showing that a writing, recording, or photograph shows that the fact is true. If a party's technique for establishing a fact is to demonstrate that a writing, recording, or photograph contains evidence of the fact, then the rule applies. As the next portions of the rule show, the requirement of producing the original is essentially a requirement to produce the original, a copy, or an excuse for having neither the original nor a copy. See pages **224-226**.

Rule 1003. Admissibility of Duplicates

A duplicate is admissible to the same extent as the original unless a genuine question is raised about the original's authenticity or the circumstances make it unfair to admit the duplicate.

> **Explanation:** Despite the existence of this original writing rule, a duplicate is almost always as acceptable as the ostensibly required original. See pages **224-226**.

Rule 1004. Admissibility of Other Evidence of Content

An original is not required and other evidence of the content of a writing, recording, or photograph is admissible if:

> **Explanation:** In the situations described in the following portions of this rule, testimony about the contents of a writing, recording, or photograph is permitted even without the introduction of either the original or a copy of the item. See pages **226-227**.

(a) all the originals are lost or destroyed, and not by the proponent acting in bad faith;

(b) an original cannot be obtained by any available judicial process;

(c) the party against whom the original would be offered had control of the original; was at that time put on notice, by pleadings or otherwise, that the original would be a subject of proof at the trial or hearing; and fails to produce it at the trial or hearing; or

(d) the writing, recording, or photograph is not closely related to a controlling issue.

Rule 1005. Copies of Public Records to Prove Content

The proponent may use a copy to prove the content of an official record — or of a document that was recorded or filed in a public office as authorized by law — if these conditions are met: the record or document is otherwise admissible; and the copy is certified as correct in accordance with Rule 902(4) or is testified to be correct by a witness who has compared it with the original. If no such copy can be obtained by reasonable diligence, then the proponent may use other evidence to prove the content.

Rule 1006. Summaries to Prove Content

The proponent may use a summary, chart, or calculation to prove the content of voluminous writings, recordings, or photographs that cannot be conveniently examined in court. The proponent must make the originals or duplicates available for examination or copying, or both, by other parties at a reasonable time and place. And the court may order the proponent to produce them in court.

Table of Cases

IN THE SHADOW
OF THE VAMPIRE

Reflections from the

World of Anne Rice

IN THE SHADOW
OF THE VAMPIRE

Reflections from the
World of Anne Rice

By
Jana Marcus

With an introduction by
Katherine Ramsland

Thunder's Mouth Press
New York

Published by
Thunder's Mouth Press
632 Broadway, Seventh Floor
New York, NY 10012

Library of Congress Cataloging in Publication Data
Marcus, Jana.
    In the shadow of the vampire: reflections on the world of Anne Rice / by Jana Marcus,
with an introduction by Katherine Ramsland.
        p. cm.
    ISBN 1-56025-147-6 (pbk.)
    1. Rice, Anne, 1941- --Appreciation. 2. Women and literature--Louisiana--New
Orleans--History--20th century. 3. Fantastic fiction, American--Appreciation. 4. Gothic
revival (literature)--United States. 5. Horror tales, American--Appreciation. 6. New
Orleans (La.)--In literature. 7. Books and reading--United States. 8. Vampires in literature.
I. Title.
PS3568.I265Z76 1997
813'.54--dc21
                                                         97-23669
                                                          CIP

ISBN 1-56025-147-6

Manufactured in the United States of America.
First Edition

To Mort

Who has taught me to embrace the world,
guides my imagination to new heights,
and always graciously corrects my grammar.

ACKNOWLEDGMENTS

I would like to thank the following people who made this book possible with their time, commitment and support:

Stuart Bernstein, my agent, for believing in this project and constantly proving he is the "Enabler."

Valerie Marcus, whose tireless commitment, ideas and humor got me through the production of this book and an endless number of adventures in the Big Easy.

Barbara Trimmer and Kim Barker, who graciously and generously placed me in the middle of the Rice whirlwind.

Anne Berest-Kopilak and Eric Sassaman, my original New Orleans crew, who supported me while stepping on new ground.

Sean Duggan, for digital enhancement of the cover photograph.

All of my family, for encouraging me and my crazy ideas over the years.

And:

Carl Battraell, George Beahm, Ritchie Champagne, Chris Cavanaugh-Simmons, Leslie Harrington-Smith, Thela Lewis, Wilma Marcus-Chandler, Morton Marcus, Thomas G. Marquez, Dan Miller, Stefanie Owens, Katherine Ramsland, Eric Schoeck, and all the participants of this book for sharing their lives.

"You convinced me long ago that the world was a Savage Garden...Well, then, in the Savage Garden you shine beautifully, my friend...In my wanderings...I always return to see the colors of the garden in your shadow, or reflected in your eyes."

—Anne Rice, *Memnoch the Devil*, (Armand to Lestat)

"...And in this Savage Garden, these innocent ones belonged in the vampire's arms."

—Anne Rice, *The Vampire Lestat*

"...No one knows what power is locked inside another; no one knows perhaps what power is locked within oneself."

—Anne Rice, *The Queen of the Damned*

PREFACE

Few writers have risen to Anne Rice's level of popularity. Her celebrity is on par with that of rock stars, generating both frenzied fans and a phalanx of security guards wherever she goes. There is an active fan club of more than 8,000, the annual Gathering of the Coven Ball in New Orleans, movies, comic book novels, audio tapes, an Anne Rice tour company, a perfume line, a Lestat wine, T-shirts emblazoned with an MRI of Rice's brain, and soon a Lestat restaurant is scheduled in New Orleans.

Thus it is not surprising that her work has created a subculture, which includes role-playing games, reading clubs, and internet groups, all of them stemming from adoration for Anne and her books. These groups have, in turn, become meeting grounds for people who otherwise may never have crossed paths. Over the past several years, however, the phenomenon has become larger than Rice and her books. As one fan mentioned, "I went from being alone and reading a book to having an extended family on the internet and making new friends that understand me through the fan club." Now many people come to New Orleans in the fall to meet internet friends, not only to go to the Ball. To some of them, Rice has become secondary to the community she has created.

This book is the outcome of my exploration into the world of the Rice reader and some of the explanations of why her work has changed so many people's lives. I have chosen to interview a cross-section of Anne's readers. They are an international group of real-life blood drinkers, gays, role-playing gamers, members of the S&M community, and many others. What they all hold in common is that they are the underground element of an emerging new culture consisting of people who often feel alone or separated from the mainstream of their society. On the other hand, Anne's work has prompted the general reader, also represented in these interviews, to explore the darker side of his imagination.

In 1976, when I was fourteen, my father and I had been wandering around a bookstore when he stopped, took a book from a shelf, and handed it to me. "A friend of mine wrote this," he said. "You might like it." The book was *Interview with the Vampire*, and needless to say it was the most powerful reading experience of my young life.

Soon I was converting everyone I knew into Anne Rice readers, and I can't recall a single Halloween since that time that I haven't dressed as a vampire. This was at the dawn of Rice's publishing history. There were no Vampire Chronicles, Tom Cruise movies, vampire comics, or television interviews. There was just this one incredible book. I had to wait nine years for the next vampire chronicle, *The Vampire Lestat*, then three more for *The Queen of the Damned*. Each time I closed the back cover on the final page of the latest volume, I was in agony, knowing I would have to wait years for the next novel.

Like so many others, I loved the Gothic atmosphere Rice's words swirled around me. They evoked a world of dark romance and lush historical backdrops that prior to reading her books only the Sandman could take me to when I closed my eyes each night. At the same time the novels were realistic in detail and often contemporary in setting, so they were fraught with possibilities, and this made them all the more intriguing.

Back then I was just a kid from an artsy family who read a lot. It wasn't until I moved to New York City at the age of eighteen to be a photographer that I realized how Anne's books had influenced my life. Her characters had not only formed a part of the person I had become, but depicted the kind of people I wanted to know, people who thought as Rice's characters did and sought to live every moment to the fullest—people who continually questioned the world around them and understood a secret part of themselves as I imagined I did.

This is what Anne has given to my generation, which has been labeled Generation X or the "slacker" generation. Many members of this age group have taken up reading for the first time and started looking at history and philosophy thanks to Anne's work. She has given many of us a window through which we can explore ourselves. In this way, Anne can be seen as a teacher. Her books allow people to think about their place in society and identify their feelings through her characters' exploration of unconventional lifestyles. More than their baby boomer parents, this new generation has delved deeper into the dark, narcissistic side of life, and Rice's books have provided the framework which has allowed them to handle those explorations.

It is extraordinary how many people I've spoken to who had never read a book before they read an Anne Rice novel. In a sense, Rice has taught an increasingly illiterate America to appreciate reading and to read for pleasure. Through her widening pronouncements, she has influenced elections, film box office results, and Gothic fashion—not to mention tourism in New Orleans.

Until I was twenty-eight, all I knew about Anne personally was what my father—an old friend of her husband Stan—told me. In the early years, I was more interested in the novels than the person who wrote them. But in the fall of 1990, when Anne was in New York for a book signing, I thought I'd introduce myself and tell her how much I appreciated her work.

It really was "dark and stormy" that October night in New York City. I shivered against the wind, clutching my copy of *The Witching Hour*, as I made my way to Barnes & Noble Bookstore to have Anne Rice autograph her latest book.

Was I in for a shock! On the wet pavement of Eighth Street, I found hundreds upon hundreds of people who had been standing for hours in a line that stretched for blocks. All of them were waiting to have copies of *The Witching Hour* signed by Anne. As I searched for the end of the line, I saw all kinds of people dressed in everything from business suits to vampire costumes. Many had painted white faces with fake blood trickling from the corner of their mouths. Inside the store, there were bodyguards all around Rice, and the fans were pushed like cattle through the lines. Get your book, pass it to Anne, have it signed, go to the register.

After three hours of being pushed and shoved, I stumbled home, dumbstruck by the bizarre scene I had just witnessed. Book signings were supposed to be sedate, art-wanker affairs, not mayhem. I was shocked at the widespread appeal of her work and the frenzied fanaticism of her fans. That scene stayed with me for many years.

Years went by, the movie *Interview with the Vampire* came out, and Anne's popularity was greater than ever. Then in 1995, when I was living in Northern California, a local paper asked me to photograph an Anne Rice book signing at a local bookstore. Sure! This time I'll be prepared....I thought. But at the bookstore everything was even bigger, grander, and more bizarre than before. During the course of the evening's event, I learned that the fans were organized into groups. There were tour groups, internet groups, reading groups, role-playing game groups. Just pick your fantasy.

When I was finally introduced to Rice at the press conference before the signing, she threw her arms around me, remembering me from my childhood. I stood frozen in shock: Dad had left that part of the story out! Anne was a captivating, intelligent, outspoken woman, and she spontaneously invited me to the Memnoch Ball, which was to take place less than six weeks later in her New Orleans mansion, St. Elizabeth's, a converted Catholic orphanage. Of course I accepted; I never miss a photo opportunity.

And so, almost before I knew it, I was on a plane heading to the Big Easy to photograph a vampire party. My real-life venture into Anne Rice's world was about to begin.

Picture six thousand people, all dressed in variations of vampire costumes, descending on New Orleans for a night. That may sound outrageous, but that was what the Memnoch Ball was like.

I remember walking through the gates of St. Elizabeth's as if I was strolling into the nineteenth century. People were everywhere, and the mansion towered above me, its windows blazing with light. The Ball—the seventh annual Gathering of the Coven—was Anne's "thank you" to her devoted readers. With the party, she was giving a piece of her world to her admirers, and she sat all night long signing autographs, atop the float of a gravestone installed in front of the house.

Mardi Gras Indians paraded through the grounds in ceremonial dress, while inside alternative bands blared in the Green Velvet Ballroom at one end of the block-long mansion and Dixieland ensembles hooted and tooted at the other.

The three-story building housed a carnival of amusements for the evening. There was The Bat Cave, a glow-in-the-dark tunnel. There was the Chamber of Les Innocents, with its bowls of eyeballs and mannequins in coffins, while in the Cabaret Room, Anne's son Christopher sang popular Broadway show tunes with several friends.

The old orphanage's second floor chapel, its holy relics still in place, had been converted into a ballroom. While a full orchestra played from the confines of the sanctuary, a troupe of dancers in eighteenth-century costumes danced the minuet and the Virginia reel on the floor of the nave, which had been cleared of its pews.

The Garden Hall downstairs contained an art exhibit of Stan Rice's paintings, and Stan gave a slide show about his work on the third floor. Anne's four hundred-piece doll collection was on display on the second floor beside the Dickens-ish Mrs. Havishman's Room, where wedding cake was served with plastic rats on the frosting.

There was food and drink all night for the six thousand guests. This included 56,000 assorted sandwiches, 58,000 cookies, 10,000 cans of Pepsi, 813 cases of chardonnay, and more than 40,000 bottles of Abita Red Ale. The Ale, specially brewed and named Ice Cold Victim, featured Anne's autograph and quotes from Lestat on the label.

Guests carried party favors consisting of cardboard fans with a drawing of St. Elizabeth's on one side, burlap voodoo bags filled with gris-gris and Spanish moss, Memnoch plastic mugs, and Mardi Gras beads. Anyone could find souvenirs commemorating the evening in bowls scattered throughout the house. As if all this wasn't enough, all night long dozens of tarot card readers could be found under a huge white canopy covering the inner courtyard, ready to read the future of anyone in the milling crowd.

For six hours I literally ran from one end of the mansion to the other, snapping photographs, trying to capture the lavishness of the event on film. As I feverishly shot roll after roll of film, I was able to observe the partygoers' camaraderie with each other and with Anne. The fans were friendly and warm and enjoyed meeting others who, like themselves, were intrigued by vampire lore and all things Gothic. They ranged in age from fifteen to sixty-five, and were of all races and backgrounds. Some were young and silly and posed in corners, muttering words like, "Yes, I bite my girlfriend." Others were committed to S&M and pagan witchcraft. Still others were merely on the lookout for a good party, so they could dress up and meet new people. They talked openly about their lives and although everyone had a different story, I became fascinated by the common link that each of them shared—Anne's books had changed their lives.

This book is about the people I met at the Memnoch Ball that Halloween and at the party held the following year. It is a book of photographs and interviews, each complementing the other.

There is another side of the Rice phenomenon which, in my role as impartial interviewer, I felt compelled to include in the book. Many fans are disappointed by Rice's growing commercialism and feel that the books have become corrupted in the face of mass marketing. One woman I met in New Orleans, who was at first excited to be interviewed for the book came to me the day of her interview and, almost in tears, told me that she had changed her mind. After reading Anne's work for eighteen years, she had become so disappointed with Rice's current novels and commercialism that she was afraid her negative feelings would outweigh what she once loved in the books. Her final comment was, "I guess after eighteen years it's time to find something new."

In compiling the interviews I included different attitudes towards Rice, and made no assumptions about the lifestyles of the people whose words appear in this book. These words are theirs. Through their unique voices I hope the reader will discover not only the source of Rice's popularity, but the sense of community that has developed among her fans. As I learned by creating this book, the dark side can be a mysterious and beautiful journey that lies inside each of us, waiting to be discovered.

—Jana Marcus

"Modern man must rediscover a deeper source of his own spiritual life. To do this, he is obligated to struggle with evil, to confront his own shadow, to integrate the devil."

--Carl Jung

SEDUCED BY SHADOWS

By Katherine Ramsland

Anne Rice is best known for a series of novels called the Vampire Chronicles. Although she writes about a diverse variety of supernatural entities, readers who respond strongly to her work typically name her vampire protagonists as their favorite characters. They read the stories over and over, create new scenarios, join Lestat fan clubs, and even dress up as vampires. It's become an increasingly popular diversion, but just who are these people who bond together in "vampire communities?" Who seek pen pals, coven mates, and kindred souls in a fetish for blood? What *is* the allure of this type of fiction?

People in search of high-octane spirituality often look to culturally defined images of iniquity. There seems to be something at the core of the forbidden that intensifies our experience and hints at more to be had. Rice understands this. She taps into a shared mystique that channels transgressive feelings into accessible form, using her own physical responses to draw out the most sublime erotic nuances. Like other authors of the supernatural, her novels map our inner darkness and provide a range of ways to explore how it feels.

Our culture lives in terror of evil. We try to keep it at bay, but that which is elusive and mysterious can exert a fascinating quality. Much as we may fear the diabolic, we are also drawn to it, for our most vulnerable feelings typically evoke the hottest pleasures. We edge closer to the psyche's deep pockets, but when those raw emotions prove too unsettling, we seek the buffer of symbols.

Here and there, courageous individuals have attempted to crystallize in literary form just what it is that most forcefully threatens us. Bram Stoker, Robert Louis Stevenson, and Johann Wolfgang von Goethe are among the authors who have explored their own dark recesses to give shape to humanity's fears. Like Rice, they instinctively recognize what the forces of darkness represent, and they set out to mold our most base desires—lust, aggression, greed—into monsters that confront us with the reality of our inner power. By giving our chaotic impressions a definite form, these writers touch a powerful subliminal chord deep within us. Swiss psychoanalyst Carl Jung called it "the shadow." It is an aspect of the subconscious. Although we cannot gaze directly at this hidden domain, we can achieve a vicarious experience of it through literary scenarios that stimulate our fears. Rice offers tales of the Mayfair witches, a powerful incubus, an immortal mummy, and a genie spirit, but it is her vampire fiction that most clearly demonstrates the compelling nature of our hidden selves.

Vampires thrive in the dark. Shocking accounts of these nocturnal plunderers date back to ancient times and appear in most world mythologies. Part human, part monster, part deity, they draw forth from our collective psyche a multitude of passions. As disturbing as their effect may be, it can also enrich us. Vampires are spiritual creatures and despite their reputation for evil, they keep alive in us the desire to transcend ourselves. As initiators into the secrets of physical transformation, they offer a bridge to another realm. Seeking new paths of divine epiphany, we return over and over to vampire fiction for its rich metaphor of seduction and surrender. The bloodsucker's predatory charm invests our anxiety with intense stimulation that pushes us toward the maximum rush.

Vampires simultaneously alarm and attract us. Magically attuned to our inward paradoxes, they are the shadow figures of a culture that denies its complexity. That's why our relationship to them is so complicated: while they survive unconscionably at someone else's expense, they also represent a heightened sense of life. As tricksters, they invite us toward death with the promise of rapture. Go for the rush, they urge, even if it means a glorious exit. There are many reasons why someone might resonate to the vampire image, from the desire for a supreme sense of power to the total indulgence of sensuality to the harrowing experience of self-laceration. Arising from the most cryptic areas of the imagination, vampires reveal many facets of our inner lives.

According to Jung, the human psyche is divided between the conscious and the unconscious. In the conscious realm, we emphasize order and rationality, but we equate the unconscious with darkness and chaos. It contains instinctual patterns, subliminal sense perceptions, and whatever is repressed—"the part of us," according to Jung, "that we don't want to be part of us." Our individual experience of this covert realm may be linked to a larger collective unconscious, and may even connect us to God.

The basic structure of the psyche is expressed in fundamental emotional patterns called archetypes, which become accessible to us though images such as the experience of rebirth, the heroic quest, or the descent into hell. Archetypes show up in the arts, literature, mythology, religion, dreams, and cultural rituals, as well as manifesting in mental disorders. They transcend time and place, and their value lies in their potency. The most forceful archetypes defy all cultural and temporal boundaries.

The shadow is one such archetype, and it takes several forms. Its abstract manifestation--Darkness itself--is viewed as autonomous evil that stands against absolute Goodness. There is also a personal shadow, which we know more intimately and which is formed by the way we are raised. We learn from our families and the culture at large what it means to be "good"—the behaviors to emulate—and what it means to be "bad"—the behaviors to shun. When we conform to these standards, we try not to feel, think, or act out anything that contradicts the self-image we seek. Traits like sexuality, rage, jealousy, and selfishness get suppressed, and they form the elusive, perverse, and mercurial shadow. We may try to block its subversive influence, but it is an inextricable part of our emotional lives.

Is the shadow evil? Many people think so. Anything so dark, mysterious, or unknown *must* be sinister. Better to keep it contained and hidden. Yet this attitude itself comes from the worst kind of darkness—ignorance cocooned in layers of fear. While evil certainly can arise from shadow traits, not all that is dark is evil. Within the shadow lies surprising potential, a sacred chaos that feeds hidden vitality. Only by acknowledging that our own dark chambers conceal a prism of energies can we discover the riches within. "One does not become enlightened by imagining figures of light," Jung pointed out, "but by making the darkness conscious."

The more we pretend that our shadow traits are alien, and the stronger our defenses against them become, the more intense their vitality grows. On a conscious level, we deceive ourselves into believing we have banished them, but they are still very much with us. "Everyone carries a shadow," Jung insisted, "and the less it is carried in the individual's conscious life, the blacker and denser it is." Even those people who believe they act out so-called shadow traits such as alienation or perversity have a dark side. Such people may shun conformity, for example, and that type of behavior then becomes their shadow. Everyone has something to push away.

Yet the shadow won't stay put in some locked container. It demands expression and thus emerges in art, mythology, and uncharacteristic behavior. It also is projected outward and, combined with the shared projections of others, becomes our monsters. We unwittingly create within ourselves the very metaphors of our terror. "Monsters," says Jungian analyst Robert McCully, "show a relationship between what is emerging in the collective unconscious of our times and the collective unconscious within us all."

Rather than try to understand what we have fashioned, we decide that monsters must be destroyed. We set up rituals to do so, like shoving a stake through a vampire's heart. We thus fail to appreciate whatever positive qualities there may be in the latent dynamism of those despised traits: rage may translate into passion, aggression into assertiveness. Yet denial only empowers the shadow. Its energy builds and eventually it may appropriate our entire being and make us obey those laws that only the shadow knows: We could become the very monsters we fear. Instead of finding ways to defuse our destructive potential, we tend to ignore our inner darkness and to inject poison into our perceptions of the world.

Nevertheless, try as we might to kill them, our monsters keep coming back. Clearly, they're telling us something.

A better approach is to mine the shadow for self-revelation and greater personal power. Examine what is there and find ways to integrate this potency into our conscious lives. The psyche craves wholeness. Self is as connected to chaos as order, and it cannot be totally structured or demystified. We can no more live totally in light than in darkness. Our unconscious potential is part of who we are. Monsters like vampires represent the vitality that culture bleeds out of us. However alarming, we should view these shadow figures as life sources to be tapped. Some fans of Rice's fiction, as evident in these interviews, seem to be doing just that.

Whatever thrives in the collective psyche conforms to mythic patterns within us. Vampire tales keep the rhythm of our emotional lives in play. Forming repressed traits into lurid but enticing scenarios provides a framework that allows us to approach forbidden desires that otherwise feel overwhelming. We retain just enough control to discover that within every shadow is some degree of light. Vampires may offer a gift. Certainly, they satisfy our craving for arousal. As preternatural creatures of hyper-sensuality, they have a magnetic allure.

Vampires are complex symbols, double-sided archetypes that give off both a positive and negative charge. They embody contradiction, uniting life and death, dominance and submission, seduction and capitulation, carnality and spirituality. Offering a fuller experience of passion, marginality, surrender, and power, vampires stretch and challenge us. They extend to us the energy of our unlived lives. Watching films, reading novels, or playing vampire roles allows us to approach the abyss emotionally and symbolically without going over the edge.

Those vampires that most inspire us are the ones who join our souls to theirs; they balance the human and the monstrous. People who view themselves as deviant or on the fringe of "normal" society often feel kinship with these creatures. The vampire as Other is about us as Other. They skirt the perimeters of society, feeling the loneliness but reaping the bounty of that roguish existence.

Rice's vampires give us the chance to explore this perspective. Through them we can see possibilities. We learn that vampires defy the limitations imposed by social expectations and can therefore realize their utmost potential. They possess heightened perception and strength. They can cultivate great focus, passion, and awareness of life. They form mental bonds that allow them to read minds; fly, project astral bodies, move fast, and jump great heights; transcend gender categories; heal themselves; fully surrender to the flow of life; and defy death. Often, they are young, beautiful, and vitally seductive, like gods of ancient times. Yet even when ugly, they possess wisdom and power. Vampires feel everything with the amplitude of the Romantic poets. They know isolation, need, and the craving for meaning. They seize the intensity of experience that many of us covet and challenge us—if we dare—to take it for ourselves.

No outside force placed vampires in our midst. We did. And we did it for our own good. Maximum life experience demands the energy of all elements, dark and light.

Vampires, as a synthesis of polarities, invite us to embrace paradox and draw close to our disparate parts. They give back in a more exciting form that which we vilify. Come, drink, they taunt. Transcend the limits. Know what lies within the deeper self and take from it the best that it can offer.

"Rice fans range from ten to eighty years of age. People will come to the bookstore and say, 'What's this about Anne? Why is she so popular and the fans so fanatic?' I've never been able to answer it. I've never seen an author have so much mass appeal before. What she writes about strikes a chord in people: the quest for good and evil, the quest for one's place in the world. Anne has said people have come to her at book signings and told her they've gotten off of heroin because of her books. She's turned a lot of people on to literature who aren't the average reader type, but they know a lot about Anne.

"Anne sells a huge number of books—no one comes close. The number of readers and fans is getting bigger and bigger. Each signing gets bigger, and wherever she goes her books sell out. I'm always amazed at the people who come to the store and New Orleans because of reading Rice. It's not anything other than that her books take place here and she lives here. It's amazing how people are drawn to her. I've become jaded because I see and talk to fans every day. I just try to keep my special and signed first editions in stock!"

—Britton Trice · Garden District Bookshop · New Orleans, Louisiana

"Reading the works of Anne Rice is not a passive activity, it is interactive: Beware the uninitiated! The experience is not contained between the covers of her books, but reaches out and pulls you into another world. Her characters are such a part of my life now that even if she never writes another word about Lestat (perish the thought), he is still alive and quite well, thank you, going about his adventures, in my imagination.

Anne is a woman I would like to be. She shares her heart with her readers and she blesses my life. I give thanks for Anne and the inspiration she gives me, for introducing me to New Orleans and last, but certainly not least, for bringing the irrepressible Lestat, that 'James Bond of Vampires' into my life. *Laissez les bon temps roulez*!"

—Teresa · 46 · Escrow Officer · Ocenside, California

The Interviews

CAROL

41 · Office Administrator · Providence, Rhode Island

"**W**hile living in North Carolina, I was introduced to *The Vampire Lestat* by a friend. Extremely overweight, involved in a very bad marriage, and often alone, I 'escaped' through books. As I suffered emotionally, mentally, and physically at the hands of an abusive husband, I escaped my unhappy personal situation by totally immersing myself in Anne's books, reading and re-reading them. I was immediately drawn in by Anne's fantastic imagery. I yearned to be a part of her world, perhaps even one of her fabulous creatures. One recurring theme spoke to me: the ability of her characters, even the mortal ones, to overcome incredible odds and circumstances. I started to lose my often overwhelming fear of loneliness, suffering, and death.

"After almost twelve years in my own private hell, I was finally able to walk away from the marriage. I continued to read Anne, devouring *Belinda*, *Exit to Eden*, and the *Beauty* trilogy. The inherent sexuality of these works awakened desires in me that were long forgotten. How liberating to explore the erotic netherworld with no sense of shame! I longed to be like those characters. Anne's world is not 'fair,' yet the characters who populate it not only survive, but thrive. Their self-awareness is always evident. These humans (or former humans) have experienced horrible, debilitating situations, dealt with them, and come out on top. I related to this, as my world was certainly unfair. She awoke my own personal rage toward the situation I was in, and that rage empowered me to make difficult changes. No longer satisfied with the woman I had become, I lost a significant amount of weight. As my confidence grew, I moved to another area of the country, found a new job, friends, and a new life.

"I continued to read Anne's books, relishing them, and became interested in Anne herself. I joined her fan club, regularly called her 'hotline' and eagerly attended the Memnoch Ball, my first Gathering of the Coven.

"Thanks to Anne, I have wonderful new friends and an exciting trip to look forward to every year. I have learned to accept (in fact, embrace!) the dark, carnal side of my personality, and if there's a dark, handsome vampire somewhere out there for me, I'm sure to find him in New Orleans.

"Anne also made me see that each individual is ultimately responsible only for himself or herself. No rationalizations allowed! That concept of personal responsibility was the key that unlocked the door to my self-imposed prison. I was the one who had to change."

JOHN

32 · Accountant · Newington, Connecticut

"I first read Anne Rice's Vampire Chronicles about seven years ago, around the time I discovered I was HIV positive. There were answers for me in those books. They were a very powerful influence, and I found much comfort in them.

"The intimacy of the vampires and the drinking of the blood deeply affected me. When I first was diagnosed I felt I was tainted. To consort with me was to consort with your own mortality. I was the walking dead. I'm much more optimistic now about my disease, but when I found out I was devastated and looked at things very dramatically. When I first read *Interview with the Vampire* I holed up in my dorm room at college and did nothing but read that book. I thought, 'This is a nice way out of my predicament!' I wanted to take out a personal ad and see if there were any vampires out there willing to take apprentices! Like the vampires, I learned that there is meaning and beauty in life: to love each other, to appreciate the here, the now, the present; to live fully and to pursue your passions. Lestat is a hero in that regard. He is always searching for new plateaus of meaning. In the end, you appreciate life through the study of death. When you have been pushed through the other side of pain, you find the meaning and derive purpose from it. How do I reconcile myself to mortality and/or immortality? The questions get bigger and bigger.

"At first I thought Rice was a gay author writing under a female pen name. Her books read like gay erotica. The way the vampires moved through crowds and could identify each other reminded me of the San Francisco cruising scene. Here were sophisticated, educated, tasteful, well-dressed men....sharing blood and hunting each other. They truly loved, appreciated, and respected each other on so many levels beyond the physical part. The vampires showed men appreciating each other's barest souls. I guess I was disappointed Rice didn't turn out to be a gay writer, posing as a woman. I thought how clever that would have been to gain credibility in the mainstream. The introspective characters like Louis would ask, 'Why are we doing this? What is the point? How do we reconcile ourselves to this fate? There better be some meaning, because this has become my life now.' Those questions are very prevalent in gay culture. Gay culture is always asking, 'What is this cruel joke?' Later on you find out it is what you make of it and whatever you create from that. Being gay is just different, it's not a joke or freak of nature; people come in all forms. With HIV you think, 'What the hell is this life, what is the point?'

"The big questions in life, as with Rice, are of purpose and being. It turns out to be really about living with yourself. Louis tried to reconcile himself and Lestat constantly grappled with good and evil. God didn't give Lestat any answers. The questions aren't easily answered; but you must keep asking them. You must keep reaching to other levels of learning. In a Buddhist sense, you must move on to different levels of enlightenment and being, reaching to higher and higher levels of awareness and consciousness. You must live to improve. Don't settle for mediocrity.

"When I read an Anne Rice book, I feel I have a friend for a while, and I'm always sad when it ends. It is an incredible place to be, asking all these questions as fast as you can, your mind racing. In our everyday lives the vital questions get pushed to the side. It is such a rich gush of those questions that Rice gives us; she brings them to the surface for us to re-analyze again and again."

D'SHAN

38 · Jewelry/Furniture Designer · New York City

"**B**ack in 1986 I was talking with a friend of mine about my love for Batman, vampires, and werewolves, and she told me about a fabulous book I had to read. It was *The Vampire Lestat* and I really related to it. I was in the military then, and the book became the structure to my chaotic thinking at the time. It solidified things for me.

"As a kid I loved vampire movies. They appealed to me and I had a primal attraction to them. The appeal of them was that they were outsiders. Rice put a structure and a history to vampires and their death, so their demise made sense. She refreshed the legend and brought it to our time period with modern day thinking. The vampires had feelings, and Rice showed how their human life influenced how they acted in their vampire life. The old Hollywood films made them monsters, like Frankenstein. Frankenstein wasn't a monster, he was a human and society projected their fears on him; therefore, he defended himself, just like me.

"Vampires are feared and chased, and yet respected. People try to kill them because they are strong and they need to be gotten out of the way. Those scenarios overlapped the reality of my life. I related not to the good guys, but to the vampires in most cases, because of my background as a black man from Texas: I was chased and hated. I had to romanticize racism because I did not understand it. Racism doesn't make sense to me; it's a ridiculous thing for people to try to wrap a logic around.

"I saw myself in Gabrielle, Lestat's mother, when she embraces the dark. In her time, women were suppressed. She had to wear corsets, which made women faint; they had no future, no job prospects, etc. She was to be a baby pumper-outer, or maybe used for sex in that patriarchal society. When she became a vampire she realized her full potential which apparently was there all the time. She didn't have to put herself into this small, square definition of a woman; her body was a round, ever-changing definition. She gained all this freedom from becoming a vampire. She knew her full potential juxtaposed to Lestat, who was frightened and bitter, or Louis, with his crying and whining and lack of understanding of the self. Gabrielle on the other hand said, 'Hey, I'm a vampire. There's no question.' She just was, and embraced it. That acceptance gave her the freedom to be the human being that she was inside. It led her to freedom, and I saw myself in that.

"The Rice books were like shelves for me. My stories and thoughts were books on the floor. *The Vampire Lestat* and all the Vampire Chronicles were the shelves upon which I could take my thoughts and place them. I could put my thoughts up on the shelves and categorize my feelings and see them more clearly.

"When I was less centered and more affected by my outside environment, as a teenager, I would get so angry and pissed off because I didn't understand the white women who would grab their purses or when people would lock their car doors as I walked by. To keep myself from being angry I would imagine I was a vampire. In that fantasy thinking I would just remember that vampires have a way of drawing out fears in folks or supressing those fears. People are naturally uneasy around them without knowing why. With the help of Anne Rice and the vampires, I came to terms with that racism. Over the years I have thought that people who are not centered will die from fear at young ages. Those people who ran from me because I was black are the kind of people who won't take a chance in life. They are the people who will try to fit themselves into the square box. When people move away from me at a bar, other people will take their places and they are a hearty people with a certain edge, that don't fear opening another door in their life. This is one way that Rice's stories have been a shelf for me to put those experiences on. For me it explained why, in a fun way, those people were so afraid. I even went so far as to think that most black people here in the U.S. have vampiric, mystic blood in them. That's why people are afraid of us, without any real reasoning behind it. They cover up all their fears with fake mumbo-jumbo excuses, like black people are inferior and so forth. I know that they are just afraid, little children.

"Most people don't want to let go of their fears; they'd rather hold onto what they know. In the book *The Messiah*, all these creatures held onto a stone, and one creature decided to let go. Instead of hitting other rocks and stones, he flew higher and higher. All the other creatures wanted to learn how to do this also and asked him to come back. He said, 'I can't show you how to do it, you have to do it yourself.' The whole idea of fear and letting go is something that the vampires understand. What is true evil? Our society tells us that power can get you anything. Our world is structured by, and people are tricked into believing, what the media says. Is that right? Isn't that evil? Gabrielle killing someone for food one night compared to wars being fought or what big industries are doing every day to our environment, is small in comparison. Which is the bigger atrocity? What is considered dark is just what our society dictates as such. What society says is bad is not what necessarily is.

"I take something from Rice's work with me every day that helps me fight what I call the 'Big Three media.' They are three large corporations that influence the media and have tried to shape what most people (or sheep) believe. I use the Rice books to counteract that way of thinking. Her stories have so many different facets of human thinking. I always believed that artists were broad-thinking and could see past the Big Three. I'm surprised that artists do get as caught up as the next guy, and say, 'that can't be done.' Rice's books say everything can be done, in your head, and that's what really matters. It has nothing to do with what's out there influencing you. Rice's books stand for a truth in human thinking, unlike the media, and that helps keep my head clear."

Vava

30 · Costume Designer · New York City

"I was very young when I got into the whole punk rock scene. I was into dressing up and the drug culture, but got that all out of the way by the time I was in high school. I was pretty sedate by my junior year, although I did get into the Goth scene. I started reading Rice then, in 1983. I read *Interview* and fell in love with Lestat. It tapped into the whole teenage angst thing for me. I was a complete outcast in high school. I grew up in a California beach town where everyone was blond and tan, and I was pale-skinned with dark hair. I was in a town where people worshipped the sun and so I naturally gravitated into this vampire, gothic chick. I did unpopular things like being involved in the theater, going to hear punk rock bands, and hanging out, staying up late. I enjoyed dressing very dark and people assumed things about me that weren't true. People saw me as they wanted to see me.

"I wasn't into vampires before Rice. I always liked murder mysteries and bad 1950's horror movies. I liked the films for their humor. Camp always appealed to me. The vampire was always that tall, handsome man in a tuxedo with a cape. I liked his outfit. I liked the persona of being the dark, mysterious person I made for myself, and Lestat's character appealed to me in my high school days. I related to Lestat's showmanship and fearlessness, and his constant seeking of answers to questions. I loved that he searched the world and crossed time and boundaries....a wild journey to find answers. I lived vicariously through him and emulated him in the daylight. I would sulk around and be very morbid, dark, and contemplative, reading a lot of existential literature (sarcastically). Rice took me to a fantasy world where I lusted after the dark side of life and the romance of the night and the moon.

"The dark side to me is an alternative lifestyle. Alternative to what people are living in the daylight. It's like light versus dark. The dark is appealing because it is taboo and it's tapping into your subconscious. You think you're being 'bad' because that's what the daylight world has told you you're being, but really it's not bad or good, it's just tapping into your fantasy life. Reading Rice's books does that. Everyone has a public life, private life, and personal life. The personal life is the secrets and fantasies that inform the private life (what you do in your off hours) that have nothing to do with the public. It is your subconscious.

"After *The Queen of the Damned* the books stopped meaning things to me. I'd pick them up and put them down. I read *Lestat* two or three times. I like what the books gave me back then. They informed my fashion life and club life. Once in college my life just changed and they stopped meaning as much to me, and Anne stopped meaning as much to me. I was so curious about her at one point. Who could have written this? Her personal story was so interesting, about her life and her family. Then I felt like the more I heard about her, as with other media figures, the less I cared. I think that her persona turned me off. I think an artist's work should stand by itself. All the mass commercialism around her was too much. Everyone loved her, and I felt like this was my special story and my special time, and it meant the most to me. Everyone has their own interpretation, but for me I felt she had become too popular as a writer.

"I joined the fan club in 1996 to go to the Ball. I was curious. I wanted to see the costumes. I had friends who had gone before, and as a designer it was important to me to see how people were interpreting her work. I wondered at what age people stopped joining fan clubs. I thought maybe I was too old at thirty to join a fan club. I was embarrassed that I sent the money in, but I did, and I got a sticker and a head shot. (Laughter). I looked on the correspondence list and was amazed at the range of ages, from thirty-three to sixty, and I thought, 'wow.' Most people in the fan club were over thirty. There were definitely places in New Orleans I wanted to see from her books. So I came this year. All the fans I met were great, no matter what they were into. Housewives with Lestat T-shirts, bondage-blood people, Goths....it was great to meet a range of people.

"I think the sheer number of fans is ridiculous. People have lost sight of the fact that it's about her writing, not her personality. As an artist it's fine for her to voice her opinions and her politics, but people take this stuff so seriously. People have to remember that she is just a human being, and a flawed human being, and that makes her a great writer. But the fans have turned her into a mythic creature. One of her own worst creations is what I see her becoming with bodyguards and being fenced off from the people. It's a shame she has to be protected. I keep hearing how she can't walk her dog. But she's created that and made herself way too accessible to people. She has created this world for herself, a castle to live in, and now she's trapped by it.

"We don't have very many heroes anymore in society. We look toward athletes, models, and movie stars with their bad attitudes, and they make so much money. But we see them as heroes. Here we have an author who is treated like a rock star, making the money of an athlete, and yet she's talking about very deep important issues...spiritual and metaphysical issues. It's almost as if no one can hear the issues anymore because marketing is clouding her message. Maybe she's clouded her message, maybe she can't hold onto it anymore. She talks about so many incredible things in every book, that it's almost impossible to remember everything she's said. She can be seen as a teacher of this generation. She's an earth mother type. She has a lot to say and a lot to teach, and people really innately respond to it. Unfortunately, the people have turned to worshipping her and have forgotten the message. It's like the Jesus complex: teaching so many great things and yet the human being can't survive because the myth must carry on, so they tear apart the human being.

"I think the wine and cologne labels she's producing are exactly what is wrong with this whole country. We take something we love and then we cheapen it, turning it into an amusement. Everything has to be taken to the umpteenth degree and made ludicrous, and you forget why it was so special and beautiful in the beginning."

AMADEUS

34 · Freelance Writer · Boston, Massachusetts

"My sister was into Anne Rice first. She had read the vampire series and kept trying to get me to read *The Vampire Lestat*. I picked it up and thought, 'Oh God, I don't want to read about some guy becoming a rock star!' I was thinking this was something I would have written when I was seventeen! Then she gave me *Interview with the Vampire* on a road trip, and when I wasn't taking my turn driving, I was reading the book, well into the night, by the reflection of car headlights behind us! It was so incredibly intriguing I just couldn't put it down. It was beyond just an interesting bestseller, it was magnetizing. I had a total identification with Louis and his views on life.

"It wasn't just Louis' pain that got me—there was a part of him that was rebellious and a part that was very honest about who he was and his life situation. Louis was very fresh, almost innocent, to the world in a way. He had a beautiful quality that was so authentic, it felt like you were talking and listening to a real human being. He didn't have defenses up, he just let everything out and said exactly who he was and what his motivations were. I couldn't believe this was a book character. I felt so close to Louis, as if he were real.

"Louis has a total lack of artifice. I think I'm rather like that in a way, and maybe that's why I appreciated him so much. I could also feel his despair. There was a quote that Armand had made in *Interview with the Vampire* about how Louis was the essence of that particular century. Louis was saying something like, 'I don't represent anything and no one has ever really cared for me. I'm just very much alone.' Armand answered, 'You represent the fall from grace.' I thought that was just so beautiful. I believe that speaks of the whole human condition as well as Louis' individual sufferings.

"I think that there is a very strong connection between vampire culture as it was portrayed in *Interview*, and alcoholism and dysfunctional families. I could relate very strongly to that, as I come from an alcoholic home. I saw Lestat as the alcoholic husband/father figure, Louis as the co-dependent wife, and Claudia as the rebellious child. That's simplifying it, but there were a lot of interplays between the characters that seemed familiar to me in that kind of family setting. There was so much love between Louis and Lestat and yet so much anger. They didn't know how to speak their feelings. A lot of times they didn't even know what they were feeling themselves, so they were pushing each other away, yet they really wanted to be together. I identified that with my own family experience.

"*Interview* helped me move through my family experience and my personal feelings. I saw how Louis perceived himself at the end of the novel, and I did not want to be what Louis had become: a person who was totally withdrawn and isolated, moving through life without any connections. I want to put my own priorities in order and really find what's important for me, and make the connections I want to make with the rest of the world. That book was my door of perception.

"To me Louis represented the light in a very dark world. I know Louis himself would vigorously disagree. I think that light is what Lestat saw in him; Louis just didn't understand that. I used to think that Anne Rice must be a beacon in the world of darkness to write something so concentrated and beautiful as that book. I'm not interested in the world of darkness for myself. I spent a lot of my life exploring my sorrow, sadness, and despair, and I would rather look at the world with fresh eyes in that respect. To me vampire culture, witchcraft, or what have you, represent things that are painful. So I try to keep away from that. I relate to Louis more on a personal level than as a vampire.

"About a year after I read *Interview*, my sister joined up on the internet. At first I was like, 'Oh no, I don't want that in my life. That's modern technology and will pull me away from people, make me even more remote.' But I gave in, and what it's done is help me hook into the creative side of myself and give all that creativity to other people, who seem to enjoy it. I became more of this person I wanted to become. I started out on a Newsgroup that talked about Anne Rice and then joined the Anne Rice Listserv. I got involved in talking about the many different aspects of Anne Rice. Then the list eventually branched into talking about Anne Rice books, more about the serious literature end of things. I love role-playing and humor, so I would write these totally bizarre things and people would write back, 'Get back on topic,' because the biggest taboo is to get off topic. I got very frustrated after awhile, so a woman on the list and I made up the 'Battlelist.' Once the 'Battlelist' was drawn up, lovers of certain characters would join forces. I know that there was a 'Church of Armand' faction and people would talk about it all serious, but I realized later, it wasn't a real church per se. I thought these people were crackpots, but I realized later it was very tongue-in-cheek, as well as the fact that these people loved Armand. I was always making cracks about Lestat on line, like, 'Le Fop de Wining Corpse,' or stuff like that. The Louisians were cheering it while the Lestatians were going nuts with rage.

"The listserv is a whole culture. We don't really see it as a game; it's more of an outgrowth of our personalities.

"I actually came to New Orleans before it was popular for Rice fans to do that, before the tours and the movie. I was seeking out Rice to sort of get a feel for whether she was this enlightened human being I'd imagined her to be from reading the books. I thought, 'Who could possibly write this? It must be somebody who has an incredible perception of the world, and I'd love to get some of that, have some sort of revelation.' My creative self owes something of its renaissance to Rice's New Orleans. It is nurtured there, through her characters. I went past her house and I saw her go off in her limousine; that was it, unfortunately. Last year I came back because I had to go to the Memnoch Ball. I was dying to see her doll collection and meet other fans. I wanted to have the whole experience. This year I'm here with my friends on the internet and to experience New Orleans with them, as a group. I think the Balls are a wonderful event for people to come to and feel that they belong. I applaud Rice for starting it off. I think it's fantastic for people to look into books and take the time to think about the characters and allow themselves to fall in love with them. My costume today is Oscar Wilde in drag. Oscar is a very sprightly character who likes being devilish and risqué, like Lestat.

"I'd like to see our group grow closer emotionally, but it's hard to say because we are all very different personalities. I definitely feel this group is like a family. We have our share of arguments, but one of us will always take the time for another if they need advice. It's really a unique friendship. You don't have the intimacy in person, but you can talk to them all the time. There's a whole other aspect of yourself that can be shown on the web that's different from just letter writing or telephone conversations. It's a whole different way of communicating. We don't always talk about Anne Rice; we talk about tons of topics. The core of us seem to have something that keeps us together. We counterbalance each other in a way."

MAN RAY

33 · Singer/Songwriter · New York City

"In the 1980's it had become an 'in' thing among friends to read Anne Rice, so I decided NOT to read the books. It was a big turn-off that it was so trendy. A long period of time transpired before I actually read the vampire series. I was always into vampires, and especially loved the visual aspect. When I finally read the books I became very excited about them. They became a part of me. The characters became friends, the kind of people I would want to hang out with. The dialogue read like a conversation I would have. I could personally identify with every character, and I really kicked myself for not having read them before. The books are written very elegantly. They are poetic. They are not as much novels as worded pictures.

"I didn't realize that all these different components that I loved--poetry, ambient music, philosophy, literature, etc.--were all mixed together in the Goth movement. When I realized that there was a Goth movement, I looked in the mirror and realized I was tailor made for it. I was pale complected, dark haired, and thin. People always thought I looked like a vampire. I used to wear my hair greased straight back years ago. I said to myself, 'This is it—this is perfect for me.'

"In the mid 1980s the whole Gothic thing exploded in New York City, and it all clicked from there for me. The Goth scene was very easy for me to adapt to. It was sophisticated, fashionable, and intellectual. At that time I was leaving the fashion industry and trying to figure out what I wanted to do, and the only thing that really appealed to me was music. A lot of Goth lyrics were inspired by Charles Baudelaire and Edgar Allen Poe, who I'd always admired. The scene was pretentious in a way, with it's references to literature and its airs, but I always kind of liked that. (Laughter)

"Around this time I read *Interview with the Vampire,* and the book completed the picture for me. The book was a text for what I was doing. I would try to do music as I imagined Lestat would. Everything described as Lestat's character was me: the deep voice, the imagery. I saw myself as a cross between the best parts of Louis and Lestat. When I first read *Interview* I didn't care for Lestat. I thought he was pompous, and wasn't very secure. Then after reading *The Vampire Lestat* I realized how weak and frail and unappealing Louis really was. Lestat was strong, aggressive, and had a zest and fervor for what he was doing. He wallowed in being a vampire and lived it to the fullest. I related to it all.

"When I was a child, about eight years old, I was afraid of horror movies. I was terrified of Frankenstein's monster and Dracula. Then, I had this very vivid, terrifying dream that Frankenstein was chasing me. When the monster was close to catching me, I turned around and pretended I was a vampire and he stopped and said, 'Oh, you're one of us.' From that day on I was infatuated with vampires. So I went from being terrified of vampires to becoming my fear, which I guess is not that unusual. Since that dream, the idea of the vampire has been a powerful one for me. Vampires were a group I could identify with. I loved the romance and elegance, the loneliness and isolation. I found my inner power through them.

"When *The Queen of the Damned* came out, of course, I had to run out and be the first one to buy the hardcover and read it. My girlfriend at the time had us buy a copy for each of us and one for the house. After reading that book she and I started arguing over who would make who a vampire first. It escalated into other things and we broke up soon after.

"There was a time when I was living in Los Angeles and had seen an ad for a 976-Vampire phone line with a cartoon of a vampire next to it. I thought it was hilarious. I was sort of out of my Gothic stage and into something else at that time, but a friend of mine worked for this company, which also had chat lines and astrology lines. I needed another job, so as fate would have it, I went to work for the vampire line. People who were interested in vampires would call up and we'd exchange stories. It was a nationwide line and I would start late in the afternoon and would read from Rice, Poe, and Baudelaire on the line. It was a nice line where people chatted. Of course you had people who called up and said they really were vampires, but, hey, I think that whatever one is into is great for them. I don't pass judgment—I think it is all very interesting.

"I've changed a lot over the years, but I'll always have a piece of the vampire and Rice with me. The experience on a whole made me realize it is okay to have insecurities. Everyone has feelings of being totally alone and thinking thoughts that they feel no one else could experience. The dark side for me is being able to look at my insecurities and be able to face them, and it has been a very healthy thing. I still wear nothing but black. The imagery is always there. The pale, dead look, the sophistication and elegance of it. I will always love that, and it is a big part of who I am. Keep on biting!"

GINGER
43 · Government Clerk · Newport Beach, California

ZENIA
21 · Student: English/History · Davis, California

Zenia: I was on a vampire kick and saw *Interview* in a store. Looked boring, but thought I'd read it anyway. I read it in one sitting. The book was so amazing—it blew me away, and then I just started reading all the vampire books I could find. *Interview* and *The Vampire Lestat* were excellent. All the emotions and feelings of the characters made them more real than any other books I'd read. They weren't just corpses that went around biting people—they were more.

The books have changed my life because I have become friends with people I normally would not have met, or even knew existed. I met Ginger and a bunch of people from the Anne Rice Listserv online. Ginger was forming a trip to San Francisco and I e-mailed her that I wanted to come along.

Ginger: I've been online for about two years now. A group of us first got together when a woman online, Amadeus, who wanted to start a role-playing game, got people from the Listserv to go to San Francisco and play it.

Zenia: I go online everyday to check what is happening. It's a big part of my life.

Ginger: We all met because of a unified love for the characters, and we all think the same way. We all have a melancholy view of life.

Zenia: Except for Lestatians like myself. We try to have a bit of a more devil-may-care attitude, or at least we'd like to think that we do.

Ginger: We have a 'Battlelist' which is our make-believe world online. All the Rice characters are represented and each of us is a member of an army, like Louis's army or Armand's army.

This is our first trip to New Orleans as a group. We aren't going to the Ball this year. It sounds boring and none of the people in our group were really interested in going. For us it's more about seeing New Orleans through the eyes of the characters than going to the Ball. We get together and wear our costumes, have dinner, and talk amongst ourselves.

Zenia: We all belong to the fan club, but the newsletters and stuff were coming very infrequently.

Ginger: I phoned the fan club and told them I hadn't gotten anything for a long time and wanted to know if I was even going to be offered a ticket to the Ball. It's been very haphazard. I don't think it's a very good club, especially the name. I'm a Louisian. Why does it have to be called The Vampire Lestat Fan Club?

Zenia: It doesn't bother me. I'm a Lestatian. My other friends don't like vampires and think I'm weird, so this trip is a chance for me to meet people who understand how I feel. When you tell people you like vampires, they think you're a Satanist who goes around biting people. They miss the point.

Ginger: I always bring vampire novels to work, and everyone thinks I'm off the wall. The point is that it's a whole way of thinking about the world, not just Gothic or blood-drinking stuff. It has nothing to do with how vampires are portrayed on TV—it's about a view of life. It's a melancholy point of view that nothing is sacred, nothing is real, life is all a dream anyway, and imagination is everything. It's not a Christian point of view. It's a way of feeling you're outside society. I enjoy that. I do feel apart from society. I don't think like the masses. The people that read these novels think like I do. Anne Rice's books brought a kind of vampire into existence unlike anything before. The way people look at me when I'm reading a vampire novel is not the way I am. Nobody understands how I feel.

Zenia: People either get these books or they don't. Members of my family have tried to read them and could only get through fifty pages. That was it. Yet other people will like them and ask where the next book is. I've always been the strange one in the family—now they just have more proof!

Ginger: I was never interested in vampires before reading *Interview with the Vampire*. Like Zenia, I had never thought of them as people with emotions or feelings, and Rice portrays them as real people. You feel as if they exist somewhere. I still feel that way, that they are here somewhere, even if it may only be in the imagination. They are more than just characters—they are alive and have substance. *Interview* is the very best book. Every book thereafter is a bit drier than the last.

Zenia: In *Memnoch The Devil*, the characters changed, like when the Armand thing happened and he goes into the sun. I felt Rice was just disposing of characters when she got tired of them.

Ginger: I feel like Anne has lost interest in these characters and she's just writing these stories because people want her to. I don't feel that she's a part of the characters anymore. I feel very betrayed by that.

Zenia: So do I.

Ginger: The characters are so real—you feel like they are friends. Especially Louis. If Louis is your favorite character and then to hear Anne say she doesn't like him anymore, it really hurts personally. Armand is one of my favorite characters and for her to just kill him off really upset me! I identified with his emotions. I understood how Louis and Armand felt inside. When you pick one of Anne Rice's characters to love, you pick a part of yourself that you identify with. I didn't like Lestat. The way he thought and things he did....I saw myself and I didn't like it, so I don't care for Lestat. The qualities of Louis and Armand I really admired. They vocalized thoughts that I couldn't. The characters we like the most aren't necessarily the sort of personality we portray in life. I admire people who are like Louis. I empathize with their loneliness and being betrayed by life. They are very deep people who feel alienated by life. Some of the things they did were evil, but I think Armand had a good soul. I don't think they tried to hurt people, but they themselves have been very hurt. I think Lestat is the opposite. He's been hurt, but he likes to hurt people in return. He handles it in the opposite way and I don't admire that kind of personality.

Right before I read *Interview* I was really depressed, and it helped me to read about other people feeling that way too. I didn't feel alone anymore.

Zenia: Lestat is my favorite character. I would like to be like him and not care what other people think and do my own thing. Louis and Armand are the parts of me I wouldn't want to have out in the open. I wouldn't want to be brooding or have the other qualities that they have, but I know they are inside of me. Lestat doesn't mean to hurt people....he just doesn't.

Ginger: Anne's characters really make you study yourself and your own personality. I have really thought more about who I am inside by studying her characters. She voices all these emotions that you never really thought about before. You become much more self-reflective by reading her books. I study other people more now also. I think Anne wrote these books to cleanse all the personalities she had inside. Now she has moved away from that part of herself and doesn't want to see Louis anymore. She wants to be Lestat now. She's on a Lestat kick, like the 'star writer,' and it seems so phony. That's why we feel betrayed. She's not real anymore. If she could get away with it, I think she would have killed off Louis. I just want her to bring back Armand. I had these T-shirts made up that said 'Armand Forever,' and I was a member of a 'church' online called, 'The Unholy Roman Armandian Church.' We wore them to book signings and Anne said, 'Oh, I'm so ashamed!' Rice had an Armand shrine at her party last year, so maybe she'll change her mind.

Zenia: Louis is a very important part of Lestat. If she had killed off Louis she'd have to kill off Lestat also. They are entwined: one can't exist without the other. We joke about how we hate each other's characters on the 'Battlelist,' but Louis is very important.

Ginger: The characters are real aspects of ourselves. That's why people love them and come to New Orleans to be part of the books and be around other people who like them also. When the internet group met, we all liked each other immediately. I think all her fans are people that think the same way. We are only interested in Rice as an author. The things she's done, like buying a church, etc., have alienated a lot of fans. For some reason she's pushing people away, and I don't know if she even realizes it.

Zenia: I wish she'd go back to how she used to write. I couldn't get through *Servant of the Bones*, and that's really rare for me.

Ginger: Bring back the old characters and tell us how they feel. All the characters have a lot to say and we already know too much about Lestat. Enough with him!

Zenia: (looking surprised) Well you *have* to have Lestat in the book, c'mon!

PAULO

26 · Hair Salon Owner · Los Gatos, California

"Taking time to read a book is next to impossible for me, but I read *The Vampire Lestat* and I got into the whole vampire thing just last year. I loved this book!

"Anne Rice has made these secretive, beautiful creatures, and immortality doesn't seem to be such a bad thing. I wouldn't mind being Lestat's buddy for all time. It would be killer to see the evolution of the world for two hundred years, and what would happen in that time frame. Marius is really cool because he's a teacher. When he told the origins of the vampires I was really moved.

"The book made me think about my homosexuality and where I fit into society. The vampires are secretive in society, otherwise they'd be destroyed, and it's the same as being gay. The religious right wants to destroy us and it's always a battle. Lestat wants to know why he came into being and why things are the way they are, which is like the gay dilemma. Nobody woke up one morning and said, I think I'll be gay today—you know what I mean? It doesn't work that way. We were born into that world and by being hated, feared, and chastised by society we were thrown underground. It's ridiculous bullshit. Lestat says to Marius, 'Didn't you ever want to tell the world about yourself and who we are?' I identify strongly with that. I'll put a gay rainbow flag on my car and tell people who I am and what I am. If they've got a problem, they have to deal with it. I'm very 'in your face' about it. I love Lestat's rambunctiousness: he dives into everything. I'm like that also, just going for it. I identify with Louis because he is caring and really into the human race and doesn't want to hurt anyone, but he finally sees the need to. That's a lot like me, also. When I was a kid I liked the vampire sense of being feared, opposed to fearing. I feel that if you look intimidating enough, no one will bother you."

"It is trippy how Anne Rice and vampires are such a household name, especially in New Orleans. Being in New Orleans was like being home. It was a strange feeling. All the smells, the people, and the architecture. It was like being in touch with a past life. The Coven Ball was beautiful. I was nervous about going; I didn't think my costume would be up to par, but now I know how to plan for next year! Watch out! I was amazed at how many people go to this thing. It's a time when your alter ego can be released. I really fell in love with my vampire costume for the Coven Ball. People would come up to me and say, 'You're so beautiful,' and I would think, 'Why? I have white skin and fangs!' But I realized vampires are very beautiful.

"When my friend and I left the Coven Ball and went to Bourbon Street and people were coming up to us, saying wild compliments, I decided, 'Fuck, I'm really into this!' In a bar, this girl came up to me and said, 'Are you a real vampire?' and I said, 'Yes.' 'Are those your real teeth?' she questioned, and I said, 'Yes, give me your wrist,' and I bit her, just sank my teeth in hard. She pulled back and said, 'You are so beautiful—do you drink blood?' I replied, 'Only on weekends.' I thought I was being a real freak, but then she said that she and her boyfriend just got into witchcraft and started drinking each other's blood. I thought, 'Okay, who's the freak now? Hello!'

"For me, this whole thing is about fun and flamboyance. What I'm learning in the vampire books is a flip side to my spirituality. I was raised Catholic, but I denounced it for a long time and was anti-religion. In high school I wore upside-down crosses on my head and black clothes and makeup. I was a mod weirdo with spiked hair. Then later I found a new sense of spirituality that had nothing to do with religion and changed my whole perspective. I believe in nature, karma, and Mother Earth. When Marius talked about taking care of the land and Mother Earth, it was almost like a little evil flip side to all of my thoughts.

"A client of mine told me I had taken on my alter ego, or my dark side, when I got so into assuming this vampire character. I know I'm not a bad person: I try to treat everyone well, so I don't think the dark side in necessarily a bad thing. I'm still trying to figure out where I stand because I do have a little dark side in me and I'm not sure where that can go. Rice brought that out in me, and now I question everything.

"I think that people who are seriously into this vampire stuff are okay as long as they don't hurt anyone. When I thought about the girl from the bar, I thought that if I had a lover and we did these ritual things, like drinking each other's blood, it could be like a ceremonial black wedding, as long as the HIV status has been checked. I think it could be beautiful and very sexy between two consenting people who understand it. But to take it overboard? I don't see the need to go on Oprah and talk about it, you know what I mean? It just makes people think you're a freak. But if you understand it and it's a part of you, I think it's great. White magic is a beautiful thing.

"I want to tell Rice, thank you for not making us monsters anymore. Oh, my God, I said 'us'! I'm an 'us' now! People tend to repress themselves, and life is to be enjoyed. People should try to have a delicious life so they can look back on it and be glad for whatever they did. People should explore how they feel about sexuality and life and just get over their inhibitions. Life is a celebration."

EVELIN MARIE

24 · Mother, wife, and "provider of all needs for the two men in my life" · Jackson, Mississippi

"I have read Rice since 1989, but I have no favorite book. Anne Rice is my favorite. She is a loving and caring person, concerned for the morals of humanity in general, and she studies the psychological impact of the daily life of humans. She puts these studies into the words of the vampire, so we can understand the psychological turmoil human beings go through.

"I feel connected to Rice. Every person sins, feels some sort of remorse, and wants to have a higher spiritual plane to return to. Anne personifies the human experience, and she has a good reflection on life. I believe Anne's spirit evolved with a higher God. Everyone is a spiritual person in their own way; everyone has his own individual view of life. Anne opens up possibilities from the very beginning of time: Mesopotamia, Sparta. She covers B.C. to twentieth century A.D. Anne gives you the options of knowing what was before you and what is to come.

"Her books are enlightening historically, psychologically, and spiritually, but I don't think there's anything that wasn't there already; it was just brought to light by Anne.

"The 1992 coven party was the first time I met other fans. They are all loving and caring people. It's a supportive family and one you can feel confident caring for. Anne has made me more confident in myself and my spirituality. I believe that I can stand up for myself and what I believe and that God, as we know it, understands and is free to walk beside us.

"If you've never read a Rice book, don't think of it as some kind of sci-fi novel. There's a lot more involved in her writing then just fairy tales. There's a lot of real human experience that can bring people to an understanding of life and spirituality and human experience. If you've never read her books you have no grounds to criticize her in any way.

"I don't think Anne is commercial. The commercialism is not something she draws, it's the people who are drawn to her that want to commercialize her endeavors. She is a loving and caring individual who wants to know her fans are there for her, and we are. I was happy to have met her in the receiving line at the party this year. Everyone was taking pictures with her and I told her I didn't have anyone to take my photo, but if it wasn't too pretentious, I would love to have a hug."

MARK

31 · Corporate Lawyer · Vancouver, Canada

"It's shocking that themes in my life I have always struggled with show up on Anne's pages. Her work has had deep personal meaning to me on several levels. I had always been into the supernatural and people thought I was weird, and here was this author writing about it. It wasn't a Transylvanian count with a red sash: the vampires were young people my age, who were modern and had more meaning to me than Dracula. The character's relationships were very insightful. People make fun of Anne's announcement at the beginning of the movie videotape, when she says, 'This book isn't just about vampires; it is about us.' I think that's true. The relationships she presents are shocking and destructive, as are so many relationships that people really have. The vampires may love each other, but for whatever reason they can't live together. You can see that with Lestat and Louis, and with Lestat and Armand. Rice's work shows how possessive relationships can become, like when we see Armand kill Claudia so he can be with Louis.

"I enjoyed the relationships between men. A lot of gay people see meaning in her books that straight people don't. I'm gay. Rice's books helped validate my feelings through her homo erotic themes. I see the books as validation for sexuality. When you are actively looking for someone to share your life, you wonder if you are going to be alone, or find someone in this world you can be in love with. In *The Witching Hour* you have Rowan and Michael who were these lonely, lost souls, having one night stands and never in relationships of duration, and then they meet and find that they are soulmates.

"I'm interested in Rice as both a writer and a person. I think her personal story is fascinating and apparently, in the *Birth of a Vampire* video, after the death of her daughter, she and her husband were in terrible grief and they overcame it through Anne writing *Interview*. There are so many autobiographical themes throughout her work: The five-year-old vampire child Claudia vs. her own daughter who died at five. Her husband serving as the model for Lestat. Her home on First Street is the home of the Mayfair witches. I love these connections. I understand that she has attended Coven parties in the past wearing a necklace similar to the Mayfair emerald. She talks about the children of these witches, Taltos, that grow incredibly tall, and then I find out that her son is 6'4"! So of course her life is interesting because it appears in the books.

"I read from a Rice book every night before I go to bed. If I have a hard day I can escape into her world and then fall asleep. Some people think I have an obsession with Anne Rice. I think it is a healthy escape. Friends don't understand my feelings. I have a friend who collects *I Love Lucy* memorabilia. He has every video, etc., but he is very judgmental of me. He has his obsession and I have mine. I like Anne Rice. But because Rice is associated with blood, witchcraft, and darkness, she is perceived as unhealthy.

"I joined the fan club last year, but only to go to the party. That was my first trip to

New Orleans. The first two days I was there I was enchanted. Walking around the French Quarter with Joy Dickinson's book, *Haunted New Orleans*, I was looking for buildings that were featured in her novels. I went to the Garden District and walked past her house, Commander's Palace, and all these places in her books. Then I got scammed by a street artist, so the bubble was popped a bit for me that all this is escapism, not reality. It disturbed me because some of my friends accuse me of living in a fantasy world through her novels, and some roll their eyes at the thought of me flying down to New Orleans for the party and buying a costume.

I come from a fundamentalist Christian background. I was a Baptist. I loved Sunday school because I was fascinated with the dark side of the Book of Revelation. I was never a morbid kid, I was just fascinated with death and darkness. I was a very gentle child. I was never into the Goth scenes or wearing black lipstick and dying my hair. I was a shy teenage kid who just read books.

"Fundamentalists believe that the King James version of the Bible is the only Bible. They are very intolerant of any alternative interpretations. I'm surprised more people haven't attacked Rice for *Memnoch The Devil*. On *Larry King*, Rice talked about what motivated her and said that if God is all powerful and the angels were created by God and knew he was all powerful, why would they rebel? That is what is laid out in *Memnoch*. Memnoch's hell is a purgatory where people must realize the evil they have done in their life so they can move on to heaven. That was an interesting theory. I liked it, but at the same time I am heavily influenced by Christianity, which states that there is an ultimate evil and good and people are drawn to one or the other. I had that in my mind, and *Memnoch* is contrary to that. It doesn't offend me; it's another view that could be valid. I believe that people are evil not because of a devil on their shoulder, but because people choose to be evil, harmful, or mean.

"I have an ongoing dilemma with being dark. When you are a teenager, you have the whole world in front of you, your dreams are fresh and new. When you become an adult your ideals start to die, and you realize that you aren't going to be what you wanted. When I started to go through my twenties, my dreams started to die; dreams of getting out of college and starting my life and having someone that would love me, buying a house, and vacations, and being happy, and finally being an adult, free of all my parent's restrictions. I started to feel very dark in my late twenties. Some people have pointed out that I was searching for darkness and I chose to see the dark side opposed to the positive side. I think life is a state of mind. If you search for darkness, you'll find it. I don't think Rice is dark. Dark and scary are two different things. I'm in transition now and working through a lot of my issues. I don't know where I'm going to end up. The literature has helped me come to terms with many things, but I realize it is also just an escape.

"There is a theme in Rice's books of domination and submission. Lestat is a dominant and Louis is a submissive. But you often wonder who is really in control. I think psychologically every relationship has a dominant and a submissive, just by who makes decisions. I understand that is often the situation in bondage relationships. Those relationships interest but also frighten me. If you get into that, do you need greater and greater thrills to maintain the excitement? You have to be able to exercise your fantasies in a safe environment, and so often people don't have that.

"It is shocking that Rice's books are everywhere in North America. I see the U.S. as very conservative with 'family values,' so to find Rice books in a store in the Bible Belt, and no one trying to burn them, is amazing. There is censorship in Canada, and you can't find the *Beauty* series anywhere. Besides, the feminist movement is intolerant of domination of woman by men in any context. Maybe I just don't know, but you never hear about her work being attacked by the forces of censorship. Knock wood.

"I had a playful relationship on the phone once. This guy from Miami was going on about *Interview* to my friends, and they told him he should meet me and gave him my number. He was fascinated that there was someone else out there into this so much. This guy was blond, 6' tall, and a mischievous spoiled brat. He had a Lestat complex. One night on my answering machine there was a message that was verbatim dialogue from the movie. I called him back and quoted from the book also. We continued this for months as Louis and Lestat talking to each other, alternating between fantasy and reality. We always talked late at night, and it was wonderful fantasy. We finally met, but leading up to our meeting the conversations became very cold and we got into arguments, because the reality was setting in, and this relationship had been sustained by a fantasy.

"I understand that when Anne finishes a book she gets very depressed that no one will like it. Don't be depressed, Anne, we love you!"

Scott

31 · Hospital Clerical · Taylor, Michigan

"I've been a lonely person most of my life. I never really fit in with any one group. When I was younger I had a speech impediment, which I have controlled now, but the kids always made fun of me. I spent a lot of time alone, and that's how I got into reading. I was never into vampires before, but liked to read about things out of the ordinary: fantasy, futuristic books, etc. Anne's characters were so much more real and human then anything I'd read before. Louis and Lestat have human feelings and foibles. When I found Louis I felt he was a kindred spirit. He was a loner trying to find himself and something to get him through his eternal life. It helped to lift my soul.

"Louis's loneliness and striving to find somebody who he could be with touched me. That's basically how I am too. I'm striving to find that one person who can help me get through life. I admire Lestat because I'd like to be more outgoing but I found comfort in Louis' struggle. I saw a lot of myself in him, and knew what he was going through. Sometimes when I'm down I'll go back and read *Interview* or *The Vampire Lestat* and I can know that there are other people out there like me, who are going through all this stuff too. Lestat's questioning and trying to find out the truth behind everything is like my own search for answers about life.

"On the internet I found the Anne Rice Listserv and met a bunch of people. To be able to talk to them about Anne Rice or about ourselves is really wonderful. On the 'Battlelist' I'm what they call an OHF (One Happy Family) because I love all the characters and can't pick one favorite. I started a mercenary group called 'whack-em-o.' Whoever sends me the most money is the one I do battle for in the game. Actually, if I had to pick one favorite character I'd probably pick Ramses the Damned. I felt very attuned to him. He and Louis are a lot alike. Ramses knew the pain of his eternal life and that he would never be able to find one person to be with him for eternity. He knew the pain of losing Cleopatra and that's why he went into the big sleep. He struggles with love like all the characters do. Can you really spend eternity with one person, no matter how much you love them?

"I went from being alone and reading a book to having an extended family on the internet and joining the fan club. A lot of people will see me reading a Rice book and come up to me and say, 'Oh, I love her too,' and then we'll sit and talk about it. I'm introverted, so when I found the Listserv I made friends easily. Anne is part of my everyday life now; I'm on the internet a lot. They are my family of friends.

"The reason I came to New Orleans was to meet my friends from the internet who I have never seen face to face before. I was a bit nervous to meet them in person. I was afraid maybe they wouldn't like me, but instead, I have a lot of new friends. Meeting people through Anne Rice has changed my life. If it was just to come to the Ball, I might have hemmed and hawed about it, but the rest of the group from the net was going to be here for the week and I thought, yeah, I'll go. The town feels like an Anne Rice town.

"I'm interested in Anne as a person, but I respect her privacy and am not going to try to dig to find out more about her. I hear people saying that Anne's writing style has changed since *Interview*. I agree. I don't think they have the same power now as they did back then. But I also think Anne isn't the same person now as when she wrote *Interview*. During *Interview* she had lost her daughter and was drinking heavily. That depression gave her work a certain power. Now her life is good and I try not to compare her work. There can never be another *Interview* or *Lestat*, because Anne is a different person now. Ten years from now she'll change yet again. So we'll find out where her life will lead her and how her books will change. I'm excited at how she will metamorphosize and what she will become. Too many fans are stuck in the past and want her to be the same old Anne. I would love to tell Anne to be true to herself. Don't try to make everyone happy and waffle about the characters you've killed off. Just keep doing the good work."

Jennifer

28 · Social Worker · Cincinnati, Ohio

"**W**hen I started reading the vampire books, I saw a listing of other books by Anne Rice. I became very curious about *The Sleeping Beauty* books. What are they? So I saved my money and went to a bookstore to buy them, but they weren't available. This was in Indiana, and they were hard to find. They don't have 'naughty' books in 'dry' (non-alcoholic) places in Indiana. So I special ordered them. At the time, I didn't know they were 'naughty' books. As I read them on the bus ride home I thought, 'Oh, my, there's no vampires here!' Friends started stealing the books from me and I had to beat them off to finish reading them! I'd never read anything like them before, and it certainly piqued my interest. I eventually read all of Anne's books, and then a friend told me about the fan club and other Rice activities.

"I like the fact that there's a lot of information in her work. It's very global. I have a liberal arts degree and I don't always get to use the information I received. Reading Rice's books gave me a place to use all my knowledge. I have a lot of friends that have read Rice and it gives us a lot to talk about. We have different opinions and share them. I'm active on the web. I read the Newsgroup postings and took the Talismanic Tour. It's great to share common interests with people that you don't have to hunt down. You can find people with your passions all over the world online. Now all my friends come to me if they need to know something about Anne Rice. I'm the source. I picked up the baton and started running. They think I'm insane.

"I love Anne's books. They feed my philosophical nature and make it a lot worse. I'm more extreme now in my philosophical thinking. I've always said that I was a closet Goth and never knew it. But when I look back on my life as a child, I was always reading books about witches, vampires, and ghosts, so of course I would do that as an adult. In Rice's work, you can sit down and take a trip with her. Being a counselor is a wonderful thing; I can speak to people who are schizophrenic and I can see what's going on in their head. Rice's books are like that also, and give me a chance to think about things. I live in a very conservative, midwestern city, and no one talks about anything there except how conservative they are. When I get to read about old things in Rice's books, it's great. We don't have any ghosts in Cincinnati, so I came to New Orleans because of Rice.

"I joined the fan club in 1991. I heard about the party to end all parties, this vampire ball, and I wanted to go. I was afraid to travel by myself to a place I'd never been, but in 1992, I got on a Greyhound by myself and came to New Orleans for the Ball. Everything was just as Anne had described it. I felt a feeling that I'd always had inside, and couldn't place. I realized that it was the trees in New Orleans. I remember having some kind of deja-vu feeling around the big trees. It was a memory I couldn't put my finger on, but in New Orleans it all clicked. I think since I moved around a lot as a kid, the trees were like the roots I was looking for, since I was born on an air force base in New Orleans.

"The party had pulled me to New Orleans, even if it meant going by myself. I read all the books and had to go. My friends saw something in me that connected to the books and they encouraged me. Rice is something that I channel all my energy into. She brings out a creativity in me and gives me a chance to dress up. In Cincinnati you can't express yourself without causing a riot. In New Orleans you don't feel like you're under a microscope. The Ball was the greatest night of my life. I went alone and met lots of people. It was a small party in Anne's house on Saint Charles that year. There were only a thousand people, and I got to talk to Anne and have her sign one of my books. I was really excited about that. She was more accessible at the old parties. Her whole family was there, even her dog. Now I come every year by myself. A lot of people I met, I meet at the Balls every year. In the last few years the parties have grown, and I understand it has to be that way. Now there are over eight thousand fans and it's a bit out of control. Some of the parties have been like concerts, but the most enjoyable ones are when you can roam around and talk to people, or sit and relax. A lot of people feel like nothing can top the Memnoch Ball in '95. The '96 party was more like a dinner party. When I joined the original fan club, founders were in charge. I don't know who these new people are. I'd like to know more about them and how they got so high up in the fan club. What are their qualifications? The fan club officers presented flowers from the club to Anne at the party in '96, but they never asked us or told us what they were going to do. I would like them to ask in the newsletters what we, the fans, would like to do. I don't feel the fan club is very accessible. I feel it is very separate from what Anne feels.

"I went to a book signing in Dayton a few weeks ago and recognized Susie Q. of Anne's staff. I talked to her, and all my friends were really impressed. It made me feel special, like I was connected to Anne's world for a moment. We all want to feel like we're part of her special universe.

"I think all artists are a bit crazy, and Anne's no different. She talks too much about movie stars in her newsletter *Commotion Strange*. I wonder what else she does with her life other than watch movies and write books. I wonder if that's what it takes to be an artist: to be a bit weird and removed from society. Whenever I read one of her books, I look for the issue that she may be going through in her life that's coming out in her writing. I think now she's processing too much of her own stuff in the books and it's not as entertaining as it used to be. In the book *Belinda*, the character who was an artist couldn't draw characters after he'd seen them on TV, and I think that was very telling on Anne's part.

"I like all the stuff Rice is coming out with now, like the wines and colognes. Some people collect things, and I collect Rice stuff. I'm disappointed that there aren't *Interview with the Vampire* action figures! I'd love those!"

JEFF

32 · State Utilities Commission · Tallahassee, Florida

"I'm a relatively new fan. In 1994 a friend of mine was giving away old paperbacks and I picked up the Vampire Chronicles. I read them all within one week, back to back. I'm not into vampires or other vampire literature. Rice is the only one for me. Then I re-read them again to get more out of the stories and discuss them on the Anne Rice Newsgroup on the web. Lots of fans want to discover Anne's meaning and find symbolism, and which character is Anne in each book. In *Interview* she was Louis. In *The Vampire Lestat* she was Lestat, and I'm guessing she was Akasha in *The Queen of the Damned.*

"I related to the kid Marcel in *The Feast of All Saints*, who didn't have a family to take care of him toward the end. I was raised in foster homes from the age of four. I really related to Marcel's feelings. I think every kid is looking for a mentor or someone to guide him. I'd been in Marcel's shoes a couple times as I was growing up. *The Feast of All Saints* and *Cry to Heaven* were stories that could have been biographical and historically accurate. The Mayfair witches are fun, but you know they're not real.

"A lot of the romance of the books is the time period of the late seventeenth century to early 1800s before the industrial revolution. It gave me a lot to sit and imagine, like an intellectual creativity. *Interview* is a tragic story, especially for Louis. Once you read *The Vampire Lestat*, you feel sorry for Lestat as well. You don't see many characters in books that on one hand you can really hate but also really envy. They are great characters with such depth, and I haven't read anything like them in the past. I envy their immortality, but like Lestat, when he tried to kill himself to end it all, I don't think I'd really want it. I think most people in their right mind don't try to think like Lestat does, or treat people as he does. I don't think people believe the stories are real; I think they like to read the books and involve themselves in the stories. Fantasy is a good thing, but you don't want to go too far and become a fanatic. I'm a fan...but not a fanatic. I write poetry and I enjoy Anne's creative spark.

"Artists and how they create interest me. I don't look for deeper meanings in Anne's work. She touches on social issues and that's nice to read and is food for thought; however, I try not to go too far into it. She's made me more interested in history and locations. I've always secretly been interested in the paranormal, but not to the degree a good number of other people are. I enjoy the books because they touch on it. For me, it's only fantasy I allow myself when I'm reading. *Memnoch The Devil* gave me a different point of view on religion. The *Beauty* series was interesting...I learned a lot. (Laughter) I'm not into that bondage thing. I've lent those books to woman friends of mine and they don't return them!

"I just read *Cry to Heaven*, which I swore I would never read until Anne died and there were no more books coming out. I was in the navy for four years and have been to Italy dozens of times. *Cry to Heaven* took me right back to when I was there. Rice takes me places, like coming to Cafe du Monde in New Orleans. I've been to New Orleans twice since reading Rice and it has more meaning to me now then ever before. I'm even considering moving to New Orleans. Last year it was an awesome trip to go to the Ball and meet the internet group.

"I have a great time at the Balls. This is New Orleans at Halloween time, and anything is possible. My memory of the Memnoch Ball was of this guy, dressed as a prince, tugging his girlfriend behind him on a leash. She was wearing a cape, and the leash was attached to her nipples and other regions...She was nude...I had to do a double take...I wasn't prepared for that. It was a topic of discussion for about three weeks afterward. The feminists in our group were upset, but I figured it was just New Orleans. Then I realized she was supposed to be Beauty. People said Stan Rice had artfully asked them to leave the party!

As a political spokesperson, I think Rice's gone too far, but that may be her press agents. Most authors don't get so politically outspoken. It's okay, I suppose, but I sit back and chuckle; it is kind of funny. Hearing the outrage of people on the internet about how she has sold out is kind of funny also. It doesn't bother me, but there are some hard-core Anne Rice people who started reading her back in 1976 when *Interview* came out, and are horrified that she would talk about politics as she does. I don't know that I'd go to a restaurant called Lestat's; I'd rather have her feed me intellectually.

"Most of her stories end in optimistic tones. I try to look at every day with an optimistic point of view; you don't need Prozac if you do. We have such a depressing society, and the endings of Anne's books are always 'happily ever after,' and I carry that with me. I talk to great people on the internet...so I take both those things with me every day. It's something to look forward to. I'm against negative people. I look at each day in a positive manner and I can thank Anne Rice for that. I do look forward to each day. It's all gonna work out and there's nothing we can do about it anyway."

CHRISTOPHER *26 · Carpenter · Charleston, South Carolina*
CHRISTINA *20 · Student: Photography · Charleston, South Carolina*

Christina: I'm an Art/English major and want to be a photojournalist. When I think about my future and talk about my work, often I look at Rice as an inspiration. She is a woman who has truly been able to express herself. She does crazy, outrageous things, but no one thinks twice because it's Anne Rice. Rice's books give me hope and let me know there is acceptance and a place in this world for the type of writing we enjoy reading and that type of thought process. It's good that she has opened a door for many others.

Christopher: I am a Goth and also a Pagan. It means a lot to me to have a good author like Anne writing about us, opposed to the terrible things that are written in the press. She's an idol to me in a lot of ways. She's a very beautiful and seductive woman.

Anne's books have really inspired me to write more and do my art and things I have passion for. The books helped me realize the horror side of life. They taught me that if someone sets his mind to it he can write something great. Maybe someday I will also. I love that she uses real places in her novels. We took a tour of New Orleans and got to see the places she wrote about. It's really nice to see it all tie together. It makes it lifelike.

Christina: I've been reading Rice since I was ten years old. Prior to that, obviously, I wasn't exposed to any of these alternative lifestyles. Her books opened my eyes to things I became interested in and then did research on. *The Claiming of Sleeping Beauty* definitely got me interested in the S&M world. Anne Rice put it in terms you could understand and identify with. The writing made it seem more appropriate. It wasn't some smutty book; it was a beautifully written novel, and that changed my outlook as well. It was a dream come true to be at the Ball this year. I've read about New Orleans in her books since I was a kid, and it meant everything to me to go there.

Christopher: We practice blood exchange together. It is an exchange of great intimacy between two people. It's a bond that is very spiritual. It also feeds my hunger, which is lust for life, energy, and happiness. It is a fulfilling act of drinking part of your partner, a way of becoming one with each other.

Christina: The drinking of blood is not something to be scared of. Blood reminds me of death, but it also is what keeps us alive. It is very erotic. The whole vampire fairy tale plays into it, to an extent, but it's not that we believe we're vampires. There isn't a room at Bellevue with our name on it. Drinking blood is almost flirting with death: you never know how much you are going to lose or how much you are going to take in.

Christopher: There is much more to drinking blood: it's an exchange with my partner of our life force. It is an energy that's transferred through the blood to one another. It has a lot of magical meanings to it. It goes back to the idea of being alive and flirting with death. I enjoy flirting with death; I'm not afraid of it. I have no fear of death. We all live and die, and our souls will go on to be reborn again. Although I don't practice blood-drinking to flirt with death.

Christina: We only do this ritual together. When we started dating we realized we were into the same kinds of things. We had the same lifestyles, listened to the same kind of music, loved Anne Rice, and our conversations built from there. As we learned more about each other and what we both wanted out of a relationship and our fantasies, we started experimenting. We took precautions, of course, and were tested first. It is a very dangerous thing. To be intimate with someone is one thing, but I find sharing blood is more intimate than sex.

Christopher: Drinking is also about pain and pleasure. All people have that dark side inside them, which has a need for pain and pleasure, and most people are too afraid to look at it. We didn't get into the blood ritual from an Anne Rice book; it came from someplace else. But it is nice to read about it, it's make believe in the books. We don't consider ourselves vampires—we consider ourselves members of the S&M community.

Christina: The fiction pulls us along and gives us a visual picture of our thoughts and the whole drinking process. It can be associated with vampirism and Anne Rice's novels, but the books for us are just a backdrop for our fantasies.

Christopher: We enjoy the nighttime better. The night is more mysterious and provocative.

Christina: We do have a lot of similarities to vampires. We like to sleep all day if we can, but we do have responsibilities we have to worry about like everyone else. My eyes are actually light sensitive. The novels are a guideline and a way of publicizing our lifestyle in a way that people can better understand it. They are a way to explain to society what our kind is like.

Christopher: The vampire lifestyle and the S&M lifestyle blend together in a lot of ways. The dark clothes, the leather. In drinking blood there is pain and there is pleasure, just as in S&M there is pain and pleasure. So they relate to one another.

Christina: I think the idea of S&M and vampirism are two separate things. The S&M lifestyle developed from the vampiric and the Elizabethan/Renaissance age type acts. A lot of things happened back then that people wouldn't dare talk about, but it was still going on concurrently with everything else. The eroticism of torture from that age definitely gave way to the S&M lifestyle. Look at Elizabeth Bathory. She had a love for the young women who were serving in her household. Her lust then turned into bloodlust. The erotic lust turned into that.

Christopher: The way we drink from each other usually begins with me biting the inside of my cheek and drawing blood, and then feeding it to Christina through my mouth. Sometimes I might use a razor on my chest and she drinks from there. Once I filled a vial of my blood for her, wax sealed it with symbols, and she wears it around her neck, so it becomes a ritual.

Christina: We don't drink a lot at one time, just as much as we can handle. Shot glass size is what we usually drink.

Christopher: I believe that drinking one another's blood does help prolong life because it is a life force. You are sacrificing part of your life to the other person.

Christina: If you believe it means vitality and will do certain things for you, then it can prove true. Your thoughts always control your actions.

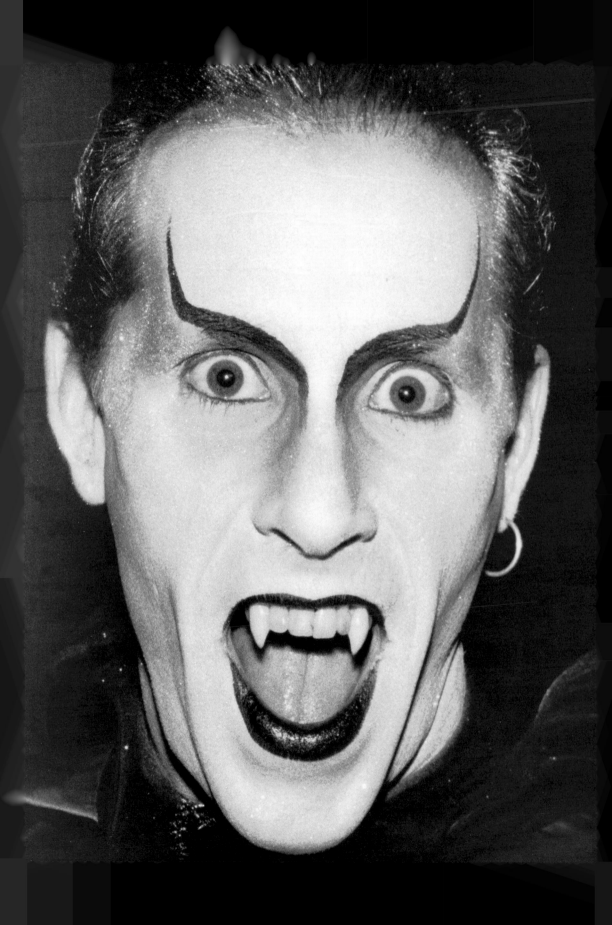

KEN

35 · Owner, "Fangs, Etc." · Houston, Texas

"**A**nne Rice is my goddess of darkness. She's written about things I'd never dreamed of. She opened my eyes to a lot of different things: witchcraft, the meaning of horror, and what terror is. It is an adrenaline rush when you think that something is going to happen in her books. I realized from reading her books how deep history was in the past, what vampires are about, and how they can change. I feel like I'm a part of it in a way. Making fang teeth propagates vampirism and makes it continue through the years.

"I read my first Rice book in 1985. All of her books had messages that applied to me, so I knew she was the author for me. What touched me was that there is no end to anything: everything is continuous. You can look at eternity as living constantly, like reincarnation. Anne's books are everlasting. They are a part of American history, and she has assured her immortality. Until the Earth is gone her books will be here."

"Reading Anne's books put my life back on track. I was in college and had read about her alcohol problems and the death of her daughter. Something devastating happened to me in college that was very personal and it almost knocked me right out of school. I stopped going to classes, etc. *The Queen of the Damned* really woke me up and gave me the incentive to go on. The message was 'never give up.' I believed in that message and picked myself up and managed to graduate with a 4.0! Her books really helped me come to terms with my homosexuality. Anne is very open and accepts people for who they are. She told me that she loves gay people more than straight, because they have these dear feelings inside and are able to show them. It was something I was struggling with, and she helped clarify it for me.

"I enjoy being around Anne Rice. It's very exciting to me, like going to a concert. I've talked to her a few times. She likes it when I show up in costume at her parties. She thanked me one time. I made fangs for her secretary Linda. Linda got me in the door, and everyone liked me and the teeth I made, and then it was like a chain reaction. I make teeth for her staff now. Anything vampire-related they let me know about. We stay in close touch. When I show up, I look real good and they know I'm there!

"My group of friends are very lax. We don't drink blood or anything; we like to dress up. When you wear your teeth that feel very real in the mouth and look at yourself in the mirror, you know you look so good, you can't help but smile. The fangs keep you smiling; you're up, you feel good. I hear about these people who think they're really vampires and drink blood, but I don't cater to them. It's a shame that they have to do that. Like those murders in Florida. Those people are not vampires; they're drug addicts and mixed-up kids. For me it's about dressing up and living out a fantasy, which I live every day. It makes me feel good to watch other people feel good and laugh when they see me. I get a lot of hugs. It's such a good feeling when you get your first pair of fangs and you feel it through and through. I like it when I see people's faces and how excited they get when they put them on.

"I've never made fangs for Anne. I think she has an image she has to keep. I remember one time she laughed at me and said, 'Ken, I write about the vampires, you make them.'"

JEFF

25 · Artist · Pinson, Alabama

"*Interview with the Vampire* is the best single piece of fiction I have ever read. I never intended to read it. I scanned the first few pages and then couldn't put it down until I was done. It opened a broad margin of fantasy for me, thinking about what it be like to live forever and if I would react to things like the vampires did. I love the seductiveness of the vampire—his power and sexiness drew me in. I related to a certain aspect of a lot of the characters. Louis has a basic kindness in him that I see in myself. I'm not a depressed person though; I don't live regretting things I've done. I strive to be like Marius and the way he relates to things. He has an overall wisdom and nobleness about him that I would like to achieve. I also related to Khayman and the way he reacts to problems. If I have a big problem I generally turn my back and walk away, and that's how he handles it. If it is too painful a situation he will turn away and forget it.

"My life was changed after *Interview*. It broadened my horizons to things out there that I never would have thought of. I was never really into books. I never really read until *Interview*. After that, I was gathering material on everything and reading as much as I could, and devouring everything by Anne Rice and other authors.

"I do a lot of painting. As a child my first pictures were of moonrises. I've always been fascinated by darkness, maybe because my mom was always reading horror books. It's always been where my fantasies lie. Anne's books opened up doors for my art and gave me ideas. I'm the king of unfinished pieces, but now I'm working in watercolor and painting seven of the major cities in the world and in a corner will be an insignificant figure in the background. I will name each piece 'Vampire on the River Thames' or wherever. She's given me so many ideas I don't have time to paint them all. *Memnoch* and the ideas of heaven and hell have given me ideas for paintings also. Anne paints pictures with words, and I like to take it one step further and put it on canvas. The paintings represent people I can't be or places I can't go.

"I'm happy that Anne has so many readers that support her, but I also feel that it's becoming too popular. I don't want to see the vampire balls become like a Trekkie convention in a few years. I like *The Queen of the Damned* because I enjoy when people band together for a cause. I loved *The Magnificent Seven* when I was a kid, and the joy of the Ball is the same, everyone coming together for Anne. I met her at a *Memnoch* book-signing. I'm fascinated by her whole world. I would love to sit with her one day over a cup of coffee. I would tell her how much I've enjoyed her work.

"I'm just thankful I was walking by the bookstore the day I saw *Interview* in the window. It's opened a lot of ideas for me on art and life. I'm a daydreamer from way back and sometimes I let fantasy get the best of me. After reading one of her books

I'll sit back and think for awhile. What would I do if I became a vampire? How would I learn? I think of what I'd do right down to the finances of it, and when ready, who would I take with me? I know it's fiction but I enjoy it. Some people like gnomes; some, unicorns. I like vampires. They're all on the same pile of goodies, but I *don't* believe there are dragons flying around."

BARBARA

39 · Co-Owner of Talismanic Tours · Red Lion, Pennsylvania

"I was in an advanced physical anthropology class in 1991, and my professor was into the occult and suggested *Interview with the Vampire*, so I read it and worked my way through all of the Vampire Chronicles. I became enthralled and obsessed.

"I connected to Lestat, as an alter ego, and to Rice and why she wrote *Interview*. We both came from dysfunctional families with alcoholic mothers. I picked up on the pain and where she was coming from. Something that ACOAs (Adult Children of Alcoholics) have are characteristics that the vampires have also. I know how hard it is to be a child when your parents are alcoholics. You become the adult and take care of the house. Anne's story eased my pain. I was fascinated with her as a person because of our shared background. Her books also gave me strength.

"I love life, and it's fun to have fun with life. Rice has provided that for a lot of people. Nobody really believes they're vampires, but to dress up and be able to go out one night and put your fangs on and pretend, isn't that great? As Lestat said, 'I'll give you the choice I never had. Life holds much fascination, look with your all seeing eyes.' And if it was offered, of course we'd go with Lestat. It's a wonderful fantasy. In a Rice book you feel the eroticism and the joy of life. Rice gave me a whole world I could get lost and meditate in. I love thinking about 'what ifs.' My favorite book is *The Vampire Lestat*. Everything about Lestat is me. He's bold and brassy with a lot of chutzpah. He speaks his mind and does what he wants to do. Maybe it's the way I want to be and I'm not; I'm not sure which it is. Rice had always said 'Lestat's my hero' and that's how it is for me as well.

"I called Rice's publisher to ask about a fan club and they gave me the address and I joined about four years ago. I saw an ad in the fan club news for Katherine Ramsland's book, *The Vampire Companion*, and once I learned these places were real I just went crazy. I got all these tour books and made a list of the places I was going to see in New Orleans. I already knew the city from the novels; I only needed to physically experience the smells and the sights.

"In 1994 the movie *Interview with the Vampire* came out. I was teaching school and was going crazy because if I talked to any of the teachers about how strongly I felt about the film they would just have thought I was totally nuts. So I started a chat room to talk about Anne Rice, the movie, and her books on America Online. The room is called Lioncourt. Once the movie hit, the chat room went crazy. Some of us had seen the movie as many as ten times! I wanted to go to the Memnoch Ball, but I wanted to go with others that felt the same way I did. I brought it up in the chat room to see if anyone was interested in going. None of us really knew each other, other than we were all crazed Anne Rice fans, but it was unanimous: everyone wanted to go! I was unbelievably obsessed with Rice and the books, and wanted to share it and show people a good time.

"Kim, who I met online, called and asked if I would like to turn the trip into a tour business. For two to three months we planned a complete supernatural tour of New Orleans and we had about fifty people lined up who wanted to go to the Memnoch Ball. Meanwhile, Britton Trice, owner of the Garden District Bookshop in New Orleans, suggested I write Katherine Ramsland and ask her if she'd be interested in leading the tour. Katherine loved the idea, and then it started becoming a big thing. We wrote a letter to Mrs. Rice asking permission to do the tours. Weeks went by and then Susie M., representing Mrs. Rice, phoned and said there was no problem, as long as we used a disclaimer that stated the tours were not authorized by the fan club or Anne Rice, which we happily did. We wanted to use the word Talamasca for the tours, but supposedly it's a word that is owned by David Geffen and the movie studios, thus we couldn't. Whether that's true or not I don't know, but according to *The Vampire Companion*, it was a word Rice found in a book on witchcraft by Jeffrey Burton Russell. Seeing how we were only doing this out of pure love for Rice's literature, we said fine. We didn't want to do anything to make Rice mad! Kim thought of the word talisman (good luck charm) and added an 'ic' to make it an adjective form, and we became Talismanic Tours. We incorporated and got everything lined up. To date, we have brought five groups to New Orleans. We toured the plantations, the Rice spots, and had a welcoming dinner with a parapsychologist, followed by a ghost tour. We did a lot of the background and history of New Orleans. The tours really tied in more than just the literature of Rice.

"For me the culmination of everything was the Memnoch Ball. I never went to my high school prom, so this was going to be it. I went all out and spent eight hundred dollars having an authentic crinoline gown made. I went to the Ball in black, in mourning for Lestat, because he basically dies in *Memnoch The Devil*. The party was wonderful, the best party I've ever been to in my life. All the lights, cameras, and costumes: you knew when you arrived it was going to be special and it really was. I love that the event of the Ball is getting bigger and bigger each year. I believe everyone should be able to share in something wonderful and it shouldn't be exclusive only to certain members.

"At this point in time Rice has started her own tour company, which is wonderful, but I have mixed feelings. I taught school until February 1996 and left my teaching position to do the tours full time. Then, days later, we received a notice from an attorney that was rather cold, ordering us to cease immediately or legal action would be taken. After all the love I had for Anne, and all the fans I got to join the club, I felt I was kicked in the teeth for being a fan. I am disappointed that I didn't get a phone call that said, 'We are going to do this now, do you mind stopping?' I am disappointed that an attorney contacted me so I had to spend money I didn't have to respond. I am disappointed that the first year we lost $8,000, but that didn't matter. This was not something that was started to make money, it was done out of love for Anne and to bring people together in New Orleans. When I heard about a very uncomplimentary comment about my persona by a Rice family member, I thought *what* are we dealing with here? It's not about Anne, it's about them, the businesspeople, and their self-importance and making money. We have legions of fans who have sided with us and are upset and angry about what has happened.

"No matter what, I still have deep feelings for Rice. I guess at this point I will bow out gracefully. Sometimes I wonder just how much Rice is aware of what's going on. Has she gotten so big that she doesn't know what's happening on the outside anymore? Has she forgotten about the 'little people' who made her writing popular? I think she does genuinely love her fans and I bow down to her out of respect. No one will know more about her life than she and her family, but the way it was handled was awful. I thought I had done everything in the world for people that love Anne Rice.

"A lot of the fans told me I shouldn't have gone to the Coven Gathering in '96, after everything Mrs. Rice had done to me. I can understand her wanting to take care of her family and sharing her business with them, but is she is leaning toward becoming a commodity? My love will always lie with the Vampire Chronicles and what they did for me. Her concept of vampires was so different—they were passionate, there was love, there were many little love stories in each book.

"Mrs. Rice has become bigger than herself now, yet it's because of her that we have all this. Many people owe her thanks. That is why I can separate what happened with the tours from my feelings for Anne Rice the writer. I have no hard feelings. I try to understand. I can see reunions with the online members going on for eternity. The camaraderie and understanding of our online group is unbelievable. I think when you connect with a book so deeply and then a number of people connect that deeply also….Well, I guess we all have something in common. Rice's books brought it out in us and put us together. There's a cohesion that holds us all together. Lioncourt is still going on over AOL. We still talk about the books and Anne Rice, but we also talk about ourselves. It's a therapy session. When the onliners get angry about how we were treated, I just have to say, look, we wouldn't have been in New Orleans together to experience all those things if it were not for Anne Rice, and because of that I could never be angry.

If I could talk to Anne I would say thank you for changing my life and adding to my world, for giving people a view of vampires that is humanistic and full of feelings. Thank you for introducing me to New Orleans, the history, and thank you for all the friends I've made because of you.

"I first met Rice at a book signing in Baltimore. I had brought the *Interview with the Vampire* movie poster framed in glass and a baseball autograph pen for her to use to sign the glass. I was first in line. She signed it and asked if she could keep the pen. I was thrilled that she wanted to keep a pen of mine. I really had this lady up on a pedestal. And she still is in many, many ways. She was very nice to me then. At the Memnoch Ball I introduced myself to her as the woman who does the tours with Katherine and she smiled and said, 'Oh.'

"I went to the coven party in '96 anyway, out of respect and love, not only for Anne Rice, but for the camaraderie of the fans and out of respect for what the books have done for my life. No matter what, the bottom line is, I fell in love with a city, an author, and a cast of vampire characters. I'm still looking for Lestat here in New Orleans, and have yet to find him. I leave Lestat and Marius messages in all the hotel guest books in New Orleans to find me. Spiritually I would like to believe they exist….in us all."

"At the Memnoch Ball I was overwhelmed by how many fans there were. When you walked into the party, there was this amazing sense of community, a sense that I'd never felt before. You knew that everyone in that place was as in love with the books, and Rice, as much as you were. I was dressed as Anne Rice that night, and everyone thought I was her. It was crazy!

"When the tours were ordered to 'cease and desist or else' by Anne's lawyers about a year later, I became very bitter. We had done everything legally, gotten an okay from Rice's assistant, and then we were suddenly threatened by Rice's army of people. We began the tours because of our love for her, the books, and the fans. We were the fans! I had an immense respect for her until this all happened. I am bitter and I do blame Rice. On the other hand, I have to wonder how much she knows about what goes on behind her back. I know she is surrounded by people who are basically 'yes' men. When you get to her level of celebrity, you tend to surround yourself with people who won't criticize you and just worship and protect you in a way that may not be good for you. Everyone has to face reality, and I don't think Rice does. Whether that's because of the people around her and how they have decided to run her businesses, I can't tell you.

"I'm bitter because of the way our company was handled. I didn't expect Anne to call us herself, but, then again, why couldn't she have called and said 'Thanks for what you started' or 'Come work for me?' People in Rice's circle know us, like Susie Q. and Susie M. We deserved something more then a cold-hearted fax. It's very hard to get to Rice. Her people surround her like a huge glass wall. If you get within two feet of this wall, you are bounced back into the next galaxy. Did someone screw up by giving us an okay? If so, it wasn't our fault. They should have taken responsibility, instead of shutting us down in mid-tour. I think they thought we were making a lot of money and/or cashing in on her name, but nothing could have been farther from the truth. We were losing money hand over fist. We felt we were on a mission to share Anne's world with people. It felt like a slap in the face to the fans that she supposedly loves and respects so much.

"I wish I could say this whole experience hasn't changed how I originally felt about Anne. I will always have a place in my heart for the books that meant so much to me at the time, but I can honestly say, I can't look at her books or read them anymore. The books I love by her are from another time, a time when I loved her, and she seemed like a different person. When I can get to the point that I can separate my feelings, maybe I can read them again. I wish I could tell her how I feel. I would be honest that I am bitter, but I would also tell her that the books have changed my life. Because of her I've met people I never would have otherwise, I have a best friend in Barbara, and I still have my beloved books to hold onto forever.

"Her mass commercialism says to me that the money is more important to her than self-respect, her fans, critical acclaim, or anything. She has become what she seemed to want to avoid: a parody of herself. She's not an institution. She is just a person with exceptional talent, which is being wasted by what she's doing now. Quality certainly surpasses quantity. All the marketing she's so enamored with is negating everything she's worked so hard for in her life. She can't stand on her past work anymore. Her castle has started to fall and it's like she's taking a wrecking ball and destroying what's left. I used to be proud to be an Anne Rice fan, but I'm not anymore. If she really loved her fans as she says she does, she'd show it in a different way. Her love seems rather hollow now."

BRADELEINE

38 · Management Consulting Firm · Redwood City, California

"**I** read *Interview* around 1980, right after I got out of college and had moved to San Francisco. Instantly *Interview* became my favorite book. I loved Louis. Life is horrible for him but, no matter how tragic things are or how dark life is, he holds onto this ability to see beauty and to go on. He stays strong and does not become cruel or bitter. That really resonated with me. He has guilt over almost everything he does. Everyone is always telling Louis how wonderful he is, but he can't see it. His depression doesn't allow him to realize that he is able to see beauty and is passionate. Louis can describe everything from becoming a vampire to the streets of New Orleans with so much love. He couldn't possibly speak that way if he were as detached, empty, and dead inside as he thinks he is.

"Louis's character was uplifting to me, and reminded me to continue to see the beauty in things around me. I'm a lot like Louis. In some ways I'm very pessimistic and have a view of life that is more dark than not, yet in between that there is all this beauty to be seen that is worth living for, even when circumstances are horrible at times. That's why I'm drawn to Louis.

"After I read about Anne's vampires, my view of vampires completely changed. It became more sympathetic. Later, I saw the stage play of *Dracula* in New York. I realized that even Dracula was sympathetic and had elements of Louis in him. He did love his victims and it was painful for him to have to kill these people all the time. Dracula loved everything, even humans who were destined to die…how lonely and painful that must have been. I never really thought about it from the vampire's point of view before. Then I started to see all vampires like that. I think that Louis has found peace. As the books go on he has become comfortable with his existence, whereas Lestat has gone the other way. He has gotten more frenzied as the stories continued.

"When *Interview*, the movie, came out it caused a huge Anne Rice resurgence for me. Seeing the movie was this cosmic thing that happened for me. It was as if Brad Pitt really became Louis for me. Louis is like a kindred spirit and seeing him come to life on the screen was a life-changing event. Brad Pitt captured everything I felt about Louis so perfectly that all I wanted to do was go back and see that movie again and again. I saw it about twelve times in the theater. I didn't have any preconceived notions before I went to see it. Some people got too wrapped up in crazy things like, 'Pitt's hair is too long, his face isn't thin enough,' that they miss what the movie had to offer. The movie came out in November '94 and then I was desperate to see New Orleans, so I came for two days and now I come every Halloween.

"The progression of the books bothered me because I loved Louis and his role became smaller and smaller and that alone was disappointing. None of the other books have been written as beautifully as *Interview*. I can pick it up and read almost any passage and it will bring me to tears, which is not the case with Anne's later novels. In *Memnoch the Devil* Anne made the characters into things they weren't. Lestat's behavior was whiny and sniveling. What happened to the guy who would look the devil in the face? The whole Armand thing is inexcusable. Not so much that Anne killed him, but that she did it in one paragraph. I had to re-read it because I had missed it the first time and everyone online in the Anne Rice Newsgroup was talking about Armand being dead, and I was shocked. Daniel disappeared as did Marius. I felt cheated. The final insult was Lestat swearing off blood forever. Vegetarian vampire? It's all horrible!

"I found my internet pals after the movie came out, because my friends were sick of me talking about vampires. I was never really interested in Anne herself during this time. I don't tend to care about author's personal lives in general. Last year there was a lot of anticipation about coming to New Orleans with all these people I'd met on-line and taking the Talismanic Tour. It was exciting to meet cyber friends in person. Everyone really bonded. We all started talking about Anne, because most of us hated *Memnoch* and in Anne's interviews she kept saying everyone loved it. She was quoted as saying anyone who didn't like it didn't understand it. It just seemed that she refused to acknowledge that there were people who were disappointed in the book. I felt that in the beginning of the Vampire Chronicles there was this story that had changed my life, and as they went on the stories became less and less powerful. I felt betrayed. Anyway, once the internet group got to know each other the talk became less about Anne and more about ourselves and life.

In the end I will be grateful to her forever, no matter what she does, for having written *Interview* because it had such a huge impact on me. I have a feeling that there may never be another great piece of work from her again, and that's a shame. But if all she had ever written was *Interview*, I would be eternally grateful."

ISILWATH 26 · *Computer Staff Assistant* · *Bellefonte, Pennsylvania*
SKYWISE 26 · *Computer Specialist* · *Bellefonte, Pennsylvania*

Isilwath: The first Rice book I read was *Interview* in 1985. I was a big Duran Duran fan, and somebody told me that Louis was a dead ringer for Nick Rhodes. I have to admit at the end of *Interview* I hated Lestat and I didn't want to read the other books. Louis comes down on Lestat very hard, and you think Lestat is a total jackass. But then I buckled under and decided I needed to hear what Lestat had to say. I really enjoyed *The Vampire Lestat*, *The Queen of the Damned*, and *The Tale of the Body Thief* more than *Interview*. Up until *The Vampire Lestat*, Louis was so depressed all the time I wanted to shove Prozac down his throat. Snap out of it!

Skywise: I haven't read any of her books. It's my wife's thing.

Isilwath: I love the vampires. They grasp the unexplainable; they are able to step outside themselves. There is power, savagery, and beauty in it all. *The Witching Hour* was too off the wall for me. (Laughter) I know that sounds strange, but I love the beauty of the vampire. They aren't evil, I think they are necessary. You have to have a predator of humans. Humans don't control their own population anymore. We are very good at killing things that kill us, so you have a niche in the web of life that has to be filled. The vampire is the perfect predator that imitates human beings, preys and feeds on them, and their greatest trick is that we don't believe in them. Since we don't believe in them, we don't actively try to get rid of them. Think about that from an ecological/biological standpoint.

The books teach that life is to be savored and you should really live life every day. Seize the day, go out and try to squeeze life out of every day, like Lestat does. He tries to squeeze every bit of life out of the night. I took a lot of that from Lestat: don't take anything for granted, notice the details, and live. Don't go through life like a bump on a log.

Skywise: I'm going to read the books one day. The problem is that Isilwath writes about the characters. She is one of the fan fiction writers online, and I tend to type for her. I love living with a Rice fan. I dealt with her Duran Duran thing for many years before she read the vampire books. It's a wonderful thing for me to watch her enthusiasm. I can see the vibrancy in her life because she lives with these things she loves. We've been married just over two years. This is our first trip to New Orleans.

Isilwath: I write speculative fiction. It's a big subculture on the Anne Rice Group online. When a new spec writer comes in and is good, they are adopted or 'minionized' by an advanced spec writer. It's very intricate. I'm someone's 'minion' and I'm 'engaged' to two other people on line. It's like keeping a writer's talent in the blood. I've written four specs so far. They are a great creative outlet for me. *Dangerous Games* and *Dagger of the Mind* are role-playing games on the internet. When I joined the List, it was already closed to new members. I do participate in the *Vampire Connection*; it's a web city where you can ask questions of the vampires and spec authors, and I'm one of the writers. People write me questions and I answer, then it appears on the web site. There are people who pretend to be Louis and Lestat. Some of the questions are serious and some funny. It's a lot of fun.

Everyone has his own vision in his head about who Louis and Lestat are. I think having a restaurant based on someone who can't eat food seems strange. Anne can do whatever she wants with her characters, but I was told that Anne wasn't interested in writing books anymore, but building an empire, and I think that is entirely true. I don't know why that shift in her paradigm has happened. I think that Rice's interests have changed, and she is using her books as a platform for those interests. By getting so caught up in her passions and what she feels very strongly about, she is losing the basic principles of writing. I know she's capable of doing better work.

Rice's world has been an exercise in escapism for me. It's not a reality to me: I'm not running around looking for Lestat to bite me. But it's nice to indulge in it and go to another reality. It has affected my writing and my thoughts and my computer time, so it is a big part of my life.

Skywise: Thank you, Anne, for all that you've given my wife.

ANNE

32 · Advertising Executive · New York City

"Anne Rice's work has two distinct facets. The mass market appeal of her work, which is not necessarily consistent with her philosophical writings. I'm an admirer of Rice's work. Her writing lets me free-associate or bring out a fantasy for myself, so I'm very drawn to her creative side. The fantasy for me is that these places and people can exist and do exist, that there's things in the world we just don't know about.

"I never really thought about the supernatural or gave it much credit before I read *The Witching Hour*. There could be something out there that we often choose to dismiss or have another explanation for. Rice shows the origin of the Mayfair spirit, so you can understand where it came from. That gives it a context. Through her books I have been led closer to an assumption that maybe the supernatural could exist. Rice's books are purely fictional, but in a way the fantasy of the story brings you to ask questions, to think that perhaps there are sprinklings that are factual. I look at the supernatural differently now. I may go to a psychic and believe her (laughter), or I won't be as quick to judge people who need to have something like that in their life.

"Through Rice's work I also became interested in things dealing with the dark side of human nature. The dark side to me is a feeling I get from her writing. It is an outside force that can go into someone's life and control them. There is a part of everyone that has that, or there is somebody who can bring that out in each person. It may not always be a bad thing, just something completely different than what we do day to day, what is accepted social behavior. It is unknown.

"I think she has a theme of forgiveness in her work. There's turmoil with her characters, but always a sense of resolve and a message of forgiveness. It appeals to my subconscious. For me, her writing is so descriptive and so uniquely crafted that wherever I am I get a veil of feelings, say the scenery of a place, and I imagine this must be exactly what it looks like in one of her books. I went to Venice, Italy, and her words in *Cry to Heaven* made me see a picture of that country completely. I adore that. There is something about her work that draws me back to her. I have to read all her books. Rice's craft for writing a cliffhanger is undeniable, you always have to get the next one. At this point though, I think she has over-cliffed her cliff.

"I had been to New Orleans several times in the past, but went again when I was reading Rice's books. The books made New Orleans much more exciting, much more rich. I remember walking down St. Charles and thinking, there's the house from *The Witching Hour*. I was staring at men in brown suits with funny hats sideways, as if they might be Lasher! (Laughter) To see New Orleans because of what is in her writing can be interesting and fun. I think that when people read her work they have a reality break. Some go to New Orleans to see all the places and streets that she describes, but some go there to just see her and touch her front yard. That's a little wacky!

"I was flying on business weeks before the party, wearing a New Orleans T-shirt and someone said, 'Hey are you going to the Anne Rice Ball?' I thought 'Oh my God, somebody affiliated New Orleans solely with Anne Rice from my T-shirt! That's amazing!' Rice has become an obsession for some. Maybe this is their way of showing devotion to her or to feel the same energy that she has felt. I'm just an average person who's read her books. I don't take it to extremes. What is it about Anne that has made these droves of people give themselves over to the world that she's created? I would never ordinarily allow myself to dive into something like joining a fan club or living like a vampire. Reading the books is a wonderful diversion, but I'm not the kind of person, in any kind of situation, that would go beyond that. I'm practical. I don't really let myself go into my fantasy world and let it become real.

"In high school I did get into Rocky Horror and got dressed up. I like dressing up. I dressed as a vampire for the Memnoch Ball. It's wonderful theater and drama for me, but for a lot of these people it's way more than that. I was very excited to go to the Memnoch Ball. Curiosity drove me there. It was like going into one of her books for a night. The party made me wonder how many of these people are really followers and how many are observers like myself. I had an overwhelming sense that all those people knew something I didn't, that they had tapped into a part of themselves I hadn't yet. I will never forget all those religious statues at the party and this guy dressed like Jesus sitting next to them, drinking coffee and wearing Converse hightops. I'll never forget that image. It makes you think: it could be God, it could really be Him—you never know who will show up at an Anne Rice party. I never knew what was going to happen next, it was an exhilarating feeling of not knowing what it was going to be like before I got there. The most striking memory that I have of the Ball is that it was just the opposite of what I expected. It was almost austere. It was so quiet. Here were thousands of people, everyone in makeup head to toe, and it *could* have been like freaks from all over the world, but all these people had so much respect for Rice's home. It was a spectacular show and a wild display of love for her fans.

"People really buy into her for more than just what she's writing. I'm not sure how truly they are looking at the whole thing. It's obvious she's trying to mass market herself as much as she can and get the dollars and exposure. I think it takes away from her writing. I made a conscious decision to not read her latest book, *Servant of the Bones*. Her other books, like *Cry to Heaven*, I adored. I am more into the romantic stories. *Taltos* made me crazy. When I finished it I threw it across the room, 'God damn it!' I thought. I felt she wrote this book to write another, which just seems horrible. I don't take stock in it any more, where in the beginning I really bought into the trilogies. Who was Lasher? We know the whole history of the Taltos and still don't know who Lasher is, and that's all we care about. It's horrible…I want my money back!

"What I do love about Anne is her sense of the quality of life. How you live and who you choose to live your life with is a message that she gets out there. It is a theme that makes one more reflective of their own life, and gives you the power to change your life."

RITCHIE

32 · President, The Anne Rice-Vampire Lestat Fan Club (ARVLFC) · New Orleans, Louisiana

"The first time I heard of Anne Rice was when Sting had that song *Moon Over Bourbon Street*, which came out in '85, and the liner notes mentioned that it was inspired by *Interview with the Vampire*. A couple of years after that I got married, and my now ex-wife had the first two Vampire Chronicles. She made me read them and I was hooked, so I owe her that much, at least.

"Anne's first two books made me run out to the bookstore and buy *The Queen of the Damned* the next day, because I had to see what happened. It was one of those rare books to me, where you care about what's happening with the characters and you feel like you know them by the time you've read so much about them. It didn't make me start dressing in black or anything; it was mostly entertainment for me. I've always rebelled against trying to read too far into things, that's why I had such a bad time in school. When people would say *Animal Farm* stood for the Russian revolution, I would think, 'No, it's a bunch of animals that can talk and take over a farm.'

"When I got divorced (smiling), I was looking for something new, a new social outlet. I read an article in *The Times-Picayune* about the fan club and so I joined in 1992. I got a newsletter and in it the staff was literally begging for help. At that time the three founding members, Susie M., Melanie, and Susie Q., were doing everything and they couldn't handle it anymore. I called them, we played phone tag, and then finally hooked up. I remember going to my first meeting and Melanie, who's a singer, sang to me the whole time I was stuffing envelopes, and I said, 'This is wonderful. I could do this every day.' So I got involved and over the years, through the parties and everything else, I started doing more 'cause I was willing to do it.

"By volunteering I found a new set of people who, even though we had Anne Rice in common, were different than people I would ever have become friends with anywhere else. I didn't have any friends who were into spiritualism, crystals, astrology, and all that stuff. Growing up I kind of stuck to the same kinds of things; I didn't venture too far from my friends because that just wasn't done. The fan club brought me to people from all walks of life and they are people I have become close friends with. The fan club officers were people who trusted me without really knowing anything about me. It felt good to show up for all the meetings and be accepted. I loved having a mission that could be accomplished at the end of the day and being proud of what I did. Melanie was retiring and I was no longer helping her with the newsletter: I was *doing* the newsletter! Now I've got people who help me. I've brought in most of the people who are on the current staff, a lot of whom are members of my family.

"Right now the staff is down to an all-time low of about nine. It takes this many people to keep the fan club running. Until I started doing it full time, we actually were looking for more people. There are calls to answer, mail, new memberships, renewals, newsletters, party organizing, etc. It can get to be overwhelming because of the sheer volume that we deal with in the fan club. The meetings are fun. Susie M. might tell us the latest 'Anne news' for ten minutes, and the rest of the time we just do our own thing. Every year at the Coven Ball, seeing the fans who I've either called or written a letter to is one of the best parts for me. I enjoy talking to all the fans. Sometimes before a party it can get overwhelming, though. At the office I'd try to get up to go to the bathroom, but the phones won't stop ringing. At the party last year there was one point when I was whispering to someone, 'Save me, save me,' because I was swamped by people. There was a crowd trying to get me to let them into The House of Blues, offering me hotel rooms for Mardi Gras, and other things, like sexual favors. Gee...uh, whatever! The fans sometimes treat the club officers like little celebrities, and I find it uncomfortable because I don't think that we are. The presentation at the Fairmont of the club officers was wild. When I introduced myself, people cheered, and I realized I had my own fan club. It's kind of weird, people wanting to take pictures with me and stuff. I like recognition, but I don't want it to be like a star thing.

"When someone joins the club they get the official newsletter—Anne's personal newsletter, *Commotion Strange*, all of which is still on no particular schedule. We try to get at least three out a year. Usually around a new book release, after the annual Coven Ball, and another one. Now that I've been declared the full-time paid officer, I'm going to try to produce at least four and maybe more. I've got tons of ideas. I'd like to do a photo tour of St. Elizabeth's. It would be interesting to show fans how much it has changed since the Memnoch Ball. I have other ideas too, like Anne's chapter outtakes, etc. I've just got to get clearance first.

"The club sponsors the Annual Gathering of the Coven Ball and that's the only event. The party's such a massive undertaking, we have to start planning it almost a year ahead of time. The '96 party was so last minute that Susie M. even suggested maybe we shouldn't have a party. The last time that was suggested, in '93, was because Anne was going to be out of town on a book tour. Fans wrote in saying, 'No! You have to have the party! So what if Anne's not going to be there!' We had the party without Anne that year and it still sold out—over a thousand people showed up, so we have to have it. The whole event really has become almost bigger than Anne, but if Anne ever said, 'Okay, that's it, it's enough,' or, 'It's gotten too big,' then that would be the end. We can't have it without Anne. I know she has talked about how it's getting too big and it may be too much for us to handle. We've always operated under the fact that we're the 'official' club. Of our founding members, Susie Q. is now Anne's personal assistant, Susie M. works in the office over at the First Street house, and Melanie does Anne's hair. It's just too intertwined to do it without Anne. It's very much a family-oriented thing at this point.

"The Coven Gathering is always held in New Orleans. The first parties, in the late '80s, were in art galleries or on a riverboat, with about a hundred people, that's how small it was. You could sit and chat with Anne all night. In 1992 the party boom really started. That party was held at the Amilia Street house, at Amilia and St. Charles, which is the

house where Mona Mayfair and her family lived in *The Witching Hour*. In '94 we participated in a citywide blood drive. If you donated blood you got a plastic squeaky rat signed by Anne. We handed out thousands of 'em in '94, at the blood drive, the Coven party, and the movie premiere of *Interview with the Vampire* in New Orleans. 1994 at Tipitina's, was really amazing; we had over 1,800 paid admissions on a place that legally holds under 700. That became a block party and the streets were closed off. That was the year the movie came out and the whole party scene really exploded. That year Courtney Love showed up and Hole played a half hour set, unannounced. Of course '95 was at St. Elizabeth's, The Memnoch Ball, and we had over seven thousand people in attendance. That party will never be repeated. It can't. The rooms at St. Elizabeth's are all bedrooms and offices now. I can't say that a party on an Anne Rice property won't happen again, but '95 was just too much, too many people, and too much superficial damage was done, I think because of the free booze.

"The '96 party was really two events. There was the Gathering, with a dinner, a mingling thing with Anne, and a ceremony at the Fairmont Hotel, with about two thousand-five hundred fans. We had to make it for club members only this year to keep the numbers down. Then there was a second party that followed at The House Of Blues, which was open to the public, and about two thousand came to that. I know there's a lot of people who think that we made a lot of money on it, but we didn't, we broke even. The fan club sustains itself basically on membership fees only. At the Memnoch Ball, Anne pretty much paid for everything, but the fan club sold the tickets. We're nonprofit and only allowed to keep so much.

"The 'phenomenon' around Anne has become bigger than that of 'Anne the writer.' It's hard for me to understand it at times because I can go to the First Street house any day, ring the bell, and go in, ya know? Sometimes I go there and groups of fans are just staring at the house and they look at me as I walk in and back out. Whether fans are coming to the party or not, they'll usually meet at Cafe du Monde with name tags, like from the internet, and get together on their own. As a social phenomenon I think it's amazing. I equate it with when I was a teenager and wanted to go to Liverpool because that's where the Beatles were from, ya know? I wanted to go see all the 'Strawberry Fields,' 'Penny Lane,' and all that stuff. But being on the inside with Rice, it doesn't get that way for me. It's great when I go to First Street and can say this is the pool where Michael drowned in *Lasher*. I know I am one of the privileged. I had a conversation with a guy who works at the Garden District Bookshop and he was complaining about how every time Anne sees him, he's all sweaty from lugging boxes of books upstairs to her library for her to sign for the bookstore. I told him, 'I could name you thousands of people who would gladly trade places with you. Don't complain.' It is kind of weird, but it's true. I did a live interview with Vancouver radio, and they asked, 'Is Anne Rice spooky? What is she really like?' And I told them she's just like my mom, she just lives a lot larger, ya know? She's really generous, down to earth, and will just talk to you. She likes to laugh and stuff like that. She's not this Gothic woman that you would picture, seeing her in the black clothes she used to wear, and all that stuff. I think if people knew her the way that I do, then it wouldn't be such a mythic thing for them. At this point she can't do a lot of public stuff anymore. She used to walk Mojo, her dog, on the street, but now there's always a tour going by, or a group of fans standing in front of her house taking pictures or just staring at it or stealing bricks from the sidewalk. That's happened!

"There are crazy fans too. There is a guy who people tell me used to be really fun and normal, but in just the last few years he's descended into fanaticism. He was on the news one time telling the cameras that Anne Rice was his priestess and her books are his bibles. Often you have thousands of people standing in line at book signings happy to say hi and move on. Then you have those who just gush about how they moved to New Orleans to be near Anne. The fanaticism is getting bigger as she gets bigger because she is one of those few authors, I think, on the level of a rock star or a movie star. You get fanatics at Anne's signings, unfortunately. It makes me uncomfortable. Most of the time the celebrity's not going to remember you five minutes later because they meet so many people, but if you do act crazy they're going to remember you. Unfortunately, it's going to be in a bad way. It gives fandom a bad light, and causes security to worry. That's the reason why Anne goes everywhere with two or three guys in suits. All the scary threats have been through the mail or on the phone machine, but the threats are out there. The people who threaten her also love her. But that's part of the sickness that's out there that threatens famous people.

"The Anne Rice empire, Kith & Kin, started out as a small idea. If Anne's cousin Bob created some really great picture frames, then she would bankroll cousin Bob selling his picture frames. It started out small and then the ball just really got rolling: Lestat Wine, Lestat perfume, the Lestat restaurant. She has this money and she has to do something with it. If she can do something that helps her family, that's great. Anne's name could become a brand name and I think there's a lot of backlash about that. The money she's getting for her books right now is up there. It's a way of supporting her family, cause a lot of them may have fallen on hard times and instead of just giving them handouts, they work for their money now. I think that's her idea for wanting to start all this stuff. If Anne takes the ball and rolls with it, then more power to her.

"I know some people were dissatisfied with the '96 party. We do try to listen to the voice of the fans, but we can't please everybody. I am trying to change the opinion of the fans who feel that their voices are never heard. I know a lot of people have been upset about unreturned phone calls, but we often do all the party organizing on our own time and couldn't answer all the calls and letters. Since I've been here full time I've returned every call that could be returned and I've answered every letter that I could answer.

"How do we keep the parties small when so many people want to participate? How do you tell somebody you can't join because we're too big, or how do you tell a member that they can't come to a party even though they're a member? We always try to give members seniority for tickets. Anne is someone who hates any kind of preferential treatment. I have to stand in line at book signings just like everybody else. That's why in '95 an extra one thousand tickets were sold to the public for the Memnoch Ball. Anne didn't want it to be such an exclusive thing. She hates the term VIP.

"I'm doing this full time to make things right for the fans. I don't like anyone to feel slighted. The personal attention that people got when the club only had a few hundred people is just not available now. It's impossible when your membership numbers are 8,500 and up. But I'm doing my best: if you have a problem, write 'Attention Ritchie' really big on the envelope. I will try to fix your problem. That's what I do. I want everybody to be happy. If you have suggestions for the newsletter or parties, send 'em in. We'll listen to them. We're doing our best and I want this to work for everybody.

"Anne Rice has definitely changed my life. I mean look, I'm finally doing something that I love for a living, ya know? It's wonderful. I get to go to good events and meet wonderful people."

AMANDA

23 · Exotic Dancer · Atlanta, Georgia

"**A**nne Rice has changed my life. I have always felt like an outsider, that no one understood me. Then I saw the movie *Interview with the Vampire*. I saw it seven times. After seeing the movie I read *The Vampire Lestat*, and then *Interview*. I've only been reading a year. I'd never read before. Rice makes me feel things I never thought anyone else felt but me. I thought I was the only one who gave a shit in this world, and now I know I'm not.

"I'm a dancer working my way through beauty school. I used to dance under the name Gabrielle, like Lestat's mother. I think I'm clairvoyant. I try to send mind messages to the clients, and when I do I get bigger tips!

"When I wear my white makeup and fangs in Atlanta everyone thinks I'm a freak. I hitch-hiked to New Orleans for this Ball because I know I'm accepted with this group of people. New Orleans is just like Anne Rice described, and so I feel at home here. I can walk down by the river and just imagine Lestat following me there. I can smell Cafe du Monde!

"I have written Anne Rice hundreds of letters. I hope she doesn't think I'm obsessed, but I love her....If Anne doesn't like women, I'd be willing to have a sex change to be with her...I love her!"

Madame Elisandrya

39 · Professional Dominatrix · Felton, California

"**I** have been a professional dominatrix for twenty-one years. This is my lifestyle of choice. I currently have seven slaves: three males and four females, but that number changes depending on my mood and their wig color. (Laughter) All of my slaves are very real and dear to me. I have a professional session dungeon, a slave training academy, and transformation weekend workshops.

"*The Claiming of Sleeping Beauty* was handed to me by a prospective slave who wanted to serve me, but was shy and didn't know how else to let me know. Many parts of myself are reflected in Anne Rice's writings. I love romance, the Gothic period, the S&M world, and vampirism, so I was naturally drawn to her writings.

"I enjoyed *Exit to Eden*. It was interesting to find someone writing about the realities of what the S&M lifestyle is and then turning it into a fantasy. The book has very strange parallels between her Lisa, the main character, and my life. My real name is Lisa and the whole book was like reading my life history, save for the going straight stuff at the end. It made me feel very exposed. People who knew about my lifestyle started asking me questions about why the book was written. I had met Rice years before on the street in San Francisco. I was with two slaves the night I met her. Although I am very open about discussing my lifestyle if someone asks, I have no idea if she knew people who knew me or wanted to find out more about the lifestyle. The way the character is treated is how I am treated on a daily basis. There is always some slave ready to do my bidding or anticipating my wants.

"What made the book interesting to me was that it exposed a side of the S&M lifestyle, that is very rich in its own merit, to the mainstream. People will never know about S&M unless they ask, and they will never know about it unless someone says, 'Here, read this book.' The book is erotic because it is very romantic and dear to the heart. It makes people think, 'I want to be spanked too,' opposed to, 'I'll never let that happen to me.' *Exit to Eden* entices people into that which they haven't experienced before. The people in my circle know me as Madame Elisandrya. I would like everyday society to see me as Lisa, the regular person. Lisa in the book never changed from when she was normal to when she was on the island or working; I make that change. I'm very grounded. I never take my aggressions out on other people. I'm very controlled. I never get angry or excited, I just do what I do and the world will fix itself. It was strange to feel exposed when it doesn't appear for all intents or purposes to be an intended parallel. But I don't know. Maybe I said too much on my brief meeting with her in San Francisco. Anne Rice would benefit from speaking with me now. I have lived the life she has written about for twenty-one years.

"People who get into the scene from reading these books need to remember they are reading a fantasy which can be recreated, but is not the real S&M lifestyle. If people find the influence of the books good as entertainment, great, but they must remember it is glorified and dressed up. Of course, the lifestyle can be whatever you want it to be. Mine is a very real living situation that resembles an actual nuclear family. Nuclear in the sense, that we are connected and rely on each other for our needs and requirements. We laugh, live, and love like any normal family should. I have recreated scenes from the Rice books because they are fun. I have done the castle scene several times. I use a lot of romance novels for ideas for S&M scene-basis.

"I am everything that is appealing in the Rice books. I've been wearing sixteenth and seventeenth century ball gowns for about sixteen years, ever since I was able to start sewing. I feel more natural that way. I am a deeply romantic person at heart. I think that my connection with the Goths and the way I portray myself has more to do with an internal calling opposed to just a visual one. This is why I read romance and Gothic novels. I want to know what I would look like wearing those clothes, so I create them so I can feel that way. I find that once I put myself into one of the outfits that I make, people respond to me differently: they decide I am a person that must be catered to, a romantic illusion, when in fact I'm very real. I express myself as I see myself. That is one of the first things I noticed about *The Claiming of Sleeping Beauty*: the way that they dressed was very appealing to me, and that was one of the first connections I made with that book.

"I also love the vampire. I was very little when I learned about vampires. To me they weren't vampires at all, but simply those who sustained a portion of their life through the blood of others, whether it was animal or human. I was introduced to what people would consider a vampiric lifestyle from my grandmother, a Santerian, who was the first person to teach me about the sacrificial use of blood. My whole personal makeup stems from Voodoo, Santeria, and Native American cultures, which my ancestors were. There's some Scottish druid culture from my father's side also. You put all these little variables together and you have a very interesting package—me—that doesn't have a fear of blood or sacrifice. I'm not squeamish about blood at all. I could see it all day and it's just very interesting to me, I love it—I like the taste of it, it's very sensual and erotic. The way I see it, a man and woman can have sex—everybody does that, it's about as close as most people get to each other. I like to go deeper than that. You can't get much more from a person then their blood, other then their heart, which I don't do. (Laughter)

"The exchange of blood, the true fluid exchange, to me, is the deepest form of conversation I can have with another human being. That kind of trust and level of commitment is not an easy one to get from most people. The slaves I have in my life, including my current husband, have given that part of their essence to me, and it is a beautiful, spiritual connection I enjoy very much. If they ask, and when they ask, I give them the same in return. If they want to know how my blood tastes, they are more then welcome to it. A lot of times I mix blood together in vials; it's a very spiritual and personal thing for me. It's difficult to explain. It means more to me then I can tell someone. I can share the thought with you, but it may never make any sense to you. Vampires have a special place in my heart because I can understand them as part of my native culture. It's part of how I breathe and live. I don't believe that without the blood of another creature I won't survive. I don't believe that at all. I do believe, however, that it makes me a part of them, and brings their essence into me in a very spiritual, romantic, and erotic way. I also enjoy the pain aspect of it.

"I am a extremely compassionate person. Anyone who knows me knows I'm the first to go and put my arms around someone and comfort them, but what inspires me to do that is their suffering. It is an emotional high for me to comfort someone who is in emotional pain. I can pull their hurt from them emotionally and give them comfort.

"I like to be the one to place the physical pain, not emotional, but physical—absolutely! I can be very controlling and controlled in my actions to the point where I can guide someone to the next level of pain without pushing them over the edge, so that emotionally the experience is one they handle and enjoy. Physical pain only lasts so long; it will go away. Emotional pain is the stuff you keep for the rest of your life, it's hard to get rid of. I like teaching people about the possibilities of exploring those feelings through S&M.

"There are no direct connections between vampires and S&M. Some people are into both, so it appears connected. For the most part the subculture likes testing their fears and limits. So it's natural to see how the whole romantic seduction of the vampire connects with the romantic seduction of S&M, when done properly. Relinquishing power to someone else, to become that vulnerable with someone, and to allow the power play, is present in both vampirism and S&M, which is why I enjoy both. I will take power any way a person wants to give it to me. If it means taking it blood-wise, I'll take it that way first. If it means S&M play and then I get what I want later, which usually is to draw blood from them, then I'll do that. The image of the vampire, as is commonly recognized, is somewhat fearful and frightening, but also erotic and sensual. It's always a person who seduces another into submission. Always.

"When I delve into vampiric activity, it is usually with a bite or with a blade. If it can bleed, I can cut it. (Laughter) I like sharp objects and sometimes that includes teeth. I like the look on a person's face who's sharing this with me. I didn't say victim, because I expect you can't really be a vampire's victim. I don't deal with the participants as if they will live forever, but they may feel that way because they are giving that much of themselves through the experience. It makes me feel I am adding life to my life, bringing new life into myself. I know in this day and age there's this freaky thing about 'don't share blood,' but if I'm going to die from blood ingestion it would have happened already. I've been doing this for years and years, and I'm very careful about who I choose. I started wearing vampire teeth fifteen years ago. It had nothing to do with anything I read or saw. I wanted them because I draw blood and I drink it. It became a fad because of the Rice books, and it is fashionable now to be a Rice vampire: a dark and sadistic person.

"I'm interested in Anne Rice as a storyteller. I respect a lot of what she's written. With all the deeply embedded fetishes she writes about, it's hard to disappoint me. I think she is compassionate enough to write the truth as she sees it, but I think she's gone beyond writing what she sees, and is writing what people want to hear. That's where she has to draw the line. I ache for another book like *Exit to Eden*, and if she needs any information

I'd love to give it to her. I'm glad that *Exit to Eden* was portrayed as a comedy onscreen; it made it more acceptable to the mainstream. I don't think there's anything wrong with trusting someone enough to let him do anything he wants with you. Most people fantasize about being taken by a strong, virile person. You simply relinquish power, give it up. I think that was clearly stated in Rice's book. The movie's comedic value stated it also, making it less frightening. When people hear about whips and chains, leather and corsets, they can at least smile about it now, opposed to putting their fingers up like a cross and saying 'no way.'"

JOY

31 · Magazine Copy Editor · Los Angeles, California

"I'm very involved in the past. I'm a member of several historical re-enactment groups that hold events associated with the eighteenth-century American Revolution to Victorian ballroom dancing. My major in college was history and I've combined that with my love for clothes and pretty things, and I do historical costuming as a hobby.

"My dress for the Coven Ball was a bustle evening gown from 1875. It was a real bustle with petticoats. I didn't have a pattern, so I drafted it myself from books. I copied the lower half from an old *Harper's Bazaar* fashion plate, and then made my own changes and pieced it together.

I like things that are dark, but I don't think of myself as a dark and brooding person at all. But there is something about it that encompasses music, art, fashion, and ambiance. There is a romance that takes you to another place. I've always been interested in 'someplace else,' because to me the modern world is very prosaic and in a lot of ways very ugly. I don't like how people act most of the time, and modern clothing is very unattractive. In Los Angeles there are a lot of these regency groups that give you avenues to explore other times and places. When an event is taking place and the location is correct and everybody's dressed up, you can almost forget you're in L.A. and it's the 1990s. That is the most interesting thing about it. When you read Rice's books, it is so well realized and sensual that again you forget where you are. I often feel that I was born in the wrong time. If I could choose between being born now and a hundred years ago…guess which I'd choose? But of course I'd want to have money. (Laughing)

"I read *The Vampire Lestat* in 1987 when I graduated from college. I always loved the historical parts of Anne's books. There's nothing better than a really good historically researched novel. You get really taken away. The vampire books gave me characters I could latch on to. I like Lestat's point of view on the world, but with Louis, I just want him to get over himself. Lestat is a very cat-like, curious person. He's very irreverent and I like that in a person. I don't like people that take themselves too seriously. He's always questioning and working out new ways to deal with who he is and how he interacts with the world around him. I think Lestat is a four-dimensional character, there is so much going on with him, that's why I like him. I think Lestat would be a great person to hang out with and go to parties with because, you know, if nothing's going on he's going to start some outrageous situation just to watch what happens.

"If I had to chose a dream lover from the books it would Aaron Lightner, from the Talamasca. He's a real gentleman. My fiancé is a real gentleman. I met him at a regency dance. It was like a storybook romance. I walked into the room and he's had eyes for no one else since then. How often does that really happen? You walk into a room in a ball gown and a handsome gentleman in a uniform comes up and asks you to dance! It was very romantic and he is my dream lover.

"I joined the fan club to go to the Balls. I believe in supporting organizations like the fan club so they can keep going. I run a fan club myself, The Star Wars Imperial Group, for bad guys only.

"I think Anne's commercialism is a symptom of late twentieth-century American culture. I don't like it, but it happens to anything that becomes popular. Why does she have so many bodyguards? We saw President Clinton at Cafe du Monde the other morning and he didn't have as many bodyguards as Anne did! She is a writer and I have great respect for that, but it seems that she is becoming more and more detached from the people that love her work.

"I consider myself a big Anne Rice fan, but I don't obsess over her books. I don't go to bed every night hoping Lestat will come sweep me away and make me live forever. The way Rice looks at the world is very sensual. I try to enjoy everything around me in the same descriptive way. I notice how the air smells, taking everything in, internalizing it, and hopefully it will come back out of me in a beautiful way. Anne's helped me to find a way to always appreciate the environment around me."

JASON

22 · Bartender/Student: Biology Major · New Orleans, Louisiana

"**A**nne's books have taught me about the beauty of family. All my family is here in New Orleans and we're very close. We have huge family get-togethers, but it was something that I took for granted. It didn't seem special, just a part of life. But when I read *The Witching Hour* I learned a new meaning for the word 'family.' Anne talked so much about how wonderful that family was; they had each other always. Then I started looking at my family in a new light, and I'm closer to my family now because of my new understanding of its importance. The history of the Mayfair family really showed where this family came from, and, in turn, I started questioning where my family came from. I started asking my grandmothers about our past, which helped me appreciate my family's present.

"The beauty of New Orleans is hidden. At first glance you just see a city that's dirty and old. With Anne Rice's books I learned to see the beauty as I'd never seen it before. I started looking at the city in a new way—I went exploring in my home town, looking for things. I was looking into alleyways and things like that, just trying to discover more about the city as Anne had described it. I started looking at the city as a whole, and how different the people are that live here. The city has a lot of character, and I feel really connected in a new way now. The books gave me a sense of beauty and history about my home. It's a crazy city, but that's New Orleans.

"New Orleans is one of the few truly Catholic cities in the United States. Part of being Catholic is that you grow up and learn that there are spirits and demons. Catholics never deny that there are ghosts in this world, especially here in New Orleans where there are ghosts everywhere, it is just an accepted way of life here. As a matter of fact, to me, saints coming back to earth is a form of ghosts. So with that, I was always interested in things other than the norm.

"I love Anne's work, but *Memnoch the Devil* was hard for me to read. It did seem sacriligious. There were so many points throughout the book when I wanted to just throw it across the room, it had upset me so much. But I'm thankful I finished the book. I didn't totally understand exactly what the book was about, but I feel that Anne resolved a lot of the issues that I was dealing with. Some of the issues that you grow up with, such as the devil always hates God, she didn't represent in that way. Anne wrote that the devil did not hate God, and that was hard for me to deal with. It definitely went against everything I'd been taught. I've learned one thing all my life, and then I read this book, because I value Rice's writing and opinions, and all of a sudden she tells you something that is totally opposite from your belief system. At first I really questioned my belief system. The book turned over in my mind for at least a couple of months. But then I got to realizing that this is just a book and her viewpoint. The way the book resolved itself is that you don't find out until the end that the devil really *does not* love God. It was probably the *most* disturbing book I've ever read. I can honestly say, I'll probably be a Catholic until the day I die, but I'm interested in different people's viewpoints. The more you understand about different people, the more you can live your life better. There's so many different types of people in this world, you have to have an open mind.

"A lot of Anne's books deal with the concept of immortality. That is such an interesting concept in itself because with immortality you don't have responsibility in a sense—you are a lot more free to do what you feel like when you want to. It's interesting to be able to see somebody who can put normal, everyday needs out of the way and concentrate more on wants. We live in a world of needs. Living for the experience opposed to daily responsibilities is interesting.

"I think the amount of fans that come to New Orleans is great. I think everyone should know about this city. One of the best things about Anne Rice as a person is that she is so publicly visible. She wants her fans to have contact with her. She doesn't hide herself away in some little house out in the middle of nowhere; whenever she can she'll make a public appearance. She realizes they appreciate her and so she tries to give that appreciation back to them. I feel more authors should be like that. If she wants to promote herself then I have no problems whatsoever with that, plus it's a good thing for the city. More people come to love the city because of Rice. They may never love it as I love it, because it's my home, but if they can appreciate just a part of it, that's great.

"I've been a member of the fan club for two and a half years now. You get newsletters, so you're up to date on the all the events: the book signings, first crack at the party tickets. I've gotten quite a few people to read her books; I am trying to convert my friends.

"I think the culture that seems to be developing around Rice is wonderful because she is such a wonderful person. The fact that she is so open to her public definitely invites this mayhem, and I think it's what she wants. The people who come to the parties are just having fun. I've heard some people are really into a vampire lifestyle, like sleeping in coffins. Personally, I'm not into that, but if they're have fun, and they aren't hurting anyone, then they should go with it. I think that's one of the problems today, not enough people having fun in this world. I know too many people who do not enjoy life at all. I guess that goes the other way too, that some people have too much fun. People who see Anne as a devil or Satanist, are people who have not read the books. They are listening to other peoples' interpretations of the books and judge her based on what they've heard about the books. Not everything that is dark is bad; that's something that Anne Rice helped me discover. I kind of knew it already: growing up in New Orleans, I knew everything is not what it seems.

"I do leave phone messages for Anne Rice on the hotline. Mostly thank yous, or I like to tell her what I think of her books, give an honest opinion. I haven't read one of her books that has sucked. If she writes a book that actually sucks, I guess I'll have to decide if I would really want to tell her that. But up until now, I haven't read a single one of her books that I didn't thoroughly enjoy, even *Memnoch*."

CONAN

29 · Special Effects Make-up Artist · Brooklyn, New York

"I'm very involved in the costume aspect of vampires. It's very fun to dress up and look right. I was raised on horror movies and sci-fi and was always doing costumes. My mom always claimed she couldn't sew, but we always pulled off something great. Being someone else was my inspiration. I was terribly shy, introverted, and repressed. Ultimately, as I grew up, I became almost disablingly shy. I didn't realize until I was in high school and getting into drama, that I was looking for an escape. Drama was a way to be someone else, to be a character, so I was saved from having to be myself, and costumes added to that.

"I got into the Goth scene in '92, at a Berkeley club called House Of Usher. Old friends from Rocky Horror days got together and scraped up outfits. The costumes and makeup worked well on me and everyone around me appreciated the look. The first night I went out in this nineteenth century costume I thought I'd just soak up the atmosphere and be part of the decorations. Socially, I was still a shut-in. A girl came up to me and said hello, and it took her three tries before I realized that she actually wanted to talk to me. I was stunned that I could be appealing. People responded to the simple elegance of my costume; it was very Victorian and different, unlike the black haired 'Cure look' you see all the time.

"I'd known about the Rice books for some time during this period. I avoided them because people were way too into them. People gushed about the books, and I thought there was too much there to be believed, so I never read them. I didn't want to be disappointed. Both my dad and brother read *Interview* and recommended it. It was surprising for them to do that; they normally don't read that stuff. I agreed to read it, and suddenly I understood what everyone saw in the books, and proceeded to tear through all of the Vampire Chronicles.

"*Interview* really hit me hard. I really identified with Louis and the idea of being trapped. I understood the concept of being locked into a situation and hating it and being thoroughly miserable based on your sensibilities. Louis was trapped, and everything that was happening in my life then was corresponding with the book. It was distinctly inspiring for me at a time when I was consciously trying to rebuild my life.

"I usually surround myself with the color blue. It is comforting, calm, and safe. But I always wanted to have red in my life. Red is vibrant, warm, and truly life-experiencing. I'd been afraid to have those colors around me, that I wouldn't be able to live up to my surroundings. I decided to redecorate my life starting with my bedroom, and I bought a fabulous four-poster bed and maroon sheets and a comforter. My life exploded. I was allowing myself to go out and be seen and meet people, and have people react to me in a positive way I could handle. Things worked out fine and I found I didn't have to live up to my bedroom sheets after all. (Laughter) So I was going out, re-did my bedroom, and was reading *Interview*. That set a backdrop for the person I was becoming. I thought I was just dressing up and going out and then I discovered my true persona inside, one I hadn't expressed before. The persona wasn't based on the book *Interview*. The book mostly fired a mood for me.

"My personal experience with going to clubs and reading the books was really good for me. It allowed me to get enough positive response to realize that I could actually— well, for a long time I thought I was a character when I would go out to clubs, but then I realized that I was finally relaxing and letting myself just be me, the person I was inside that I was hiding from. I had a transformation, and was very aware of all the stages as I went through them. I had to accept that the 'uncovered' me was every bit as much me as the shy person I was used to being. I'm much more open, outgoing, and sure of myself now than I was five or six years ago. Dressing up and having enough people around go, 'oooh, awwww' has let me be confident.

"I'm also a fan of erotica, and read the *Beauty* series as well. I was interested in S&M for quite some time, to a small degree, but it never went very far until a couple of years ago when I got into fetishism and started playing at a club called Bondage A Go-Go in San Francisco. I know the fetish scene has become very mainstream in the last couple of years and people liked it when it was more underground and secret. I like the fact that it has opened up and people can be exposed to it and can explore if they'd like to. Information is important. People don't know how to change their minds if they aren't exposed to ideas. The appeal of Rice's books is that they touch on a lot of different subjects for people, both socially and psychologically.

"In my experience, people who are into Goth clubs, the fetish scene, renaissance fairs, Rocky Horror, etc., are all the same people, part of the same group. Ultimately they are over–intelligent, over–sensitive theater geeks who need an outlet. I certainly put myself right in the middle of that. It is a way of expressing yourself without fear. Being yourself is dangerous. You might be judged harshly for how you act or dress, or what you say. When you put on the other persona, it frees you to be who you've always wanted to be, or who you really are inside and haven't let out.

"There is a connection between vampires and D/S (Dominance and Submission) in a whole psycho-sexual context, when you talk about power exchange, roles of D/S and surrendering yourself to another person. When I would go to Bondage A Go-Go it was in a much different way than at the Goth clubs. I still dressed Victorian, but since it wasn't typical rubber fetish wear you see in that scene; people really responded to the elegance of the clothes. People thought 'vampire' without seeing the teeth. Once they did see the teeth, they *really* responded. Several people at the club wore fangs. The fangs represent power. The vampire being dominant and the victim submissive. I'm a dom because I'm a wimp and can't handle pain. I became a fang-slut. Lots of people want to be chewed on. People would see these beautiful strangers come up to me and say, 'would you bite me the way you bit her?' I make fangs, and the teeth caused my social life to increase a thousandfold. It was a huge ego boost for me. I made my first pair of fangs for a cat costume in high school, but I didn't do anything with them until I started going to the Goth clubs and realized the open market for good quality acrylic vampire teeth. It's amazing how many people have always wanted a pair of fangs!

"I've been through so much since I read the Vampire Chronicles, but they were there at an important time and essentially triggered what happened in my life. They gave me inspiration and style, and a character to have in the back of my head to then filter through and use for who I was becoming socially. I'm not afraid anymore of people thinking I'm a geek for dressing up on a day-to-day basis. Despite how many people have decided to call me Lestat, I never wanted to be Lestat or assume that role. Many people have told me I am their fantasy of Lestat. There are too many people who want Lestat to exist, and believe he does exist, and I'm not going to get in the way of that. So, it's always bothered me a bit when people say it.

"I'm not fascinated with Rice as a person; her fans are so fanatical about her. People who live deeply in the Goth scene—I couldn't do that either. I'm far too rational and grounded. I'm one of the least spiritual people you will ever meet. I'm far too agnostic to accept anything that isn't clear to me. This is all very much fantasy for me. It's dressing up, it's theater, it's having a good time. It has become more of a lifestyle now than I ever would have thought I would admit, but I don't dress that way at home and I don't think I could live that way every day. But I do live out my fantasy world, and it is a real part of who I am now.

"Taking all factors into account, the starting point for this and my dive into the Goth and fetish world, my fang-making success and current self image, can be traced back to that year I started reading Rice's books. Her books expose people to ideas, and everyone needs information to work with. Here were characters that affect and have affected millions of people, and I know I was affected right along with them. I still can't verbalize it completely, but the books floored me, they were amazing. Everything the vampires were, and why they lived, was so rich. It was a completely believable world. You can really imagine them living among you. You might have walked past them in the street one night. Maybe you could be one of them someday. They could choose you. You could be part of the story too."

LUCINDA

30 · Receptionist · Santa Cruz, Caifornia

"**E**ver since I was a kid I have been fascinated by vampires and the ghoulish. I would watch all the old vampire movies with Christopher Lee, and there was always a beautiful woman in a white gown that the vampires went after. I wanted to be one of those sexy woman that was pursued. There is an erotic quality about the feeding and an intimacy to sucking out somebody's juices. It is very sensual. Besides, the mysterious Count with the accent always turned me on. Anne Rice made the whole vampire world come to life in a new way for me, as if it could be real. I have always felt I have an evil twin, my dark side. Having the fangs and doing the whole vampire trip opens that up and makes my dark side more complete for me. I feel dangerous and sexy wearing the clothes and the fangs. I love the teeth and the undead aspect of being immortal and coming back.

"For me the Vampire Chronicles were a fantasy world I enjoyed. After the first three vampire books I couldn't keep up with all the new ones coming out all the time. It fed the vampire fetish in me for awhile. When her subculture started appearing, it was time for me to disappear. It was no longer alternative, it had become a fad, and was losing its uniqueness for me. She had originally made it seem so plausible. It's still a wonderful idea to think that Lestat might really be out there. I would like to switch bodies with him, like in *The Tale of the Body Thief*, and experience life through his 'vampire eyes.'"

SHANNAN

25 · Student: Speech Pathology · New Orleans, Louisiana

"**W**hen I was a freshman in college, a friend gave me *Interview* to read and I've read every one of Anne's books since then. I love the Vampire Chronicles because of the passion she puts into the books. I'm in love with Louis, Lestat, and Armand. I love Lestat's personality and demeanor. He is so outgoing, which I'm not. Since I've been reading the books, I feel bolder. This is the first year I've come to the Coven Ball. I was going to come even if I didn't have a date…and Lestat gave me the strength to do that. I'm dressing up for the party, which is a big deal for me. (She opens a box and shows me her fangs.) I'm wearing an old antique dress.

"I have hope, in the back of my mind, that Anne's characters are real. The vampires are a fantasy world that is always with me. When I come to the French Quarter I'm always looking over my shoulder to see if Lestat may be there. Anne's work has helped me to learn more about the city I live in. I live further out in Louisiana, but since reading the books I've come uptown looking at all the buildings in the Garden District. When the movie came out, I went to all the sites where it was filmed. I've been walking around a lot more and thinking about different scenes from the movie and where Louis and Lestat would be.

"I joined the fan club because of my love for Anne's work. I couldn't put the Chronicles down, so I figured it would be good to join the club and the internet to talk to people who are interested in the same things I am. I've made a lot of new friends. On the Newsgroup, I am somebody's minion. That means he is my master, and I do little things he tells me. We play parts written for the on-line role-playing game. I answer him, 'Yes, master,' or 'Your loyal servant here'….I love that. We are more into vampire things than sexual things. He'll say to me, 'Do I have to take a little drink to keep you in line?' It has really drawn me in. I would love to have a vampire lover. The fantasy world of being submissive to the vampire's power is a role I'd love to play and let my inhibitions go. It makes me feel sexy and desirable. I think normally I'd be the dominant one, but in the game I want to be submissive. If there was really an Eden, like in *Exit to Eden*, I'd go there in a heartbeat.

"I couldn't get a date when arranging to go to the Coven party. Friends assumed there would be freaks there, scary people with black lipstick, and they said they didn't want to be associated with people like that. I tried to explain to them that I'm not like that, but I'm into this vampire thing, and there are normal people into it also. That's why it's great to find people who you can share these common interests with. I can communicate and express things they understand, that my other friends think is just weird. Everyone at the Gathering of the Coven has been brought into this fantasy world, and it's good to be around each other."

Eiko

43 · Translator · Yokohama, Japan

Ichiko

34 · Office Worker · Hokkaido, Japan

Eiko: My first access to Anne Rice was her *Sleeping Beauty* trilogy. I had always been interested in women who write about love and sex between males, and also quite intrigued by the dynamics of violence and love, including dominance and submission. That will be also the reason why I am intrigued so much to the Vampire Chronicles. They are the monsters out of this world, desperately seeking for love and yearning, but never able to get it.

Ichiko: When the first Japanese edition of *Interview* was released in 1987, I bought one, but I quit after only a few pages. At the time, I felt the story was too long and it seemed boring. In 1994, I happened to buy a manga magazine (Japanese comic book). I read the article about the movie *Interview*, and then I found the graphic novel was serialized in the magazine. It reminded me that I had bought the novel before, and I came to be interested in it again very much. Once I started reading the novel, I found it was very great, then I became a fan of Rice. The stories aroused various interests of me, for example foreign cities like New Orleans, American history, internet, etc. In Japan, even now Anne Rice is not familiar to the ordinary people. Thanks to the movie, *Interview with the Vampire*, she has become one of the cult novelists, especially among young women. Homosexual novels are very popular among Japanese teenage girls. By reason of that, Rice's novels are acceptable to these girls in my country.

Eiko: I like the vampires' loneliness and their agony, instead of their power. I'm not sure if I can call it attractive, but their loneliness is our loneliness, which we are trying desperately to forget in our daily life. Oh, I must not forget that they are very beautiful creatures!

Ichiko: I love the vampires' beauty, their gracefulness, and even their aristocratic pride. I would love to experience the ecstasy that I would have if a vampire sucked my blood! The most attractive aspect of them is their tragic fates brought by their immortality. I love *Interview* best because I love Louis. The reason why I love Louis is that he has much humanity and good common sense, weakness and perseverance, fragility and stability—though I know he is a cruel killer, on the other hand. He has almost the same point of view as me, so I can identify with him, and with Daniel also.

Eiko: Anne Rice has become my bread of life, literally, because I am now the translator of the Vampire Chronicles. When *Interview with the Vampire* was first published in Japan, I was not a translator yet, but almost ten years later, when I had read the sequels, I was. I made a phone call to the Japanese publisher, and told them 'let me do it!' I must confess that I did the same thing when I first read Poppy Z. Brite's *Lost Souls*. I don't understand the exact meaning of the word 'darkness,' but I should say I like the books because they are so often full of eroticism and violence.

Ichiko: Anne Rice's world is rather secure, and less terrifying than the horror stories in Japan. Before I read her novels, I had very little interest in America. If not for Anne Rice, I would never have bought a personal computer to get more information about her on the internet.

Eiko: I am especially intrigued by the vampire Armand, to his despair, loneliness, and desperate need of love, however evil he is. In a way, as somebody has said before, he is the child inside me, needing to be fed and nurtured and loved. I wish Anne would write much more about him; I think he has much more things to say.

Ichiko: I had already been into vampires before I read Anne Rice. I loved Dracula movies starring Christopher Lee and Japanese comic books like *The Tribe of Poe*, created by Moto Hagio, which has influenced me very much.

Eiko: I love vampires. I believe in vampires partly, but who cares if they're true or not! The Japanese comic which is called *The Tribe of Poe* is a story about two boy vampires, and they are interwoven into the great chronicle of vampires. There are also stories about love between two immortal boy characters and a little girl who is also immortal. The vampires have extraordinary powers, but they are isolated from time, living in solitude, and desperately seeking the love and company of others, and their eternal home. It is a surprise that it was written in 1972, years before *Interview*, but I don't think Anne had ever read it.

Ichiko: I do *not* believe in vampires. I have heard about some blood-sucking people, but I think they are merely some kind of cannibalistic perverts and they are not immortal. To tell the truth, I wish there were vampires just like the ones in Rice's world.

Eiko: I belong to the fan club. This is my second visit to New Orleans, and the first time to attend the party. I think the fan club is doing very well, considering the recent expanding growth, but I also wish they could respond much more swiftly to the fans living overseas. I wish that Anne had as much popularity in Japan as in the United States, so that I can translate another series of her books, but they aren't violent enough for Japanese readers.

Ichiko: Even now, in our country, she is not so popular, and she will not be in the future either, I think. I wish she were more famous in Japan. On the other hand, I do not like the commercialism such as the web page of 'The Official Anne Rice Home Page.' I personally put out newsletters about the Vampire Chronicles in Japan and am a member of the fan club. Ten Japanese fans of Anne Rice all went to the Coven Party last October. That was our first visit to New Orleans. I was very sorry not to have communicated with other fans at the party because of my lack of knowledge of English. I was surprised there were various kinds of people at the party, young and old, male and female, and so on. In Japan, almost all Rice fans are young women.

AUDREY

32 · Occult Shop Owner · Columbus, Ohio

"I was born interested in the occult. I grew up in the Appalachian tradition of herbalists and witches who worked with cards, the signs of the moon, and using herbs for healing. I have a mix of southern culture and my father's family, who are from Europe, so I grew up knowing a lot about witchcraft and ghosts.

"Like Anne's characters, my family were elegant, fallen outcasts. In my family history we had a lot of money, but by the time it got to my generation we had to start all over again with nothing. My grandfather was the mayor of Columbus. My sisters and I grew up rather wild. We had this big house and no money to maintain it. It was like growing up in a haunted house; it was in a constant state of disrepair. That kind of situation contributes to an outsider status, and you have to learn to embrace it. I found Rice to be a writer who celebrates the elegance of the fallen outcasts. Louis was in a family where he felt guilty and miserable; yet there is another side of life for Louis, as there is for all of us.

"The vampire is present in many legends, especially eastern European legends. One of the girls that worked for me in my store, Bell, Book & Candle, was a direct descendant of Murray Brown, the vampire of Exeter, Rhode Island. The legend of Murray Brown is from the late eighteenth century. Supposedly, after her death, she was spotted around town, and soon afterwards all her family members started to die, one by one. Townspeople started to call her a vampire. The town decided to dig up her grave and found the coffin open and empty!

"In the store, we had tons of Rice fans come in and people who thought they were really vampires. It was strange—they weren't always looking for vampire stories but stuff about Satan. We'd tell them to go to a Christian bookstore, because they would know more about the devil than we did.

"Anne's work has allowed people to look at the occult in a different way. It may not seem so strange and weird to people anymore. Often we see a negative portrayal of witches and paganism, but there is a wealth of historic knowledge that is not biased, and Anne brings it to life with characters that have human questions, frailties, and struggles. Anne is a kindred Celt to me. Anne is someone who has grown up in an old city with its legends and history, and brings that past to life. She brings the human experience alive with all our questions of mortality vs. immortality. You can feel yourself in her characters. She has a dreamy disposition and understands a connection between times and worlds. She can write about the seventeenth century and then about rock bands and Porsches and it's all right in step. She brings the past and present together, and it all works.

"Vampires have a timeless sensuality to them. As a kid, I always thought, 'Wow, I know there'd be bad consequences if they bit me, but hey, they make it look good!' (Laughter) In *Ed Wood*, the movie, Bela Lugosi says there is a sexuality to the vampire, and I think he's right. Woman find it irresistible. The blood is the essence of a person, which is why it is used in magic, along with hair.

"The idea of forever is intriguing. Time being infinite and life being infinite, it's like frozen fireworks. It would be exhausting, though, to have nothing to do but go on and on. I believe in reincarnation; we just don't have memory of each lifetime, like a complete thread, which is probably a blessing. But every once in a while a piece if it will come back to you, like déjà vu. I feel really at home in New Orleans, and I'd never been here before this Coven Ball. That was a definite déjà vu experience for me.

"Sometimes you feel like you're alone in this love for Rice, but to go to the party and see people that appreciate her too makes it all come together. Anne has made me feel less alone, that there is an aesthetic that is out there, and I'm not the only one into it. I feel an intense kinship with what she writes about. She describes other dimensions as if they might be just around the corner. Life can be so ordinary sometimes, it's nice to know it can be more than what we see."

Judy

52 · Writer/Southern Nights Bed & Breakfast · New Orleans, Louisiana

"I'm a romance writer. I started writing when I was fifteen years old. My mother gave me *Forever Amber*, a romance novel, and I wanted to write like that. I wanted to create books like *Gone with the Wind* and *Shana*. I grew up in a time when carnivals came to the outskirts of town and I would walk over there barefoot and spend a lot of time alone. After my mother's death I had a lot of time to let my imagination grow. You could give me five words and I could make a story for you. I haven't been published yet, but I'm close. I've written five novels.

"Anne's work is among my favorites. She has the ability to put you right there in the moment. I try not to delve to deep into the work for meaning. I love a good story that is descriptive with good locations and good dialogue and at the end it has you crying or smiling or something. Anne has been a big influence for the vampire and gothic genres, which is very exciting to me. I love the paranormal and science fiction, and Anne combines that with romance, which I love. I became more aware of things reading her books; my senses became heightened.

"*Interview with the Vampire* is my favorite book. The setting was so vivid for me. The whole theme of *Interview* was about someone imparting knowledge to someone else, telling them their deepest, darkest secrets. It was romance interwoven with horror and other whiffs of smoke that come and go and disappear. Anne inspires me to keep writing.

"I think it's wonderful that she is so popular. What writer doesn't want to be popular? If it makes her happy to open restaurants, I think it's great. When you write you don't want to write in a vacuum. You want to know that people have been affected by it. I know many people are affected by her work. I look at her from a writer's point of view and appreciate her. She's really stuck with her vision, and that's what writing is: determination and not stopping. You have to keep going. I heard she had many rejections at first, which is encouraging to me.

"Right now I'm living *The Witching Hour*. I bought my property a year ago, to open as a bed and breakfast. It is 7,000 square feet, and has three active ghosts: Cecilia and little Katie, who are from the 1880s, and Warren, a neighborhood salesman from the 1920s. They are very nice entities. They give me a very relaxed feeling. So many things happened when I first moved here, even a police officer asked if I had a ghost when my alarm kept going off! Ghosts go with the territory here in New Orleans. Hauntings Today, a group of parapsychologists, have an official overnight ghost expedition at my bed and breakfast now. They use special equipment, and each participant of the expedition stays in a different room. We don't tell them which ghost appears where, but Cecilia loves room number two, the main suite, and going out on the porch."

GINA *31 · Nurse · New Orleans, Louisiana*

JOSEPH *30 · Architect · New Orleans, Louisiana*

Joseph: I'd like to thank Anne for what she's done for me. If it wasn't for her I wouldn't have Gina in my life. We met at a Coven party, got engaged at another Coven party, and almost got married at one.

Gina: In 1983 I read *Interview* and *Lestat* and loved them. I always adored vampires, which was definitely based on the sexuality aspect. I would stay up on Saturday nights watching science fiction theater, praying they would have a vampire movie on. I didn't understand it then, but the dark, enigmatic stranger who takes you against your will into some sinful, lustful decadence was a wonderful idea to me. In addition to that, I was always a strange and sick child that worried about issues of mortality and God, and this was an erotically charged immortality that looked damn good to me! The movies were always pretty bad, so I was disappointed that I never found anything that really fulfilled what I was looking for. When I found Rice, that was it. So I became rabid for all of her work from the erotic to everything else. Whatever Anne writes about really touches on a lot of things that I never understood about myself, but interested me.

Joseph: I usually read Dickens and Arthur Conan Doyle, but I bought a copy of *Interview* in 1976. It was this strange book that was very cool, and I loved it. The book was modern and old at the same time. I wasn't into vampires before this book. I wasn't into running around in black. I was just an average teenager with normal reading habits. I got a little strange, though, and started collecting thousands of books. I have all of Anne's first editions, signed.

Her writing style clicked with me. She can capture a feeling in a few words and convey an emotion in a short space, where other writers ramble on. My favorite is *The Mummy*. It was a departure for Rice, and it was fast-paced. Then of course, I love *Interview*. The vampire genre is interesting. I like the way she writes about it best. It has a lot of sexual and spiritual overtones. It's a powerful story, and I think that's why it hits so many people. For me, it hits the spiritual and immortality issue and she does a good job of tying it all together and leaving you with the possibility that it is true. It's always plausible—a rich tapestry.

Gina: After reading her novels and being so touched by her work, I decided to write Anne and say thank you. I sent her a gift package with CDs of Tori Amos and Sisters of Mercy (what I thought Lestat would sound like singing); I don't know if she ever got it. Hopefully someone in the fan club is enjoying them now. So after that I was sent information on a fan club I didn't know existed. It was 1990 and I had heard rumors of this party that happened every year and I really wanted information on it. You could only buy tickets in New Orleans at the time and I desperately wanted to go. I had been saving my money for years to take a vacation or to take my parents to Europe, so, since that was never going to happen, in 1994 my mother and I decided to go to New Orleans. We decided we were going to the party, had costumes made from the late seventeenth century period, spent exorbitant amounts of money we didn't have, and came to New Orleans.

We got to the party, and there were thousands of people in line. As we stepped out of a cab, a woman said, 'There is no way in hell you are going to get in.' We did finally, as the party was ending. Everyone seemed glorious and ethereal. Suddenly I noticed Joseph in a corner, and I just thought he was gorgeous in his costume, and I wanted to have my picture taken with him, and mother made me go ask him.

Joseph: I'd watched her peek around corners all night, and whenever I got anywhere near her, she would dash away. I was really looking forward to meeting her all night. Gina's mother is a trip. They were trying to get a car back to the airport after the party and I saw her talking with a policeman about how to get there. So I cruise up and ask if they need a ride someplace. So her mother says, 'Sure!' and grabs Gina and starts walking toward my car…not like they'd ever met me before!

Gina: At this time New Orleans was the murder capitol, and I realized this was someone I'd only had my picture taken with and it was quite stupid. But he gave us an architect's tour of the city and drove by Rice's homes.

Joseph: I asked them if they'd been to Cafe du Monde, and they didn't know what it was, so I said, 'OK, that's our next stop.' Now it's four o'clock in the morning, we're still in costume, and we cruise into Cafe du Monde and have some coffee, and get strange glances. I gave them the nickel tour of the French Quarter. I was quite infatuated with Gina by that point.

Gina: I thought Joseph was fabulous, but I was in an unhappy marriage and had my walls up: I'm not a tramp. There was an undeniable attraction, and after all of this was said and done, and poor Joseph had limped all over the Quarter with a bad knee, he asked if we wanted to get some breakfast, as the sun was coming up. I really wanted to have breakfast with this marvelous man, but my mother was tired, so Joseph left us at our hotel at the airport.

Joseph: I was thinking, 'Damn.' I had given them my number if they were going to be here for a while so they could give me a call.

Gina: My mother has no compunctions and was eager to have a tour guide for the rest of the week, so we made an arrangement to meet on All Soul's Day at his family's tomb, and participate in the washing ceremony. I talked myself up to this romance and then right back out of it so I would be in control, but when we met him at the tomb I was terribly jealous that he was talking to my mother more than me. We asked him out to dinner at Commander's Palace that night, and then to O'Brien's, and we had Hurricanes by the flaming water fountain. After two glasses of wine and a Hurricane I was tipsy and it was the perfect excuse for him to put his arm around me and lead me along. It was wonderful. After that night, it was love.

Joseph: It was great. We met every day they were in New Orleans. We took a boat ride on the river, had coffee with the Goths at Cauldie's. I invited them to Mobile, anoth-

er old southern town, because I was going to see my parents, and thought I'd show them a little southern hospitality, but Gina's mother said they were leaving.

Gina: Basically, after his invitation, we restructured our lives, to spend the weekend in Mobile and meet his family. Two days before we left New Orleans I started dreaming out loud and said Joseph's name, which my mother gave me great grief about. I thought this was going to be this great romance that was never going to develop into anything, because it couldn't. Mother mentioned to Joseph that I cried out in my sleep. Which was all he needed to go forward.

Joseph: I didn't go that forward...

Gina: So we spent all night talking and baring our souls to one another. My first kiss was a bite on the neck.

Joseph: That's as far as it went, though...

Gina: As we were driving back to New Orleans after three sleepless days in Mobile, there were tears and desperation. On the airplane home I made a list of all the pros and cons of my life, and how I could not stand to go back to my old life. I thought Joseph and I could maintain a friendship, but it didn't happen that way. I was desperate within days; my life was falling apart. Within a month I'd filed for divorce, quit my job, left my house. All I needed was my furniture and a truck. Joseph flew to San Diego and drove back across the country with me.

Joseph: Never drive through Texas....

Gina: We moved in together and had two blissful months of nothing but honeymoon.

Joseph: We bought this house (in the Garden District), and Gina was asking if I wanted to marry her when we bought the house. For a year I was planning the engagement...a friend was making the ring, and I was trying to put Gina off, while the whole time I was trying to get the ring finished, and have our period costumes fitted for the next party, the Memnoch Ball. I was planning to propose at the party. Everyone knew I was going to propose at the party, except Gina. How that family kept a secret I'll never know. It was right before the last waltz, with the huge orchestra in the chapel.

Gina: One woman from the party flew all the way from Rhode Island to be at our wedding because she photographed the proposal. We would have gotten married at the '96 Coven Ball, but because of family we had to have a traditional Catholic wedding.

Joseph: For me, Rice has been about the fan club and meeting people. Once you meet people who are really 'out there' and say, 'Hey, I'm a vampire,' and bite their arm and start bleeding, you think, well, I'm pretty normal. Having fetishes or leanings of that sort is okay. There's always someone who's further 'out-there' who you can get along with and like. So, it's freeing in that respect. I went to the party in 1991 and in 1994, when I met Gina. All the pretentious people that were at the Memnoch Ball because of the movie are gone now. They were there for the show and the press, not the Gathering, and I think now it's going back to the group of people who are really there for each other. We are into the clothing, 'Where did you get that corset?' stuff like that. Like bondage, you put that corset on till it hurts. It's fun and puts you into the novels. I like to make sure that everything down to the underwear is right. It's easier to become the character when the clothing is right. You carry yourself differently and think differently. The clothing is a constant reminder so you can lose yourself, and be whatever you want to be that evening. It's fun.

Gina: As an author Rice has helped me get in touch with things inside of myself that normally I would have thought were too strange. She has opened me up to the strangeness that can be normal. If you can reach an acceptance of things, it's wonderful. Ever since I was a child, I have had bondage dreams, and I couldn't come to terms that I was inherently evil inside. I grew up Mormon. Reading her work I realized I wasn't the only person that had those thoughts. It put me in touch with an openness about my sexuality. After reading the *Beauty* series and meeting other people who enjoy S&M too, I thought, hey, this is okay. It gives you permission to accept yourself. I remember one of the first conversations I had with Joseph—I perked up when he mentioned handcuffs. It's been a rich life since then.

The popularity that surrounds Rice now makes it feel less exclusive—less unique these days. Not a private little cult anymore; perhaps it never was a small thing. But you felt this kinship when it was a smaller group. Also, the more popular Rice is, the more the public wants to give its opinion of her, and there's a lot of negativity about her now.

Joseph: A lot of people who have joined from that commercial spurt are here for different reasons. Some people now aren't into sharing stories and having their pictures taken. It's like, 'go away.' Attitude grows, and the family feeling goes. It's a cool group of people when you find the ones who are in it for similar reasons. I think Anne managed to bring together all these groups like the Goths, S&M and costuming groups, and the teenagers with no meaning. It's still focused on her, but it's also focused on the group now.

Gina: For some it's a real pilgrimage to come to New Orleans. By pursuing her own thing, Anne's changed a lot of lives. I focus all year long on the magical event of the Ball. It provides me with the opportunity to pretend to be anything I want to be. For a little while you can be that, in a crowd that lets you. She's created a great fantasy world. Living in New Orleans brings the fantasy to life. You can live it all year long here if you want to.

One of Rice's characters has the realization that this life is all we have, and nothing should be more precious than the here and now. It's true. That was one of the most meaningful things in her books for me. Living for the moment has changed my life in every respect.

Tommi Tommie Tommy

36 · Costume Designer/Performance Artist · Los Angeles, California

"I have friends who have read Rice's books, and I thought, 'Oh, another vampire book.' Whenever I see a sci-fi or monster movie title I stay away from it. If it says 'love story' or 'kooky comedy,' I like it. To me *The Tale of the Body Thief* was a love story between David and Lestat. I kept thinking to myself, do people really know what she's writing about? Am I the only one who is clicking into the fact that these two men are turned on by each other? It was nice to read a book about two men in love that wasn't in the 'gay section' of a bookstore or a piece of trash, although it got trampy-trashy in my mind. (Laughter) If you don't believe in vampires, Anne takes you to places that you never thought of before and it becomes a journey.

"Anne's books have made me interested in vampires; they're 'cool.' But when I see people who really act this stuff out, I feel there is a line that needs to be drawn between fantasy and reality. In the '90s can you really drink anyone's blood? We're not immortal, and by doing that we may be killing someone or ourselves with the AIDS epidemic. In love stories they leave out the condoms. When it comes to reality it might be something you want to do, but you have to think, 'Am I dating a loony-tune?' Where's the passion going to go? You might love to be a vampire, but are you going to be a good or bad vampire? People acting out blood drinking is very scary, as it would be if there really were vampires. I think the scary thing is this: You walk into a bar and you want to hook up with someone. You may fall in love or nobody will talk to you at all; it's hit or miss. Well, what if you were chosen by a vampire? What if you could be immortal? Is that vampire going to bite you and leave you, or are you the chosen that gets the bite of immortality? In her books, you think it would be so romantic and cool to have Lestat choose you, but what if I was the one left to die? I've never really been in love or love at 'first bite.' It is romantic, but I could be dead. That's a metaphor for life and love: the chances you take, to be chosen or not.

"I feel Anne's books are erotic love stories with conflicts and broken hearts. I enjoy the books as long as they don't get too wordy. Anne can describe a doorknob for twenty-five pages. I already know what a door knob looks like and I may not like Anne's door knob. (Laughter) Although she's explaining it for a reason, I need room for my own interpretation of what that doorknob means. She takes us on a journey, but it's nice to have a little imagination of our own as well. The magic of imagination is beyond what someone tells us or shows us in the movies. To visualize for yourself is very important to that reading journey.

"Being in the theater business, I see plays that are about the harsh realities of life. But my take on performance art isn't always to teach you something. I don't have to give a history lesson. I can take you to the theater and make you laugh, and take you away from the real world. I want to give fun and escapism, like you may find in one of Anne's books. They are fantasies, whether it is the dark side or the light side.

"My outfit is one I chose for the occasion. I don't walk around like this, but Memnoch in heels is my interpretation for the moment. If I were in an Anne Rice book, this is how I'd dress. Why not put him in high heels so he can tower over everyone? Why not make him an S&M dark angel? I'm not into vampires, so I don't do that look. I'm drawn to the kitsch, the theatricalism of it all. Fans go to the parties dressed in their interpretation of how the characters would dress. We all know what Lestat looks like, so let's bring the other characters to life as well."

SHER

33 · Hair Designer · San Jose, California

"The vampire series is very homo-sensual. The books are not really heterosexual, just more homo-sensual, which I think is very provocative. Anne is very much a bisexual thinker and you see that in *The Claiming of Sleeping Beauty* series. In the *Beauty* books the characters were challenged by their bodies, degradation, and humiliation, so they were forced to become very open, which made them more complete people, who didn't fear anything or have insecurities. I thought it was brilliant. It really affected the way I think about bondage and pain. You find that it is really not about pain, but the psychology of an individual, sensation, and who we really are inside.

"I became very interested in S&M because Rice's work was the first that didn't degrade women. It wasn't volatile, it was erotica for women written by a woman, but could also be loved by a man. *The Story of O* is always held as the book that started the whole S&M ruckus, but it has nothing compared to the *Beauty* series. It opened up a thought pattern for me that has become my fantasy. I learned that the whole dominance and submission thing isn't about inflicting pain as commonly thought, but more about the psychological aspects of people. It opened a lot of doors for me to understand different people.

"I've been reading Rice since 1983. I loved *The Mummy* and *The Witching Hour*. I always keep one of her books in the wings that I haven't read, while waiting for a new one to be published. I don't like not having one of her books around. Got to have them all the time!

"I am devoted to Anne as an author. I collect all of her first editions. She takes me places I've never been, like Europe. She challenges the readers to open their minds. She is an educator as well as a dream maker, who takes you into fantasies and helps you create your own. I wasn't raised religiously, but Anne took all the myths and religious ideas and explained them and how they evolved. I believe her to be a spiritual educator as well. I've learned a lot about religion through her. If I could go back to school I'd study religion and history, but I'm not lucky enough to do that, so Anne is my teacher."

"I don't think Anne is commercial—I think she's finally getting the recognition she has coming to her. I really respected her for putting a two-page ad in *The New York Times* about the movie scandal and saying Tom Cruise was good in the movie. I thought, let's see how commercial she is, did she sell out? But Tom Cruise *was* great and I respected her for coming out and saying that. I don't want to say anything negative about Anne. I don't know what it is to be a writer and what it takes. I often wonder if she's bored with it all. I feel she has given me so much, that if anything in her books is mediocre, I hold her editors accountable. I think she's gotten so big now that the editors aren't saying, hey, this is over-done. She's had so many good books, I think now she may need a sounding board, and the editors aren't doing their job. I don't think she would just pump out books; she has too much integrity for that."

MARIA

28 · Singer/TV Production · Hollywood, Florida

"I have always dressed like a vampire, even when it wasn't Halloween. I adore vampires. They are nocturnal and romantic. I don't find them evil at all. They are all emotional, spiritual, romantic, and loving to me. My perception is that when someone is bitten by a vampire they have to stay here on earth because they have unfinished business which is spiritual. It's a soul kind of thing that they have to stay and figure out.

"I love a vampire's pasty white skin; it's very close to death. I'm attracted to people who are different looking—like pale white skin and unusual eyes—I wonder about them and what darkness lies inside them. I think that someone who is too beautiful doesn't have a dark side, so to me they aren't very real. The ultimate dark side is someone who is very loving and yet can totally understand how much pain is involved in pleasure, both in life and sexuality. A loving, caring person who can go into the depths of his pain and other people's pain, and feel emotion, that is a beautiful dark side. People don't tend to have a lot of emotion, and I think that's because life isn't always very pretty. I'm more afraid of the living than the dead.

"The vampire can make others immortal. You die but you're not a ghost: you're still here and moving and doing. You are undead, still passing through time, living on the outside of life, not playing by the rules. You just are, and go with it; I love that. I'm fascinated with death.

"I discovered Anne Rice books in an airport. It was Halloween, 1994, and I was on my way to New Orleans for Halloween. I thought, 'Mmmm, *Interview with the Vampire*? Let me read this!' I read the entire book on the plane. There I was on my way to New Orleans and dressed as a vampire, but I had no clue about Anne Rice before seeing that book. I got really into it and decided I had to do more, so I came back to New Orleans the following year for the Memnoch Ball and wore white contacts and fangs, put veins on my face, and got really into the characters.

"Rice made me want to see everything in New Orleans in a new way. I wanted to know what it would be like to be bitten, what it would be like to live like that forever, and to change with time periods. I believe that vampires really do exist. I have a friend I really believe is a vampire. He has a love of life but also a love of death. He's an interesting guy. We talk about the underworld and vampires a lot. He had chrome fangs permanently put into his mouth.

"I loved *The Claiming of Sleeping Beauty*. I'm fascinated with the different facets of sex. I was mostly fascinated with the torture aspect in the series and how it became pleasurable to Beauty. I was never interested in S&M before I read this book. The guy I was dating at the time was reading the *Beauty* trilogy. He gave them to me to read on a weekend ski trip and I could not put them down. The books opened up a whole new part of me. I felt more comfortable with myself and even my boyfriend noticed a difference.

"The correlation between vampires and S&M is the taboos and forbidden aspects of both: they are dark, mysterious, and unknown. What is that? Can I do that? If I do, will it hurt me? And if it does, will that be bad or good? It's all the not knowing and then being able to reach out and discover it. I think Rice's books allow people to experience their dark side. They can experience it through the books without really doing it, or they can take it one step further.

"I grew up in traditional Spanish culture and this is not normal thought. Today my mother thinks I'm a complete freak. But I know there's nothing wrong with me, I'm just expressing a side of myself and acknowledging that it exists. Coming to New Orleans every year allows me the freedom to express this side of myself and not feel uncomfortable or weird. Even in my sexual relationship, I did some things I read in the book and it became part of my lifestyle with that partner. We were so close, and the book opened up a special part of our relationship. I was always taught that love was romantic and prince charming-ish. That's all wonderful and nice, and I do want that, but there is also that other side of me where I want to be a little deviant. I want to be on the darker side of something and experience a little pain, a little torture, a little abandonment. When I'm a vampire I can be the dominant one. When I'm not, I can be the submissive one.

"That first year I came to New Orleans and I had read *Interview*, I'd heard about the Coven parties and I had to go! I didn't expect so many people! I didn't know if they were all there because of Rice or because of vampire culture in general. It was both. The people I talked to at the Ball were more interested in having the freedom of that night to be as close to a vampire as they could get and not be looked down upon for doing that. The Memnoch Ball was amazing. I heard conversations about the books and people's dark sides. 'Would you…Could you…Should you?' This one couple was having a whole conversation about biting and how deep you could go into someone's skin before drawing blood. I thought, 'Whoa! Okay!'

"One of my memories of the Memnoch Ball was when I was walking toward the courtyard at St. Elizabeth's, and there was a woman who was totally nude. She had on nipple rings, a collar, and a clitoris ring all hooked together. She had no problem being naked and that was really amazing. I asked her who she was and she said Sleeping Beauty. It was just as I had visualized it!

"I'm not in the fan club. I don't consider myself a fan, only because I don't really follow her fanatically. I'm more interested in vampires in general. I acknowledge that Rice opened me up sexually. Thank you for changing my sex life! I always tell friends to read *The Claiming of Sleeping Beauty*. It will change everything for you! Maybe not what you do physically, but it'll change how you think. I believe people are too repressed and don't allow themselves to think about things that might be a little darker, and to feel it's okay to explore that. Anne lets us know it's okay."

KATJE

26 · Professional Dominatrix · San Francisco, California

"I like vampires. At the time I read Anne Rice I was hanging out in Goth circles and it was the whole vampire thing I could get lost in. The Gothic clothes add to all the eeriness, and you can tune into the darker side of yourself. For some people it's just about vampires, but for me it's the whole darker side of things. At Goth clubs it's a spiritual experience to trance out to the music. It's almost like I'm not really there, but transcending into another space and time. The source of that space is calm and not grounded in material things. It is also a sadness that I embrace and am comfortable with. It's like going into a beautiful tragedy, a dream space. I don't always experience it, but when I do it's usually at night, in the rain, or when I'm alone. It's very personal, and I don't experience it with others. It's an inside, core feeling. I use it as a way to express myself. It helps me with my feelings.

"*Exit to Eden* was cute. I smiled while reading it. There were parts that were realistic, but it is definitely a fantasy. The fantasy and pain of S&M all involve a transcendence. I go to a different part of myself when I'm doing a S&M scene. It is similar to the space I'm in at a Goth club, except one is more interactive than the other. I'm oblivious when I'm dancing, but in a scene I purposely shut things out. Both experiences are very powerful; they reach deep inside me to a strong place. The inner strength I find when doing a scene is very romantic to me. It's almost like an energy goes through me and I'm an instrument. The experience taps something spiritual. The spiritualness in a scene is the ritual, it's a mediation, a feeling that tells me the experience is real. So much S&M is insincere. Working as a dom I don't always have that magical feeling, but when I do, it's invigorating and touches a real place in me.

"Going to the Coven Ball was fun. The people were beautiful. I felt like they were my people; I related to them like in a Goth club. Rice is not a major force in my life, but I think she is a figurehead for something bigger by bringing all those people together. There was definitely more than Anne in common with these people: several different and dark lifestyles. It was nice to be in that space and have that community together."

ALIA

20 · Student: Computer Science/Bio-Chemistry Major · Santa Cruz, California

"When I was a little kid I was intensely attracted to anything mythical. I went through volumes of mythos, including *The Mabinogion* and Viking mythology, when I was eight. I didn't understand a lot of it, but I had figurines of unicorns and fairies and all the good creatures. Then I started thinking about what their enemies would be like. Vampires fell under that category, and from there it became a question of why they were so bad. I tried to figure it out. When you're eight it's hard to find books about the evil creatures because the children's section is full of goodness and light. (Laughter)

"I've always been attracted to the wisdom that one would gain from the experience of immortality. Lately I've started hoping that when I get to be an old woman I will have been around enough to be able to pass my wisdom on to other people. That is my romantic vampire view, to have a wise, older, caring vampire-mentor who can teach me all those wonderful things. For me, it isn't the horror aspect at all. I know it's there, but there's more to it than that. Vampires are beautiful and romanticized to the point of being extraordinary. What an intriguing romantic encounter they would be! I always wanted that to happen to me. As a child I wondered if vampires existed. I hoped they did and that they didn't. Between the two, I found a compromise. If they do exist it would be cool, but I'm not sure I'd let one bite me. Then I read *Interview*. I hid in the book, and it gave me a lot to think about. Would I want to be a vampire? I decided I would be fair vampire bait, but I'm skeptical enough that it would take a lot of proof, and they would have to lay their cards on the table for me, prove that they aren't just blood-sucking creeps. If they presented a rational argument I very well might go for it. I would love to be immortal. The idea of living forever is both terrifying and intriguing.

"I love *Interview* the most. I fell in love with Louis and his frank viewpoint that was so colored by opinions. There was no fancy-schmancyness, just, 'I'm a vampire, and it sucks.' I loved Claudia too. I always liked that she was a little girl who never got to grow up and she hated that. She becomes immortal very young and is surrounded by all these little things her size, but it wasn't enough for her. I couldn't fathom her predicament myself, so I fell more into her story line.

"I've read the Vampire Chronicles through *The Tale of the Body Thief*. I loved that the books expanded. We got to see how a group of vampires interacted, from different viewpoints. There were scenes that I fell in love with, such as when Lestat and Akasha meet and the description of the two of them drinking from a continuous circuit (she from him, he from her, so they never drain each other). It's rather orgasmic. I like Akasha also; she is an empowered female. Her presence alone is so big that she doesn't have to speak or run around—she just is.

"Anne's vampires are very familiar with each other. They are all part of the same species. In Poppy Z. Brite's *Love in Vein* books you come across every kind of vampire: gross ones, emotional ones—they are all over the map—they are very graphic. She really goes into the gory details. You don't try to read one of her novels and eat at the same time. Anne's books are less about feeding and more about the society the vampires exist in. It's an anthropological viewpoint that I really liked. We know how they eat, so let's get on with life, and Rice shows us that.

"I had a friend in college who was playing *Vampire: The Masquerade*, which is one of the White Wolf games, and introduced me to it. There are seven major clans, and each person who joins writes his own character. There are basic character concepts, but you can create your own history that explains your character on your first night. I gave it a try, and it was a lot of fun.

"The storyteller is the game master. He is in charge of the rules and directing the plot to some extent. It's not law, but he guides the characters within the boundaries of the basic plot. 'Live-action' for us means everything *but* physical contact. It is a safe situation where physical contact would not be what it is in real life. Instead, you do what's called a 'physical challenge.' If I'm bringing one of my fighters to defend me in a scene, I don't actually touch you: I bid a physical trait, that describes what the particular challenge is. I would say, 'I'm brawny enough to deck you,' and you would respond with, 'I'm dexterous enough to dodge you.' Then we do rock, paper, scissors, and whoever wins that wins the challenge. There's never any biting. Any faux biting is between two players outside the game. We try to discourage couples acting like couples. When you have sixty people to keep track of, you forget which are couples that like to be kissing and who is a guy just bugging a girl.

"We meet once a week. In the beginning of an evening we first gather and have a meeting called 'listen up' where we discuss what happened during the week in the game time. Sometimes we incorporate real news stories. If something happens in real life that pertains to the game, the storyteller decides if it happened in the game, to add to the plot. When real life is so beautifully obvious that we should use it, by all means we do.

"My current character, Alía, is a mixed–up vampire. She is Malkavian, the crazy clan. She was embraced much like Lestat in the sense that her sire took her back to this beautiful mansion, embraced her, and told her nothing about who she was or her clan, then threw himself into a fire. Alía goes through a discovery of who she is for the next fifty years, living off deer and animal blood in the forests of France, which is tacky, but eventually she gets taken in by the Toreador Clan and learns about other vampires. There are deceptions, adventures, etc. I'm a narrator in the game now, so I get to play lots of characters.

"There are people that think we are Satanists. They don't understand that it is just a game. We don't *really* think we're vampires. All the press about the Florida vampire murders was upsetting to me. I find it disturbing that people are so out of touch with reality that they think they can do things like that. I hate that they blame the writers. Anyone's ideas can be taken out of context and stretched to an extreme; it doesn't make it their fault. I was raised in a family that taught me what I could do that was reasonable within the boundaries of society. It worries me to see people that have lost touch with those boundaries and don't think of the consequences that exist.

"Playing the game is a release. People need a little fantasy in their lives to get away from mundania. As a student, my life is about labs and tests and pounding through assignments. To be able to get away once a week, avoid my current life, and fulfill my vampire fantasies is stress relief. You get to be whatever you want to be. It's grown-up make believe. I love playing the game. I miss it when I can't go. It hurts when I spend my Friday night in the computer lab working and I know where I'd really like to be...that really sucks."

DENISE

46 · Artist's Model · Los Angeles, California

"I was in a shop when a woman came up to me and said I looked just like Jesse in *The Queen of the Damned*. So I went and bought the book and then read four more books by Rice. I loved all of them; they left a mark on me. Anne makes you feel like you're part of the story with the characters, having the adventures with them. I've never seen a writer become so popular, but, then again, I've never found a writer who made me feel that a story was so real or took me into it like that before either. It makes you wonder about who Anne is. I like the history in her books. I'm actively involved in an eighteenth century reenactment group called Brigade of the American Revolution. We dress in traditional costumes and have a ball once a year. I love it because it let's you be another person, dress-up, and create a fantasy. Thinking fantasy isn't enough for me, I like to do things. I love the romantic eighteenth century feel, but there is my dark side also that likes to dress like a vampire in a black velvet cape and do that thing too. I go with my mood—whatever strikes me at the time.

"I relate to Lestat. We are similar people personality-wise, and as I'm reading I think, 'Oh, are you going through this now? I've already been there; don't get stuck there too, Lestat!' I consider myself a person who likes to try a lot of things. I'm a jokester, outspoken. I'm tough on the outside, but my feelings get hurt very easily if you hit the right button, and Lestat is similar. I believe if you want your life to be interesting, then you have to investigate. The vampires are very sensual and I like the powers they have.

"I loved Akasha in *The Queen of the Damned*. She said something like, 'Why don't all the guys drop dead and there will be no problems.' I said that when I was fourteen, and my father blew a fuse, so I found it all very amusing. I really do like men a lot, though. (Laughter)

"Anne has had a lot of personal loss. She needs to know people care about her. I saw her interviewed on *Rosie O' Donnell* and she seemed like a very nervous person: hyper, scattered, and proud. I liked her! Rice is very outspoken about politics. But I don't think Anne likes to sound rude or have people think badly of her.

"I read the Anne Rice Listserv every day. No one ever likes what I write, but that's okay; I've made lots of friends online that I've met and hung out with. The books changed my life because I met people through the internet that I would not have met otherwise.

Someone put my photo on a web page with my picture as Jesse. I had no idea how many people were into this Rice stuff, but a friend and I decided to take a vacation and party and check out the Coven Ball. There were a lot of people there from the internet, which was amazing.

"Going to New Orleans was very quaint and perverted at the same time. It was like seeing a background for her books, and then I would think, 'Well, where are these vampires?' I have no problem waiting for Lestat to show up and take me. I told my husband if I left New Orleans without being bitten by a vampire I would really be disappointed. Well, I did get bitten…by two mosquitoes!"

ANNE RICE APPENDIX

Books By Anne Rice:

THE VAMPIRE CHRONICLES
Interview with the Vampire, Knopf, 1976
The Vampire Lestat, Knopf, 1985
The Queen of the Damned, Knopf, 1988
The Tale of the Body Thief, Knopf, 1992
Memnoch the Devil, Knopf, 1995

LIVES OF THE MAYFAIR WITCHES
The Witching Hour, Knopf, 1990
Lasher, Knopf, 1993
Taltos, Knopf, 1994

Erotica: Writing as Anne Rampling
Belinda, Arbor House, 1986
Exit to Eden, Arbor House, 1985

Writing as A.N. Roquelaure
The Claiming of Sleeping Beauty, Dutton, 1983
Beauty's Punishment, Dutton, 1984
Beauty's Release, Dutton, 1985

OTHERS:
The Mummy or Ramses The Damned, Ballantine,1989
Cry to Heaven, Knopf, 1982
The Feast of All Saints, Simon & Schuster, 1979
Servant of the Bones, Knopf, 1996

Books about Anne Rice:

Prism of the Night: A Biography of Anne Rice, Katherine Ramsland, Dutton, 1991

The Vampire Companion: The Official Guide to Anne Rice's The Vampire Chronicles, Katherine Ramsland, Ballantine, 1993

The Witches' Companion: The Official Guide to Anne Rice's Lives of The Mayfair Witches, Katherine Ramsland, Ballantine, 1995

The Anne Rice Trivia Book, Katherine Ramsland, Ballantine, 1995

The Roquelaure Reader: A Companion to Anne Rice's Erotica, Katherine Ramsland, Plume Books, 1996

The Anne Rice Reader, Katherine Ramsland, Ballantine Books, 1997

Anne Rice: A Biography, Bette B. Roberts, Twayne Publishers, 1994

The Unauthorized Anne Rice Companion, Edited by George Beahm, Andrews and McMeel, 1996

Haunted City: An Unauthorized Guide to the Magical, Magnificent New Orleans of Anne Rice, Joy Dickinson, Citadel Press, 1995

Conversations with Anne Rice, Michael Riley, Ballantine, 1996

Fan Club

You must be a member of the fan club to attend the Annual Gathering of the Coven which happens at Halloween time, in New Orleans. For information send a stamped, self-addressed envelope to:

The Anne Rice Vampire Lestat Fan Club (ARVLFC)
P.O.Box 58277
New Orleans, LA. 70158-58277
Att: Ritchie Champagne

Web Sites

These are just a few of the dozens of Rice related websites on the internet. Check the "links" section of each site which will guide you to additional websites. Some favorites worth checking out are:

Anne Rice Home Page : www.annerice.com
Rice/Random house: www. Random house.com
About Anne Rice: www.personal.psu.edu/users/l/m/lms5/aboutar.html
Dracula's Daughter: html://users.aol.com/mishian/DD/DD.html
The Brat Queen: www.eskimo.com/~talset
Commtion Strange: www.ecosys.drdr.virginia.edu/~jsm8f/commtion.html (with complete links section)
ShadowFox's AR Page: www.geocities.com/Athens/6638/rice.html
Novel Photo Gallery: www.zilker.net/~kyle/Dave/ARMPG html
Newsgroups: www.alt.books.anne-rice
www. salon1999.com
The Black Rose: www.eskimo.com/~ash/ (ARListserv archives & specs)

"Coming to the ball is about taking all of Anne's books, compiling them together, and for a night living-out what you've read."

—**Sherilynne, 25, Arizona**

"My family did a lot of moving around which meant many different schools, homes, and cultures for me. The result of this was that I never had time to establish good friendships. Add this to a domestic misunderstanding with my step-father and you have my difficult upbringing. This all led to me becoming a manic-depressive and I was not a very happy person to say the least.

"When I finally made good friends at my university and in America, I found that it was easy for me to become depressed when I thought about my life and family, which I had left a few years before. However, I always managed to make myself happy even when I was sad because I knew that there was nothing else to do but keep on trying to make myself a better life. Anne Rice wrote in *The Vampire Lestat*: 'You can only try and get what you want in life, the only other choice is death.'

A quote from *Body Thief* has also reminded me time and time again of the fact that if I do try, then there is hope, even if it seems at times that I will be overwhelmed by pain. Rice spells out for me that there is nothing else to do but put on a brave face and get back into life. The only alternative is death, letting the pain drown you. My life is spent sailing the thin line between the two. I quite honestly believe that these quotes made me think before I might have acted unwisely and this has brought me to what I am today: a much more stable, happier person."

'And my dark soul is happy again because it does not know how to be anything else for very long and because the pain is a deep dark sea in which I would drown if I did not sail my craft over the surface, steadily towards a sun which will never rise.'

-Anne Rice, *The Tale of the Body Thief*

— **CAL, 18, Student: Environmental Biology, Scotland**

THE PARTIES

The Memnoch Ball, 1995

The Annual Gathering of the Coven, 1996

in New Orleans, LA.

TOMMI TOMMIE TOMMY

36 · Costume Designer/Performance Artist · Los Angeles, California

SHER

33 · Hair Designer

San Jose, California

MARIA

28 · Singer/TV Production

Hollywood, Florida

KATJE

26 · Professional Dominatrix

San Francisco, California

ALIA

20 · Student: Computer Science

Bio-Chemistry Major

Santa Cruz, California

DENISE

46 · Artist's Model

Los Angeles, California

"Anne Rice is my most beloved author...person... everything. By reading her books it made me appreciate beauty in a way that is so often taken for granted. People never seem to notice how wonderful life is; they're too busy complaining about what they don't have, rather than what they do have. She always talks about how

happy she is to see her fans, rather than complaining about how naggy they are. She seems to trigger a place in my heart that nobody has before by talking about the tiniest details. She makes me want to smile and laugh and cry and observe and create and...live. She makes me live. I appreciate everything so much more because of her and I know I'm not the only one."

**—SERENA, 16,
Student, Garland, Texas**

in a mirror because they are a one-way reflection of humanity. We only see the ugliness that is within us reflected in the vampire. I'm drawn to the vampire in admiration of his nature and purity, the essence of what it is. I don't know if I'd want to be a vampire. A lot of people say they would, but if you really think about it, is it something you would want to become? I don't know. By living forever, you cheat your soul out of a chance to grow."

**— RIP, 29, Film Maker,
Hollywood, Florida**

"**H**ave you ever really thought, if the option was presented to you to become a vampire, would you do it? I have pondered that thought a lot. The vampire is really a very ugly creature. He will kill whatever is necessary for him to survive. But he only destroys because he must. The vampire is a thing of beauty and ugliness because he is pure. Human Beings are more evil than true vampires, because they destroy because they want to. Vampires can't be reflected

"first discovered Anne Rice in 1995. I saw the movie, *Interview With The Vampire*, one night when I was semi-suicidal. I am a transsexual and because I wasn't doing anything about it and couldn't tell my family, I hated life. With Anne I had finally found something to identify with. When I found out who Anne Rice was and about her books, I held on tight. I pored over all the Vampire Chronicles in one-and-a-half weeks, forgoing sleep. It was a lonely time but also a happy one. I joined the fan club and decided I was going to the Memnoch Ball even if I had to sleep in the

street. What followed was the best time of my entire life. It wasn't just the Ball, it was the city, the friends I made, and Anne herself. I felt alive for perhaps the first time in my life. I owe a heartfelt debt to Anne I can never repay. She is a part of me, of who I am. I dunno what would have happened had I not discovered her. For all I know, I might be dead. She and her fans have shown me a lot of acceptance overall and as I sit in my apartment alone, I miss that. Although things are still very tough. I hold on to those memories and I hope to create more soon, when I move to New Orleans in 1998."

—**Nicole, 22,**
Student: Political Science,
Athens, Georgia